Best Practices for Trauma-Informed School Counseling

Angela M. Powell
Lone Star College, USA

A volume in the Advances in Early Childhood and K-12 Education (AECKE) Book Series

IGI Global
PUBLISHER of TIMELY KNOWLEDGE

Published in the United States of America by
IGI Global
Information Science Reference (an imprint of IGI Global)
701 E. Chocolate Avenue
Hershey PA, USA 17033
Tel: 717-533-8845
Fax: 717-533-8661
E-mail: cust@igi-global.com
Web site: http://www.igi-global.com

Library of Congress Cataloging-in-Publication Data

Names: Powell, Angela M., 1970- editor.
Title: Best practices for trauma-informed school counseling / Angela M. Powell, editor.
Description: Hershey, PA : Information Science Reference, 2022. | Includes bibliographical references and index. | Summary: "This edited book will prepare potential and current school counselors to handle the challenges and responsibilities they may face as professional school counselors, preschool through high school by providing a wide range of topics including: effective interventions for racism, recognizing trauma, a school counselor's relationship with administrators, working with diverse students, a model for advocating on behalf of, and providing services to children with disabilities"-- Provided by publisher.
Identifiers: LCCN 2021051909 (print) | LCCN 2021051910 (ebook) | ISBN 9781799897859 (hardcover) | ISBN 9781799897866 (paperback) | ISBN 9781799897873 (ebook)
Subjects: LCSH: Students with social disabilities--Counseling of--United States. | Students--Mental health--United States. | Students--Mental health services--United States. | Psychic trauma in children--United States. | Educational counseling--United States.
Classification: LCC LB3430 .B47 2022 (print) | LCC LB3430 (ebook) | DDC 371.826/94--dc23/eng/20220124
LC record available at https://lccn.loc.gov/2021051909
LC ebook record available at https://lccn.loc.gov/2021051910

This book is published in the IGI Global book series Advances in Early Childhood and K-12 Education (AECKE) (ISSN: 2329-5929; eISSN: 2329-5937)

British Cataloguing in Publication Data
A Cataloguing in Publication record for this book is available from the British Library.

Advances in Early Childhood and K-12 Education (AECKE) Book Series

ISSN:2329-5929
EISSN:2329-5937

Editor-in-Chief: Jared Keengwe, University of North Dakota, USA

MISSION

Early childhood and K-12 education is always evolving as new methods and tools are developed through which to shape the minds of today's youth. Globally, educational approaches vary allowing for new discussions on the best methods to not only educate, but also measure and analyze the learning process as well as an individual's intellectual development. New research in these fields is necessary to improve the current state of education and ensure that future generations are presented with quality learning opportunities.

The **Advances in Early Childhood and K-12 Education (AECKE)** series aims to present the latest research on trends, pedagogies, tools, and methodologies regarding all facets of early childhood and K-12 education.

COVERAGE

- Urban K-12 Education
- K-12 Education
- Diverse Learners
- Learning Outcomes
- Curriculum Development
- Individualized Education
- Reading and Writing
- Special Education
- Common Core State Standards
- Early Childhood Education

IGI Global is currently accepting manuscripts for publication within this series. To submit a proposal for a volume in this series, please contact our Acquisition Editors at Acquisitions@igi-global.com or visit: http://www.igi-global.com/publish/.

The Advances in Early Childhood and K-12 Education (AECKE) Book Series (ISSN 2329-5929) is published by IGI Global, 701 E. Chocolate Avenue, Hershey, PA 17033-1240, USA, www.igi-global.com. This series is composed of titles available for purchase individually; each title is edited to be contextually exclusive from any other title within the series. For pricing and ordering information please visit http://www.igi-global.com/book-series/advances-early-childhood-education/76699. Postmaster: Send all address changes to above address.

Titles in this Series

For a list of additional titles in this series, please visit:
http://www.igi-global.com/book-series/advances-early-childhood-education/76699

Disciplinary Literacy as a Support for Culturally and Linguistically Responsive Teaching and Learning
Leslie Haas (Xavier University of Louisiana, USA) and Jill T. Tussey (Buena Vista University, USA)
Information Science Reference • © 2022 • 391pp • H/C (ISBN: 9781668442159) • US $195.00

Handbook of Research on Using Motor Games in Teaching and Learning Strategy
Pedro Gil-Madrona (University of Castilla-La Mancha, Spain)
Information Science Reference • © 2022 • 511pp • H/C (ISBN: 9781799896210) • US $245.00

Modern Reading Practices and Collaboration Between Schools, Family, and Community
Ana Patrícia Almeida (Universidade Aberta, Portugal) and Sandrina Esteves (ISEC Lisboa, Portugal)
Information Science Reference • © 2022 • 304pp • H/C (ISBN: 9781799897507) • US $195.00

Preparing Early Childhood Teachers for Managing Emergencies
Hannah O. Ajayi (Obafemi Awolowo University, Nigeria) Emmanuel Grupper (Ono Academic College, Israel) Simeon Sunday Fowowe (Adeniran Ogunsanya College of Education, Nigeria) Tom Cassidy (Cambridge Leadership College, UK) and Emily Ashton (University of Regina, Canada)
Information Science Reference • © 2022 • 280pp • H/C (ISBN: 9781799870203) • US $195.00

For an entire list of titles in this series, please visit:
http://www.igi-global.com/book-series/advances-early-childhood-education/76699

IGI Global
PUBLISHER of TIMELY KNOWLEDGE

701 East Chocolate Avenue, Hershey, PA 17033, USA
Tel: 717-533-8845 x100 • Fax: 717-533-8661
E-Mail: cust@igi-global.com • www.igi-global.com

Table of Contents

Detailed Table of Contents

role responsibilities with their administrators. The goal of this chapter is to prepare school counselors to establish a clear professional identity through role advocacy. Ultimately, unambiguous role definition serves to advocate for students who need the services that professional school counselors are uniquely trained to provide.

Providing trauma-informed school counseling is imperative to implementing quality school counseling. The purposes of this chapter are to provide readers with a foundational understanding of trauma-informed school counseling, to emphasize the importance of trauma-informed school counseling, and to explain how to apply trauma-informed school counseling. Therefore, the chapter will offer a simplistic model to aid in understanding trauma-informed care, an overview of trauma-informed care guiding principles discussed in the literature, a case-study analysis using trauma-informed care guiding principles, questions for consideration, and general trauma-informed school counseling interventions. The chapter will also include a discussion on the importance of considering contextual and cultural factors in trauma-informed care.

Individuals and school communities are often faced with unexpected events. While some unexpected events bring joy and happiness, others cause fear and helplessness. Stability is crucial during an unexpected crisis, and crisis management planning helps create processes, frameworks, and response protocols, reducing further trauma. According to the National Education Agency (NEA), schools must focus on safety to prevent incidents and a foundation of this work is supporting the community's mental health needs. Crisis management planning is critical to help reduce secondary trauma in the lives of others. School counselors should be leaders when helping their school systems prepare for these unexpected situations. They are seen as an essential resource in planning for crisis situations.

purpose of this chapter is to serve as a resource for school counselors to implement trauma-informed, culturally-sensitive practices, using the multitiered systems of support (MTSS) as a guide, when working with Asian American youth affected by COVID-19-related racial discrimination.

The purpose of this chapter is to provide students with a primer for assessing for and reporting child abuse and neglect on K-12 campuses. The authors highlight physical abuse, emotional abuse, sexual abuse, and neglect, which may manifest in a variety of different forms. Prevalence rates of abuse and neglect in the United States are reviewed, along with statistics reflecting the most common types of abuse as well as specific groups at greater risk for victimization. Guidelines for assessing and reporting allegations to Child Protective Services are presented, along with a case study to support students in the application of chapter constructs and procedures. The chapter ends with a discussion of specific post-reporting self-care strategies that may be implemented by school counselors.

Children of incarcerated parents may have traumatic experiences that correlate with negative educational and mental health outcomes. School counselors are ideally suited to provide trauma-informed school counseling for children of incarcerated parents through individual, group, or classroom counseling interventions while also collaborating with stakeholders. This chapter provides school counselors an overview of the possible trauma of parental incarceration while describing approaches to help meet the needs of students. The authors describe the importance of collaborating with caregivers, administrators, school nurses, and teachers to help promote a positive school climate, offer support, and reduce the possible stigma connected to parental incarceration. The authors recommend advocacy practices and future research areas to continue to promote trauma-informed school counseling for children of incarcerated parents.

Preface

"My students are acting out and I don't know what to do!" is by far the most common outcry heard from school counselors. In 2005, the author of this book took on the challenge of pursuing her passion of becoming a school counselor. Surprisingly, she received the offer just before the new school year and quickly moved into the position one day before school began. As a new school counselor, she had many questions but had prefaced her new journey by reading many recommended books and speaking with a few seasoned school counselors on how to be successful in this position. Approximately, two weeks into the new school year, a tragedy hit. Hurricane Katrina made landfall in southeast United States, specifically Louisiana and Mississippi. The Hurricane devastated the city of New Orleans. Hurricane Katrina was the largest and third strongest Hurricane to strike the United States. It was the deadliest Hurricane to strike the country within the past 70 years and by far the most expensive costing over $150 billion in property damage (United States Department of Homeland Security, 2006).

In the aftermath of the Hurricane, many citizens relocated to Texas seeking refuge. Suddenly, the author's school received over 200 displaced students who had lost their parents or even witnessed them drowning in the storm. As a new school counselor, she was stunned and desperately seeking ways to work with those students in need. The behaviors and symptoms they exhibited were significantly different from what she had learned in her graduate program and she quickly began to shift gears in seeking knowledge to assist them.

In the past decade, there have been increasingly more natural disasters, such as Hurricane Harvey in 2017 and the unexpected Texas freeze in 2021. Across the United States, there have been mudslides, tornadoes, and wildfires just to name a few of the catastrophes that claim lives and threaten the safety and mental well-being of children. With the onset of the Coronavirus in 2020 (COVID-19), there has been a surge in food disparity, medical care, and disproportionate accessibility to the COVID-19 vaccinations. School counselors were faced with the challenge of attempting to locate students who were not attending virtual classes, either due to the lack of internet or truancy. Whereas prior to this shift in the learning environment, School counselors had in-person access to students and could detect behavioral changes and/or some physical injuries related to child abuse. During the pandemic, social distancing and online learning was implemented in an effort to alleviate the spread of the virus. During this time, the number of child abuse cases spiked (Kovler et. al, 2021). Students were not in school and the indicators of child abuse could not be identified and reported by educators and School counselors. Consequently, there have also been reports of increased domestic and family violence when children were spending more time at home and likely the target of violence and neglect (Campbell, 2020).

Racism and social unrest has again come to the forefront. Many students are directly or indirectly affected by various racial injustices that have plagued our country. Additionally, increased gun violence has caused many children to experience heightened anxiety due to either witnessing violence or fearing that they will become a victim. Taking into consideration the plethora of adversities that children face, many do not receive counseling outside of the school system. It is vital for students' mental well-being and academic success that School counselors are able to recognize the impact of such events and identify trauma or signs of toxic stress among students. When these symptoms are identified, trauma-informed practices may be beneficial to their mental health and success.

CHALLENGES

During her early years as a school counselor, the author recognized the gap between the knowledge she obtained in my graduate program and the actual knowledge required to work with students with trauma. She diligently sought out various trainings and workshops to build her skillset in providing more trauma-informed care in the school setting. While the concerns and needs of students with trauma can be overwhelming, it is crucial for school counselors to recognize environmental, social, and psychological triggers of students in order to provide a safe space for them. Becoming aware of trauma-informed practices could assist School counselors in making a greater impact on students and placing them on the right track to be successful in school and the community.

Most graduate school counseling programs do not elaborate on the trauma-informed practices and techniques that would be beneficial in working with students with trauma. In fact, most programs do not require school counseling interns to work with students with trauma during internship and practicums so as the interns progress into school counseling positions, they may feel unprepared or even overwhelmed when it comes to providing services to address those needs.

Since the learning opportunities are not available in most graduate programs, the new School counselors may not readily identify signs of trauma. As time progresses and the students' needs are not identified or addressed, developmental and academic disruptions may occur. Trauma and adverse childhood experiences may exacerbate children's inability to cope, causing more toxic stress and trauma. When trauma is untreated or unresolved, it can negatively impact children's mental well-being, physical health, increase the likelihood of substance abuse, and decrease their potential for a quality of life.

At a broad contextual level, although School counselors are not required to be Licensed Professional Counselors, there are a number of trauma-informed practices that could be utilized within their scope to assist students. There are perhaps limitations to time with students and interventions; however, in many cases trauma-informed care can be successfully intertwined with School Counseling.

SEARCHING FOR A SOLUTION

In a previous study, the author of this book found that school counselors believed that they were not adequately prepared by their graduate school counseling programs to work with students with trauma. Given their charge to adhere to the counseling standards set forth by their school districts, administrators, and state requirements, many school counselors often find themselves serving in ambiguous capacities and have little time to focus on extra training.

Solutions to the problem of working with students with trauma hark back at shifting emphasis from generic graduate school counseling programs to incorporating trauma-informed practices within the graduate curriculum. Although many researchers have indicated the relationship between trauma and academic success, traditional school counseling practices still dominate.

ORGANIZATION OF THE BOOK

The book is organized into 12 chapters. A brief description of each of the chapters follows:

Chapter 1: Elementary Counselors' Perspectives of Trauma-Informed Preparedness

This chapter presents a research study focusing on the perceptions of school counselors and how well they believed they were prepared by their graduate counseling programs to work with students who have experienced trauma. The chapter sets the scene for discussions presented by various authors in subsequent chapters. In particular the chapter identifies the global perception of school counselors and the related problems they encounter when working with students with trauma. It also identifies the importance of incorporating trauma-informed practices in graduate-level school counseling programs.

Chapter 2: School Counselor Role Advocacy

The authors establish the need for a positive working relationship between school administrators and school counselors. Successful collaboration is critical to the development of successful student-centered programs and increased counselor self-efficacy. The authors of this chapter contend that by investing in the administrator-counselor collaboration, school counselors may be more successful in working in alignment with the vision of the program, providing enhanced services, and fostering positive student well-being and academic achievement.

Chapter 3: Trauma-Informed School Counseling – Foundations and Interventions

In this chapter, the author reviews the foundational underpinning of trauma-informed care and how it applies to school counseling. The author expounds on these principal aspects in the following chapter sections: a) What is Trauma-Informed Care?, b) The Importance of Trauma-Informed Care in School Counseling, c) Guiding Principles to Taking a Trauma-Informed Approach: Theory and Application, d) Recognizing and Responding to the Systemic and Contextual Factors Surrounding Trauma, e) Trauma-Informed Care in Action: Case Study Examples, and f) Conclusion. The author contends that the awareness of trauma and its impact on children and adolescents is a growing concern for school counselors. The author further suggests that trauma exposure in children and adolescents have been linked to several barriers including academic success, socioemotional and physical health, behavior, and overall well-being.

Chapter 4: Preparing for the Unexpected

The author takes philosophical orientation and describes the four critical components of the crisis management planning process. The author discusses the importance of developing and maintaining an ongoing process of planning practicing, and evaluating to be prepared for unexpected crises. Having a system in place to prevent, prepare, respond, and recover affords the school counselor to act expediently in providing crisis counseling services to students in need. The author examines some challenges in systematic execution of crisis management. The overall aim of the chapter is to prepare school counselors to answer the question "are you prepared for the unexpected?"

Chapter 5: Servant Leadership – School Counseling During the Pandemic

The authors review the importance of becoming a servant leader in the role of a school counselor. The authors of this chapter classify a servant leader as one who values their caretaking efforts of others while providing optimal support. As school counselors implement the Multitiered System of Support (MTSS) framework in working with students as an effort to ensure that students are receiving equitable resources. In this chapter, the authors delineate the MTSS process and how it benefits the well-being of students. The authors also discuss how school counselors were forced to pivot the MTSS framework during the pandemic. Best practices for this process are discussed.

Chapter 6: Virtual School Counseling

The author of this chapter presents an analysis of issues and concerns in the sudden shift in the learning environment after the onset of the COVID-19 pandemic. In this regard, the author reviews the response to the pandemic and discusses best practices for schools who temporarily shifted to virtual settings. The author disproves the notion that virtual learning is a novel concept and explores best practices of pre-existing virtual school systems. The author examines how the virtual learning format aligns with the American School counselor Association (ASCA) National Model, and reviews special consideration specifically for school counselors.

Chapter 7: Gifted and Talented – Not Always a Gift

The authors address the traumatic issues of gifted and talented (GT) students. Contrary to popular belief, GT students may experience a unique type of traumatic stress. The authors suggest that there seems to be reluctance on part of GT students to express themselves. Being categorized as smarter than average and set aside brings about new challenges such as bullying, isolation, and stress for GT students. In most cases although there may be a few variations, GT students bring unique abilities and may have cognitive processes above the norm. The authors discuss ways to work with GT students facing trauma as their exceptional cognitive abilities may be taken for granted and misunderstood.

Chapter 8: Addressing Social Justice Issues in Schools Utilizing Trauma-Informed Care

The authors of this chapter addressed trauma and its impact on children and adolescents. They explain that as a possible outcome of childhood adversity, trauma affects students' social/behavioral skills and academic performance. They present research-based evidence contending that traumatic exposure is positively associated with social justice. The authors conclude the chapter by providing recommendations on implementing trauma-informed care to address social justice issues in schools.

Chapter 9: Trauma-Informed School Counseling Practices to Address COVID-19 Fueled Discrimination and Racial Trauma in Asian American Youth – A Multitiered Systems of Support

This chapter reviews issues surrounding racial bias and discrimination among Asian American youth. There was a marked escalation in violence towards Asian American youth after the onset of COVID-19. Since the virus was presumed to have originated in China, many Asian Americans became targets of racial discrimination and violence. The authors of this chapter further discuss how historical stereotypes and misconceptions of Asian Americans were exacerbated through media coverage and social media. This massive outbreak in the United States cause many Asian American youth to become targets of violence and bullying. The focus of this chapter is to provide school counselors recommendations of best practices in addressing racial trauma within this population. They discuss using the MTSS as a tool to help in achieving this purpose.

Chapter 10: Reporting Child Abuse and Neglect on K-12 Campuses

The chapter encompasses the practice of recognizing and reporting child abuse on K-12 campuses. The authors define and discuss the prevalence of child abuse by highlighting the four primary forms: 1) physical, 2) sexual, 3) emotional, and 4) neglect. The authors provide detailed information how and when to report child abuse, how to request an escalation of priority, as well as provide a checklist for school counselors to use in organizing the process. The authors conclude the chapter with a case study and discussing post-reporting self-care strategies for school counselors.

Chapter 11: School Counseling for Children of Incarcerated Parents

The authors of this chapter address working with children of incarcerated parents. The authors indicate the necessity of school counselors having the ability to recognize the stress and trauma experienced by children of incarcerated parents. In this chapter, the authors delineate the needs of CIP paying close attention to how school counselors could best serve those students. They will discuss strategies and provide recommendations for school counselors to develop appropriate plans, coordinate their plans and programs, and facilitate small group counseling session for CIP.

Chapter 12: The Elephant in the Room – Using AAI in a School Counseling Program

This chapter concludes the book with a unique research-based intervention that could be used in schools. The author presents a single case study involving the implementation of canine-assisted animal intervention (AAI). The author will discuss the study to explain the benefit of AAI in working with children and adolescents with trauma.

Angela M. Powell
Lone Star College, USA

REFERENCES

Cambell, A. M. (2020). *An increasing risk of family violence during the Covid-19 pandemic: Strengthening community collaborations to save lives*. doi:10.1016/j.fsir.2020.100089

Kovler, M. L., Ziegfeld, S., Ryan, L. M., Goldstein, M. A., Gardner, R., Garcia, A. V., & Nasr, I. W. (2021). Increased proportion of physical child abuse injuries at a level I pediatric trauma center during the Covid-19 pandemic. *Child Abuse & Neglect, 116*(2), 104756. Advance online publication. doi:10.1016/j.chiabu.2020.104756 PMID:33004213

United States Department of Homeland Security, Federal Emergency Management Agency. (2006). *Designated counties for Alabama Hurricane Katrina*. Available from: https://www.fema.gov/news/eventcounties.fema?id=4825

Introduction

School counselors have been a vital component in school systems for many years. There is a great deal to be understood in working with children and adolescents who have experienced trauma during their early stages of life. Research and discussions of the relationship between mental well-being, trauma, academic success, and quality of life have been moving at a steady pace to the forefront of education. Yet, there is documented evidence of the unrelenting need for more trauma-informed school counseling programs (Rawson, 2020a). Perhaps since the onset of the pandemic of the Coronavirus, the topic of school counselors being prepared to work with students with trauma has become more prevalent. However, in addition to adjusting to the crises related to the pandemic, there are many other sources of trauma that school counselors should be aware of as it relates to implementing appropriate interventions and providing quality services.

Many researchers have discussed the prevalence of childhood trauma and the staggering toll it takes on mental health. Developing and implementing trauma-informed practices ca be a slow process in order to shift the culture and existing systems (Rawson, 2020b). This shift will come with patience and research based evidence to present to administrators. In order for the shift to be successful, the school counselor must have the support from fellow educators as well as administration.

During the process of shifting the mindset among faculty and staff, school counselors may be charged with engaging others, sustaining motivation, and maintaining systematic planning. Osher (2018) described the importance of being intentional in developing and sustaining a positive school climate and creating a collaborative system of change. The Trauma and Learning Policy Initiative involves six elements that should be incorporated in order for a school to become successfully trauma-informed with sustainable practices (2018).

- Leadership
- Professional Development
- Access to Resources and Services
- Academic and Non-academic Strategies

- Policies and Protocols
- Collaboration with Families

Rawson (2020b) noted that to develop a successful trauma-informed program, this framework must be aligned with the school's policy and vision. Developing and implementing The school counselor would need the support of administration in order to enforce standard policies and procedures. Leadership and strategic planning teams should meet to form guidelines, action plans, and evaluation strategies to carry out the program.

Teachers should receive training on how to communicate with students and families in order to build connectivity and positive relationships. They should also be provided access to resources to assist students. This may include outside training for the teachers as well. The school counselor could consider inviting mental health professionals outside of the school to host a training for teachers to foster trauma awareness. Having the proper knowledge and training will give the teachers the tools they need to help students to improve their emotional regulation, improve social skills, and support their social emotional learning overall.

While school counselors are privy to a wealth of knowledge and resources to assist students and families, being the sole person with this information can become overwhelming at times. In action planning and setting the stage to provide a more well-rounded trauma-informed program, some resources may be shared with other school personnel such as the nurse, or front office staff. In the event that a parent should have questions regarding outside resources, one of these staff members could offer immediate support rather than taking the school counselor away from their current schedule or even frustrating the awaiting parent as the staff member locates someone else with answers. Not only does this intervention allow the school counselor more time to focus on students, but it could also lend itself to other staff members becoming more trauma sensitive and connecting with the stakeholders (Rawson, 2020b).

As training is made available to all staff members, academic and non-academic strategies may be helpful in building relationships with students and encouraging them to become more comfortable at school feeling secure and a part of a caring "community." Supporting student participation, having a strength-based approach when discussing their interests, and implementing positive behavior interventions will all be beneficial in working with students with trauma.

This book is a collaborative project designed to assist school counselors in designing a comprehensive counseling program utilizing trauma-informed practices. It focuses on the skills and strategies that will enable the school counselor to work more effectively with children and adolescents from a trauma-informed viewpoint. There are methods described to begin the process and to encourage a new mindset among faculty and staff. The introductory chapter activates this discussion with a study conducted by the author of this book. The author described the overall common perception of school counselors not feeling prepared to work with students with trauma. After reading this book, school counselors are encouraged to seek further consultation and training to gain more substantial knowledge in utilizing trauma-informed practices in school counseling.

REFERENCES

Osher, D. (2018). *Trauma and Learning Policy Initiative (TLPI): Trauma-sensitive schools descriptive study.* American Institute for Research. https://traumasensitiveschools. org/wp-content/uploads/2019/02/TLPI-Final-Report_Full-Report-002-2-1. pdf

Rawson, S. (2020a). *Applying Trauma-sensitive Practices in School Counseling: Interventions for Achieving Change*. Routledge.

Rawson, S. (2020b). Trauma-Sensitive Schools: Reframing the “Why” Not the “How”. In Applying Trauma-Sensitive Practices in School Counseling (pp. 61-76). Routledge.

Chapter 1
Elementary Counselors' Perspectives of Trauma-Informed Preparedness

Angela M. Powell
Lone Star College, USA

ABSTRACT

Nearly half of all students in primary and secondary school in the United States have experienced trauma. As a result, school counselors' preparedness to work with those students may affect the traumatized youths' overall mental, academic, social, and physical well-being. This phenomenological study explored the degree to which elementary school counselors perceived their level of preparedness to work with children who have experienced trauma. Elementary school counselors within a Texas urban school district completed an in-depth interview. The emerging themes from this study delineated consistent perceptions of inadequate graduate school training to work with traumatized youth. Implications for counselor educators are discussed.

INTRODUCTION

Youth trauma and crisis is a well documented issue and the number of impacted youth continues to increase across the United States (Finkelhor et al., 2015; Ports et al., 2016; Ruiz, 2016; Saunders, & Adams, 2014). School counselors are charged with the task of implementing strategies for all students in order to assist them in reaching their potential in school (American School Counselor Association (ASCA), 2012), including students who may be experiencing some type of trauma symptomatology (Brown et al., 2008). Although mental well-being and high academic

DOI: 10.4018/978-1-7998-9785-9.ch001

achievement (ASCA, 2012) are the expectations, there is a question of how well school counselors are trained to work with students who have experienced trauma. Although there is a great amount of research that describes the increasing number of students experiencing trauma (Briere & Scott, 2015; Bücker et al., 2012; Cohen et al., 2010; & Finkelhor et al., 2015), there is a paucity of literature that discusses the level of training that school counselors receive to assist them, particularly at the elementary level.

The purpose of this study was to explore the perceptions of school counselors and how well they believed they were prepared by their graduate counseling programs to work with students who have experienced trauma. In order to better serve the elementary school student population, it is critical to understand the counselors' perceptions of their preparedness to work with them. In response to the documented prevalence and impact of youth trauma and the apparent scarcity of literature that addresses school counselor training with this population, the author of this chapter explored the perceptions of elementary school counselors and addressed the research question: How do elementary school counselors perceive their graduate counseling program's preparation for work with students who have experienced trauma?

LITERATURE REVIEW

Fitzgerald (2013) conducted a qualitative study that explored the perceptions of six counselors-in-training as it related to their training and level of confidence when counseling youth who have experienced interpersonal trauma. She reported that trauma exposure most often has dire effects on youth, thus asserting that counseling graduate programs should have "intensive training and supervision specific to traumatology" (p. 3). More importantly, Fitzgerald noted that counselor educators have an ethical obligation to provide adequate training pointing out the sensitivity and risks involved in counseling youth who have experienced trauma. Ironically, in her study of six counselors-in-training, Fitzgerald found that participants were not academically prepared to provide adequate trauma counseling.

Grubbs (2015) conducted a similar study as Fitzgerald (2013) focusing on "school counselors' perceptions of job preparedness based on their graduate training programs" (p. 1). Upon completing her study of six school counselors, Grubbs (2015) discovered that school counselors perceived their graduate training as inadequate preparation for the arduous and ambiguous responsibilities of school counselors. Given the fact that Texas school counselors are required by the Texas Education Agency (TEA, 2014) to work with students according to the state mandated comprehensive guidance model, many school counselors' job requirements are dictated by the school principal. School counselors may be inundated by various miscellaneous duties leaving minimal time to adequately work with students who need counseling interventions. Further, with TEA's focus being on the comprehensive model (TEA, 2014), many graduate programs provide training to meet those standards; consequently, there is not enough training on trauma to meet the needs of the increased number of students who have experienced traumatic events. Koeller and Bertel (2006) noted that there has been a significant increase in the number of students who need mental health interventions in schools; however, with school counselors' lack of the knowledge and skills to work with those students, it is suspected that school counselors may perceive that their graduate training to work with children who have experienced trauma would be even more unlikely.

Impact of Youth Trauma

Academic impact. Researchers have found that trauma has a negative effect on children's and adolescents' emotional well-being, cognitive ability, and memory (Briere & Scott, 2015; Brown et al., 2008; Cohen et al., 2012). These symptoms could have significant adverse effects on the child's academic achievement in the school setting (Brown et al., 2008). School counselors are vital in assisting traumatized children by identifying trauma symptoms (Cohen et al., 2012) and referring them to the proper mental health professional. Although therapy is not appropriate in all school settings, school counselors should be trained to recognize trauma symptoms and collaborate with teachers and administrators in providing a safe and nurturing environment for them (Brown et al., 2008; Cohen et al., 2012).

In a qualitative study of 21 adolescent students from two predominantly African American low socioeconomic (SES) schools, Thomas et al. (2012), reported that a recurrent theme emerging from the adolescents' responses was that adults in their schools mostly focused on their academic performance and rarely addressed their stressors associated with violence and family issues. Not being provided with the proper interventions and support to process their trauma may leave students confused and frustrated with their emotions, leading to more difficulties in the future.

This suggests that the direct negative effects from violence exposure may be exacerbated by the lack of opportunity to process these issues with significant adults in their lives, placing them at greater risk for developing internalizing difficulties and externalizing behaviors (Thomas et al., 2012, p. 60).

According to Crozier and Barth (2005), maltreated children are more likely to exhibit aggression, poor peer relationships, and a variety of emotional problems. Without the intervention of a trauma informed school counselor, traumatized students' undesirable behaviors may be misinterpreted as disruption and aggression in the school environment, leading to unduly disciplinary actions (Cohen et al., 2012; van der Kolk, 2014). Such discipline and ridicule often leads to students becoming disengaged from school and isolating themselves from their peers, cycling more undesirable behaviors (Cohen et al., 2012).

Cognitive impact. Several researchers have contended that trauma physically restructures the brain, especially in young children (Bücker et al., 2012; Cohen et al., 2010; Perry, 2002; van der Kolk, 2014; Wilkinson, 2016). Trauma has been linked to the physical alteration and defragmentation of the hippocampus and the prefrontal cortex, areas most affected by stress (Bücker et al., 2012, p. 759). van der Kolk (2014) stated that when individuals experience trauma, their brains become locked in the present state of the trauma making it difficult to develop or incorporate new experiences in their lives.

Social impact. Severe trauma poses a negative course of direction on youth's social interactions with others (Perry, 2002; van der Kolk, 2014; Wilkinson, 2016). Properly trained school counselors may be able to identify youth trauma prior to the onset of a host of negative trauma related social behaviors including, but not limited to conduct disorder, oppositional defiant disorder, isolation, distrust in others, substance abuse, and early sexual activity which in many cases positions to be unpopular among their peers (Wilkinson, 2016). As such, Wilkinson (2016) and Perry (2002) reported that since many youth repeatedly experience trauma, their social skills are markedly affected having a negative impact on their interpersonal relationships with others as well as their academic performance. These adverse effects from trauma may be offset by early detection, interventions, and outside referrals by properly trained school counselors.

Theoretical Framework

School counselors are obligated to implement comprehensive school counselor programs that meet the needs of students, school staff members, and parents. Several standards have been set in order to provide school counselors a guide to develop their school counseling programs, assuring quality counseling services to students and support to staff, parents, and the community.

The ASCA model (2012) entails four major components: foundation, management, delivery, and accountability. School counselors have a broad range of responsibilities including referrals and consultations with other mental health professionals. According to the Council for Accreditation of Counseling & Related Educational Programs (CACREP) standards, school counselors are required to have professional knowledge of trauma (2016) and should be able to identify characteristics of "students at risk for mental health and behavioral disorders" (Sec. 5.g., 2.g). CACREP accredited programs must account for the implementation of these components in their programs (2016); however, it is not clear as to the intensity or depth of training required.

The Texas Education Agency (TEA) (2014) requires school counselors to provide a guidance curriculum to all students, to respond to students who exhibit personal issues that may interfere academically, to assist students in individual personal and social goals, to consult with teachers, and to support parents through parent educational programs and community connections. This model outlines the format and time allotted for school counselors to work with students in the school setting.

Studies of youth trauma conducted by several researchers have led those researchers to indicate that there is a tremendous prevalence of trauma among youth in the United States (Finkelhor et al., 2015; Ports et al., 2016; Ruiz, 2016). It is not clear; however, that this phenomenon has been addressed in counselor education programs by adequately preparing school counselors-in-training to work with students who have experienced trauma. Through previous research studies, researchers have pointed out the profound physical, cognitive, social, and academic impact of trauma on youth (Cohen et al., 2010; Perry, 2002; van der Kolk, 2014, Wilkinson, 2016). The general population of individuals outside of the educational realm may assume that school counselors are properly trained to assist students presenting a plethora of symptomatology, yet extant research on this issue is scant. Ultimately, what is at stake here is the overall well-being of youth. In order to assist traumatized youth with proper school-based interventions, it is important to understand the training and preparation of school counselors to determine any necessary adjustments relevant to graduate counseling programs and counseling supervision.

Methodology

A phenomenological study consists of describing the common experiences of participants and focusing on a "common meaning" among their "lived experiences" (Creswell, 2013, p. 76). Using a phenomenological approach (Creswell, 2013; Moustakas, 1994), the researchers conducted face-to-face interviews with ten elementary school counselors to investigate their perceptions of their preparation to work with traumatized children. Given this process, the phenomenological approach (Creswell, 2013; Miles et al., 2014) was suitable for this study.

The semi-structured face-to-face interview questions were derived from a review of the literature of school counselor training and their perceptions of their training. The questions inquired about the participants' definition of trauma, how they viewed their work with students who have experienced trauma, how they viewed their graduate program preparing them to work with this population, how their graduate program preparation impacted their effectiveness as a school counselor, and how they perceived their level of competence in working with students with trauma histories. Participants offered more information which led to a more detailed and enriched insight of their perceptions.

Participants

Purposive sampling was used to enlist participants for this study. Purposive sampling was determined to be most suitable for this study due to the characteristics of the population and the objective of the study. Ten state certified elementary school counselors in an urban school district in Southwest Texas participated in the study. Their school counseling experience ranged between 3 and 15 years. Eight of the 10 participants were female, and two were male, with 80% African American and 20% Hispanic. According to self report, all were state certified school counselors according to Texas standards (TEA, 2014) with a Masters' degree being the highest degree obtained, and one being a Licensed Professional Counselor-Intern. None of the participants were Licensed Professional Counselors. Pseudonyms were used instead of the counselors' names throughout this study to protect their identity.

Results

As a result of organizing and coding the data, several themes emerged across the interviews with the participants. The three main themes were *self-efficacy, lack of competence, and self motivation*. Following is a discussion of the categories of participants' themes.

Self-efficacy. There was a positive relationship between self-efficacy and performance. Self-efficacy is referred to as an individual's belief that he or she has the ability to successfully complete a given task. Therefore, as the school counselors' self-efficacy increases, so will his or her performance (Sawyer et al., 2013).

Three out of 10 participants endorsed self-efficacy during their interview. As Nova reflected on the question regarding how she perceived her effectiveness as a school counselor, her voice became softer as she looked downward. "I wish I could help them more. I focus more on guidance lessons. At times, I don't know if I'm being effective as a counselor because I don't feel [like] I'm being helpful to them in being more resilient." Leonard reported feeling stressed when students act out because he is uncertain about his worth as a counselor. "I don't know if I am ready to handle it. It seems like it's getting worse."

Michelle revealed her apprehension about working with students with trauma stating that she can not afford to attend trainings to learn more about trauma. "I get nervous every time I have to work with one [student with trauma] because I don't want to make matters worse."

Lack of competence. Of the 10 participants, nine admitted to having minimal training during their graduate programs to work with traumatized students. Participants' perspectives were very similar in how they viewed their own levels of competence when working with students who have experienced trauma. Although the participants appeared to understand the importance of their roles as school counselors, they were also shaken when working with this population. They entered the school counseling profession believing they had been thoroughly prepared for their responsibilities but have come to realize that there was an important component to their training curriculum that was missed. When asked to describe how she viewed her work with students who have experienced trauma, Jamie stated,

At times it can be difficult, you know, I think as you get more training and learn more about trauma from the beginning you really didn't.... I really didn't know what it was until I actually found out what it was. So I guess the experience has been.... Early on in my career... (took a deep breath and hesitantly stated) ... not knowing was frustrating. Even though I have gone to trainings throughout my career but I had my first trauma training after 10 years of counseling this year, I still feel unprepared. I'm still not comfortable.

Brenda admitted to having little knowledge about how to work with traumatized students and described how she does not mention the trauma unless the student initiates the conversation. She discussed not having time to spend with students as she should due to "duties, visiting classrooms, and meetings." She believed that with her lack of counseling techniques when working with students with trauma she would "cause more harm than good."

Self-motivation. "I go to conferences on my own once a year," Nova stated and "my school [university] did not prepare me at all for what I deal with every day as a school counselor." Leonard also mentioned his self-initiative to attend conferences, "Well, I seek out conferences to find out more about how to work with them [traumatized students]. It's kinda difficult though because their situations are so different and it's hard to know what's what." All of the participants stated that they actively attend trainings and enjoy learning more about how to work with students with trauma. However, there is the underlying obstacle of being absent from work to do so. We also identified two additional issues, graduate training and school counselors' ambiguous duties, that seemed to be dominant in the lives of the participants of this study.

Graduate Training

Ninety percent of the participants shared the same perspective about their graduate school counseling program. They consistently stated that they did not receive any trauma training while preparing to become school counselors. Although trauma was briefly mentioned, they had "no idea what that looked like", Jamie stated. Ms. Jackson proudly reported being trained and exposed to working with students with trauma through an extensive practicum in her graduate program although school funding limits her ability to efficiently work with the students. She stated that training has proven to be helpful in the school counseling setting as the trauma symptomology is recognizable among the student body. She also reported being happier as a result of her training as opposed to some of her "counselor friends".

Nikki felt comfortable in her ability to provide guidance and other components of counseling; however, where trauma is concerned, she withers. On a scale of 1-5 with 1 being not prepared at all and 5 being well prepared to work with students with trauma, she rated her competence level as 2. She explained

I don't think that my program prepared me to work with traumatized students the way that I would have loved them to. In my opinion, they focused more on theories and not on real world situations and experiences like trauma.

Ambiguous Duties

Limited resources have forced many school counselors to take on ambiguous responsibilities that do not pertain to school counseling. Although Ms. Jackson believed that she was well prepared by her graduate program, she still has to balance her time between administrative duties which limits her time to work with students in need. During a normal day, she spends a considerable amount of time monitoring the hallways, disciplining students, serving as an administrator in committees, and attending various meetings that she described as "frustrating and time consuming".

Discussion

Through this study, the author gained insight into the frustration experienced by school counselors who felt unprepared to help children who have been impacted by trauma and the implications for counselor educators and administrators as well as it relates to adding traumatized children. Regardless of the critical numbers of students with trauma and crises in the community, researchers have imparted the tremendous need for school counselors to be prepared to work with traumatized students. Sawyer et al. (2013) contended that "only 10.6% of school counselors reported taking a specific course involving school crisis interventions and 57% reported feeling inadequately or minimally prepared to handle crisis situations" (p. 31).

Because many graduate counseling curriculums do not provide direct instruction and practicum in working with students with trauma, it is apparent that school counselors are entering the profession ill prepared. As the demands of school counselors increase, they may become frustrated and begin to experience burn out due to their lack of knowledge and stress in attempting to complete their tasks. As reflected by Gündüz (2012), school counselors may experience burn out as a result of feeling overwhelmed by a lack of self-efficacy. Consequently, "counselors may have decreased confidence in their skills and self-efficacies thus eroding their talents and competencies" (Gündüz, 2012, p. 1762). Such distortions may be prevented with the incorporation of a thorough curriculum for school counselors-in-training that includes crisis and trauma counseling.

Additionally, school counselors are inundated with ambiguous duties that remove them from their counseling roles. Many students, in turn, are not provided adequate services and are left in the hands of uninformed teachers and administrators. With proper training, school counselors' self-efficacy could increase as they would be able to identify trauma symptomatology and either provide proper school interventions or refer to outside professionals.

The findings clearly indicate that elementary school counselors do not feel prepared to work with students who have experienced trauma. Interestingly, all participants in this study defined trauma; however, some could not identify symptomatology, and most all desire more training on the topic. As noted by the participants, providing adequate time and mental health care to traumatized students has not been the general occurrence which adds to the significance of this study. The results add to the knowledge base by highlighting the increased number of students who are being referred to the office and receiving punitive consequences for behaviors that should be addressed by the school counselor; and noting the increase in out of school suspensions, over-crowded response-to-intervention programs, and special education programs.

Implications

School counselors are essential to the success of students who have experienced trauma. They are the connection between the students' mental well being and successful education; therefore, trauma and crisis training is needed to equip school counselors in assisting youth in schools. The data collected in this study should increase the understanding of the lack of trauma and crisis training for school counselors in their graduate programs and its impact on students. Trauma courses incorporated into the graduate school counseling curriculum would be beneficial to the developing school counselor. Because there has not been much research on school counselor supervision of youth with trauma, graduate counseling programs that offer youth trauma training and school counseling practicums that include trauma cases should be explored further. Additionally, more research to focus on the relationship between trauma counseling and academic success should be undertaken so that a greater understanding of the relationship between the two can be realized. Helping students relieve the symptoms of trauma can lead to great academic success and improved graduation rates, which is the goal of private and public education.

Limitations

In this study, we explored the experiences of 10 elementary school counselors who are employed in a specific school district in Southwest Texas. There are limitations to this study that should be considered when interpreting the results. First, due to the participants being located in one general area, there is a chance that many if not most of the participants attended the same university. Moreover, a larger and possibly more diverse sample would yield more generalizable results. Since the participants' definitions of trauma may vary, their responses may reflect their differing meanings of trauma.

REFERENCES

American School Counselor Association. (2012). *ASCA national model: A framework for school counseling programs* (3rd ed.). Author.

Briere, J., & Scott, C. (2015). *Principles of trauma therapy: A guide to symptoms, evaluation, and treatment* (2nd ed.). Sage.

Brown, S. D., Brack, G., & Mullis, F. D. (2008). Traumatic symptoms in sexually abused children: Implications for school counselors. *Professional School Counseling Journal, 11*(6), 368–379. doi:10.5330/PSC.n.2010-11.368

Bücker, J., Kapczinski, F., Post, R., Ceresér, K. M., Szobot, C., Yatham, L. N., Kapczinski, N. S., & Kauer-Sant'Anna, M. (2012). Cognitive impairment in school-aged children with early trauma. *Comprehensive Psychiatry, 53*, 758-764. doi:10.1016/j.comppsych.2011.12.006

Council for Accreditation of Counseling & Related Educational Programs. (2016). *2016 CACREP standards*. Retrieved from https://www.cacrep.org/section-5-entry-level-specialty-areas-school-counseling/

Cohen, J. A., Berliner, L., & Mannarino, A. (2010). Trauma focused CBT for children with co-occurring trauma and behavior problems. *Child Abuse & Neglect, 34*(4), 215–224. doi:10.1016/j.chiabu.2009.12.003 PMID:20304489

Cohen, J. A., Mannarino, A. P., & Deblinger, E. (2012). *Trauma-focused CBT for children and adolescents: Treatment Applications*. Guilford Press.

Creswell, J. W. (2013). *Qualitative inquiry and research design: Choosing among five traditions* (3rd ed.). Sage.

Crozier, J. C., & Barth, R. P. (2005). Cognitive and academic functioning in maltreated children. *Children & Schools, 27*(4), 197–206. doi:10.1093/cs/27.4.197

Finkelhor, D., Turner, H. A., Shattuck, A., & Hamby, S. L. (2015). Prevalence of childhood exposure to violence, crime, and abuse: Results from the national survey of children's exposure to violence. *Journal of the American Medical Association, 169*(8), 746–754. PMID:26121291

Fitzgerald, E. (2013). *Perceptions of counselors-in-training regarding preparation and level of confidence when counseling children who have experienced interpersonal trauma* (Doctoral dissertation). Retrieved from ProQuest. (3575109)

Grubbs, L. (2015). *Texas school counselors' perceptions of job preparedness based on their graduate training programs* (Doctoral dissertation). Retrieved from ProQuest. (3664337)

Gündüz, B. (2012). Self-efficacy and burn out in professional school counselors. *Educational Sciences: Theory and Practice, 12*(3), 1761–1767.

Koeller, J. R., & Bertel, J. M. (2006). Responding to today's mental health needs of children, families and schools: Revisiting the preservice training and preparation of school-based personnel. *Education & Treatment of Children, 29*(2), 197–217.

Maxwell, J. A. (2013). *Qualitative research design: An interactive approach* (3rd ed.). Sage.

Miles, M. B., Huberman, A. M., & Saldana, J. (2014). *Qualitative data analysis: A methods sourcebook*. Sage.

Moustakas, C. E. (1994). *Phenomenological research methods*. Sage. doi:10.4135/9781412995658

Perry, B. D. (2002). Childhood experience and the expression of genetic potential: What childhood neglect tells us about nature and nurture. *Brain and Mind: A Transdisciplinary Journal of Neuroscience and Neurophilosophy, 3*(2), 79-100.

Ports, K. A., Ford, D. C., & Merrick, M. T. (2016). Adverse childhood experiences and sexual victimization in adulthood. *Child Abuse & Neglect, 51*, 313–322. doi:10.1016/j.chiabu.2015.08.017 PMID:26386753

Ruiz, E. (2016). Trauma symptoms in a diverse population of sexually abused children. *Psychological Trauma: Theory, Research, Practice, and Policy, 8*(6), 680–687. doi:10.1037/tra0000160 PMID:27243569

Saunders, B. E., & Adams, Z. W. (2014). Epidemiology of traumatic experiences in childhood. *Child & Adolescent Psychiatric Clinics, 23*(2), 167–184. doi:10.1016/j.chc.2013.12.003 PMID:24656575

Sawyer, C., Peters, M. L., & Willis, J. (2013). Self-Efficacy of Beginning Counselors to Counsel Clients in Crisis. *The Journal of Counselor Preparation and Supervisor, 5*(2), 28–43. doi:10.7729/52.1015

Texas Education Agency. (2014). *A model comprehensive, developmental guidance and counseling program for Texas public school: A guide for program development pre-K-12th grade*. Author.

Thomas, A. J., Carey, D., Prewitt, K., Romero, E., Richards, M., & Velsor-Friedrich, B. (2012). African-American youth and exposure to community violence: Supporting Change from the inside. *Journal for Social Action in Counseling and Psychology, 4*(1), 54–68. doi:10.33043/JSACP.4.1.54-68

van der Kolk, B. (2014). *The body keeps the score: Brain, mind, and body in the healing of trauma*. Viking.

Wilkinson, I. G. (2016). Why some children come to school with "baggage": The effects of trauma due to poverty, attachment disruption and disconnection on social skills and relationships. *Canadian Journal of Family and Youth, 8*(1), 173–203. doi:10.29173/cjfy27147

Chapter 2
School Counselor Role Advocacy

Donna L. Hickman
Texas A&M University, Commerce, USA

Samantha L. Klassen
Texas A&M University, Commerce, USA

ABSTRACT

School counselors play a crucial role in the personal, academic, and career development of all students. With the delivery of a developmental, comprehensive counseling program, school counselors respond to a wide variety of student needs while supporting the school's academic vision. According to the American School Counselor Association (ASCA), school counselors should spend the vast majority of their time at school providing direct and indirect services to students. However, school counselors are often given responsibilities that do not fall under the umbrella of appropriate activities for school counselors and have little to do with counseling. Trauma-informed school counselors must be prepared to advocate for appropriate role responsibilities with their administrators. The goal of this chapter is to prepare school counselors to establish a clear professional identity through role advocacy. Ultimately, unambiguous role definition serves to advocate for students who need the services that professional school counselors are uniquely trained to provide.

INTRODUCTION

School counselors play a crucial role in the personal, academic, and career development of all students. With the delivery of a developmental, comprehensive counseling

DOI: 10.4018/978-1-7998-9785-9.ch002

program, school counselors respond to the social and emotional needs of students while supporting the school's academic vision (ASCA, 2019b). According to the American School Counselor Association (ASCA), school counselors should spend the vast majority of their time at school providing direct and indirect services to students (ASCA, 2019b). Direct services are defined as "in-person interactions between school counselors and students" (ASCA, 2019b, p. 77). Direct student services include the delivery of social/emotional curriculum instruction and individual and group counseling. Conversely, ASCA defines indirect student services as "services provided on behalf of students as a result of the school counselor's interactions with others" (ASCA, 2019b, p. 77). Indirect student services include consultations with parents and teachers, outside referrals, and interactions with people in the community. Overall, ASCA requires school counselors to prioritize the delivery of student services.

School counselors are tasked with facilitating the social, emotional, and academic growth of all students through the implementation of a comprehensive counseling and guidance program. Moreover, school counselors are mental health professionals who are specifically trained to identify and work with students who have been impacted by trauma. However, school counselors are often given responsibilities that do not fall under the umbrella of appropriate activities for school counselors and have little to do with counseling (Wilder, 2018). Trauma-informed school counselors must be prepared to advocate for appropriate role responsibilities with their administrators. Research has shown that school counselors experience higher levels of job satisfaction and have more time to provide services to students when they are assigned appropriate duties that align with the ASCA National Model (Hickman, 2020; Kim & Lambie, 2018; Mullen & Gutierrez, 2016). Professional advocacy in the field of school counseling is critical to promote the profession and help school counselors establish a clear professional identity. Ultimately, unambiguous role definition serves to advocate for students who need the services that professional school counselors are uniquely qualified to provide.

Defining the School Counselor Role

The school counseling profession emerged in response to social, educational, political, and economic changes in society (Gysbers, 2010). School counselors have had an impact on student development since the early 1900s. However, trends in society and movements within the profession have resulted in various interpretations and misconceptions about the school counselor's role. As Dahir (2004) stated, "The history of school counseling has depicted a profession in search of an identity" (p. 345).

BRIEF HISTORY OF THE SCHOOL COUNSELING PROFESSION

The role of the school counselor has changed significantly over the last 100 years. The school counseling profession began as vocational guidance in the early 1900s. During this time, teachers and administrators served in the role. Other than a list of responsibilities, a clear definition of the role did not exist. In the 1920s, the role shifted from vocational guidance to a clinically-focused approach emphasizing personal adjustment and "mental hygiene" (Gysbers, 2010). During the 1930s, a new organizational structure known as **pupil personnel services** emerged. This shift resulted from discussions within the field about how school counseling services were delivered and who was responsible for providing them. In the 1940s and 1950s, the profession shifted again as a result of efforts related to World War II. After World War II ended in 1945, discussions within the field resumed on how to provide counseling services in schools. With the passage of the Vocational Education Act in 1946 and the National Defense Education Act in 1958, the hiring and training of school counselors received additional attention and support. Additionally, the **American School Counselor Association** was established in 1952 to provide structure and guidelines for a rapidly growing field (Gysbers, 2010).

During the 1960s and 1970s, the identity of the school counseling profession was again under debate. Leaders in the field were divided about the nature and purpose of the profession: Should school counseling be viewed through a psychological lens with counseling as a major focus? Or should the profession be conceptualized through an educational lens, including activities such as assessment, placement, and follow-up services in addition to counseling? Another major development during this time was the separation of training practices and procedures for elementary school counselors and secondary school counselors. Although elementary school counseling had previously been discussed, the implementation of school counseling services for elementary school students finally became a reality in the 1960s (Gysbers, 2010).

The 1960s and 1970s also saw the beginnings of a **comprehensive program** approach to school counseling. Calls for change within the field led to a movement that lasted into the 1980s, 1990s, and beyond. During this time, states began developing their own models and additional training programs were implemented. A related concern during this period was related to terminology: Should the role be referred to as guidance, guidance and counseling, or school counseling?

Although progress was made towards the implementation of comprehensive school counseling programs during this time, the debate over the exact nature of the role continued. Should the work of school counselors focus on academic, career, or social/emotional concerns? What specific content should be included in a comprehensive school counseling program? During this period, the school counseling profession began to focus on using **data** to identify student needs and concerns. In the early 2000s, the standardization of school counseling programs across the country increased with the publication of the first edition of the ASCA National Model (ASCA, 2003). The ASCA National Model provided much-needed structure, consistency, and standardization to the field of school counseling. A second edition of the ASCA National Model was published in 2005, followed by the third edition in 2013. The most current edition of the model was published in 2019 (Gysbers, 2010).

Over the last 10 years, the concepts of data and **accountability** have been at the forefront of the profession. Literature in the field has focused on the use of data to demonstrate the efficacy of school counseling programs in schools. Professional school counselors must be able to use data to continuously improve their work and advocate for their roles with administrators. Furthermore, school counselors should be prepared to use data to identify student needs, plan their interventions, and prove that their interventions are working.

While it is impossible to predict the next 100 years of the profession, it is clear that students benefit from the implementation of a comprehensive, developmental school counseling program. Although the exact nature of the role has evolved over time, the overarching goal has always remained the same: to support students. Professional school counselors can honor the past and greet the future by focusing on supporting students through the implementation of a comprehensive school counseling program.

ASCA Role Statements

The American School Counselor Association defines the role of the school counselor in this way:

"School counselors are highly educated, professionally certified individuals who help students succeed in school and plan their career. An integral part of the total education system, school counselors help students form healthy goals, mindsets and behaviors. With the aid of a school counselor, students learn to develop effective collaboration and cooperation skills, to practice perseverance, to develop time management and study skills, and to learn self-motivation and self-direction habits" (2021, para. 1).

The ASCA website contains a variety of resources for school counselors to use to support their role at school, including infographics, research articles, and position statements. In addition to the school counseling role resources, the ASCA website includes 49 position statements describing the organization's stance on specific education topics that have an impact on students. The ASCA position statements include topics on contemporary issues such as Anti-Racist Practices, Child Abuse and Neglect Prevention, Credentialing and Licensure, Discipline, High-Stakes Testing, Student Mental Health, Trauma-Informed Practice, and Virtual School Counseling. The authors encourage school counselors to utilize these resources when advocating for their role with administrators, parents, students, and the school community.

School Counselor vs. Guidance Counselor

As discussed earlier in this chapter, the terminology used to describe the role of the professional school counselor has evolved and changed over time. Historically, the title of "guidance counselor" was used to refer to counselors working in schools. However, the term has evolved into "school counselor" as the job description and duties have changed. Although some school districts still refer to professional school counselors as "guidance counselors," the American School Counselor Association encourages the use of the term "school counselor" to more accurately reflect the duties and responsibilities associated with the role.

Two recent research studies (Zyromski et al., 2019; Baker, Zyromski, & Granello, 2021) investigated the impact of terminology on perceptions of school counselor competency. A 2019 study of 200 professional school counselors found that "guidance counselors'' were perceived as less competent by study participants than "school counselors." A similar study replicated with members of the public found that participants who completed surveys with the term "guidance counselor" were statistically less likely to believe that school counselors were able to perform the duties associated with their role. These findings emphasize the importance of language and titles when advocating for the school counseling profession. Although confusion still exists to this day, school counselors can help reinforce their own professional identity by encouraging the use of the term "school counselor."

Questions for Reflection and Discussion

1. After reading about the history of the school counseling profession, what is your perception of the role confusion that exists within the profession?
2. As a professional school counselor, how can you advocate for the use of the term "school counselor" instead of "guidance counselor"? Why is this so important?

Administrator Perceptions of the School Counselor Role

The literature indicates that some principals are unaware of the existence of ASCA guidelines and standards (Wilder, 2018; Zalaquett & Chatters, 2012). Many principal training programs fail to provide adequate information about school counselor roles and responsibilities, and the majority of principals do not learn about the school counselor role until they assume their positions as building principals (Amatea & Clark, 2005). If principals are encouraged to establish an effective working relationship with school counselors, both parties will be prepared to form a collaborative partnership that helps students succeed (Wilder, 2018; Zalaquett, 2005). To that end, "understanding the diverse roles, responsibilities, and impacts of school counselors on students' success is crucial to the effective partnership between counselors and administrators" (Yavuz, Cayirdag, Dahir, & Gumuseli, 2017, p. 177).

When principals are unclear about appropriate roles for campus counselors, they may delegate responsibilities that are incongruent with ASCA standards. Although ASCA clearly delineates appropriate school counselor activities, principals often assign inappropriate activities to their school counselors. Some principals believe that school counselors should have responsibilities such as cafeteria duty, campus testing coordination, data entry, and other administrative tasks. One study found that a majority of secondary school principals thought that duties such as student registration and testing coordination fell under the umbrella of appropriate counselor duties (Pérusse, Goodnough, Donegan, & Jones, 2004). In general, research findings have indicated that professional school counselors have a responsibility to educate administrators on the role of professional school counselors and the standards of the profession (Amatea & Clark, 2005; Duslak & Geier, 2016; Lane et al., 2020).

PRINCIPAL TRAINING AND PREPARATION

The National Policy Board for Educational Administration's (NPBEA) *Professional Standards for Educational Leaders* (2015) include measures that directly relate to the school counselor's role as articulated in the ASCA National Standards. For example, the training standards for principal preparation include the ability to create "an inclusive, caring, and supportive school community that promotes the academic success and well-being of each student" and the principal's responsibility to honor the professional capacity of school personnel "to promote each student's academic success and well-being" (NPBEA, 2015, pg. 27). In essence, principals must understand how to create trauma-sensitive campus environments that attend to the mental health needs of students. Allowing school counselors to utilize their skills as mental health professionals is a natural way to accomplish these aims.

In practice, these standards should lead to principals' awareness of the social and emotional needs of learners as well as respect for the capacity of the school counselor to foster a positive campus climate, promote well-being, and cultivate academic success. However, many principal training programs fail to foster a genuine understanding of the school counselor's role as a school-based mental health professional. Principal certification programs often focus heavily on educational administration to the exclusion of intentional conversations and building collaborative relationships with colleagues to improve instruction, support achievement, and create a positive school culture. Next, perceptions that principals may hold about school counselors are examined and circumstances under which school counselors are better able to perform their job duties are identified.

Principal Perceptions of School Counselors

Given the challenges to principal training and preparation described above, it may be unsurprising that ambiguity and confusion around the school counselor's role present significant challenges for school stakeholders, including administrators, counselors, parents, and students (Yavuz, Cayirdag, Dahir, & Gumuseli, 2017). Principal-counselor collaboration can be a struggle in any school setting, though these issues seem to be particularly salient for school counselors who serve in public school settings.

Research by Yavuz and colleagues (2017) revealed that school counselors in private school settings were more likely to take on appropriate roles as articulated in the ASCA National Model, with private school counselors having more clarity around their job functions; being more directly involved with efforts to improve school climate; participating in key campus decision-making processes; and counseling students with social and emotional problems more frequently than their public school counterparts. In contrast, their public school counterparts were less likely to work alongside teachers and school administrators on campus improvement issues, including the development and implementation of prevention programs and professional development activities (Yavuz et al., 2017). In summary, school counselors, particularly in public school settings, must be intentional about advocating for their role as a school-based mental health professional.

CASE STUDY: ELEMENTARY SCHOOL COUNSELOR

Jasmine is a 28-year-old first-year elementary school counselor in a K-5 Title I school serving approximately 750 students. Jasmine was thrilled to be offered her first school counseling job right after she graduated from her master's degree program, but her school year is not turning out the way she expected. The night before the first day of school, Jasmine's principal told her that she had to give up her office due to overcrowding in the building. Although she was devastated to lose her cozy office space, Jasmine was determined to move forward and be a team player. Every morning, she loads up a cart with her school counseling supplies and moves from class to class teaching her district's social/emotional curriculum. Recently, however, Jasmine's principal has been asking her to cancel her school counseling lessons so she can cover classes. Her school district is experiencing a substitute teacher shortage, and Jasmine doesn't feel like she can say no. Her principal has stated that with her background in counseling, he trusts her to handle behavior issues and discipline concerns on her own. Jasmine reaches out to her assigned counseling mentor for help, but her mentor works at a school on the other side of the district and rarely returns her phone calls or emails. Jasmine knows that she needs to talk to her principal about her job responsibilities, but isn't sure what to do next.

Questions for Reflection or Group Discussion

1. What would you do in Jasmine's situation? In your opinion, are her principal's requests unreasonable?
2. What would be the best way for Jasmine to advocate for appropriate role responsibilities?
3. What are some self-care strategies that Jasmine can implement to cope with her current job situation?

SCHOOL COUNSELOR ROLE ADVOCACY

What Is Role Advocacy?

According to Hall (2017), "Advocacy ensures that stakeholders understand the role of the school counselor and the importance to students of implementing a comprehensive school counseling program" (para. 3). Simply stated, school counselors must be able to communicate **what** they are supposed to be doing and **why** it is important for students. In addition, school counselors must describe their unique qualifications when it comes to identifying and working with students affected by trauma. According to Wilder (2018), school counselors should not passively accept unclear role responsibilities. Instead, school counselors must continuously advocate for their role with administrators, parents, teachers, and students. Although it may feel uncomfortable to be assertive about appropriate role responsibilities, school counselors can minimize the risk involved by focusing on relationship-building first (Wilder, 2019). For example, during a beginning-of-the-year staff meeting, a school counselor can introduce themselves with a short presentation focusing on their background, interests, hobbies, pets, and family information, and then briefly explain what they will be doing to support their school community. In follow-up presentations throughout the school year, school counselors can introduce and explain each component of their comprehensive school counseling program. When practiced regularly, these role advocacy activities can support and clarify the crucial role of a school counselor in addressing the academic, career, and social emotional needs of all students.

ASCA Standards and Competencies

The ASCA School Counselor Professional Standards & Competencies (2019a) provide specific guidance for school counselors on role advocacy. Specifically, school counselors should demonstrate the following behaviors in regards to role advocacy (B-PF8):

- Model advocacy competencies to facilitate program development and student success;
- Advocate for local school board policy and laws and regulation in the best interest of students;
- Describe the benefits of a school counseling program for all stakeholders;
- Advocate for appropriate role responsibilities;
- Advocate for the removal of inappropriate role responsibilities;
- Use data to promote lower school counselor-to-student ratios;
- Participate in professional school counseling organizations (ASCA, 2019a).

The authors encourage both new and experienced school counselors to utilize these guidelines when creating, implementing, and evaluating their comprehensive school counseling program.

Opportunities for School Counselor Advocacy

While advocating for the school counselor role may seem daunting, particularly for early-career professionals, its importance cannot be overstated. In fact, Trusty and Brown (2005) stress the importance of school counselor role advocacy in their conceptualization of advocacy competencies for professional school counselors. The professional school counselor's advocacy competencies encapsulate the dispositions, knowledge, and skills required to "(a) eliminate barriers impeding students' development; (b) create opportunities to learn for all students; (c) ensure access to a quality school curriculum; (d) collaborate with others within and outside the school to help students meet their needs, and (e) promote positive, systemic change in schools" (Trusty & Brown, 2005, pg. 259). One advocacy competency of particular relevance is the **advocacy disposition**, which necessitates that school counselors be aware of and embrace their roles as advocates and be willing to take risks in order to support individuals and groups of students in getting their needs met (Trusty & Brown, 2005). If the school counselor is not empowered to act in their capacity as a school-based mental health professional, the campus suffers.

Some practical steps for advocating for the school counselor role include educating school administrators about appropriate activities for school counselors, which include activities such as:

- Advisement and appraisal for academic planning;
- Interpreting cognitive, aptitude, and achievement tests;
- Providing short-term individual or group counseling to students;
- Consulting with teachers about classroom climate and management; and
- Consulting with school principals to identify and resolve student issues, to name just a few (ASCA, n.d.).

Beyond these appropriate school counselor duties, ASCA (n.d.) also provides a list of inappropriate activities for school counselors, which could be useful for identifying specific work tasks unrelated to the school counselor role that may need to be delegated to another professional. The authors recommend having a printed or electronic copy of resources such as ASCA's (n.d.) *Appropriate and Inappropriate Activities for School Counselors* to reference for support during meetings with school administrators. Dollarhide, Smith, and Lemberger (2007) also stress the importance of "document[ing] [the school counselor's] value as a resource to the entire school community," and using that documentation to advocate for a meaningful allocation of their time in support of student success and well-being (pg. 367).

Last but not least, school counselors should be aware of the other administrative professionals on their campus or district offices who can support their work with students. Beyond lead principals, school counselors should also consider leveraging the support of assistant principals, directors of counseling, central administration, school board members, and the parents of the students they serve. Working in schools sometimes requires out-of-the-box thinking and reaching for non-traditional sources of support to accomplish important aims. To that end, the authors encourage school counselors to advocate for their roles as campus-based mental health professionals with other avenues of support.

Advocacy With Students

One of the most effective strategies school counselors can use to advocate for themselves is by clearly communicating their role to students. The authors recommend that counselors prioritize these introductory activities at the beginning of the school year and revisit them as needed. First, school counselors should plan to briefly introduce themselves to all students during the first few days of school. This can be accomplished by making a guest appearance during morning announcements, taking a few minutes to talk to each grade level during lunch, or stopping by each classroom for a quick introduction throughout the day. The goal of this brief introduction is for each student to know your name, where your office or classroom is located, and a quick summary of your role. Next, school counselors should plan a classroom lesson to teach students about your role and how you can support them at school. For younger students (K-3), the authors recommend reading a book such as Mrs. Joyce Gives the Best High Fives (Winnett, 2013) or My Counselor is a Princess (Acker, 2018). For upper elementary or middle school students, the counselor could share an interactive power point presentation or play an online game to introduce the school counselor's role. With high school students, the counselor could spend a few minutes introducing themselves to each homeroom class and then ask students to participate in a needs assessment to help plan their topics for the year. Finally, school counselors should capitalize on their introductory lesson by staying visible throughout the first few weeks of school. For example, the school counselor could spend time greeting students at the front door each morning, eating lunch with students in the cafeteria, or high-fiving students on their way out the building at the end of each school day.

NATIONAL SCHOOL COUNSELING WEEK

A unique advocacy opportunity that occurs yearly is National School Counselor Week. The purpose of National School Counseling Week is to focus public attention on the contributions that school counselors make in schools throughout the United States. National School Counseling Week is sponsored by the American School Counselor Association and is always celebrated during the first full week of February. The ASCA website (https://www.schoolcounselor.org/Events-Professional-Development/Events/National-School-Counseling-Week) contains a plethora of resources to help school counselors promote the week, including sample morning announcements, a sample press release, posters, stickers, door hangers, and bookmarks. The theme for each year and planned events are announced each December.

Case Study: Middle School Counselor

Lynn is a 26-year-old first-year school counselor at a large middle school (6th-8th grade) serving approximately 4,500 students. She works alongside six other school counselors in her campus Counseling and Guidance Department. Her school district also has funding to employ clinical mental health counselors (CMHCs) in addition to school counselors, who are primarily responsible for intervening when students experience mental health crises while at school (e.g., self-harming in class, aggressive outbursts towards teachers or other students, using drugs or alcohol while on campus). Because she is a recent graduate from a CACREP-accredited school counseling program, Lynn came into her first job as a school counselor with what she believed to be a comprehensive understanding of her job and responsibilities. However, Lynn has had the unfortunate experience of "butting heads" over her responsibilities with some of her school counseling colleagues, including her assigned campus mentor Karen, who has worked for the district longer than Lynn has been alive.

Lynn is frustrated with what she perceives to be Karen's unhelpful guidance about managing her large caseload. In a recent meeting, Lynn lamented that she was having difficulty finding time to provide the level of mental health support that many of her students require. Karen's primary encouragement was to "let the real counselors handle that" so that Lynn does not fall behind on her paperwork and important state-mandated data collection measures. Lynn is considering requesting a meeting with one of the assistant principals (APs) on her campus to express her frustration with her mentorship relationship and clarify the parameters of her responsibilities as a school counselor. However, she is feeling overwhelmed by the possibility of being perceived as confrontational or ungrateful for her job. Lynn's hesitation is compounded by the fact that she was a successful teacher at the same campus prior to transitioning into her school counseling role, and she's worried the AP may think she was "better off in the classroom."

Questions for Self-Reflection or Group Discussion

1. What feedback might a seasoned school counselor from another campus give Lynn about navigating relationships with the counselors in her department?
2. How should Lynn prepare for her meeting with the assistant principal?
3. What resources might Lynn utilize to advocate for her role as a school counselor?
4. Assuming Lynn's advocacy efforts go as planned and she has more time to fulfill her actual job duties, how should she utilize this time?

Best Practices for Principal-Counselor Communication and Collaboration

Clear, unambiguous understanding of the school counselor role is crucial when building a successful counselor-principal partnership. This partnership is a key factor in counselor efficacy (Armstrong et al., 2010). Successful collaboration between administrators and counselors is essential to the development of student-centered school counseling programs, while poor communication and collaboration result in higher stress levels and lowered job satisfaction for school counselors (Zalaquett & Chatters, 2012). As Mullen and Gutierrez (2016) noted, high levels of stress and burnout in school counselors could have a negative impact on the provision of direct student services. Therefore, school counselors must be prepared to educate administrators and advocate for appropriate role responsibility.

The principal-counselor relationship is influenced by many factors. These determinants include trust, confidence, open communication, and a shared vision (Armstrong et al., 2010; MacDonald et al., 2008; Wilkerson & Bellini, 2006). Researchers have found that strong principal-counselor collaboration may lead to increased alignment with professional standards, enhanced services, and improvement in student achievement (Dahir et al., 2011). Furthermore, a national study by Duslak and Grier (2016) found that frequent principal-counselor meetings were associated with higher ratings of relationship quality. School counselors and principals can translate this research into practice by intentionally creating opportunities to connect, communicate, and collaborate.

Before diving into specific strategies for connection, communication, and collaboration, consider these **ten characteristics of effective principal-school counselor relationships**, which include:

1. Open communication that provides multiple opportunities for input to decision making;
2. Opportunities to share ideas on teaching, learning and schoolwide educational initiatives;
3. Sharing information about needs within the school and community;
4. School counselor participation on school leadership teams;
5. Joint responsibility in the development of goals and metrics that indicate student success;
6. Mutual trust between the principal and school counselor;
7. A shared vision on what is meant by student success;
8. Mutual respect between the principal and school counselor;
9. Shared decision making on initiatives that impact student success; and
10. A collective commitment to equity and opportunity (College Board, 2011).

Strategies for Connection

In busy day-to-day campus operations, the time available for making meaningful connections with administration can be limited. However, connection requires a commitment to continuous dialogue between both parties around expectations for work and support. To that end, the authors recommend taking advantage of both formal and informal opportunities to foster a strong principal-school counselor working alliance. While formal opportunities for connection can and should occur in the form of standing meetings between campus administrators and the school counseling department, school counselors should find opportunities for frequent, informal contact to enhance collaboration and foster joint responsibility for campus outcomes. Informal communication opportunities could occur wherever and whenever needed, such as in the morning before students arrive for the day, during study hall duties, in passing in the lunchroom, or stopping by one another's offices for an impromptu conversation about a specific need or situation.

Strategies for Communication

Effective communication between principals and school counselors involves specific conversational skills, including the ability to formulate a consensus by merging diverse perspectives to create common goals; an appreciation of divergent perspectives about strategies for goal attainment; flexibility in communication styles; strong listening skills; professional engagement through shared responsibility for communication; and the ability to establish commonality to align overarching campus goals with the goals of the school counseling program (College Board, 2011). Beyond these communication skills, the authors also recommend the following practical tips for enhancing communication between school counselors and principals:

- Keep a running tab of items to communicate with the principal, including how the counselor spends their time each week. Touch base in person whenever possible, but don't be afraid to utilize technology such as e-mail to provide updates when needed as well.
- Track specific campus needs, especially those that are tied to school counseling operations (e.g., a list of materials or time required to facilitate a group over an issue noted in meetings with students and teachers).
- When making a request that requires administrator input or approval (e.g., a request to dedicate one hour/week of instructional time for classroom guidance on social-emotional issues), be prepared to justify the request with campus data and/or school counseling research.
- Keep the principal apprised of situations germane to school operations and safety (e.g., aggressive interactions between students during passing periods). Maintain clear boundaries around the school counselor role and defer to the principal as the disciplinarian for student conduct issues.

Case Study: High School Counselor

Jeff is a 42-year-old third-year counselor at a large suburban high school serving approximately 1,800 students. Jeff recently transferred from a middle school in the same district and is looking forward to working with older students. Jeff is aware that his new principal has worked with many different school counselors and wants to start the school year off with strong principal-counselor collaboration in place. Jeff emails his principal and assistant principals and asks if he can meet with them during lunch before his contract starts in late July. His goal for this first meeting is to start building a positive working relationship with each of his administrators. Jeff shares about his background, education, and family and encourages each of his administrators to do the same. He ends the meeting on time and thanks his administrators for taking the time to meet with him. He follows up the next day with an email thanking them for their time.

The week before his contract starts, Jeff arrives at school early each day to organize his office. He takes a few minutes each morning to greet his administrators and ask if there is anything he can do to support them. During his first week back at school, Jeff schedules another meeting with his administrators to communicate his ideas for his comprehensive school counseling program and ask for their feedback. He focuses on the themes of trust, transparency, and accountability and asks to share his electronic calendar with his administrators. He follows up with an email including his school counseling program outlined by month and a link to his needs assessment for students, parents, and teachers. He also requests a few minutes to do a short presentation at the first PTA meeting of the year to introduce himself to parents.

During the first month of school, Jeff focuses the majority of his attention on his students. He spends time introducing himself to the students in each of their homeroom classes and during their lunch periods. He schedules "minute meetings" with his high-needs students and documents a quick follow-up step from each meeting. At the end of the first month of school, Jeff creates an electronic newsletter to share with students, teachers, and parents focusing on the goals of his school counseling program.

Beginning in October, Jeff begins using a data tracking app on his phone to record how he spends his time at school. He enters each activity as it happens in real time (individual counseling, group counseling, classroom lessons, parent meetings, etc.) and compares his results with the ASCA model time recommendations. During his yearly evaluation meeting with his administrator, Jeff creates a spreadsheet detailing how he spends his time at school and includes this data in his self-evaluation.

Questions for Reflection or Group Discussion

1. How would you describe Jeff's working relationship with his campus principals?
2. What do you notice about Jeff's communication style? How do you think it influences his relationship with his administrators?
3. What did you notice about Jeff's advocacy efforts with his administrators and school community?

SUMMARY

In this chapter, the authors discussed the role of today's trauma-informed school counselor. The chapter began with a definition of the school counselor role, including a brief history of the school counseling profession, ASCA role statements, and a comparison of the terms school counselor vs. guidance counselor. Next, the authors discussed how school counselors can advocate for appropriate role responsibilities with administrators, teachers, and students. Finally, the authors outlined best practices for successful principal-counselor collaboration. Three school counselor case studies and discussion questions were included to apply these concepts to real-life situations.

REFERENCES

Amatea, E. S., & Clark, M. A. (2005). Changing schools, changing counselors: A qualitative study of school administrators' conceptions of the school counselor role. *Professional School Counseling*, *9*(1), 16–27. doi:10.5330/prsc.9.1.w6357vn62n5328vp

American School Counselor Association. (2016). *The school counselor and trauma-informed school practice*. Author.

American School Counselor Association. (2019a). *ASCA school counselor professional standards & competencies*. Author.

American School Counselor Association. (2019b). *The ASCA national model: A framework for school counseling programs* (4th ed.). Author.

American School Counselor Association. (n.d.). *Appropriate and inappropriate activities for school counselors*. https://www.schoolcounselor.org/getmedia/8fe536c2-7a32-4102-8ce7-42e9b0683b3b/appropriate-activities-of-school-counselors.pdf

Armstrong, S. A., MacDonald, J. H., & Stillo, S. (2010). School counselors and principals: Different perceptions of relationship, leadership, and training. *Journal of School Counseling*, *8*(15), 1–27. http://jsc.montana.edu/articles/v8n15.pdf

Baker, E., Zyromski, B., & Granello, D. H. (2021). School or guidance counselor: How the title influences public perception. *Professional School Counseling*, *25*(1), 1–8. doi:10.1177/2156759X20981034

Dahir, C. A. (2004). Supporting a nation of learners: The role of school counseling in educational reform. *Journal of Counseling and Development*, *82*(3), 344–353. doi:10.1002/j.1556-6678.2004.tb00320.x

Dollarhide, C. T., Smith, A. T., & Lemberger, M. E. (2007). Critical incidents in the development of supportive principals: Facilitating school counselor-principal relationships. *Professional School Counseling*, *10*(4), 360–369. doi:10.5330/prsc.10.4.k111116677917913

Duslak, M., & Geier, B. (2016). Communication factors as predictors of relationship quality: A national study of principals and school counselors. *Professional School Counseling*, *20*(1), 115–126. doi:10.5330/1096-2409-20.1.115

Gysbers, N. C. (2010). *Remembering the past, shaping the future: A history of school counseling*. American School Counselor Association.

Hall, M. (2017 November). *Advocating for your school counseling program using ASCA resources*. MASCA News. https://www.schoolcounselor.org/Newsletters/December-2017/Advocating-for-Your-School-Counseling-Program-Usin?st=ma

Hickman, D. (2020). *The impact of role ambiguity, stress, and burnout on professional elementary school counselors* (Publication No. 28029586) [Doctoral dissertation, Texas A&M University-Commerce]. Proquest Dissertations & Theses Global.

Kim, N., & Lambie, G. W. (2018). Burnout and implications for professional school counselors. *The Professional Counselor*, *8*(3), 277–294. Advance online publication. doi:10.15241/nk.8.3.277

Lane, J. J., Bohner, G. L., Hinck, A. M., & Kircher, R. L. (2020). Current administrative perceptions of school counselors: Kansas' administrators' perceptions of school counselor duties. *Journal of School Counseling*, *18*(2). http:/www.jsc.montana.edu/articles/v18n2.pdf

Mullen, P. R., & Gutierrez, D. (2016). Burnout, stress, and direct student services among school counselors. *The Professional Counselor*, *6*(4), 344–359. doi:10.15241/pm.6.4.344

National Policy Board for Educational Administration. (2015). *Professional standards for educational leaders*. Author.

Pérusse, R., Goodnough, G. E., Donegan, J., & Jones, C. (2004). Perceptions of school counselors and school principals about the National Standards for school counseling programs and the Transforming School Counseling Initiative. *Professional School Counseling*, *7*(3), 152–161.

The College Board. (2011). *Enhancing the principal-school counselor relationship*. https://secure-media.collegeboard.org/digitalServices/pdf/advocacy/nosca/enhancing-principal-school-counselor-relationship-111018.pdf

Trusty, T., & Brown, D. (2005). Advocacy competencies for professional school counselors. *Professional School Counseling*, *8*(3), 259–265.

Wilder, C. (2018). Promoting the role of the school counselor. *Journal of Professional Counseling, Practice, Theory, & Research*, *45*(2), 60–68. doi:10.1080/15566382.2019.1646085

Wilkerson, K., & Bellini, J. (2006). Intrapersonal and organizational factors associated with burnout among school counselors. *Journal of Counseling and Development*, *84*(4), 440–450. doi:10.1002/j.1556-6678.2006.tb00428.x

Yavuz, O., Cayirdag, N., Dahir, C., & Gumuseli, A. I. (2017). Improving student achievement through strengthening principal and school counselor partnership. *International Journal of Educational Reform*, *26*(2), 176–201. doi:10.1177/105678791702600205

Zalaquett, C., & Chatters, S. (2012). Middle school principals' perceptions of middle school counselors' roles and functions. *American Secondary Education*, *40*(2), 89–103. https://www.jstor.org/stable/43694132

Zyromski, B., Hudson, T. D., Baker, E., & Granello, D. H. (2019). Guidance counselors or school counselors: How the name of the profession influences perceptions of competence. *Professional School Counseling*, *22*(1), 1–10. doi:10.1177/2156759X19855654

Chapter 3
Trauma-Informed School Counseling:
Foundations and Interventions

Danielle Render Turmaud
https://orcid.org/0000-0002-5239-6970
Multnomah University, USA

ABSTRACT

Providing trauma-informed school counseling is imperative to implementing quality school counseling. The purposes of this chapter are to provide readers with a foundational understanding of trauma-informed school counseling, to emphasize the importance of trauma-informed school counseling, and to explain how to apply trauma-informed school counseling. Therefore, the chapter will offer a simplistic model to aid in understanding trauma-informed care, an overview of trauma-informed care guiding principles discussed in the literature, a case-study analysis using trauma-informed care guiding principles, questions for consideration, and general trauma-informed school counseling interventions. The chapter will also include a discussion on the importance of considering contextual and cultural factors in trauma-informed care.

INTRODUCTION AND BACKGROUND

Makayla, a Caucasian, cisgender, female-identifying 12-year-old, walks through her school each day with warmth and a smile on her face. Her teachers, school counselor, and school administration see her as "bright", engaged, and eager to learn. Yet, they don't see the intense anxiety and fear of failure that, at times, leave Makayla

DOI: 10.4018/978-1-7998-9785-9.ch003

feeling like she is suffocating or lead to panic attacks in the bathroom. Makayla carries an invisible backpack from her trauma history that no one sees or expects.

The awareness of trauma and its impact on children and adolescents is a growing concern for schools and school counselors (Cole et al., 2013; Rumsey & Milsom, 2019). Children's exposure to trauma has been linked to several challenges and barriers with learning, socioemotional health, behavior, physical health, educational engagement and success, and overall well-being (Evans & Coccoma, 2014; Morton & Berardi, 2018; Perry & Daniels, 2016; Rumsey & Milsom, 2019). An unfortunate reality is that an alarming number of children and adolescents experience or are exposed to traumatic events that may contribute to distress and many of the consequences stated above (Miller, 2019; Morton & Berardi, 2018; Santiago et al., 2018). In fact, according to the Substance Abuse and Mental Health Services Administration (SAMHSA, 2020), "more than two thirds of children report at least one traumatic event by age 16" (para. 1). The field is increasingly recognizing that traumatic experiences and exposures in youth are likely norms rather than exceptions (Santiago et al., 2018). It is important for school counselors to be aware that many students, like Makayla, may be carrying "invisible backpacks" and wounds to school with them (Santiago et al., 2018).

As discussed by the American School Counselor Association (ASCA, 2016), school counselors play an important role in supporting students and promoting a trauma-sensitive and trauma-informed environment in their schools. Mental health professionals openly acknowledge that trauma occurs and that it can lead to several consequences for victims/survivors, yet this knowledge does not always translate well into practice and interventions (Evans & Coccoma, 2014). The literature notes concern about the level of training and competence counselors have surrounding trauma, trauma-informed care, and trauma-informed interventions and practices (Padden, 2021; Morton & Berardi, 2018; Sorrentino, 2020). In response, it is crucial for school counselors to have a foundational understanding of trauma-informed care and of how to implement it into their practice. This chapter provides school counselors with the necessary foundation for defining trauma-informed care, recognizing its importance in school counseling, learning its principles and how they apply to school counseling, and understanding the importance of systemic and contextual factors. The chapter includes applications, interventions, and case study examples to illustrate how school counselors can practice trauma-informed care.

WHAT IS TRAUMA-INFORMED CARE?

Defining Trauma and Trauma-Informed Care

At the center of trauma-informed care is the understanding of what trauma is, what types of experiences may elicit a trauma response, and what potential impacts trauma might have on individuals or groups of people (SAMHSA, 2014). As discussed by Sweeney et al. (2018), a trauma-informed care approach involves moving away from the question of "What is wrong with you?" and moving towards the question of "What has happened to you?". Although definitions of trauma can vary greatly depending upon the source, an inclusive definition provided by SAMHSA (2014) that is commonly cited in the literature and accepted by mental health professionals states:

Individual trauma results from an event, series of events, or set of circumstances that is experienced by an individual as physically or emotionally harmful or life threatening and that has lasting adverse effects on the individual's functioning and mental, physical, social, emotional, or spiritual well-being. (p. 7)

Put differently, trauma is an event that overwhelms an individual's psyche and can lead to several negative consequences (Eriksen, 1976). Some traumatic experiences (e.g., childhood abuse and neglect, sexual trauma, intimate partner violence, car accidents, etc.) may involve an individual, a family, or a few people, while others, termed collective trauma, (e.g., pandemics, wars, mass shootings, systemic oppression, natural disasters, etc.) may involve a group of people, a community, or a society (Aydin, 2017; Erickson,1976; Shamai, 2016).

Trauma's effect on an individual can vary greatly depending upon typology of the adverse experience(s), duration of the experience(s), age at which the traumatic event(s) occurred, neurobiological differences, comorbid disorders/mental health challenges, environmental and social supports available, cultural and intersectionality factors, systemic and sociopolitical factors, other compounding health issues or traumatic experiences, and more. Although trauma's impacts are highly individual and may look different based on one's developmental stage, some common effects on children can include traumatic stress symptoms, Post-Traumatic Stress Disorder, depression, anxiety, fear or worry, behavioral problems, difficulties concentrating, challenges with schoolwork, withdrawal, or substance abuse (Gerrity & Folcarelli, 2008; Perfect et al., 2016; Santiago et al., 2018). In a school setting, impacts of trauma can manifest in a variety of ways including but not limited to: isolation/withdrawal, aggression, non-attendance or attendance inconsistencies, delayed speech development, delayed cognitive development, relationship difficulties, focus difficulties, inattentiveness, hyperactivity, hypoactivity, missing or late assignments, physical illness, impaired memory, and challenges with schoolwork (ASCA, 2016; Cavanaugh, 2016; Cole et al. 2005; Cole et al., 2013; Gerrity & Folcarelli, 2008; Lansford et al., 2002; Petersen et al., 2013; Veltman & Browne, 2001). Given trauma's invasive nature and its detriment to students and their educational progress, a trauma-informed care approach is a critical component of school counseling (Cavanaugh, 2016).

Cole et al. (2013) denotes how assuming a trauma lens can guide school counselors and school personnel because it allows for "students and their learning, behavior, and relationships" to be "seen and understood" (p. 7). While this is true, it is important to clarify that trauma-informed care is not a lens that one takes on and off like a pair of glasses. It is not a selective approach but, alternatively, is one that is essential in all environments, systems, and settings. Taking a trauma-informed care approach is a vital paradigm shift that influences how we view, interact with, and engage with the world around us (Harris & Fallot, 2001). Trauma-informed care provides a foundation for students to be understood for who they are within the context of their environment and met right where they are, wherever that is.

The Who, What, When, How, and Why of Trauma-Informed Care

Providing care from a trauma lens is nuanced and multifaceted. Before diving into an in-depth analysis of the principles of trauma-informed care and of how to use them in practice, having a foundational understanding of trauma-informed care and a palpable model to reference when working with students can be helpful. To provide a simplified model of the components of trauma-informed care, the author of this chapter developed the "Who, What, When, How, and Why Model of Trauma-Informed Care." This model was created based on both trauma-informed care literature and the author's experiences as a therapist who specializes in trauma. A diagram depicting this model can be seen in Figure 1.

Figure 1. The "Who, What, When, How, and Why Model of Trauma-Informed Care"

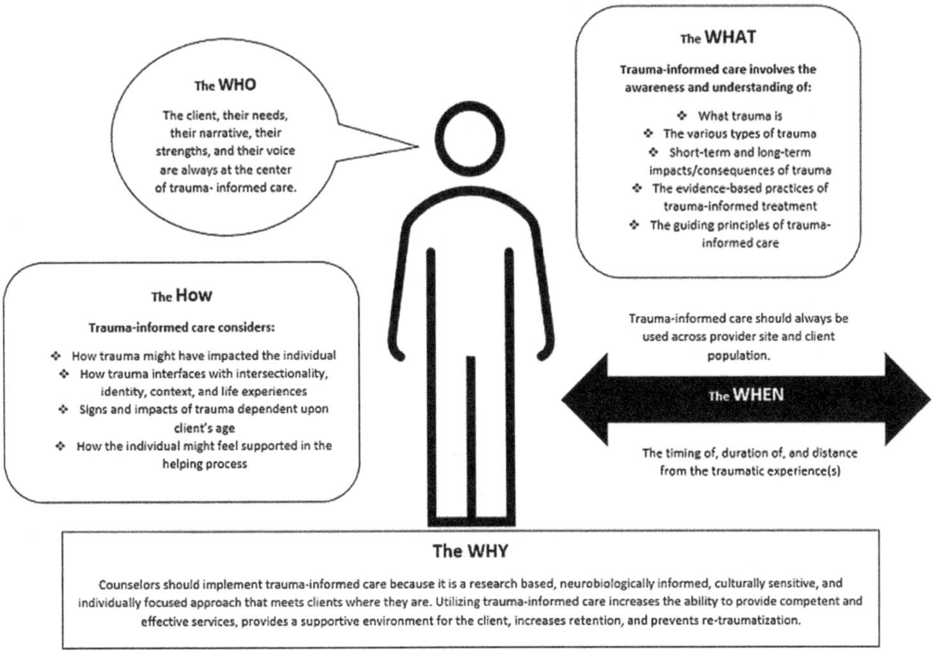

The "Who" of Trauma-Informed Care

The "Who" of trauma-informed care answers the question, "Who is the focus?". As demonstrated in Figure 1, trauma-informed care always centers around the student's needs and voice, and it champions and builds off the student's strengths (Cavanaugh, 2016; Harris & Fallot, 2001; SAMHSA, 2014; Sweeney et al., 2018). In other words, the "Who" of trauma-informed care is and should always be the student. This definition includes acknowledgment that each student comes into the office with their own experiences, neurobiological differences, sociocultural identities, contexts, and beautiful complexities (Harris & Fallot, 2001; SAMHSA, 2014b). The "Who" of trauma-informed care means meeting a student right where they are, just as they are, and for "Who" they are.

The "What" of Trauma-Informed Care

The "What" answers the question, "What is trauma-informed care?". It involves awareness of what trauma is, of the various types of trauma, of the short and long-term consequences of trauma, and of the evidenced-based practices that can support students (SAMSHA, 2014; Sweeney et al., 2018). Additionally, the "What" of trauma-informed care involves the guiding principles surrounding putting trauma-informed care into practice, like those offered by Sweeney et al. (2018) and discussed in this chapter.

The "When" of Trauma-Informed Care

The "When" of trauma-informed care involves two different components. The first component is the question, "When should trauma-informed care be used?". The answer to this question is always. Regardless of a school counselor's work environment or the population they are serving, applying trauma-informed care is always necessary to promote safety, inclusion, care, and appropriate coordination of resources in the school setting.

The second component in the "When" category considers the timing of the trauma and the duration of the traumatic experience(s) (Gerrity & Folcarelli, 2008; Santiago et al., 2018). When considering the "when" of trauma-informed care, the school counselor should ask the questions: When did the traumatic experience(s) happen? Was/Were the experience(s) ongoing or incidental? Is the experience(s) still ongoing? When did the traumatic experience(s) occur in relation to the treatment?

The "How" of Trauma-Informed Care

The "How" of trauma-informed care considers the following: a) how trauma might have impacted the individual cognitively, neurobiologically, behaviorally, emotionally, relationally, and spiritually, b) how the trauma interfaces with aspects of intersectionality, the individual's socio cultural identities, and other life circumstance/ experiences, c) how the trauma might manifest in the individual based upon their age (keeping developmental differences under consideration), and d) how the individual might feel supported or benefitted by the helping process (e.g., considerations given to what resources are needed, treatment steps are taken, etc.) (Ano & Vasconcelles, 2005; Gerrity & Folcarelli, 2008; Goodman, 2014; Harris & Fallot, 2001; SAMSHA, 2014b; Santiago et al., 2018; Sweeney et al., 2018). These aspects of trauma-informed care assist school counselors as they engage in case conceptualization, conduct treatment planning, and support the student they are helping.

The "Why" of Trauma-Informed Care

The final piece of the model answers the question, "Why should a trauma-informed approach be utilized?". Trauma-informed care is a neurobiologically informed, culturally sensitive, and individually focused approach that allows school counselors to meet a student where they are, wherever that is. Taking a trauma-informed care approach strengthens their ability to provide a supportive environment for students, improve retention, prevents re-traumatization, increases the effectiveness of counseling, and raises the capacity for students to reach their goals (SAMHSA, 2014; Santiago et al., 2018). A trauma-informed care approach provides the needed foundations for growth and recovery, including unconditional positive regard, acceptance, empathy, and care (Rogers, 1957). Put simply, as depicted in Figure 1, a trauma-informed care approach should be the ever-present base, as it provides both students and school counselors with a solid ground on which to stand in an often chaotic system and world.

The Foundations of Trauma-Informed Care

The literature, mental health professionals, and victims/survivors of trauma have recognized that simply understanding trauma is not sufficient in practice (Evans & Coccoma, 2014; SAMHSA, 2014). In response, there has been a global interest in and call for taking a trauma-informed approach in counseling and other helping professions (Evans & Coccoma, 2014). As with the term *trauma*, the literature has provided several definitions for trauma-informed care (Bendall et al., 2021). One framework of trauma-informed care that has been widely adopted is SAMHSA's (2014) four "R's" approach. This approach to care involves a) a basic *realization* about trauma and the impact that it can have, b) the ability to *recognize* the signs and impacts of trauma, c) a *response* of integrating trauma-informed care principles, and d) the creation of environments that foster recovery and safety and *resist re-traumatization*. As discussed by the literature, a vague definition of trauma-informed care might lead to some ambiguity surrounding how to implement it (Bendall et al., 2021). Following SAMHSA's (2014) proposed framework, for the purpose of this chapter, trauma-informed school counseling will be defined as utilizing the understanding of trauma, its signs, its potential impacts on the lives of individuals and groups, and factors of intersectionality to intentionally inform: the conceptualization and treatment of cases, the interactions and relationships with students, advocacy efforts conducted in the school and community, and allocation and provision of appropriate resources.

As can be seen in the framework provided by SAMHSA (2014), trauma-informed care does not involve a specific set of interventions or rules, but instead involves an approach focused on fostering environments and relationships that promote empowerment, safety, and recovery for victims/survivors of trauma (Sweeney et al., 2018). Although those relationships are important, as trauma-informed care is inherently tailored to the unique experiences and needs of students, the lack of specific interventions might leave school counselors feeling ill-equipped to implement trauma-informed care in their case conceptualization, treatment planning, assessments, and daily work. To guide understanding of how trauma-informed care can be moved from "a big idea to everyday practice" (Berliner & Kolko, 2016, p. 169), Sweeney et al. (2018) offers 10 key principles of trauma-informed approaches. As seen in Table 1, the 10 guiding principles of trauma-informed care suggested by Sweeney et al. (2018) and adapted from Elliott et al. (2005), Bloom (2006), and SAMHSA (2014), include a) seeing through a trauma lens, b) appreciation of invisible trauma and intersectionality, c) sensitive discussions about trauma, d) pathways to trauma-specific support, e) preventing trauma in the mental health system, f) trustworthiness and transparency, g) collaboration and mutuality, h) empowerment, choice, and control, i) safety, and j) survivor partnerships. The 10 guiding principles of trauma-informed care can be used as a foundational roadmap and can aid school counselors in both the conceptualization and treatment planning processes. Further information on these guiding principles will be provided in this chapter along with a case example of how they can be implemented in practice.

Table 1. Ten key principles of trauma-informed care (Sweeney et al., 2018)

Trauma-Informed Care Guiding Principles	
Principle #1:	Seeing through a trauma lens
Principle #2:	Appreciation of invisible trauma and intersectionality
Principle #3:	Sensitive discussions about trauma
Principle #4:	Pathways to trauma-specific support
Principle #5:	Preventing trauma in the mental health system
Principle #6:	Trustworthiness and transparency
Principle #7:	Collaboration and Mutuality
Principle #8:	Empowerment, choice, and control
Principle #9:	Safety
Principle #10:	Survivor Partnerships

THE IMPORTANCE OF TRAUMA-INFORMED SCHOOL COUNSELING

The literature is clear that school counselors can play an important role in supporting the healthy socioemotional development of students, promoting students' academic success, linking students to needed resources, and fostering a supportive school environment (ASCA, 2019; Martinez et al., 2020; Perry & Daniels, 2016). An important factor in school counseling assistance includes the use of trauma-informed counseling. Although the depth and breadth of reasons for trauma-informed care's importance in school counseling cannot be adequately addressed in one chapter, this section will examine a few of the reasons surrounding its significance.

An Unparalleled Setting

The importance of a trauma-informed school environment is unparalleled; with "students spending a significant portion of their daily lives in school, this social context is surely one of the most powerful social institutions shaping the next generation of youth" (Basch, 2011, p. 594). Due to the frequency and regularity with which students attend school, school settings are an important touch point and access to services for all students, and as such, may be the primary mental health provider for students (Cavanaugh, 2016; Evans et al., 2014). Many students encounter structural barriers in obtaining mental health services outside of the school setting, especially children who are marginalized or live within the context of lower socioeconomic status (Garrison et al., 1999). School counseling services overcome many of these barriers and can provide support and resource coordination that can be of great benefit to students, including those who have been impacted by trauma (Garrison et al., 1999; Martinez et al., 2020). Because of their work setting, school counselors are in a unique position that may allow them to identify students who might be affected by traumatic events and, in turn, provide them with the support and resources needed (ASCA, 2016).

The Benefits of Trauma-Informed Care

In addition to the unparalleled nature of the school setting, trauma-informed care can lead to several benefits for students, parental/guardian relationships, families, the school environment, and even communities (ASCA, 2016; Cole et al., 2013; Gherardi et al., 2020; Martinez et al., 2020). Some of these benefits might include culturally responsive practices, advocacy efforts that lead to positive partnerships and change within families and communities, safety for students, consistency, empowerment, dismantling of systemic barriers, improved parental/guardian relations, improved student relations, improved school counseling outcomes, support for the development of students, and more (Cole et al., 2013; Gherardi et al., 2020; Martinez et al., 2020). In fact, within the school environment alone, ASCA (2016) notes that a trauma-informed school counseling approach can lead to several benefits: a decrease in excessive disciplinary actions, a decrease in bullying and harassment, improvement of academic achievement, and the formation of student coping skills.

In addition to wider-reaching systemic impacts, trauma-informed care can also have important implications for the therapeutic alliance between students and school counselors. As substantiated by several decades of counseling research, "the quality of the therapeutic alliance is the most robust predictor of treatment success" (Safran & Muran, 2000, p. 1). These findings suggest that both the quality of the therapeutic alliance and the ability of the counselor to provide a therapeutic environment that promotes safety, empowerment, collaboration, and empathy are of extreme importance. Trauma-informed care is uniquely positioned to foster a strong therapeutic alliance as its ultimate goal is to meet students right where they are with care, empathy, support, respect, and curiosity. An improved therapeutic relationship leads to improved therapeutic outcomes.

School Counselors as Allies

The unfortunate reality is that many "young victims of trauma suffer in silence, due to shame, fear, difficulty putting their experiences into words, and stigma" (Santiago et al., 2018, p. 18). School counselors can be powerful allies to students who have experienced trauma by letting them know that they are seen, valued, and heard. Research suggests that nurturing and healthy relationships with adults, such as school counselors, can foster healthy development for students and can have several positive consequences for their well-being (Brooks, 2014; Martinez et al., 2020). In some cases, school counselors might be the first individuals to whom students ever disclose their traumatic experiences or the first providers in their lives to inquire about their well-being. The ability of a school counselor to serve as a receptive and responsive ally for students can be instrumental to student development.

A Protective Factor from Re-Traumatization

As addressed and discussed throughout trauma literature, the potential for re-traumatization by the systems or providers whose aim is to support victims/survivors of trauma is of great concern (ASCA, 2016; SAMHSA, 2014; SAMHSA, 2014b; Sweeney et al., 2018). Promoting trauma-informed care practices in school counseling is critical to aid school counselors in their ability to decrease or avoid practices that might lead to re-traumatization (ASCA, 2016; SAMHSA, 2014b). With an awareness of trauma and competency in trauma-informed care, school counselors have an increased ability to assess policies, practices, treatment interventions, and assessments for improvement (SAMHSA, 2014b). SAMHSA (2014b) provides some tips to aid counselors in prevention of re-traumatization, which include being sensitive to their students' needs surrounding potentially harmful or re-triggering techniques or interventions, being intentional in attending to a student's symptoms and needs when traumatic stress surfaces, avoiding what might be disempowering, and being attentive when identifying a student's trauma triggers and supporting them through their traumatic stress. When school counselors anticipate the re-traumatization risk for students with trauma histories, whether individual or collective/systemic, they can actively utilize trauma-informed treatment practices in their work and can advocate for the use of trauma-informed policies and practices in the school environment to increase positive outcomes for students in their care (SAMHSA, 2014b).

GUIDING PRINCIPLES TO TAKING A TRAUMA-INFORMED APPROACH: THEORY AND APPLICATION

To further support readers in understanding how to implement trauma-informed school counseling, this next section will provide 10 key principles of trauma-informed care. These 10 guiding principles proposed by Sweeney et al. (2018) and adapted from Elliott et al. (2005), Bloom (2006), and the SAMHSA (2014) include a) seeing through a trauma lens, b) appreciation of invisible trauma and intersectionality, c) sensitive discussions about trauma, d) pathways to trauma-specific support, e) preventing trauma in the mental health system, f) trustworthiness and transparency, g) collaboration and mutuality, h) empowerment, choice, and control, i) safety, and j) survivor partnerships. The following paragraphs will elaborate on each of these guiding principles and will demonstrate through a case study specific applications, interventions, and examples of ways to implement these principles in school counseling practice. A summary of these principles can also be found in Table 2.

Guiding Principle One: Seeing Through a Trauma Lens

The first trauma-informed care guiding principle offered by Sweeney et al. (2018) entails an approach to care that is viewed through a trauma lens. Conducting practice through a trauma lens involves being aware of the prevalence of trauma, the effects of trauma, and the signs of trauma (Sweeney et al., 2018). Additionally, viewing students through a trauma lens supports school counselors in understanding both the complexities of trauma and the ways in which it might influence a student's emotions and behaviors and lead to maladaptive coping strategies. Seeing through a trauma lens allows the school counselor to further understand how a student's experiences and story have impacted them developmentally, neurobiologically, emotionally, mentally, physically, spiritually, and relationally.

Table 2. A summary of the ten key principles of trauma-informed care (Sweeney et al., 2018)

Trauma-Informed Care Guiding Principles and Summaries	
Principle #1: Seeing through a trauma lens	Acknowledging and understanding the prevalence, signs, and effects of trauma
Principle #2: Appreciation of invisible trauma and intersectionality	Having a consideration for aspects of intersectionality and the cultural, experiential, and historical contexts surrounding trauma
Principle #3: Sensitive discussions about trauma	Discussing trauma in a way that is sensitive, appropriate, timely, and fostering agency for the student in deciding to share or not
Principle #4: Pathways to trauma-specific support	Connecting the student to trauma-specific services as needed
Principle #5: Preventing trauma in the mental health system	Deliberate utilization of interventions, protocols, policies, and steps to prevent the re-traumatization of students
Principle #6: Trustworthiness and transparency	Utilizing transparency, openness, and respect to foster trust in the therapeutic alliance and process
Principle #7: Collaboration and Mutuality	Dismantling a hierarchical approach and instead fostering a relationship built upon collaboration and shared power
Principle #8: Empowerment, choice, and control	Taking a strengths-based approach that fosters empowerment, autonomy, and agency
Principle #9: Safety	Implementing measures that foster emotional, psychological, social, gender, cultural, and physical safety for all parties
Principle #10: Survivor Partnerships	Creating collaborative partnerships with individuals, families, groups, and communities impacted by trauma

Guiding Principle Two: Appreciation of Invisible Trauma and Intersectionality

A trauma-informed care approach takes a holistic view of trauma and considers the "community, social, cultural and historical traumas such as racism, poverty, colonialism, disability, homophobia and sexism and their intersectionality" (Sweeney et al., 2018). A trauma-informed care approach considers the environmental and socio-cultural contexts that impact the life of the student, recognizing that the "content" of trauma cannot be separated as an isolated entity. This approach values and champions' students' perspectives, views, and experiences. Although trauma can impact anyone, an important aspect of trauma-informed care is considering child populations that are at risk of traumatic experiences. Some populations that might experience a disproportionate risk to trauma and its consequences include children in poverty, ethnic minorities, immigrant youth, children with disabilities, sexual orientation minority youth, transgender or non-binary youth, and children who have faced multiple types/experiences of trauma (Santiago et al., 2018). Traumatic incidents are not isolated, but interwoven, into the beautiful and complex fabric of students' identities and narratives.

Guiding Principle Three: Sensitive Discussions About Trauma

Trauma-informed care not only guides counselors in knowing elements of which they should be mindful, but it also guides them in how to have discussions surrounding trauma. If a school counselor inquires about trauma or participates in a discussion about trauma, they must do it in a way that is respectful and that fosters autonomy and choice surrounding what the student will share and how much they will share (Sweeney et al., 2018). It is important for school counselors to recognize that pursuing details of trauma narratives and histories can be re-traumatizing for students (SAMHSA, 2014b). This principle is specifically pertinent to school counselors because of their inability to provide trauma counseling in their role.

As a note from the author, although it is important for school counselors to consider the way in which they communicate and what they say in discussions surrounding trauma, an even more important aspect of this guiding principle may be the counselor's ability to listen empathetically to a victim/survivor. As discussed by Corey (2013):

When people are in crisis, one of the first steps is to give them an opportunity to fully express themselves. Sensitive listening, hearing, and understanding are essential at this point. Being heard and understood helps ground people in crises, helps to calm them in the midst of turmoil, and enables them to think more clearly and make better decisions. (p. 187)

Where someone's words and the provision of resources can validate and empower, listening communicates acceptance, worth, understanding, and connection, and it also provides a crucial foundation in trauma-informed care.

Guiding Principle Four: Pathways to Trauma-Specific Support

As discussed by Harris and Fallot (2001), when clients seek mental health support, often it is not to receive treatment for their trauma, but to obtain support for their current presenting problems or symptoms. This is particularly true in the school counseling world as students often come into the office with the presenting problems focused on challenges with schoolwork, difficulties in peer or teacher relationships, inability to pay attention, difficulties with coping, struggles with anxiety, and other issues pertinent to the school environment. Yet, solely serving victims/survivors is insufficient in the mental health field, as mental health providers need to both be aware that trauma is a potential factor in the client's life and be prepared to treat the consequences of trauma (Harris & Fallot, 2001).

According to the roles and responsibilities of a school counselor, they can serve and support survivors, but conducting trauma therapy and treating trauma are not within the scope of their work. Because of this reality, it is imperative to recognize that there is a difference between trauma-specific services and trauma-informed care (Sweeney et al., 2018). Where trauma-informed care involves being "informed about, and sensitive to, the potential for trauma-related issues to be present in clients" (Butler et al., 2011, p. 178) so that counselors can welcome victims/survivors with appropriate support, trauma-specific care involves treatment or services aimed at targeting the symptoms and challenges related to the trauma (Harris & Fallot, 2001). Although school counselors can powerfully impact students' lives by utilizing trauma-informed care, providing trauma-specific support and services are outside the scope of practice in the school setting. In response, it is paramount to connect students experiencing the consequences of trauma to trauma-specific resources and other needed supports. These connections might involve making a child abuse report and connecting a child to social services, referring the student to a practitioner who can provide trauma counseling and treatment (e.g., Eye-Movement Desensitization therapy, Trauma-Focused Cognitive Behavioral Therapy, play therapy), making referrals to victim/survivor counseling groups, connecting the student to in-patient services, and more.

An important factor of the trauma-informed care that school counselors can provide is the use of a Multi-Tiered System of Support (MTSS). A MTSS incorporates "tiered models of academic, behavioral, and mental health service delivery" (Reinbergs & Fefer, 2018, p. 251). As discussed by Reinbergs and Fefer (2018) and Cole et al. (2013), school counselors cannot stand alone in supporting students, and involving other stakeholders in the use of interventions and student support is crucial. MTSS incorporates school-wide interventions and supports, promotes student safety, promotes culturally responsive practices, engages peer support, and has several other benefits (Cavanaugh, 2016; Santiago et al., 2018). As an African proverb states, "It takes a village to raise a child." In the context of trauma-informed school counseling, it takes the entire school community to support a child and provide the comprehensive trauma-informed care needed (Reinbergs & Fefer, 2018).

Guiding Principle Five: Preventing Trauma in the Mental Health System

As noted in the literature, the potential for re-traumatization when victims/survivors seek help for trauma or when they are involved in different systems is significant (SAMHSA, 2014; SAMHSA, 2014b, Sweeney et al., 2018). As discussed by the

Institute on Trauma and Trauma Informed Care (ITTIC, n.d.) and SAMHSA (2014, 2014b), re-traumatization can occur at all levels of care, unintentionally, and without the awareness of the service providers. According to Sweeney et al. (2018), re-traumatization "occurs when something in a present experience is redolent of past trauma" (p. 322). Re-traumatization can involve interactions and situations which resemble past traumas; it may trigger similar feelings, sensations, or experiences as those of individual traumas or experiences of collective, cultural, or historical traumas (Jackson, 2002; Sweeney et al., 2018). A trauma-informed care approach seeks to avoid any action of coercion, control, or force, and it aims to mitigate the potential for any accompanying traumatic stress triggers (Sweeney et al., 2018). As discussed previously, school counselors can serve as a protective factor for students in preventing or minimizing the likelihood of re-traumatization within school settings. Therefore, promoting trauma awareness is critical to giving school counselors the ability to decrease and prevent re-traumatization (SAMHSA, 2014b).

Guiding Principles Six and Seven: Trustworthiness, Transparency, Collaboration, and Mutuality

For many victims/survivors of trauma, specifically surrounding trauma that is perpetrated by others, trusting others can be challenging (Bell et al., 2019). This response is understandable given that many victims/survivors have experienced coercion, manipulation, betrayal, secrecy, abandonment, and controlling relationships (Sweeney et al., 2018). As discussed by Sweeney et al. (2018), taking a trauma-informed care approach involves more than just a focus on the interventions; it also requires an emphasis on the relationship. Interactions between the client and clinician are characterized by transparency, truthfulness, authenticity, genuineness, unconditional positive regard, empathic understanding, and acceptance (Rogers, 1957; Sweeney et al., 2018). Additionally, a trauma-informed care approach does not mirror a medical model where the counselor is a helper to the "helpee" who is expected to comply (Butler et al., 2001; Sweeney et al., 2018). Instead, a collaborative approach is taken in the therapeutic process such that the student is invited into all aspects of the process (e.g., goal setting, treatment planning, etc.). In trauma-informed care, the expertise of both parties is valued, as the expertise that the student has on themselves, their needs, their story, their strengths, and their hopes is championed.

Guiding Principle Eight: Empowerment, Choice, and Control

Trauma, at its core, involves an event, experience, or series of events/experiences in which the control, choice, and power is stripped away from the victim/survivor (Sweeney et al., 2018). Regardless of the type of traumatic incident experienced, the root of trauma involves the brain feeling helpless, powerless, and as if one's world is being flipped upside down. In recognizing this, a foundational aim of trauma-informed care is to empower the victim/survivor both in the therapeutic process and in their lives. The trauma-informed care process is not one in which the school counselor is in control, but is one where the student is empowered in their autonomy, in sharing their voice, and in making choices.

An important aspect of empowering students involves taking a strengths-based approach to care (Cavanaugh, 2016; Harris & Fallot, 2001). Instead of focusing on their struggles or growth areas, the counselor recognizes each student as having existing capabilities, strengths, and resilience, and they implement interventions to engage and enhance these already present resources (Butler et al., 2001). In trauma-informed care, the counselor emphasizes the student's abilities to adapt to, cope with, and survive the trauma (in whatever form) (Butler et al., 2001; Sweeney et al., 2018). As discussed by Cavanaugh (2016), "finding times for students to showcase their strengths and offering choices during the day to provide opportunities for students to engage their interests are also critical" (p. 44). For example, Matthew's history teacher has asked him to write a paper on World War II. After losing his father last year in combat, Matthew begins to have panic attacks whenever the assignment is discussed in class. Matthew's teacher and school counselor, recognizing the way in which the assignment's content is re-traumatizing for Matthew, offer an alternate assignment to write a paper on a time in history that is meaningful for him. Providing this option supports Matthew in completing the assignment and meeting the needed academic outcomes while simultaneously fostering a sense of agency. As is highlighted in Matthew's case, an empowering environment for students involves one where resilience is emphasized over the struggle or the pathology (Butler et al., 2001).

Guiding Principle Nine: Safety

As described by the Diagnostic and Statistical Manual of Mental Disorders (American Psychiatric Association, 2013) trauma involves "exposure to actual or threatened death, serious injury, or sexual violence" (p. 271). The root of trauma and the negative impacts it leaves on victims/survivors involve experiences of threats to one's physical safety, emotional safety, or integrity of their identity (SAMHSA, 2014; Sweeney et al., 2018). In response, trauma-informed care is intentional in providing an environment that promotes students' physical, emotional, psychological, social, and cultural safety (Sweeney et al., 2018). Steps towards this goal might include but are not limited to informed consent and choice, cultural competence in service providers, physical environments characterized by safety and warmth, collaboration, shared decision-making, advocacy efforts, trauma-sensitive policies and procedures, inclusivity, a systemic and intersectionality lens, and more (Anderson, 1998; ASCA,

2016; Harper & Singh, 2013; Hernandez et al., 2004; Sweeney et al., 2018). As denoted by ASCA (2016), school counselors play an instrumental role in fostering a school environment that feels safe, welcoming, and supportive to all students.

Guiding Principle Ten: Survivor Partnerships

The final trauma-informed care guiding principle proposed by Sweeney et al. (2018) involves providing services that are founded upon partnerships. As discussed previously, trauma-informed care is not characterized by a hierarchy but by collaboration. School counselors and those practicing trauma-informed care do not see themselves as "providers" but of partners in the student's journey and process. Additionally, dismantling a hierarchy means that there is more balance between service providers and the victims/survivors, as it is recognized that many service providers may be victims/survivors of trauma themselves (Sweeney et al., 2018).

In addition to partnering with the student, Gherardi et al. (2020) discusses the importance of partnering with the family as well as that of fostering community engagement. Although trauma-informed frameworks that consider the individual student's partnership are important, those frameworks alone may insufficiently support the student and may further marginalize both the student and the communities a counselor is trying to support (Gherardi et al., 2020). In response, it is important that the school and the community form partnerships "that are grounded in mutuality and empowerment" and "avoid the stigmatization of communities and families impacted by trauma" (Gherardi et al., 2020, p. 490). Those partnerships involve considering that "while not everything that happens within families may be okay, families themselves are critical partners in making things okay" (Gherardi et al., 2020, p. 494). In summary, the tenth guiding principle of trauma-informed care involves shared power amongst the school counselor, the student, and the family/community.

TRAUMA-INFORMED CARE IN ACTION

To foster a deeper understanding of how to implement trauma-informed school counseling, one may examine the fictional client case study below. The case study will be analyzed and discussed through the lens of Sweeney et al.'s (2018) 10 trauma-informed care guiding principles, and specific trauma-informed action steps and interventions relevant to school counseling will be provided. Questions for consideration will also be offered in Figure 2.

Case Study

Marcus is a 12-year-old, Black, cisgender, heterosexual, male identifying student. Christine, the school counselor, has asked to see Marcus because teachers have identified him as acting "unruly", "unmotivated", and "disruptive" in class. In the classroom, Marcus frequently balls up paper and throws it at other students and his teachers, responds with verbal aggression toward his peers, and consistently taps or fidgets with various supplies in response to his anxiety. Marcus' teachers and school administration are frustrated with his behaviors and inability to respond to directives.

Figure 2. Case study questions for consideration

Question 1:

In what ways can a trauma-informed perspective aid in the understanding and conceptualization of Marcus' behaviors?

Question 2:

How might a trauma-informed care approach be beneficial to Marcus and the interactions of school personnel supporting Marcus?

Question 3:

As his school counselor, what are some steps and strategies that you might take to support Marcus?

Case Study Analysis

Guiding Principle One: Seeing Through a Trauma Lens

An important aspect of trauma-informed school counseling involves moving away from the "what is wrong with you?" and towards the "what has happened to you?" (Bloom, 1995; Sweeney et al., 2018; Winfrey & Perry, 2021). Although possibly unaware of his experiences and history, when seeing Marcus' behaviors through a trauma-informed lens, stakeholders at his school can begin to consider how his experiences and needs inform his behaviors. Instead of prioritizing school success, remembering that trauma experiences can interfere with school success is crucial (SAMHSA, 2014). Without doing so, schools can quickly pigeonhole themselves into trying to change the "problematic" behaviors interfering with a student's academic success, without considering the non-academic challenges a child may be experiencing. It is essential for schools to address students' needs in holistic ways and to take into account their relationships, self-regulation, academic competence, and physical and emotional well-being" (Cole et al., 2013, p. 21).

The neurobiological impacts of trauma can be meaningful when considering how trauma has impacted a child. Experiences of trauma or chronic stress can activate the brain's stress response (Ford, 2013; Perry, 2000; Perry & Daniels, 2016; Schore, 2001; Van der Kolk, 2015). Activating the brain's stress response, especially in the long-term, can lead to challenges with memory consolidation, concentration, sustained attention, irritability, anxiety, and more (Van der Kolk, 2015; Conradi & Wilson, 2010). As discussed by Perry and Daniels (2016), Basch (2010), and Stevens (2012), when children struggle with these consequences of trauma, it can lead to them being labeled as "unruly", "disruptive", or "unmotivated". Labeling a child based upon their behaviors and struggles can be counterproductive and harmful. As discussed by Dr. Bruce Perry, "I've found that seemingly senseless behavior makes sense once you look at what is behind it" (Winfrey & Perry, 2021, p. 23). The reality is that schools and school counselors frequently serve students with a trauma history while being unaware that any trauma occurred (Harris & Fallot, 2001). Unfortunately, when systems are unaware of trauma and operate without a trauma-informed lens, there can be "inadvertent re-traumatization when a service system's usual operating procedures trigger a reemergence or an exacerbation of trauma symptoms" (Harris & Fallot, 2001, p. 3).

Instead of labeling Marcus' behavior as "unruly" or difficult, it can be helpful for the school counselor and school personnel to "attempt to understand the distress and fears that underlie particular ways of trying to get needs met and difficulties expressing them" (Sweeney et al., 2018, p. 327). Through a trauma-informed lens, one can ascertain that behaviors might be victims'/survivors' means of understanding, coping with, and communicating their pain (Filson, 2013; Sweeney et al., 2018). As Filson provides (2016):

I was essentially disconnected from any context that could have explained the chaos in and around me. This is what happens when the individual is viewed as the problem, rather than the world the individual lives in. When the actions we take to cope, or adapt, or survive are deprived of meaning, we look – well, crazy. (p. 21)

A child's behavior is only a part of the story, or a response to the story, not the story itself. Students' experiences and stories matter; they are more than their presenting problems or behaviors. When school counselors hear student labeling or identifiers focused on challenging behaviors, they should facilitate a conversation with stakeholders where they can explore, "What has happened to them?" or "What need is their behavior trying to meet?" versus "What is wrong with them?". This might also include speaking with teachers to see what resources or supports they might need to care for students well. Consultations among teachers, administrators, and parents is an important step in protecting students like Marcus from further re-traumatization or harm.

Guiding Principle Two: Appreciation of Invisible Trauma and Intersectionality

A trauma-informed lens does not solely consider individual traumatic experiences, but views the student in a holistic way, considering their history of experiences, context, and socio-cultural identities (Goodman, 2014; Gherardi et al., 2020; Sweeney et al., 2018). An important aspect of trauma-informed care involves avoiding simply focusing on the student's symptomology and seeing the entirety of the student's experiences in context. As described by Harris and Fallot (2001), where a traditional approach to therapy might ask, "How do I understand this problem or these symptoms?", a trauma-informed care approach asks the question, "How do I understand this person?" (p. 13). To understand Marcus and his challenges, a school counselor must see him within context.

An unfortunate reality is that individuals who identify as Black or African American, particularly Black males, might often be identified as unruly, aggressive, problematic, or disruptive in school systems (Kinsler, 2011; Okonofua et al., 2016; Riddle & Sinclair, 2019). In fact, research suggests that Black and minority students are more likely than Caucasian students to experience stricter disciplinary actions, like suspension or expulsion, within the education system (Morgan et al., 2014; Riddle & Sinclair, 2019; Santiago et al., 2018). In conceptualizing and working with youth, it is important not only to consider the impacts that individual trauma has had on their lives, but also how one's socio-cultural identities might involve experiences where they are stigmatized or experience collective trauma and systemic oppression. In Marcus' case, the narrow and stigmatizing view of his behaviors might involve several factors including his trauma history, race, and gender. Recognizing the intersectionality of Marcus' experiences is vital in knowing what types of support, individual and systemic, that Marcus and other students like him may need.

Guiding Principle Three and Four: Sensitive Discussions About Trauma and Pathways to Trauma-Specific Support

Understandably, there are several reasons why practitioners, especially school counselors, may be reticent to question a client surrounding their trauma history (Read et al., 2007; Sweeney et al., 2018). Included in the questioning is the potential for re-traumatization for the student, fear of causing additional distress, lack of training on how to ask questions related to trauma, and more (Read et al., 2007). To recognize the challenges that trauma can bring for many students, research suggests that counselors can use universal screening surrounding mental health, relational, and behavioral challenges that may surface in response to trauma (Reinbergs & Fefer, 2018). In Marcus' case, conducting universal screening before challenges arise can provide a foundation for proactively supporting him, versus the alternative of responding when challenges arise, which can contribute to potentially shaming responses.

As discussed by Read et al. (2007) and Sweeney et al. (2018), any question or discussion surrounding trauma should be done sensitively, at the student's pace, and in a way that is empowering to the victim/survivor. A victim/survivor should never be forced to disclose or answer questions about trauma or abuse (Read et al., 2007; Sweeney et al., 2018). Instead, it is vital that school counselors recognize the signs and common responses of trauma without a disclosure and that they are able to support the student with school specific supports and connect them to external trauma-specific support as needed (Harris & Fallot, 2001; Read et al., 2007; Sweeney et al., 2018). In the case of Marcus or other students, if a disclosure about trauma and abuse were to occur, Read et al. (2007) provides the following recommendations: avoid questioning or trying to obtain details of the trauma, offer trauma-specific support and resources, ask if and how trauma might be related to current challenges, assess current safety, reassure the student, conduct an emotional check-in after the disclosure, and end the session with plans for an additional session or with a concrete support plan for the student. Trauma-specific support might entail contacting Child Protective Services regarding a trauma or abuse disclosure to ensure the safety of the student.

As previously discussed in this chapter, it is important to recognize that although school counselors can be of immense support and a resource to victims/survivors of trauma, particularly within the school setting, providing trauma-specific processing or conducting "trauma counseling" and trauma-specific care is not within a school counselor's scope of practice. Trauma-specific therapy is a specialty area, involving specific competencies, which often involves more ongoing treatment than school counselors can provide. As such, in recognizing that Marcus may be experiencing consequences of trauma, connecting his family and him to trauma-specific resources (e.g., trauma-focused therapy) can be invaluable.

Although much of the "trauma work" will be done outside of the school setting, it is important to recognize that school counselors are not powerless in helping victims/survivors who are experiencing traumatic stress during the school day. For example, Christine has several tools that can be immensely helpful when Marcus' anxiety and traumatic stress symptoms surface. These can include supporting Marcus in utilizing coping skills and regulatory grounding techniques at times when his nervous system is experiencing high levels of stress (e.g., ice cube technique, deep breathing exercises, engaging his senses to ground him to the present moment, acupressure rub, counting, holding an item of comfort, etc.). Additionally, Christine can be an instrumental link in providing a supportive school environment for Marcus. By engaging the MTSS, Marcus' teachers may also be instrumental in the support plan and they can be informed of his coping/grounding plan. This would allow teachers to support Marcus with his coping skills while in the classroom environment.

Guiding Principle Five: Preventing Trauma in the Mental Health System

Feelings of worthlessness and shame are commonly experienced effects of trauma (Jeon et al., 2014; Platt & Freyd, 2012). If Marcus' school counselor, teachers, and school administration participate in shaming reactions toward Marcus, it may foster increased struggles with self-identity, self-esteem, and self-worth. Additionally, if school staff use more aggressive or shaming language as they become frustrated with Marcus, it might lead to traumatic stress and re-traumatization as Marcus' brain associates the current situation with previous individual or collective trauma experiences. As discussed by SAMHSA (2014), harsh or intimidating disciplinary actions in school settings can be trauma-inducing themselves. For example, for Marcus, who experienced verbal and physical abuse from his grandmother as discipline in early childhood, replicating this cycle through shaming or disciplinary actions can be contraindicated, triggering, and harmful. Additionally, the perpetuation of systemic oppression and the harsher disciplinary measures that Marcus might face as a Black male student can lead to several negative short-term and long-term consequences (Riddle & Sinclair, 2019).

To support Marcus and students like him, it is vital that schools take an MTSS approach to care where all school personnel are trained and able to provide trauma-informed and culturally sensitive support to students (Harris & Fallot, 2001; Reinbergs & Fefer, 2018). In Marcus' case, this might include the school counselor taking an advocacy role for him by working with his teachers and the school to ensure that he receives any needed training, coaching, or support and that his teachers receive clinical consultation as needed (Reinbergs & Fefer, 2018). Advocacy involves supporting students individually and at the school environment level. This might include implementing necessary trauma awareness training and multicultural/diversity training for all school stakeholders (Santiago et al., 2018). A school counselor's role in preventing re-traumatization does not solely involve the work done in their office, but also involves fostering a school culture and environment that seeks to prevent re-traumatization and promote safety for all students in classrooms, hallways, playgrounds, and within the school community (Santiago et al., 2018).

Guiding Principle Six, Seven, and Eight: Trustworthiness, Transparency, Collaboration, Mutuality, Empowerment, Choice, and Control

For victims/survivors of abuse, trusting others can be challenging, particularly for those whose trauma was inflicted by others in their lives (Bell et al., 2019; Harris & Follet, 2001). Trust is earned over time through an emphasis of openness, transparency, and respect (Harris & Follet, 2001; Sweeney et al., 2018). Sweeney et al. (2018) discusses the importance of collaborative, compassionate, authentic, and nonhierarchical relationships in trauma recovery. As many types of trauma exist in the context of relationships, recovery, too, takes place in the context of relationships (Herman, 1992).

An unfortunate reality that many victims/survivors of trauma encounter is a lack of power and control (Sweeney et al., 2018). Fostering empowerment, choice, and control in school counseling is paramount, especially for students who have endured experiences of trauma. Herman (1992) emphasizes this importance by noting that core experiences of trauma are disempowerment and disconnection. Due to the trauma that he has experienced, Marcus has learned coping strategies that help him feel in control and safe in the world around him, such as engaging in protective strategies when interacting with others. Where some might see Marcus' behaviors as "problematic" or "challenging", a trauma-informed lens recognizes that these behaviors might be trauma responses that have helped Marcus to have some sense of control, to adapt, and to survive the threatening world around him (Harris & Fallot, 2001).

In recognizing this, a trauma-informed care approach with Marcus would involve providing support that invites, includes, collaborates with, and partners with Marcus and his family as often as possible. This collaborative exploration might involve seeking support options that could be helpful for Marcus within the classroom, linking him to support networks within the school, and exploring from what other resources or supports the family might benefit (e.g., family counseling, trauma-specific counseling for Marcus, etc.). By focusing on the victims/survivors' voices, trauma-informed care allows the student to write their story instead of others fostering ongoing powerlessness by taking the pen from their hands. Herman (1992) articulates this point by sharing that "The first principle of recovery is the empowerment of the survivor. They must be the author and arbiter of their own recovery" (p. 133).

For example, while speaking with Marcus and his mother about his challenges in the classroom, Christine learns that Marcus struggles with high levels of separation anxiety from his mother in response to the tragic loss of his father the year earlier. This struggle with separation anxiety, coupled with the school's disciplinary measures in response to his behaviors, contribute to Marcus' sense of feeling unsafe within the school environment. Taking an active approach to foster safety for Marcus will be paramount to his progress. This will include taking measures to promote a safe environment both within and outside the counseling office. Partnering with Marcus by asking *him* what helps him feel safe reveals that having his stuffed bunny and feeling as if his family is with him help to navigate fear. Through collaboration, Christine, Marcus, and his mother discuss a plan where he will keep a "safety box" in his backpack to aid in times of anxiety. Marcus decides that in his box, he would like to put his stuffed bunny, a picture of his family, a letter from his mother, and a fidget spinner. School stakeholders setting up a foundation for Marcus to feel safe creates a foundation for recovery and learning.

Guiding Principle Nine and Ten: Safety and Survivor Partnerships

As discussed by Sweeney et al. (2018), central to trauma-informed care is the ability to provide physical, emotional, social, cultural, gender, psychological, and social safety. Concisely, "children are only able to learn within the context of safety and security" (Bloom, 1995, p. 1). For Marcus and other students who may benefit from additional support, implementing a student success team or MTSS within the school can provide several outlets and pathways for support. By setting up a student success meeting with Marcus, his guardian(s), the school counselor, teachers, and any other possibly helpful stakeholders, the stakeholders can collaboratively create a student success plan to promote safety and support for Marcus at school. This might involve providing Marcus with choices inside the classroom, delivering training for teachers surrounding trauma-informed communication or discipline, promoting engagement in a mentorship or tutoring program, utilizing external resources, and more. Employing a student success plan through a MTSS can provide consistent support that will aid the student in feeling safe, heard, seen, and valued in the school environment.

Additional Interventions in Trauma-Informed School Counseling

As shown in the case of Marcus, supporting victims/survivors of trauma can be nuanced and can involve a number of individual, cultural, and developmental factors. As such, there is no "one-size-fits-all" approach in trauma-informed care (Lawrence, 2014; Sorrentino et al., 2020). School counselors need to meet students where they are as individuals, within their contexts, and within the context of their school and resources available to them. However, in addition to the interventions that were discussed in the case studies above, school counselors could benefit from implementing additional common interventions or tools. These include but are not limited to using universal screening and assessment, creatively creating support networks within the school environment, and leading specified group counseling interventions (Cavanaugh, 2016; Reinbergs & Fefer, 2018).

In addition to responding to students' needs as they surface, an important aspect of trauma-informed care involves taking a prevention approach (Reinbergs & Fefer, 2018). One method the literature discusses is utilizing universal screening measures to help identify students who may need additional support (Cavanaugh, 2016; Oakes et al., 2014; Reinbergs & Fefer, 2018). Screening can help identify challenges that may be a response to traumatization, including but not limited to anxiety, aggression, and behavioral challenges (Reinbergs & Fefer, 2018). Various universal screening aids exist. Some include Systematic Screening for Behavior Disorders (Walker & Severson, 1992), Behavioral and Emotional Screening System (Reynolds & Kamphaus, 2015), Strengths and Difficulties Questionnaire (Goodman, 1997), and Social, Academic, and Emotional Behavior Risk Screener (Kilgus et al., 2016). Through screening measures or needs assessments, school counselors can gain insight into which students may need additional support and can provide interventions which may be useful (Reinbergs & Fefer, 2018).

Utilizing already established networks within a school can be a useful tool for school counselors. Options might include peer support networks such as counseling support groups, peer mentorship or tutoring programs, teacher mentorship opportunities for students, and more (Cavanaugh, 2016). As discussed by Cole et al. (2013) "it is critical that children feel safe and connected to others in all parts of the school, not just in one program or with one teacher" (p. 3). Although the value of a safe and meaningful therapeutic relationship with a school counselor cannot be understated (Safran & Muran, 2000), connecting students to other support networks within the school can be empowering and meaningful. For Marcus, for example, engaging with his peers in a counseling support group for anxiety could be instrumental in helping him feel less alone, in providing meaningful connections, and in gaining new coping skills. Additionally, if a similar group does not already exist, creating a Black Culture Club for students in the school to find community and celebrate their heritage and culture could support Marcus in feeling affirmed in his culture.

To conclude the discussion surrounding trauma-informed care interventions for school counselors, it can be helpful to note additional interventions discussed by the literature. In research conducted by Reinbergs and Fefer (2018), there are some school counseling group interventions that may be useful in supporting students who have been impacted by trauma and its effects. These interventions might include but are not limited to conducting Cognitive Behavioral Intervention for Trauma in Schools groups (for 11 years and older), Bounce Back (for K-5), and dialectical behavioral therapy (DBT) skills groups.

RECOGNIZING AND RESPONDING TO THE SYSTEMIC AND CONTEXTUAL FACTORS SURROUNDING TRAUMA

The calling for and implementation of trauma-informed care is a critical step forward in counseling as it provides a framework that "acknowledges that trauma can have complex and long-lasting impacts on clients" which need to be addressed for counseling to be effective (Goodman, 2014, p. 55). Although this is the case, Goodman (2014) notes that utilizing trauma-informed practices that ignore societal, systemic, and contextual factors of trauma may perpetuate injustice and limit trauma treatment. Gherardi et al. (2020) echoes this sentiment stating that "current research and practice around trauma-sensitive schools is largely decontextualized, with the complex intersectional and sociocultural realities of student experiences either overlooked or viewed from a deficit orientation" (p. 494). Implementing a social justice-based and decolonizing approach to trauma-informed care involves counselors taking a more systematic and comprehensive approach to the conceptualization and treatment of trauma and involves transparency, the sharing of power, and partnership with the students and the community (Gherardi et al., 2020; Goodman, 2014; Sweeney et al., 2018).

Gherardi et al. (2020) notes that although trauma-informed models might recognize the relationship between trauma and identity, full contextualization of trauma and intersectionality often remains unconsidered. In response, trauma-informed models may see the "disproportionate impact of trauma as a symptom rather than acknowledging the root causes of this reality" (Gherardi et al., 2020, p. 489). For student treatment and support to be decolonized and comprehensive, one must consider the social causes of disproportionality and sociopolitical factors that might contribute to a student's trauma (Gherardi et al., 2020). This approach can include considerations regarding the varying privilege and subjugation surrounding ability, race, ethnicity, nationality, religion, gender, sexual orientation, socioeconomic status, and other sociopolitical factors in a student's life. For example, although trauma impacts individuals from various racial and socio-economic backgrounds, "the impact of these experiences on specific subpopulations and the complex interrelated experience with individuals' social identities are factors to address in considering equity" (Gherardi et al., 2020, p. 490). Individual trauma experiences are pieces to a larger experiential, cultural, familial, and personal context that is inextricably linked. As described by Sonya Renee Taylor (2018), humans are each complex tapestries. Decolonized trauma-informed care is an approach that takes the entire complex and beautiful tapestry into account, alternative to looking at a single thread that is interwoven within the student's identity, life, and community.

CONCLUSION

As discussed by Morton and Berardi (2018), trauma-informed care practices bring hope, break down walls, and build community. School counselors play a vital role in supporting students who have been impacted by traumatic events and in providing them with or linking them to the resources that they need (ASCA, 2016; ASCA, 2019; Martinez et al., 2020). If counselors take a trauma-informed school counseling approach, they, in collaboration with their school and community partners, "can help transform the school into a safe, supportive, trauma-sensitive learning environment for all students" (ASCA, 2016, p. 4). The calling for further training, knowledge, and competence in trauma-informed care school counseling is an important one that should not be ignored.

ACKNOWLEDGMENT

The author of this book chapter would like to acknowledge Kim Severn and Robbie Cox for their valuable contributions as school counselors, counselor educators, and colleagues who offered valuable insight and contributions to this chapter. The author of this book would also like to acknowledge her husband, daughter, family, and loved ones who continue to provide her with unwavering support and love.

REFERENCES

American Psychiatric Association. (2013). *Diagnostic and statistical manual of mental disorders* (5th ed.)., doi:10.1176/appi.books.9780890425596

American School Counselor Association. (2016). *The school counselor and trauma-informed Practice*. https://schoolcounselor.org/Standards-Positions/Position-Statements/ASCA-Position-Statements/The-School-Counselor-and-Trauma-Informed-Practice

American School Counselor Association. (2019). *ASCA school counselor professional standards & competencies*. https://www.schoolcounselor.org/asca/media/asca/home/SCCompetencies.pdf

Anderson, D. C. (1998). Curriculum, culture and community: The challenge of school violence. In M. Tonry & M. Moore (Eds.), *Youth violence* (pp. 317–363). University of Chicago Press.

Ano, G. G., & Vasconcelles, E. B. (2005). Religious coping and psychological adjustment to stress: A meta-analysis. *Journal of Clinical Psychology*, *61*(4), 461–480. doi:10.1002/jclp.20049 PMID:15503316

Aydin, C. (2017). How to forget the unforgettable? On collective trauma, cultural identity, and mnemotechnologies. *Identity*, *17*(3), 125–137. doi:10.1080/15283488.2017.1340160

Basch, C. E. (2010). *Healthier students are better learners: A missing link in school reforms to close the achievement gap*. http://www.equitycampaign.org/i/a/document/12557_Equitymatters vol6web03082010.pdf

Basch, C. E. (2011). Healthier students are better learners: A missing link in school reforms to close the achievement gap. *The Journal of School Health*, *81*(10), 593–598. doi:10.1111/j.1746-1561.2011.00632.x PMID:21923870

Bell, V., Robinson, B., Katona, C., Fett, A.-K., & Shergill, S. (2019). When trust is lost: The impact of interpersonal trauma on social interactions. *Psychological Medicine*, *49*(6), 1041–1046. doi:10.1017/S0033291718001800 PMID:30043717

Bendall, S., Eastwood, O., Cox, G., Farrelly-Rosch, A., Nicoll, H., Peters, W., Bailey, A. P., McGorry, P. D., & Scanlan, F. (2021). A systematic review and synthesis of trauma-informed care within outpatient and counseling health settings for young people. *Child Maltreatment*, *26*(3), 313–324. doi:10.1177/1077559520927468 PMID:32536207

Berliner, L., & Kolko, D. J. (2016). Trauma informed care: A commentary and critique. *Child Maltreatment*, *21*(2), 168–172. doi:10.1177/1077559516643785 PMID:27152025

Bloom, S. L. (1995). Creating sanctuary in the school. *Journal for a Just and Caring Education*, *1*(4), 403.

Brooks, J. (2014). *The process of parenting*. McGraw Hill.

Butler, L. D., Critelli, F. M., & Rinfrette, E. S. (2011). Trauma-informed care and mental health. *Directions in Psychiatry*, *31*, 197–210.

Cavanaugh, B. (2016). Trauma-informed classrooms and schools. *Beyond Behavior*, *25*(2), 41–46. doi:10.1177/107429561602500206

Center for Disease Control and Prevention. (2020). *Six guiding principles to a trauma-informed care approach*. https://www.cdc.gov/cpr/infographics/6_principles_trauma_info.htm

Cole, S. F., Eisner, A., Gregory, M., & Risuccia, J. (2013). *Helping traumatized children learn: Creating and advocating for trauma-sensitive schools, safe, supportive learning environments that benefit all children* (Vol. 2). Massachusetts Advocates for Children.

Cole, S. F., Greenwald O'Brien, J., Gadd, G., Ristuccia, J., Wallace, L., & Gregory, M. (2005). *Helping traumatized children learn.* Massachusetts Advocates for Children.

Conradi, L., & Wilson, C. (2010). Managing traumatized children: A trauma systems perspective. *Current Opinion in Pediatrics, 22*(5), 621–625. doi:10.1097/MOP.0b013e32833e0766 PMID:20717037

Corey, G. (2013). *Theory and practice of counseling and psychotherapy* (9th ed.). Cengage Learning.

Elliott, D. E., Bjelajac, P., Fallot, R. D., Markoff, L. S., & Reed, B. G. (2005). Trauma-informed or trauma-denied: Principles and implementation of trauma-informed services for women. *Journal of Community Psychology, 33*(4), 461–477. doi:10.1002/jcop.20063

Erikson, K. (1976). *Everything in its path.* Simon and Schuster Paperbacks.

Evans, A., & Coccoma, P. (2014). *Trauma-informed care: How neuroscience influences practice.* Taylor and Francis. doi:10.4324/9781315815572

Evans, S. W., Stephan, S. H., & Sugai, G. (2014). Advancing research in school mental health: Introduction of a special issue on key issues in research. *School Mental Health, 6*(2), 63–67. doi:10.100712310-014-9126-8 PMID:25067959

Filson, B. (2013). *Self-injury: The attempt to cope, connect and communicate* [Webinar]. MA Department of Public Health. https://www.youtube.com/watch?v=JfapTE0R6g0

Filson, B. (2016). The haunting can end: Trauma-informed approaches in healing from abuse and adversity. In J. Russo & A. Sweeney (Eds.), *Searching for a rose garden: Challenging psychiatry, fostering mad studies* (pp. 20–24). PCCS Books.

Ford, J. D. (2013). *Treatment of complex trauma: A sequenced, relationship-based approach.* Guilford Press.

Garrison, E. G., Roy, I. S., & Azar, V. (1999). Responding to the mental health needs of Latino children and families through school-based services. *Clinical Psychology Review, 19*(2), 199–219. doi:10.1016/S0272-7358(98)00070-1 PMID:10078420

Gerrity, E., & Folcarelli, C. (2008). *Child traumatic stress: What every policymaker should know*. https://www.nctsn.org/sites/default/files/resources/child_traumatic_stress_what_policymakers_sh ould_know.pdf

Gherardi, S. A., Flinn, R. E., & Jaure, V. B. (2020). Trauma-sensitive schools and social justice: A critical analysis. *The Urban Review*, *52*(3), 482–504. doi:10.100711256-020-00553-3

Goodman, R. (1997). The Strengths and Difficulties Questionnaire: A research note. *Journal of Child Psychology and Psychiatry, and Allied Disciplines*, *38*(5), 581–586. doi:10.1111/j.1469-7610.1997.tb01545.x PMID:9255702

Goodman, R. D. (2014). A liberatory approach to trauma counseling: Decolonizing our trauma-informed practices. In R. D. Goodman & P. C. Gorski (Eds.), *Decolonizing "multicultural" counseling through social justice* (pp. 55–72). Springer.

Harper, A. J., & Singh, A. A. (2013). Counselor agency and action in developing safe schools: Six directions for systemic change. *Journal of LGBT Issues in Counseling*, *7*(4), 405–415. doi:10.1080/15538605.2013.839346

Harris, M., & Fallot, R. D. (2001). *Using trauma theory to design service systems*. Jossey-Bass.

Herman, J. L. (1992). *Trauma and recovery*. Basic Books.

Hernandez, T. J., & Seem, S. R. (2004). A safe school climate: A systemic approach and the school counselor. *Professional School Counseling*, *7*(4), 256–262.

Institute on Trauma and Trauma Informed Care. (n.d.). *What is trauma-informed care?* https://socialwork.buffalo.edu/social-research/institutes-centers/institute-on-trauma-and-trauma-informed-care/what-is-trauma-informed-care.html

Jackson, V. (2002). In our own voice: African-American stories of oppression, survival and recovery in mental health systems. *International Journal of Narrative Therapy and Community Work*, *2002*(2), 11–31.

Jeon, H. J., Park, J.-I., Fava, M., Mischoulon, D., Sohn, J. H., Seong, S., Park, J. E., Yoo, I., & Cho, M. J. (2014). Feelings of worthlessness, traumatic experience, and their comorbidity in relation to lifetime suicide attempt in community adults with major depressive disorder. *Journal of Affective Disorders*, *166*, 206–212. doi:10.1016/j.jad.2014.05.010 PMID:25012433

Kilgus, S. P., Eklund, K., von der Embse, N. P., Taylor, C. N., & Sims, W. A. (2016). Psychometric defensibility of the Social, Academic, and Emotional Behavior Risk Screener (SAEBRS) Teacher Rating Scale and multiple gating procedure within elementary and middle school samples. *Journal of School Psychology*, *58*, 21–39. doi:10.1016/j.jsp.2016.07.001 PMID:27586068

Kinsler, J. (2011). Understanding the Black–White school discipline gap. *Economics of Education Review*, *30*(6), 1370–1383. doi:10.1016/j.econedurev.2011.07.004

Lansford, J. E., Dodge, K. A., Pettit, G. S., Bates, J. E., Crozier, J., & Kaplow, J. (2002). A 12-year prospective study of the long-term effects of early child physical maltreatment on psychological, behavioral, and academic problems in adolescence. *Archives of Pediatrics & Adolescent Medicine*, *156*(8), 824–830. doi:10.1001/archpedi.156.8.824 PMID:12144375

Lawrence, J. A. (2014). Managing dissonance: Implications for therapeutic practice with partner violence. *Partner Abuse*, *5*(2), 119–151. doi:10.1891/1946-6560.5.2.119

Martinez, R. R., Gavin Williams, R., & Green, J. (2020). The role of school counselors delivering a trauma-informed care approach to supporting youth in foster care. *Professional School Counseling*, *23*(1), 2156759.

Miller, E. (2019). Trauma-informed approaches to adolescent relationship abuse and sexual violence prevention. *Pediatric Annals*, *48*(7), e274–e279. doi:10.3928/19382359-20190617-01 PMID:31305945

Morgan, E., Salomon, N., Plotkin, M., & Cohen, R. (2014). *The school discipline consensus report: Strategies for the field to keep students engaged in school and out of the juvenile justice system*. The Council of State Governments Justice Center.

Morton, B. M., & Berardi, A. A. (2018). Trauma-informed school programing: Applications for mental health professionals and educator partnerships. *Journal of Child & Adolescent Trauma*, *11*(4), 487–493. doi:10.100740653-017-0160-1 PMID:32318170

Oakes, W. P., Lane, K. L., Cox, M. L., & Messenger, M. (2014). Logistics of behavior screenings: How and why do we conduct behavior screenings at our school. *Preventing School Failure*, *58*(3), 159–170. doi:10.1080/1045988X.2014.895572

Okonofua, J. A., Walton, G. M., & Eberhardt, J. L. (2016). A vicious cycle: A social–psychological account of extreme racial disparities in school discipline. *Perspectives on Psychological Science*, *11*(3), 381–398. doi:10.1177/1745691616635592 PMID:27217251

Padden, J. V. (2021). *Urban trauma: Mental health clinicians' perception of trauma informed care, trauma responsive practice, and trauma resilience* [Doctoral dissertation, Morgan State University]. ProQuest Dissertations and Theses Global.

Perfect, M. M., Turley, M. R., Carlson, J. S., Yohanna, J., & Saint Gilles, M. P. (2016). School-related outcomes of traumatic event exposure and traumatic stress symptoms in students: A systematic review of research from 1990 to 2015. *School Mental Health*, *8*(1), 7–43. doi:10.100712310-016-9175-2

Perry, B. D. (2000). Traumatized children: How childhood trauma influences brain development. *The Journal of the California Alliance for the Mentally Ill*, *11*(1), 48–51.

Perry, D. L., & Daniels, M. L. (2016). Implementing trauma-informed practices in the school setting: A pilot study. *School Mental Health*, *8*(1), 177–188. doi:10.100712310-016-9182-3

Petersen, A., Joseph, J., & Feit, M. (Eds.). (2013). *New directions in child abuse and neglect research*. National Academies Press.

Platt, M., & Freyd, J. (2012). Trauma and negative underlying assumptions in feelings of shame: An exploratory study. *Psychological Trauma: Theory, Research, Practice, and Policy*, *4*(4), 370–378. doi:10.1037/a0024253

Porche, M. V., Costello, D. M., & Rosen-Reynoso, M. (2016). Adverse family experiences, child mental health, and educational outcomes for a national sample of students. *School Mental Health*, *8*(1), 44–60. doi:10.100712310-016-9174-3

Read, J., Hammersley, P., & Rudegeair, T. (2007). Why, when and how to ask about childhood abuse. *Advances in Psychiatric Treatment*, *13*(2), 101–110. doi:10.1192/apt.bp.106.002840

Reinbergs, E. J., & Fefer, S. A. (2018). Addressing trauma in schools: Multitiered service delivery options for practitioners. *Psychology in the Schools*, *55*(3), 250–263. doi:10.1002/pits.22105

Reynolds, C. R., & Kamphaus, R. W. (2015). *Behavior Assessment Systems for Children* (3rd ed.). Pearson.

Riddle, T., & Sinclair, S. (2019). Racial disparities in school-based disciplinary actions are associated with county-level rates of racial bias. *Proceedings of the National Academy of Sciences of the United States of America*, *116*(17), 8255–8260. doi:10.1073/pnas.1808307116 PMID:30940747

Rogers, C. R. (1957). The necessary and sufficient conditions of therapeutic personality change. *Journal of Consulting Psychology*, *21*(2), 95–103. doi:10.1037/h0045357 PMID:13416422

Rumsey, A. D., & Milsom, A. (2019). Supporting school engagement and high school completion through trauma-informed school counseling. *Professional School Counseling*, *22*(1), 1–10. doi:10.1177/2156759X19867254

Safran, J. D., & Muran, J. C. (2000). *Negotiating the therapeutic alliance: A relational treatment guide*. The Guilford Press.

Santiago, C. D., Raviv, T., & Jaycox, L. (2018). *Creating healing school communities: school-based interventions for students exposed to trauma*. American Psychological Association. doi:10.1037/0000072-000

Schore, A. (2001). Effects of a secure attachment relationship on right brain development; Affect regulation and infant mental health. *Infant Mental Health Journal*, *22*(1-2), 7–66. doi:10.1002/1097-0355(200101/04)22:1<7::AID-IMHJ2>3.0.CO;2-N

Sorrentino, A. E., Iverson, K. M., Tuepker, A., True, G., Cusack, M., Newell, S., & Dichter, M. E. (2020). Mental health care in the context of intimate partner violence: Survivor perspectives. *Psychological Services*. Advance online publication. doi:10.1037er0000427 PMID:32237873

Stevens, J. E. (2012, May 31). *Massachusetts, Washington State lead U.S. trauma-sensitive school movement* [Blog post]. ACES Too High. https://acestoohigh.com/2012/05/31/massachusetts-washington-state-lead-u-s-trauma-sensitive-school-movement/

Substance Abuse and Mental Health Services. (2020). *Understanding child trauma*. https://www.samhsa.gov/child-trauma/understanding-child-trauma

Substance Abuse and Mental Health Services Administration. (2014). *SAMHSA's concept of trauma and guidance for a trauma-informed approach*. Substance Abuse and Mental Health Services Administration. https://ncsacw.samhsa.gov/userfiles/files/SAMHSA_Trauma.pdf

Substance Abuse and Mental Health Services Administration. (2014). *Trauma-informed care in behavioral health services: TIP 57*. Substance Abuse and Mental Health Services Administration. https://store.samhsa.gov/product/TIP-57-Trauma-Informed-Care-in-Behavioral-Health-Services/SMA14-4816

Sweeney, A., Filson, B., Kennedy, A., Collinson, L., & Gillard, S. (2018). A paradigm shift: Relationships in trauma-informed mental health services. *BJPsych Advances, 24*(5), 319–333. doi:10.1192/bja.2018.29 PMID:30174829

Taylor, S. R. (2018). *The body is not an apology: The power of radical self-love.* Berrett-Koehler Publishers.

Van der Kolk, B. A. (2015). *The body keeps the score: brain, mind, and body in the healing of trauma*. Penguin Books.

Veltman, M. W. M., & Browne, K. D. (2001). Three decades of child maltreatment research: Implications for the school years. *Trauma, Violence & Abuse, 2*(3), 215–239. doi:10.1177/1524838001002003002

Walker, H. M., & Severson, H. H. (1992). *Systematic Screening for Behavior Disorders (SSBD)* (2nd ed.). Sopris West.

Winfrey, O., & Perry, B. D. (2021). *What happened to you?: Conversations on trauma, resilience, and healing*. Flatiron Books.

ADDITIONAL READING

Crenshaw, K. (1991). Mapping the margins: Intersectionality, identity politics, and violence against women of color. *Stanford Law Review, 43*(6), 1241–1299. doi:10.2307/1229039

Evans, A. & Coccoma, P. (2014). *Trauma-informed care: How neuroscience influences practice.* Taylor and Francis.

Goodman, R. D., & Gorski, P. C. (2014). *Decolonizing multicultural counseling through social justice*. Springer New York.

Rawson, S. (2021). *Applying trauma-sensitive practices in school counseling: Interventions for achieving change*. Routledge.

Sibbald, L., & Weed Phifer, L. (2020). *Trauma-informed social-emotional toolbox for children and adoescents: 116 worksheets and skill-building exercises to support safety, connection, and empowerment*. PESI.

Sporleder, J., & Forbes, H. T. (2016). *The trauma-informed school: A step-by-step implementation guide for administrators and school personnel.* Beyond Consequences Institute.

Sweeney, A., Filson, B., Kennedy, A., Collinson, L., & Gillard, S. (2018). A paradigm shift: Relationships in trauma-informed mental health services. *BJPsych Advances*, *24*(5), 319–333. doi:10.1192/bja.2018.29 PMID:30174829

Van der Kolk, B. A. (2015). *The body keeps the score: brain, mind, and body in the healing of trauma*. Penguin Books.

Winfrey, O., & Perry, B. D. (2021). *What happened to you?: Conversations on trauma, resilience, and healing*. Flatiron Books.

KEY TERMS AND DEFINITIONS

American School Counseling Association (ASCA): The primary American school counselor association supporting school counselors in providing resources and professional development.

Intersectionality: The intersection between various socio-cultural identities and the way in which these intersections can impact an individual within their context.

Multi-Tiered System of Supports (MTSS): An integrated system of school support that responds to academic and mental health needs.

Trauma: An experience, or series of experiences, which are perceived as threatening to an individual, group, community, or society and lead to various negative impacts and consequences for the victims/survivors.

Trauma-Informed Care: Care that is informed by an understanding of trauma, its effects, and best practices in supporting victims/survivors of trauma.

Trauma-Informed School Counseling: School counseling that utilizes the understanding of trauma, its signs, and its potential impacts and consequences on the lives of individuals and groups of people, and factors of intersectionality to intentionally inform the: conceptualization and treatment of cases, interactions and relationships with students, advocacy efforts conducted in the school and community, and providing of and linking to appropriate resources.

Trauma-Specific Support: Services provided to victims/survivors of trauma that provide direct support surrounding the trauma's impacts.

Chapter 4
Preparing for the Unexpected

Kristen Ascencao
Liberty University, USA

ABSTRACT

Individuals and school communities are often faced with unexpected events. While some unexpected events bring joy and happiness, others cause fear and helplessness. Stability is crucial during an unexpected crisis, and crisis management planning helps create processes, frameworks, and response protocols, reducing further trauma. According to the National Education Agency (NEA), schools must focus on safety to prevent incidents and a foundation of this work is supporting the community's mental health needs. Crisis management planning is critical to help reduce secondary trauma in the lives of others. School counselors should be leaders when helping their school systems prepare for these unexpected situations. They are seen as an essential resource in planning for crisis situations.

INTRODUCTION

A crisis is defined as an unexpected event that interrupts routines, behaviors, and emotions. These unexpected interruptions can "shatter students' assumptions of school safety, order, and predictability" according to Elbedour et al. (2020, p. 208). Schools may assume that a crisis will never happen to them and, consequently, may not adequately prepare for emergencies and be overwhelmed when facing the unexpected (Schonfeld & Newgass, 2003). Preparing for the unexpected helps ensure school leaders, including the school counselor, have an initial game plan to approach any type of crisis. During a crisis, an individual may feel emotionally or physically threatened. In addition, a crisis may result in the compromised safety of students, staff, and community members. Crises can occur with an individual or

DOI: 10.4018/978-1-7998-9785-9.ch004

impact a group of individuals. A traumatic experience limits one's ability to regulate stress healthily or safely (Erbacher et al., 2014; National Education Agency [NEA], 2018; Giboney Wall, 2021; Wiest-Stevenson & Lee, 2016; Wolpow et al., 2016b). Adrenaline is often running high during a crisis, and information processing is often compromised. When school leadership and the school counselor approach crises systematically, it reduces the potential for overlooking steps, enabling the leaders, including the school counselor, to address the crisis in question without wondering, "What is next?" School systems and campuses can approach the unexpected event using best practices, including trauma-informed principles, given the opportunity to plan. According to the American School Counselor Association (American School Counselor Association [ASCA], 2019) School Counselor and Safe Schools and Crisis Response Position Statement, "School counselors are a vital resource in preventing, intervening, and responding to crisis situations" (p. 1). Therefore, the objectives of the chapter include discussing how school leadership, including the school counselor, can prepare for unexpected crises, recognize the different types of traumas, understand the importance of creating trauma-sensitive practices in the school setting, and the importance of self-care in highly stressful, unexpected situations.

BACKGROUND

The American School Counselor Association (ASCA) has several standards that direct school counselor behaviors before, during, and after a crisis (American School Counselor Association [ASCA], 2016). The ASCA Standards speak to the school counselor's role as a leader in the school. Leadership is an essential aspect of crisis response, as it helps set the tone for how others will prepare and react to the unexpected. Additionally, school counselors should respond with appropriate strategies to address the specific needs of individuals, groups, or the school community during the crisis response process (ASCA, 2016). The ASCA (2016) Standards also remind school counselors of the limits of school counseling and the importance of referrals to community agencies to maintain the continuum of care.

Many situations can lead to a crisis. According to Erbacher et al. (2015, p. 39), the criteria of a crisis may include:

1. High levels of subjective discomfort.
2. Individual(s) temporarily unable to act to modify stress.
3. Situations overwhelm an individual's ability to cope or their knowledge of coping strategies.

4. Situations or events that an individual perceives as negative, harmful, or threatening.
5. Seemingly unsolvable problem.

The National Education Association (NEA) further iterates that a crisis may create a "sense of helplessness, hopelessness, and vulnerability combined with a loss of safety" (National Education Association [NEA], 2018, p. 7). Crises come in all sizes and might include acts of school violence, natural disasters, unexpected death of an individual, destruction of property, hate crimes, pandemic/health crisis, vehicle/pedestrian accident, or any other event that causes a disruption that results in an individual's inability to regulate stress or utilize healthy coping strategies (NEA, 2018). Regardless of the type of crisis, individuals may experience a type of trauma.

According to Starr Commonwealth (2019), more than half of children today in America have experienced a type of childhood trauma or been involved in a crisis. With the arrival of COVID-19, we could say that all of America's children have been involved in a crisis. Trauma is an experience and could stem from home, school, personal, social, or health issues. Some examples of crisis events that could result in trauma include the death of a loved one/student/teacher, abuse, neglect, community violence, lack of basic needs, suicidal ideation, illness, pandemic, bullying, conflict with others, car accident, or witnessing bullying/fighting/violence, just to name a few (NEA, 2018; Starr Commonwealth, 2019). As previously discussed, a traumatic experience limits one's ability to regulate stress healthily or safely (Erbacher et al., 2015; NEA, 2018; Giboney Wall, 2021; Wiest-Stevenson & Lee, 2016; Wolpow et al., 2016b). In addition, these traumatic exposures impact a student's "process of learning, forming relationships, and behaving appropriately in school" (Wolpow et al., 2016b, p. xi) and place the student in a type of survival mode.

The Adverse Childhood Experiences (ACE) Study (Felitti et al., 2019) connected these traumatic experiences with a greater risk for risky behaviors and chronic health conditions. The short-term and long-term effects of trauma include chronic fatigue, low self-esteem, anxiety, hypertension, depression, and aggressive tendencies (STARR Commonwealth, 2019). Given these emotional and physical connections, it is critical for the campus to use trauma-informed principles to help turn the school environment from chaos to calm for students (and staff members). When school systems actively work to prevent adverse childhood experiences, children and adults can more successfully thrive, reducing potential risky behaviors and changing the generational cycle of adverse childhood experiences (Texas Education Agency [TEA], 2021). Thus, trauma-informed principles can help students (and staff members) succeed regardless of the circumstances of the trauma experienced, and an emphasis is placed on "validating and supporting student trauma" (Haviland, 2017, p. 18) through respect and compassion. The trauma-informed approach helps instill hope and light, "minimizing trauma's harmful grip" on the life of an individual (Giboney Wall, 2021, p. 2).

DIFFERENT TYPES OF TRAUMAS

The Substance Abuse and Mental Health Services Administration (SAMHSA, 2014) defines trauma as the:

results from an event, series of events, or set of circumstances that are experienced by an individual as physically or emotionally harmful or life-threatening and that has lasting adverse effects on the individual's functioning and mental, physical, social, emotional, or spiritual well-being. (p. 7)

Thus, one could define trauma as an event that results in one's inability to regulate stress healthily or safely (Erbacher et al., 2015; NEA, 2018; Giboney Wall, 2021; Wiest-Stevenson & Lee, 2016; Wolpow et al., 2016b). According to SAMHSA (2014), there are three "E's" in trauma: the event or events, perception or experience of said event(s), and effect. We can categorize these traumatic experiences into specific types based on frequency or intensity. A Type 1 trauma is a single exposure, while a Type 2 trauma could be a single incident that includes abuse over a period or multiple exposures. A Type 3 trauma is considered toxic stress, where the student's emotional or physical safety is threatened multiple times (Mann, 2019; NEA, 2018; STAAR Commonwealth, 2019; Walkley & Cox, 2013). SAMHSA (2014) stated that "traumatic events by their very nature set up a power differential where one entity (whether an individual, an event, or a force of nature) has power over another" (p. 8).

Within the school setting, there can be organizational, community, or personal crises which result in trauma (Elbedour et al., 2020). Organizational crises are those large-scale events that impact all students and staff, like a tornado, flood, or campus-based shooting (Elbedour et al., 2020). In contrast, community crises are those defined as "chronic environmental stressors that adversely disrupt the entire school," like "chronic community violence or bullying" (Elbedour et al., 2020, p. 209). Personal crises initially affect individuals (like divorce, gender issues, domestic violence, or abuse) and unfortunately, the trauma experienced in these personal crises can ultimately also negatively impact the child's relationships with others (Elbedour et al., 2020).

Trauma can create different reactions or symptoms, including hyperarousal, intrusion, or constriction (Wolpow et al., 2016b). Wolpow et al. (2016b) indicated that students might experience hyperarousal when they continually expect danger, even if danger is not present. Intrusion may occur when a student experiences flashbacks during the day or nightmares at night. Constriction is the final reaction, and it is what some may call the "deer in the headlights" look, where the student is checked out or disconnected from their surroundings. Examples of these different reactions may include but are not limited to asking "why me," having trouble sleeping, being easily startled, becoming hyper-vigilant, looking for "safe" places in a room, becoming aggressive or irritable, withdrawing from friends or activities, forgetting known skills, or a drop in grades (Elbedour et al., 2020: Mann, 2019; SAMHSA, 2014; STAAR Commonwealth, 2019). These reactions impede students' ability to feel safe in their environment and negatively impact their learning and development.

A crisis affects individuals differently, and some students and staff members will need more support than others. Remember, a student or staff member's response to a traumatic event is primarily connected to their perception or experience of the particular trauma and coping skills (Haviland, 2017; SAMHSA, 2014; Wiest-Stevenson & Lee, 2016). An individual's adverse response to the effect of trauma may occur immediately or have a delayed onset, and in many situations, the student or staff member may not recognize the connection between past trauma and a current event (Martin et al., 2017; SAMHSA, 2014). Trauma significantly impacts learning, as acquiring academic subjects requires lots of "attention, organization, comprehension, memory engagement in learning, and trust" (Wolpow et al., 2016b, p. 12). Teachers and staff members may find that students cannot process verbal and nonverbal information, such as assignment instructions, or cannot participate effectively in class. They may lack specific social skills, struggle with relationships, or have difficulties with school transitions.

TRAUMA-INFORMED PRINCIPLES

According to the SAMHSA, the goal of trauma-informed principles is to help promote an environment that prioritizes "safety, trustworthiness and transparency, peer support, collaboration, and mutuality, empowerment/voice/choice, and cultural/historical/gender issues" (2014, p. 14). SAMHSA (2014) indicated that four key assumptions need to be understood by all school stakeholders for trauma-informed principles to be effective: realization, recognition, response, and resisting re-traumatization. First, all individuals must have a "basic realization about trauma and understand how trauma can affect families, groups, organizations, and communities as well as individuals" (SAMHSA, 2014, p. 9). Trauma-informed principles take into consideration that trauma(s) may directly impact a student's learning and development, and it is crucial for staff members to have a shared understanding of these trauma connections (Haviland, 2017; SAMHSA, 2014; Giboney Wall, 2021).

Second, the school community must recognize the specific signs of trauma and know what is not developmentally appropriate (SAMHSA, 2014). Wolpow et al. (2016b) stated "that learners cannot meet academic goals until their more basic human needs are met physically and emotionally" (p. 1). Schools might use a universal trauma screening tool to help identify students with trauma needs. Universal recognition and prevention include skill-building, promoting positive relationships, and creating a safe and inclusive school environment (TEA, 2021). Trauma-informed principles move from a "what is wrong with you" lens to a view of "what has happened to you" (Bergren, 2021, p. 145; McInerney & McKlindon, 2014, p. 2). In other words, how can the school community help students or staff members reconnect? How can the school community be taught to be more patient in heated situations that appear out of control? How can emotional vulnerabilities in our students or staff members be recognized? How can the stigma of mental health issues be reduced? School mental health practices should be a priority and embedded in the fabric of the school's framework and assessment procedures (TEA, 2021).

Third, a campus's response to trauma is critical and is one of the four critical assumptions required with a trauma-informed approach (SAMHSA, 2014). Howell et al. (2019) stated that this means:

all adults (a) realize the impact of trauma and pathways to healing; (b) recognize the signs and symptoms of trauma in students, staff, and families; (c) respond to trauma by incorporating knowledge into practices, procedures, and policies, and (d) resist traumatization of students by eliminating practices that can trigger students exposed to trauma. (p. 28)

When a school system responds to student behavior through a trauma-informed lens, one can see these efforts' directly and indirectly in various ways. For example, the traumatic experiences of children will be accounted for when formulating school policies, such as the mission statement or handbook; staff language, responses, and behaviors will be grounded in trauma-informed principles; and staff training will be an ongoing focus on the campus (SAMHSA, 2014). Resilience, recovery, and healing should be at the heart of the campus's culture, which will move the school community beyond the typical at-risk scenarios to create a more holistic approach to understanding student and staff behavior.

Finally, SAMHSA (2014) believes it is critical to resist re-traumatization. Re-traumatization occurs when a practice or situation unintentionally triggers a painful experience, resulting in the re-traumatization of the individual. Schools should establish a compassionate school culture that minimizes re-traumatization and effectively implements trauma-informed principles and strategies. It will be critical to evaluate current practices and policies to ensure the proper framework is in place to embrace these principles. On the Washington Office of Superintendent of Public Instruction website, Wolpow et al. (2016a) list ten strategies used to create compassionate schools, which help create an environment that embraces students (and staff members) with a trauma history. The strategies include:

1. Focus on culture and climate in the school and community.
2. Train and support all staff regarding trauma and learning.
3. Encourage and sustain open and regular communication for all.
4. Develop a strengths-based approach in working with students and peers.
5. Ensure discipline policies are both compassionate and effective (restorative practices).
6. Weave compassionate strategies into school improvement planning.
7. Provide tiered support for all students based on what they need.
8. Create flexible accommodations for diverse learners.
9. Provide access, voice, and ownership for staff, students, and community.
10. Use data to identify vulnerable students and determine outcomes and strategies for continuous quality improvement. (Wolpow et al., 2016a, para 5)

School systems can use trauma-informed and compassion-focused strategies to establish a learning environment that promotes supportive relationships, safety, wellness, and resiliency while encouraging students' healing, learning, and growth (TEA, 2021). Together the trauma-informed principles and the compassionate school strategies can help foster a learning community focused on the holistic needs of the students.

CRISIS MANAGEMENT PLANNING PROCESS OVERVIEW

There are four critical pieces to the crisis management planning process. These steps include prevention, preparing, responding, and recovering (Elbedour et al., 2020; NEA, 2018). During the prevention stage, crisis management planning should "foster and protect both physical safety and psychological safety" (NEA, 2018, p. 7). Utilizing a multi-tiered approach to prevention will help ensure the net is cast wide enough to capture the needs of all students. These prevention tiers might include school-wide (universal) interventions, selected interventions for groups of students, and targeted interventions for individual students. Universal mental health prevention is rooted in education, including school-wide teaching on substance abuse education, dating violence and suicide prevention, intervention, and 'postvention.' When campuses understand mental health and a culture of care, they are more apt to respond to situations orderly and with compassion. The school community should cultivate a connected culture that embodies trust, respect, and caring relationships. Creating a positive school climate can reduce situations that directly contribute to a crisis and increase the potential for students to work together with staff to establish a safe environment (NEA, 2018). There should be a system "to identify, refer, and support any student who is struggling academically, behaviorally, or socially in school," in addition to a "means of addressing any signs of troubled behavior or a student at risk of harming themselves or others" (NEA, 2018, p. 6). Preparation involves routinely practicing respectful behaviors throughout the school. Preparing the culture is one ingredient, while the other involves preparing the campus from a protocol standpoint. This preparation begins with developing collaborative district and campus-level crisis teams, determining the roles of each individual, and establishing a chain of command. The crisis management team should create step-by-step plans that address a variety of potential crises or threats. While we cannot plan for every crisis situation, plans should be created and modified based on the situation, as there is no "one size fits all" crisis plan (NEA, 2018). It is vital in the preparation stage for staff training to occur regarding the nature of crises, trauma, available crisis response resources, and the response process. Staff members should have a clear understanding of potential threats, hazards, and what to do in a time of crisis.

Preparation also involves creating a communication plan for students, staff, and the community, including social media protocols. Schools should create a culture and climate during the response phase that enables students and staff members to manage their emotions and stress level during an unexpected event or emergency (NEA, 2018). If staff members have been given clear roles and responsibilities, the response phase will run smoother, even when faced with adversity. "Knowing how to respond in a crisis is a key to restoring order and supporting the school community" (NEA, 2018, p. 36). Responding includes those first critical steps of addressing priority needs, assessing the crisis, and contacting applicable individuals (like 9-1-1 or district leadership) for support. In comparison, the recovery phase focuses on the emotional and mental health well-being of students, staff, and the community. NEA states that "a good school crisis plan will foster and protect both physical safety, such as a secure building, and psychological safety of a safe and supportive environment" (NEA, 2018, p. 6). Recovery helps restore the "social and emotional equilibrium of the school community by promoting positive coping skills and resilience" (NEA, 2018, p. 48). Recovery will take time, and everyone's recovery will be at a different pace and potentially require different interventions. It will be necessary for the school community to maintain routines and activities while also providing both short-term and long-term interventions to those affected by the crisis (NEA, 2018).

PREVENTION: TRAUMA SENSITIVE STRATEGIES

Trauma-Informed Policies and Procedures

Schools should develop trauma-informed policies and procedures that help prevent secondary trauma and reduce further harm to students and staff (Elbedour et al., 2020). For example, imagine walking past someone who wears a familiar fragrance linked in one's brain to past trauma or the startle reaction that occurs when a balloon pops, reminding an individual of an experience tied to a shooting? A trauma trigger occurs when a circumstance reminds an individual of a previous distressing situation or memory (Martin et al., 2017). These trauma triggers are not necessarily life-threatening situations but are emotional responses tied to sights, sounds, smells, touches, or tastes (Martin et al., 2017). Understanding specific triggers and recognizing the impact of trauma on students (or staff) allows for better preparation to react in a manner that understands student behavior, what has indeed happened to an individual, and the importance of helping the individual regain their emotional stability (Martin et al., 2017; Giboney Wall, 2021).

Teachers work with students on a day in, day out basis, and in a way, they are on the frontline for triage-based emotional support. Teachers should consider adding coping techniques and relaxation skills for all students. As a reminder, most students will have experienced at least one traumatic event in their lifetime. Weist-Stevenson and Lee (2016) suggest that teachers regularly educate all students on positive stress management skills or coping skills techniques such as deep breathing, positive imagery, or brief breaks for students to have dedicated time to refocus and reduce their daily stress levels. Many students also need tactile ways to reduce stress like stress balls, fidget toys, or a chair that allows movement. Regularly practicing stress management techniques and skills helps create healthy habits for students and gives them tools to handle stress in the future (Weist-Stevenson & Lee, 2016).

When preparing for the unexpected, crisis management planning, also known as crisis intervention planning, should involve a "continuous cycle of planning, practicing, and evaluating" to ensure a school community has a "system in place for immediate and effective response and recovery" (NEA, 2018, p. 15). All levels of administration must embrace preparation and planning, starting at the top with district and campus leadership. The outcomes of planning help outline the response process and articulate the roles and responsibilities of all parties. As a reminder, steps or protocols outline what must be accomplished but may not give the specifics needed to implement the process (Steele et al., 2003). School Counselors and campus leaders should have conversations about the specifics and practice through various scenarios to better understand the implementation process. These conversations also help flesh out additional questions and clarify understanding or intent. Schonfeld and Newgass (2003) indicated that the plan should address three areas, including "safety and security; dissemination of accurate information to school crisis response team members, school staff, students, parents, and, when appropriate, the general public; and the emotional and psychological needs of all parties" (p. 3).

According to Esquith (2013), preparation means that all settings, building configurations, transportation options, resources, and times of day should be considered. Planning cannot be limited to during the day, as students are often involved in various events off-campus and outside typical school hours (Esquith, 2013). Planning must also provide for:

the access and functional needs of the whole school community. The whole school community includes children; individuals with disabilities and others with access and functional needs; those from religiously, racially, and ethnically diverse backgrounds; and people with limited English proficiency. (Esquith, 2013, p. 1)

We must prepare schools beyond the traditional fire and evacuation drills. School members should brainstorm all potential threats and hazards that may affect the school community to ensure they are prepared for the unexpected. It is also critical that the plan complies with local or state guidelines to ensure a more seamless implementation. There may be times when school boundaries extend into multiple cities, and it will be essential to have a working relationship with all first responder groups (like police or fire) of the different municipalities, so everyone knows their role in a crisis.

Multi-Tiered System of Support and Response to Intervention

According to NEA (2018), "trauma can change the way those involved look at the world and make them feel less safe and secure" (p. 50). The School Counselor can lead by supporting the school community through staff and student learning/educational opportunities, ensuring student prevention and intervention strategies have a grief and trauma-sensitive lens, creating safe spaces for all, and routinely assessing student and staff needs to direct counseling services (Howell et al., 2019). Using a multi-tiered system of support (MTSS) or response to intervention (RTI) will help ensure a systematic approach to trauma prevention. This multi-tiered approach uses three distinct tiers of interventions. Tier 1 trauma-sensitive strategies should begin with building school-wide relationships and interventions to ensure a connectedness between students and staff (Giboney Wall, 2021). Is there structure and stability within the school? Are all stakeholders working together and fostering shared control? Are there "clear and predictable school structures with consistent routines, expectations, and limits" (Giboney Wall, 2021, p. 2). Some other ways to build these relationships include using needs assessments to learn social and emotional priorities; empowering students to use their voice; allowing students to share their opinions; identifying at-risk behaviors; and ensuring the campus has an articulated referral process for students in need of emotional, behavioral, or physical interventions (Giboney Wall, 2021). Trauma-informed prevention practices also encourage active listening, using both ears, and attending to the spoken words and body language (Giboney Wall, 2021). Tier 1 strategies help establish universal support for all students. These strategies might include classroom guidance, staff training, and consultation regarding common language and the effects of trauma on learning and behaviors, Positive Behavioral Interventions and Supports (PBIS), restorative practices, and social-emotional character education development (Dorado et al., 2016).

The school community must understand when a student referral is needed for Tier 2 selected intervention strategies; therefore, it will be necessary for the staff to "recognize behaviors which may be reactions to trauma and to whom to refer children and their families if services are needed" (Wiest-Stevenson & Lee, 2016, p. 500). When teachers can distinguish between a reaction to trauma and typical developmental behaviors in the classroom, they will create a more trauma-informed classroom, allowing them to become more aware of potential triggers that affect students (Giboney Wall, 2021). Common reactions include shock or disbelief, fear, sadness, guilt, shame, grief, confusion, pessimism, or anger (NEA, 2018). Tier 2 selected strategies would be used for students identified as more at-risk (typically about 15% of the student body), and these supports might include psychoeducational skill-building interventions. Tier 2 supports also include helping school staff understand and recognize their own stress and wellness, and ensuring that a student intervention team or care team meets regularly to discuss the needs of at-risk students and determine additional supports and interventions (Dorado et al., 2016). We would consider students with the most intense needs for Tier 3 targeted interventions, typically about 5% of the student body. These targeted and intensive supports may include trauma-specific brief one-on-one counseling, small-group skills-building support, case management, safety plans, and potential referrals to outside resources for more long-term therapy (Dorado et al., 2016; TEA, 2021). Tier 3 support would also include crisis support for affected staff members and outside referrals if needed. It is crucial for students who have experienced trauma to learn to recognize their triggers to improve their emotional instability during stressful moments (Giboney Wall, 2021). Teaching students techniques like mindfulness and a personal awareness of their triggers will allow them to reduce their stress level by signaling the teacher discretely or stepping away from the situation, triggering the emotional response (Giboney Wall, 2021).

Collectively, this three-tiered preventative approach meets the holistic needs of students and help address the trauma reactions students and staff face because of unexpected events. Examples of trauma-informed interventions/programs include Cognitive Behavioral Therapy (CBT), Cognitive Behavioral Intervention for Trauma in Schools (CBITS), Healthy Environments and Response to Trauma in Schools (HEART), Grief and Trauma Intervention for Children (GTI), and Trauma-Focused Coping in Schools (Chafouleas et al., 2015; Dorado et al., 2016).

PREPARING: CRISIS RESPONSE PROCESS

School Crisis Team and Crisis Management Planning

Creating a collaborative school crisis team is one of the initial preparedness steps and is crucial for the crisis response process (Esquith, 2013; Mann, 2019; NEA, 2018). When considering which people to invite to serve on the crisis team, consider the strengths and expertise of individuals within the school system. School crisis teams are often composed of the principal, assistant principal, school resource officer, campus nurse, one or more department chairs, special education lead, community members, and the school counselor (NEA, 2018; Schonfeld et al., 2002). Having the right team at the table will help ensure a comprehensive approach to the logistics of crisis management planning. Once the crisis team is established and roles have been determined, it will be essential to ensure all parties are well-versed in their role in the crisis management process, understand the effects of trauma and grief on individuals, and any potential supports available to staff members that can provide support to others in times of crisis (Mann, 2019; NEA, 2018). Preparedness should also include practicing appropriate drills to safeguard students and staff and regular education and training on-campus procedures and protocols (NEA, 2018). Types of drills or training exercises might include a traditional drill used to practice a specific emergency (fire, tornado, lock-down, shelter-in-place, evacuation), a tabletop exercise where key personnel evaluate response plans, and a full-scale exercise that simulates an actual emergency response scenario (NEA, 2018). While the crisis team cannot predict a crisis, they can also prepare for the unexpected by developing tools for the communication of information. These communication tools might include drafting sample letters, scripts, social media, or regular media releases to help reduce campus administration stress during the actual incident and help provide a template for disseminating information during a crisis (Mann, 2019; NEA, 2018). Several organizations have developed crisis response protocols, processes, and tools that schools and school counselors may find useful when planning for the crisis response process. The National Education Agency has a detailed handbook called the NEA

School Crisis Guide that can be accessed online at https://www.nea.org/resource-library/neas-school-crisis-guide. In addition, the Federal Emergency Management Agency (FEMA) also has a detailed guide for schools to assist with school emergency operation plans. This resource is available at https://www.fema.gov/sites/default/files/2020-07/guide-developing-school-emergency-operations-plans.pdf. Finally, there are several resources for crisis planning available at the Texas State Texas School Safety Center at https://txssc.txstate.edu/tools/.

According to Schonfeld and Newgass (2003), it is also essential to "avoid plans that replace staff members with experts from outside the community" (p. 2). Many find that the teachers have the relationships with students, staff, and the community when a caring culture has been established in a school. While the teachers may also be hurting, they are going to have better insight into the behaviors of their students and notice reactions that are not typical for a student. In addition, the teachers will continue to be on the front line in their classrooms throughout the long-term recovery phase (Schonfeld & Newgass, 2003). That being said, a teacher or staff member may need assistance or a substitute person if they are too impacted to be effective in the classroom or unable to keep students safe due to their reaction to the crisis. Preparation takes time and cannot be a last-minute thought or a plan that is created when an actual crisis occurs. The crisis response process is an ongoing endeavor, meaning it should be refined and revised based on information learned during previous crisis incidents, changes in school policies or procedures, or changes in school leadership or staff configurations. The preparation phase should not be overlooked and should not add to the trauma others are experiencing because crisis management planning was not prioritized.

Sample Crisis Scenarios

To properly prepare for the unexpected, crisis teams should consider various scenarios that may require crisis response. On-campus and off-campus scenarios should be evaluated and dissected to determine appropriate preparedness steps. In addition, scenarios should reflect different times of day, including before school, after school, and on the weekends.

Consider the following scenarios and think about the sequence of steps that would need to be taken to address the mental health and physical well-being of students, staff, and the school community.

Scenario #1: The high school senior class is on their annual overnight trip to the coast (about three hours away). Three buses leave the high school on Friday morning around 10 am. About an hour outside of town, the first bus is driving through a green light and is t-boned by a dump truck. The impact of the crash causes the bus to flip over. The two other buses are behind the first bus and drive up on the crash scene. The first bus driver is unconscious, and an undetermined number of students appear to have sustained injuries. People who witnessed the crash at the intersection are in the process of checking on casualties, and sirens can be heard in the distance.

Scenario #2: During lunch, an 8th grade middle school student is texting a friend in 9th grade about how they feel depressed. The student is upset over a recent breakup with a boyfriend. The student mentions that they cannot live without the boyfriend and uses emoji's that depict different methods to die and faces with tears. The depressed student stops texting, and the friend is worried. Less than five minutes later, the bell rings, and the worried friend goes to the school counselor to report their concern. The 8th grade student never shows for class and is found fifteen minutes later in the girl's bathroom unresponsive in a corner stall. There is an open bottle of sleeping pills sitting on top of her backpack.

Scenario #3: The 3rd grade is at an outside gym when a tornado warning sounds. The students take cover in the gym bathrooms as they do not have time to get to the main building. The storm quickly passes over the school. Broken windows are visible in the main building, downed trees are noticeable throughout the property, and mangled playground equipment is strewn across the playground. People quickly notice that one of the gym walls collapsed and part of the roof is missing. Students can be heard screaming and crying. Cell phone contact has not been established with the adults in the gym. It is unknown what casualties may exist in the gym or the main building.

RESPONDING: DURING A CRISIS

The response phase "includes the steps taken to minimize harm to people and property during an incident. Its focus is on the short-term, direct effects of an incident and requires tight coordination and rapid action among all participants" (NEA, 2018, p. 3). Communication is vital in the response phase. If a crisis team cannot communicate efficiently and effectively, the crisis response process could become delayed or appear unorganized (Razi & DeChillo, 2005). Consider creating different levels of crises (like the tier intervention process) as schools will have isolated crises (e.g., death of a student's parent or guardian), district and campus crises (e.g., car wreck involving one or more students), or large-scale community crises (like a natural disaster) (Mann, 2019; NEA, 2018; Schonfeld & Newgass, 2003). These different levels of crises will help the crisis team plan for the scale of the crisis incident response. Having a flowchart or checklist to ensure steps are not overlooked or missed is helpful. When an initial crisis occurs, and a staff member is made aware, what happens next? Having a chain of command will help ensure a more seamless crisis response process. For example, maybe the first step is contacting the campus principal when one is aware of a crisis. Who will the principal contact? What will happen next? It is vital to obtain the relevant details from a credible, first-person source. The crisis team needs to know who, what, when, where, why, and how. Who will notify the school superintendent? Who will enact the crisis team and set up a meeting's location, date, and time? Is the meeting in-person, virtual, or via phone? A word of caution: given the ease of texting, it is never recommended that texting replace an actual conversation among the crisis team members.

The crisis team should meet before they disseminate additional information to staff members. It is essential to know the facts and the appropriate information to be shared. However, time is of the essence, as cell phones and social media can cause crises to unfold quickly (NEA, 2018). According to Esquith (2013), "school counselors play a pivotal role in the social fabric of a school and are uniquely positioned to make a significant contribution" during the crisis response phase (p. 2). The school counselor is an excellent person to bring pertinent student information to the crisis meeting. For example, the school counselor could bring a copy of the student's school schedule, the student's school photo (if available in the student information system), information on any known siblings in the school system, parent names and contact information, and information on whether the individual rides the school bus or participates in any known extracurricular activities. It will be necessary for the crisis team to establish timelines and next steps. Are subs needed, or additional staff members from another campus or neighboring school district? Does an emergency faculty meeting need to occur? What will teachers say in the classroom? How will office personnel respond to phone calls or emails?

RECOVERING: AFTER A CRISIS

After a crisis, it is common for people to experience the five stages of grief: denial, anger, bargaining, depression, and acceptance (Grief.com, 2021). Addressing grief will be a critical component of the recovery phase and should be at the heart of crisis intervention and counseling services for students (and staff). Schonfeld and Quackenbush (2021) gave four goals when supporting students, "normalize common experiences of grief, help students express and cope with feelings, help students find resources and strategies for coping with difficult feelings, and clarify concepts for younger students" (pp.123-124). Most students (and staff members) will create a "new normal" and resume functioning appropriately, depending on the individual's coping skills, prior trauma history, resiliency, and support system (NEA, 2018). However, it is essential to note that some individuals may continue to struggle and need additional crisis interventions, including potential referrals for community support.

Individuals experiencing grief will frequently want to create a memorial of the event. School counselors should encourage school systems to have specific procedures for establishing memorials. Often, the crisis site becomes a makeshift memorial, and individuals feel compelled to leave flowers, pictures, stuffed animals, or other forms of remembrance. How is the school system going to handle these temporary memorials? Because of the vast types of crisis events, schools should be cognizant of how the decision to memorialize one event will impact the memorials of future events. Memorials should be handled systematically, and careful thought should be given to establishing permanent memorials (NEA, 2018; Schonfeld & Newgass, 2003). Schonfeld and Quackenbush (2021) discussed several challenges for schools in their book, *The Grieving Student: A Guide for Schools*. What happens if the building is remodeled, a memorial has to be removed due to construction or expansion, or a memorial is vandalized or damaged accidentally? Will the school allow memorialization for all types of deaths, including suicide? Is the school okay with setting a precedent? Removing a permanent memorial could re-traumatize individuals and set precedents that could create emotionally charged situations in the future; therefore, it is crucial for school systems (and school counselors) to take time to discuss and develop appropriate practices and procedures before a crisis occurs.

School counselors should also take the lead to remember that specific dates (anniversary of the event) or transitions, like the beginning of a new school year or graduation, can trigger other grief reactions (NEA, 2018). While the school counselor may be the primary individual responding to student and staff needs, the National Education Agency (2018) noted that "with the proper training and resources, school personnel can be empowered to support students and respond appropriately in times of grief and crisis" (p. 52). The school counselors must work with campus administrators to ensure they offer staff development to build capacity in times of crisis (NEA, 2018; Schonfeld & Quackenbush, 2021).

ROLE OF THE SCHOOL COUNSELOR

The School Counselor should help identify mental health resources within the school and community that could assist during a crisis, determine potential types of services needed, and oversee the mental health triage of students and staff members (Mann, 2019; Schonfeld & Newgass, 2003). Schonfeld and Newgass (2003) indicated that "mental health triage during a school crisis means that children in need of immediate evaluation and services by a mental health professional should be referred directly to appropriate community resources and should not receive extensive evaluations or counseling services by school personnel" (p. 5). School Counselors can also prepare by creating campus crisis kits to aid in the response phase (Mann, 2019; Schonfeld et al., 2002). These crisis kits are designed to be used in student/staff crisis areas and provide tactile ways for individuals to work through the intense emotions that often occur with traumatic events. These kits or bags or backpacks, whatever the campus calls them, should contain developmentally appropriate items to reduce stress. Examples include coloring books, picture books, markers, crayons, Play-Doh, paper, pencils, journaling pages, stress balls, or fidget toys. The crisis kit should also contain Kleenex, visitor badges, sign-in sheets, and other campus-specific items to help the response phase run smoothly. Maybe include a school map or the bell schedule or key contact numbers on campus, the list is endless. Regardless of what they include in the kit, the key is to have items that meet the students' social, emotional, and development needs.

School crises can cause various levels of trauma to students and staff. Therefore, the school counselor's role in the response phase must include trauma-informed practices and procedures. One example of a crisis intervention technique is a short-term, seven-phase, supportive group discussion process developed by Dr. Jeffrey Mitchell called CISD or *Crisis Incident Stress Debriefing,* which typically occurs 24-72 hours after the initial traumatic event (Mitchell, n.d.a). This model uses small group discussions to help debrief the crisis or incident. The CISD model consists of at least two to four trained team members who facilitate discussions with groups of 10 to 14 participants. Dr. Mitchell noted that the typical formula is "one team member for every 5 to 7 participants" (Mitchell, n.d.a, p. 2). CISD is designed to empower individuals after a traumatic situation and is considered a type of "psychological first aid" (Mitchell, n.d.a, p.2). During the group discussion, individuals will be taken through seven phases that focus on introductions, facts, thoughts, reactions, symptoms, teaching, and re-entry. Dr. Mitchell noted that "the CISD process does not constitute any form of psychotherapy, and it should never be used as a substitute for psychotherapy" (Mitchell, n.d.a, p. 1). In turn, CISD is designed to be a "crisis-focused discussion" that aids individuals in processing a traumatic event (Mitchell, n.d.a, p. 1). The CISD process also helps school counselors identify students or staff members who need more intensive support like individual counseling or referrals to outside professionals.

The recovery phase will usher in another set of responsibilities for the school counselor. Razi and DeChillo (2005) discussed the various ways a school counselor can assist in the recovery phase, including "educational initiatives, prevention programs, individual and group counseling, crisis intervention, advocacy, policy developmental school-based family counseling, case management, consultation, and service coordination as liaison between school, families, and the greater community" (p. 117). In addition, due to the unexpected nature of a crisis, the recovery phase will involve mental health triage and referrals to resources within the school and community (Schonfeld & Newgass, 2003). One best practice, evidence-informed approach is the six-hour online Psychological First Aid (PFA) course designed by the National Center for PTSD and the National Child Traumatic Stress Network. This course helps responders understand how to assist students, staff, and families in the aftermath of a tragedy or crisis (NEA, 2018). Another crisis intervention example is the Critical Incident Stress Management (CISM) system. According to Dr. Mitchell (n.d.b), CISM is a "comprehensive, integrated, systematic and multi-component crisis intervention program" (p. 1). CISM is a group of intervention strategies designed to be used together. These strategies include reducing the impact of the traumatic event, facilitating typical recovery processes, restoring adaptive functioning, and identifying those in need of additional support services or referrals (Mitchell, n.d.b).

SECONDARY STRESS, SELF CARE, AND COMPASSION FATIGUE

Crisis intervention work is complex and emotionally draining. It will be necessary for school leadership to recognize the toll that crisis response has on the crisis team, especially the school counselor. School counselors are on the front lines of crisis response and can easily experience emotional overload. This overload can lead to compassion fatigue, also known as secondary traumatic stress. In general, school counselors might also face compassion fatigue if they have unresolved issues related to a personal history of trauma or they rarely express their feelings in stressful situations. Significant life changes (e.g., moving, getting married, or having a child) can also cause compassion fatigue if they do not use appropriate coping skills. There are many symptoms of compassion fatigue, including feelings of isolation, anxiety, helplessness, confusion, lack of interest in enjoyable events, illness, depression, lack of concentration, or sleeping difficulties. One of the most widely used tools to measure the positive and negative aspects of the helping profession is the Professional Quality of Life Scale (ProQOL), a 30 item self-report screening instrument (Stamm, 2010). The ProQOL scale measures Compassion Satisfaction and Compassion Fatigue. The Compassion Fatigue portion has two subscales: burnout and secondary trauma. The instrument is straightforward to use and can be administered individually or in group settings. The ProQOL is a free screening tool and is available at https://proqol.org/.

The U.S. National Institutes of Health (2021) developed an emotional wellness toolkit that provides tips for reducing stress and adjusting to difficult situations. The U.S. National Institutes of Health (2021) recommends several steps to improve one's mental health, including developing a more positive mindset, reducing stress, getting quality sleep, utilizing mindfulness, and strengthening social connections. To develop a more positive mindset, also known as resiliency, school counselors should consider generating positive emotions through thankfulness, creating healthy habits, or spending more time with friends. Stress management is another vital aspect, and they might accomplish this by setting priorities, showing compassion for oneself, or exercising regularly. School counselors must also get quality sleep, as tired individuals will struggle to function and be limited in how they can help others. To get better quality sleep, NIH recommends setting a schedule and going to bed and getting up each day around the same time. It is also helpful if sleep time occurs in a dark, quiet place with limited use of electronics. Mindfulness is another crucial ingredient in emotional wellness. According to the U.S. National Institute of Health (2021), several techniques can help with self-awareness. For example, "take some deep breaths in through your nose to a count of 4, hold for 1 second, and then exhale through the mouth to a count of 5. Repeat often." (U.S. National Institute of Health, 2021, p. 2). Other mindful techniques include taking a stroll and noticing the sights, sounds, or smells or doing a mental scan to bring awareness to how the body feels. Finally, they should strive to strengthen social connections. Humans were made for connections, and spending time with others can positively influence emotional wellness and mental well-being. Regardless of the wellness tool or technique, school counselors must make intentional time to reduce compassion fatigue or secondary traumatic stress.

Secondary stress "affects one's capacity to feel empathetic or capable and can significantly impact mental, psychological, and physical well-being" (Howell et al., 2019, p. 32). Staff members will need access to appropriate supports, including mental health counseling for themselves and resources to assist students in the classroom environment. All parties involved directly or indirectly in the crisis response process will need to be reminded of the importance of self-care. School counselors and staff members can only fill the cup of others if their cup is full. How should the school counselor fill their cup? In what ways can the school counselor restore their mental health and emotional well-being? Self-care has to be a priority for school counselors to ensure their well-being and to ethically meet the needs of students, staff, and families.

FUTURE RESEARCH DIRECTIONS

Trauma-informed school counseling continues to evolve as students, staff, and the community needs change. School counselors are the face of mental health expertise and support in the school setting. More and more school communities are confronted with tragedies and crises, and school counselors can positively impact the school culture and climate through the crisis response process. Future research should continue to explore the role of trauma-informed principles in response to the COVID-19 pandemic and the long-term needs of the school community. School counselors should continue to be on the frontline when helping their school systems prepare for unexpected situations. Advocating for trauma-sensitive practices is critical to equipping students (and staff members) with the skills needed to mitigate the negative effects of a traumatic event or crisis. School counselors should encourage school administrators and staff members to seek opportunities to increase their knowledge of trauma-sensitive practices, not just to manage crises effectively, but to create a learning environment that approaches education from a holistic manner where students heal, grow, and thrive.

CONCLUSION

Preparing for the unexpected is a crucial topic that must be considered in the school setting. Every crisis will create trauma, and the school counselor is strategically positioned to help students and staff "rebound, recover, and reengage learning on campus" (Giboney Wall, 2021, p. 2). School systems must take a team approach to ensure the campus has been engaged in a culture of trauma-informed practices and has a well-articulated and comprehensive protocol in place to address the unexpected.

While school counselors are trained mental health professionals and have the specialized training needed to meet the social and emotional needs of students, staff, and their school community during times of crisis, the school counselor cannot be the sole person responsible for the crisis management process. Best practices demonstrate that preparing for the unexpected involves a comprehensive approach to crisis management and should involve a team of professionals focused on the importance of prevention, preparing, responding, and recovering. Crises are unexpected, but a collaborative team, with the mental health leadership of the school counselor, can provide hope and healing to the school community.

REFERENCES

American School Counselor Association. (2016). *ASCA ethical standards for school counselors*. Schoolcounselor.Org. https://www.schoolcounselor.org/getmedia/f041cbd0-7004-47a5-ba01-3a5d657c6743/Ethical-Standards.pdf

American School Counselor Association. (2019). *The school counselor and safe schools and crisis response*. Schoolcounselor.Org. https://schoolcounselor.org/Standards-Positions/Position-Statements/ASCA-Position-Statements/The-School-Counselor-and-Safe-Schools-and-Crisis-R

Bergren, M. D. (2021). Post-COVID-19: Trauma-informed care for the school community. *The Journal of School Nursing: the Official Publication of the National Association of School Nurses, 37*(3), 145. doi:10.1177/10598405211004709 PMID:33969768

Chafouleas, S. M., Johnson, A. H., Overstreet, S., & Santos, N. M. (2015). toward a blueprint for trauma-informed service delivery in schools. *School Mental Health, 8*(1), 144–162. doi:10.100712310-015-9166-8

Dorado, J. S., Martinez, M., McArthur, L. E., & Leibovitz, T. (2016). Healthy environments and response to trauma in schools (HEARTS): A whole-school, multi-level, prevention and intervention program for creating trauma-informed, safe and supportive schools. *School Mental Health, 8*(1), 163–176. doi:10.100712310-016-9177-0

Elbedour, S., Alsubie, F., Al'Uqdah, S. N., & Bawalsah, J. A. (2020). School crisis management planning. *Children & Schools, 42*(4), 208–215. doi:10.1093/cs/cdaa021

Erbacher, T. A., Singer, J. B., & Poland, S. (2015). *Suicide in schools: A practitioner's guide to multi-level prevention, assessment, intervention, and postvention (School-Based Practice in Action)* (1st ed.). Routledge.

Esquith, D. (2013, November 1). *Plans, processes, and procedures*. Schoolcounselor. Org. https://www.schoolcounselor.org/Magazines/November-December-2013/Plans,-Processes-and-Procedures

Federal Emergency Management Agency. (2013). *Guide for Developing High-Quality School Emergency Operations Plans*. https://www.fema.gov/sites/default/files/2020-07/guide-developing-school-emergency-operations-plans.pdf

Felitti, V. J., Anda, R. F., Nordenberg, D., Williamson, D. F., Spitz, A. M., Edwards, V., Koss, M. P., & Marks, J. S. (2019). REPRINT OF: Relationship of childhood abuse and household dysfunction to many of the leading causes of death in adults: The Adverse Childhood Experiences (ACE) Study. *American Journal of Preventive Medicine, 56*(6), 774–786. doi:10.1016/j.amepre.2019.04.001 PMID:31104722

Giboney Wall, C. R. (2021). What hurt and what helped: How one school's trauma-informed approach provided support during the pandemic. *Journal of Loss and Trauma*, 1–14. doi:10.1080/15325024.2021.1943127

Grief.com. (2021, March 31). *Five stages of grief by Elisabeth Kubler Ross & David Kessler*. https://grief.com/the-five-stages-of-grief/

Haviland, S. (2017). A districtwide effort. *ASCA School Counselor, 54*(3), 14-18. https://asca-prod.azurewebsites.net/asca/media/asca/ASCAU/Trauma-Crisis-Management-Specialist/DistrictwideEffort.pdf

Howell, P. B., Thomas, S., Sweeney, D., & Vanderhaar, J. (2019). Moving beyond schedules, testing and other duties as deemed necessary by the principal: The school counselor's role in trauma informed practices. *Middle School Journal, 50*(4), 26–34. doi:10.1080/00940771.2019.1650548

Mann, S. (2019, January). *Critical incident response training* [Workshop]. East Central Bexar County Regional Crisis Team Cluster Training, San Antonio, TX.

Martin, S. L., Ashley, O. S., White, L., Axelson, S., Clark, M., & Burrus, B. (2017). Incorporating trauma-informed care into school-based programs. *The Journal of School Health, 87*(12), 958–967. doi:10.1111/josh.12568 PMID:29096416

McInerney, M., & McKlindon, A. (2014). *Unlocking the door to learning: Trauma-informed classrooms & transformational schools*. Education Law Center. https://www.elc-pa.org/wp-content/uploads/2015/06/Trauma-Informed-in-Schools-Classrooms-FINAL-December2014-2.pdf

Mitchell, J. (n.d.a). *Crisis incident stress debriefing*. Info-Trauma.Org/En/e-Library. http://www.info-trauma.org/flash/media-f/mitchellCriticalIncidentStressDebriefing.pdf

Mitchell, J. (n.d.b). *Crisis incident stress management*. Info-Trauma.Org/En/e-Library. http://www.info-trauma.org/flash/media-e/mtichellCriticalIncidentStressManagement.pdf

National Education Association. (2018). *NEA's school crisis guide*. https://www.nea.org/resource-library/neas-school-crisis-guide

Razi, A., & Dechillo, N. (2005). High schools respond to crises. *Journal of School Violence, 4*(2), 115–131. doi:10.1300/J202v04n02_07

Schonfeld, D., Lichtenstein, R., Kline Pruett, M., & Speese-Linehan, D. (2002). *How to prepare for and respond to a crisis* (2nd ed.). Association for Supervision and Curriculum Development.

Schonfeld, D., & Newgass, S. (2003). *School crisis response initiative*. U.S. Department of Justice, Office of Justice Programs, Office for Victims of Crime. https://ovc.ojp.gov/sites/g/files/xyckuh226/files/publications/bulletins/schoolcrisis/ncj197832.pdf

Schonfeld, D. J., & Quackenbush, M. (2021). *The grieving student: A guide for schools* (2nd ed.). Brookes Publishing.

Stamm, B. H. (2010). The Concise ProQOL Manual (2nd ed.). ProQOL.org.

Starr Commonwealth. (2019). *Children of trauma & resilience guidebook.* Starr Commonwealth.

Steele, W., Ingle, D., Nelson, M., & Porter, P. (2000). *Trauma response protocol manual for schools* (Rev. ed.). National Institute for Trauma and Loss in Children.

Substance Abuse and Mental Health Services Administration. (2014). *SAMHSA's concept of trauma and guidance for a trauma informed approach* (HHS Publication No. SMA 14-4884). https://store.samhsa.gov/product/SAMHSA-s-Concept-of-Trauma-and-Guidance-for-a-Trauma-Informed-Approach/SMA14-4884

Texas Education Agency. (2021). *School mental health practice guide and toolkit.* https://schoolmentalhealthtx.org/

U.S. National Institutes of Health. (2021, August 26). *Emotional wellness toolkit.* https://www.nih.gov/health-information/emotional-wellness-toolkit

Walkley, M., & Cox, T. L. (2013). Building trauma-informed schools and communities. *Children & Schools, 35*(2), 123–126. doi:10.1093/cs/cdt007

Wiest-Stevenson, C., & Lee, C. (2016). Trauma-informed schools. *Journal of Evidence-Informed Social Work, 13*(5), 498–503. doi:10.1080/23761407.2016.1166855 PMID:27210273

Wolpow, R., Johnson, M., Hertel, R., & Kincaid, S. (2016a). *Compassionate Schools – Learning and Teaching Support.* https://www.k12.wa.us/student success/health-safety/mental-social-behavioral-health/compassionate-schools-learning-and-teaching-support

Wolpow, R., Johnson, M., Hertel, R., & Kincaid, S. (2016b). *The heart of learning and teaching: Compassion, resilience, and academic success* (3rd ed.). Office of the Superintendent of Public Instruction. https://www.k12.wa.us/student-success/health-safety/mental-social-behavioral-health/compassionate-schools-learning-and-teaching-support

ADDITIONAL READING

Frydman, J. S., & Mayor, C. (2017). Trauma and early adolescent development: Case examples from a trauma-informed public health middle school program. *Children & Schools*, *39*(4), 238–247. doi:10.1093/cs/cdx017

KEY TERMS AND DEFINITIONS

Compassion Fatigue: The physical, emotional, and psychological remnants from helping others experiencing emotional distress or trauma.

Crisis: An unexpected event that interrupts routines, behaviors, and emotions.

Crisis Management: A systematic approach to response and recovery that assists students, staff, and the school community during an unexpected event that interrupts routines, behaviors, and emotions.

Secondary Traumatic Stress: Also referred to as compassion fatigue, secondary traumatic stress results from helping those who have experienced trauma.

Trauma: An event that results in one's inability to regulate their stress in a healthy or safe manner.

Trauma-Informed: Choosing to recognize an individual's symptoms and reactions and acknowledging how trauma may impact their life.

Trigger: A reminder of a past traumatic event that is experienced through the five senses.

Chapter 5
Servant Leadership:
School Counseling During the Pandemic

Maritza Cha
Claremont Graduate University, USA

Andrea Perez
Claremont Graduate University, USA

ABSTRACT

This chapter explores how school counselors are servant leaders through the MTMDSS Framework in K-12 and how they practice servant leadership skills pre- and post-pandemic. School counselors are servant leaders in their school communities. They lead with their hearts to serve students through their academics, social-emotional needs, and post-high school plans. They collaborate with staff to ensure students get the personal support needed. In addition, they develop school culture with faculty and administrators. As school counselors return to campus, they face challenges since they have large caseloads and new responsibilities, but their ability to multitask, connect with others, and provide help when needed will help guide their work. School counselors demonstrate servant leadership values in their work. As school counselors, their goal is always the greater good. School counselors are student-centered and strive to help their students be the best possible version of themselves.

INTRODUCTION

School counselors can hone important leadership skills since they have been able to serve students through their programming. However, when the pandemic started, they had a short time to make their programming virtual and enhance their servant

DOI: 10.4018/978-1-7998-9785-9.ch005

leadership role. Servant leadership will be defined as empathetic leaders willing to put their students first, help students develop their full personal capacities, and find ways to empower the community they serve (Northouse, 2019).

School counselors looked to the American School Counselor Association (ASCA) for guidance for the best ways to serve their students during the pandemic. Specifically, there is a focus on how to serve within the three main domains of academic, social-emotional, and college-and-career readiness (American School Counselor Association, 2018). The ASCA's National Model states that school counselors' programming should advance student learning while enhancing the quality of education (Goodman-Scott et al., 2020). ASCA aligns its National Model for the school counselors program with the Multi-Tiered Multi-Domain System of Support (MTMDSS) to help school counselors strengthen their programming. While the ASCA has 100 years of history, the ASCA National Model established in 2003 has subsequently been through four editions to respond to the cultural shifts within school counseling (ASCA, 2019).

Each decade has brought change to the profession since the implementation of school counseling over 100 years ago. The National Model establishes alignment throughout the different districts and states, leaving enough room for school counselors to make it their own (ASCA, 2019). ASCA recommends that school counselors spend 80% of their time in direct services and 20% in indirect services. Indirect services include school counselors' time to collect school-wide data, find outside resources, collaborate with stakeholders, plan classroom lessons, and other duties. School counselors' direct services are individual student planning, facilitating group counseling sessions, delivering classroom lessons, and providing responsive services (Bemak & Chung, 2005, p. 196). The objective of this article is to explore the role of school counselors as servant leaders, how school counselors demonstrate their leadership skills, and how returning to in-person instruction after the pandemic will allow school counselors to continue to serve students at this critical juncture.

BACKGROUND

Bishop and Noguera (2019) argue that schooling in the United States attempts to address students' social-emotional and academic needs. While there was an emphasis on standardized testing in the United States over the last 30 years, now the focus has turned to the social-emotional state of students, which affects students' academic performance. In addition, schools have reopened after eighteen months of being on distance learning. For California, distance learning meant school districts rushing to get computers in the hands of students so they could log on to Zoom for class. California school districts faced multiple challenges during distance learning. For example, some school districts had students with connectivity issues, attendance dropped, and many students had distractions at home that did not allow them to focus on schoolwork. As a result, the instructional quality was compromised, and it was difficult for both school staff and students to stay motivated. On top of all that, lack of social interactions and losing family members and loved ones due to COVID-19 made it challenging for students to stay focused.

Schools across the nation are now seeing the repercussions of these issues as students return to in-person school. Schools are currently facing student fights. School counselors are constantly supporting students who have suicide ideation, and they are conducting suicide assessments more than before. Additionally, students are now having difficulty communicating their needs to school staff, so it becomes harder to know which students need additional support and resources.

School staff must constantly juggle supporting students' needs while they might be personally struggling to recover over the continuing pandemic. School districts have tried using the Positive Behavior Intervention and Supports (PBIS) and Multi-tiered Multi-Domain System of Support (MTMDSS) models to help their faculty transition back to in-person school. PBIS is an evidence-based three-tiered framework to improve and integrate all data and practices affecting student outcomes (PBIS, 2021). MTMDSS is a systemic framework in which data-based problem solving and decision-making is practiced across all levels of the educational system for supporting students (Goodman-Scott et al., 2020). In addition, it would behoove school districts to tap into their resources, such as school counselors, to help transition back to in-person school.

School counselors are servant leaders. As servant leaders, they search for data-informed practices that would benefit the general student body, and they look for ways to create a positive school culture. Servant leadership is defined by Northouse (2019) as a person who places the good of followers over their self-interests and supports the followers' personal development. Servant leaders also demonstrate a strong moral behavior towards their followers, the organization they are part of, and toward others. School counselors can be leaders as they return to on-campus instruction by helping facilitate students' needs and giving teachers tools to use in their classrooms.

There is limited research on counseling and leadership frameworks. This chapter can add to the research of school counselor leadership and provide practical suggestions as school counselors enter a new phase in education. In this chapter, the researchers will address the possible tools of how school counselors can manage their time, provide social-emotional support and collaborate with all stakeholders. This chapter will discuss the role of school counselors in K-12, school counselor's role as educators return to in-person, and educators concerns as they return to in person learning. The chapter will also discuss how school counselors are leaders on their school site, school leaders in social emotional programming, and how to further collaboration and communication among all stakeholders. Lastly, the authors will address future research ideas based on current challenges school counselors face in choosing graduate programs that develop them as leaders.

MAIN ISSUE

Multi-Tiered Multi-Domain System of Support (MTMDSS)

School counselors demonstrate their servant leadership in the MTMDSS Tier 1 by taking an active role in delivering classroom lessons and helping to plan district/school-wide activities. School counselors can teach classroom lessons on social-emotional learning (SEL), character traits, positive decision making, setting and achieving goals, and other various topics that can support the healthy development of students. Additionally, school counselors can also create school-wide programs and activities. These programs and activities can be Red Ribbon Week, The Kindness Challenge, Spirit Week, and other fun interactive activities to lift students' school spirit. School counselors help with the school-wide implementation of programs and activities for the student population (Hatch et al., 2018; Goodman-Scott et al., 2020). School counselors support students under the social-emotional domain in Tier 1 by creating a school-wide behavioral expectations matrix that supports the school climate. Schools can use a matrix table to list different campus locations and the expected student behavior at each specific location (Goodman-Scott et al., 2020). School counselors under this same domain can also design a curriculum that aligns with universal behavior instruction (Hatch et al., 2018). For example, school counselors can reinforce behavioral expectations through classroom lessons and acknowledge students' behavior through incentives (Goodman-Scott et al., 2020). Creating, developing, and managing a school-wide behavioral expectation matrix shows the school counselor's servant leadership because they actively work with staff to implement this support.

In addition to supporting students under the social-emotional domain with their social-emotional development, school counselors also support students under Tier 1 with their academics and college and career readiness. Students in all grade levels need academic support regardless of their academic achievement. School counselors need to discuss with students about their academic achievements, particularly for students who might be at-risk or struggling academically. School counselors under Tier 1 support can teach students how to read and understand their report cards. They can also deliver classroom lessons on study skills and study habits to help students develop strategies that will help them long term. At the middle school and high school level, school counselors can teach classroom lessons about culmination requirements and graduation requirements to ensure that all students know what they need to do to culminate or graduate. A way school counselors can integrate parents under Tier 1 is through hosting parent workshops. The parent workshops can be about the same topics the students are learning through their classroom lessons, and parents can reinforce and help students at home. Tier 1 interventions for college and career for school counseling include core curriculum classroom lessons for school counselors in their state (Hatch et al., 2019). For individual planning, school counselors can use Naviance to help complete individualized plans or present post-secondary pathways for students to explore. Lastly, for school-wide programs and activities under Tier 1, schools can celebrate all of their seniors' decisions with Decision Day instead of a college signing day. Another opportunity is an 8th-grade virtual college tour where all students participate.

In addition to school counselors supporting Tier 1 interventions, school counselors practice servant leadership skills in MTMDSS Tier 2. School counselors provide identified students with additional support and supplemental interventions by using small groups, referral to resources, and consultation or collaboration with stakeholders (Hatch et al., 2018). Under the social-emotional domain, school counselors can support students through counseling groups that focus on a specific skill-building or social-emotional need. For example, if through the data collection, the data shows that some students have been experiencing anxiety when they return to campus after distance learning, the school counselor can create a counseling group that focuses on supporting students with anxiety by providing them with tools and strategies (Hatch et al., 2018). Another Tier 2 data point school counselors can use is attendance data and grades. These two data sets can help school counselors identify students struggling academically and at risk of not passing their courses. When school counselors meet with students struggling with their academics or have excessive absences, school counselors demonstrate servant leadership because they want to ensure that all students have an equal opportunity to graduate and be academically successful. Tier 2 interventions are for a targeted group of students. For example, a school counselor can create a small group if a group of students whose admissions were rescinded. In addition, school counselors can create small groups on career exploration or introducing college basics.

In MTMDSS Tier 3 supports, school counselors demonstrate servant leadership by using data to collaborate with school staff about specific students they might be concerned about. Through this process and under the social-emotional domain, school counselors individually meet with the students for individual short-term counseling. School counselors can also regularly meet students and parents to discuss external support. While in Tier 2 and Tier 3, the school counselor analyzes data, in Tier 3, school counselors interact with the students' needs individually and not in a group setting. Students who require Tier 3 support are usually the students with the highest level of need. In these cases, school counselors provide referrals to outside agencies to support the students and families. These more intense supports are tailored to meet individual students' needs (Hatch et al., 2018). Providing Tier 3 support to students who have a high level of need is essential because, as Northouse (2019) points out, servant leaders are committed to the growth of others.

When it comes to academic support under Tier 3, school counselors can set individual appointments to meet with students who are not completing their A-G high school requirements and/or their graduation requirements. These individual meetings are vital to support students since the school counselor can further inquire what might be affecting the student in their academics, and they can together plan what would be best to support this student in this area. Also, school counselors can include parents in these conversations. Collaborating with parents and students can help the student long-term because they will be getting the help and assistance they need both at home and school. Tier 3 intervention would be individual counseling for students using college data. For example, if a specific sub-population is not applying to college, then using that data to target those students to help them apply to college.

School Counselors in Grades K-12

School counselors are leaders in all grade levels. However, not all grade levels have a school counselor. For example, high school counselors are more common than elementary and middle school counselors. School counselors in high school focus most of their time on college, career readiness, and making sure they equip students with post-secondary choices. However, K-8 school counselors are equally important. K-8 school counselors teach students social-emotional skills through lessons and in small groups. School counselors also use the MTMDSS framework to identify and place students in intervention programs (Betters-Bubon et al., 2016).

Additionally, school counselors work closely with administrators since K-8 settings may only have one school counselor. The constant collaboration makes school counselors an informal part of the school leadership team. Northouse (2019) states that a servant leader is empathetic, a good listener, and fosters community. School counselors, as servant leaders, tend to spend time with administrators creating behavior support for MTMDSS Tier 2 students, and listen to students' and administrators' concerns. Taking this role allows the school counselor to be part of the decision-making team without the title of administrator or coordinator.

K-8 school counselors are vital leaders. Research indicates that when students have access to a school counselor early on, students are more likely to succeed academically (Parzych et al., 2019). In addition, Parzych et al. (2019) point out that students in districts with K–12 counselors have higher graduation rates, higher college entrance numbers, and fewer out-of-school suspensions. These outcomes demonstrate that students benefit from the guidance of school counselors and that early interventions impact a student's educational outcome. As servant leaders, school counselors in K-8 settings spend time with stakeholders to ensure that students' needs are met through early intervention plans.

High school counselors are also leaders in their own right. A high school counselor's role is to provide direct and indirect student services as students transition to adulthood. Direct services can include advisement, short-term counseling, and instruction. Indirect services can include consultation with other stakeholders, collaboration with community partners, and referrals to appropriate mental health agencies or other support systems. Thus, high school counselors can be leaders if provided the opportunity. However, a significant obstacle to high school counselors' leadership opportunities can be the relationship between the school counselor and the principal. Studies have proven that principals frequently assign duties to school counselors not related to their role (Leuwerke, Walker & Shi, 2009; Nelson, Robles-Pina, Nichter, 2008).

As a consequence, school counselors cannot dedicate time to support each student. Principals do not deny school counselors leadership out of malice; sometimes, principals have limited information about school counselor duties. School counselors, as servant leaders, want to share control and influence; as Northouse (2019) points out, this is part of the definition of servant leadership. However, it is hard to do when principals do not understand the role or know of the existence of ASCA. Some principals are unaware of the appropriate and inappropriate duties outlined in the National Model unless they are explicitly told or have done their research. Reference to the National Model helps leaders advocate for themselves, their school's comprehensive counseling program, and their students.

Williamson et al. (2015) explore different SEL programs that could work at the high school level, but there is a need for more evaluation, as not all the programs analyzed had published results. Williamson et al. (2015) provide an overview of eight promising programs that could be modified to fit the needs of high school students, but none of the programs mentioned in the article have had three or more successful evaluations. The programs are Positive Behavior Interventions and Supports, Too Good for Drugs and Violence High School, Teenage Health Teaching Modules, Facing History and Ourselves, Check and Connect, Changing Lives Program, Positive Life Changes, and Positive Psychology for Youth Program. Most SEL programs are focused on grades K-8, not specific to high school levels for SEL programming. The suggestion by the researchers is to make the high school level SEL programming more youth-friendly, which includes having digital applications (Williamson et al., 2015).

Another consideration is implementing SEL competencies in structures already built into the school site, other than in the classroom, perhaps having those SEL competencies at a club or sports. This approach to implementation introduces the competencies; if school leadership wants to have them school-wide, this would be an excellent opportunity to have buy-in, as many high school athletes and clubs are an essential social aspect for teenagers.

Williamson et al. (2015) also contemplated whether it was better to approach SEL at the high school level, not necessarily with a separate program, but through Deeper Learning. Marzano (2015) also, seconded this idea, stating that embedding the SEL curriculum within the school day allows students to track their progress in the specific SEL skills learned. Deeper Learning would allow students to showcase their growth in SEL competencies throughout the school day by project-based learning. The shift of approach would require buy-in by the school community.

School Counselors and Returning to In-Person Learning

During the pandemic, school counselors had to reimagine the MTMDSS framework and practice their servant leadership skills to provide indirect and direct student services at a distance. Schools in various parts of the country decided it was safer for students and school staff to stay home and continue school lessons online due to COVID-19. As schools reopen buildings, school counselors have utilized their servant leadership skills by working on collaborative plans with stakeholders to ensure students get the social-emotional support needed. While simultaneously keeping up with new college requirements and new graduation requirements some school districts adopted in the school year. School counselors are adapting the MTMDSS framework because they are putting the needs of their students first.

As previously mentioned, the MTMDSS framework focuses on academics and behavioral support for students (Hatch et al., 2018). Experts are concerned that many students will reenter schools after spending the COVID-19 lockdowns with family and potentially experiencing or witnessing multiple traumas (Pincus et al., 2020). As a result, school counselors must be alert to support students who might be going through traumatic experiences. One way to ensure students receive support at schools is by tailoring supports to students' needs.

The California Association of School Counselors (CASC) has developed a tool to help school counselors transition back to campus. CASC (2020) recommends that when schools reopen their campuses, they should build a system of care. Teachers and school staff are provided opportunities to receive professional development in self-care and trauma-informed practices (California Association of School Counselors, 2020). CASC also recommends that schools create emotionally safe learning environments where students can identify one or more trusting adults on-campus to support them (California Association of School Counselors, 2020). These suggestions align with MTMDSS Tier 1 framework. School counselors can implement these other support systems by offering professional development to staff on healing-informed care (Pincus et al., 2020). If the school counselors need support in these areas, they can collaborate with their school district to put students first and embrace mental health agencies to find trained personnel.

Additionally, MTMDSS Tier 2 support will be helpful as schools transition from online to on-campus learning. School counselors can collaborate with stakeholders to identify students who might need more help as students transition back to the school building. Before the pandemic, school counselors were disaggregating and analyzing school-wide data to identify students who may be historically underserved and disproportionately disciplined (Olsen et al., 2016). Now, school counselors should use this data to inform the support students need. School counselors provide Tier 2 support by conducting group counseling on stress, coping strategies, and other specific needs (Pincus et al., 2020). As servant leaders, school counselors understand that being a servant leader means putting students first and embracing the group's growth.

School counselors understand that after the pandemic, there will be a higher need for individual student support. Tier 3 interventions can give this support. School counselors collaborate with school personnel about students' specific needs; or create individual support plans for the students (Goodman-Scott et al., 2020). Due to the pandemic, families and students might have different stressors affecting their lives. School counselors must develop and maintain community partnerships and provide students and families with referrals (Goodman-Scott et al., 2020). Families need access to health agencies, food banks, social services, after-school programs, and other agencies to assist them. School counselors helping coordinate this effort become an integral part of the community, and it further demonstrates that school counselors are servant leaders since they serve all of their students and families.

School counselors are leaders in their school community. They are on the front line, assessing needs and providing care throughout the day (Pincus et al., 2020). As servant leaders, school counselors proudly take on this role because they care about their schools. Returning to the campus presents challenges since school counselors have large caseloads and new responsibilities, but their ability to multitask, connect with others, and provide help will help guide their work.

Educators and the Current Continuance of the Pandemic

As students and school staff return to in-person instruction, school districts must remember that educators also went through a pandemic. Many people in the education sector know that burnout is real, and many folks are leaving education.

The grace that is expected for students should also be extended to educators. Grace can be extended by understanding that staff can experience burnout from being in a pandemic. Grace means that teachers might need invaluable professional development and meeting time to work together. It can be an opportunity for school counselors and other school staff to teach one another about Tier 1 interventions they can try with their students to reconnect. School administrators can use school counselors who have the ears of the staff, students, and parents to guide them as they think of their district and school site needs.

As school districts are thinking of having students come back in person, it would behoove them to have a systematic way of assessing the needs of the students. School counselors should be involved in the process of assessing the needs and the interventions needed. The needs assessment can be district-wide, but we must allow for individualization as each site is unique and their needs are as well. In building a needs assessment, schools must consider that elementary, middle school, and high school students might have different needs, so space for individualization will be needed. The school district can have a resource folder that all school counselors can tap into, upload information, and adapt to their site as they see fit.

School districts and administrators must remember that morale is low due to the pandemic. It is important to ensure the staff is heard, supported, and can voice their needs during this difficult time. Schools must not go back to "normal" as the pandemic continues to impact school staff, students, and families as well. A reversion to past practices would be detrimental to our students and school staff. School districts must acknowledge that education has changed. Educators must learn the lessons from distance learning and continue the good things that distance learning brings.

SOLUTIONS AND RECOMMENDATIONS

Virtual Learning Continued

In California, due to Senate Bill 130 (2021), parents have the opportunity to have their students continue Virtual Learning. SB 130 creates new provisions for distance learning and independent study (Johnson, 2021a). Families in California may pick Virtual Learning for many reasons, such as medical concerns, fears of COVID-19, anxiety, familial, or economic needs. For example, some high school students went to work during distance learning in the year 2020, while they continued to attend school virtually because their family members were at-risk and they were young enough to bounce back from COVID-19 if they got sick.

SB 130 would help students and families who depend on the flexibility of Virtual Learning. The bill will ensure students can access a competitive learning curriculum since school districts are responsible for meeting specific requirements. The requirements include: curriculum, instructional minutes, and student-to-teacher ratios must be equivalent to what is offered in-person. Access to technology and Wi-Fi must be made available for all students. Schools must keep records of student participation, teachers must constantly communicate with parents/guardians to discuss academics, and schools have to find ways to keep students engaged so their attendance does not drop. Also, there needs to be additional support for English Learners, students in foster care, or other high-needs populations. Meals must be available for students if they qualify for free or reduced lunches. School districts must also plan to transition students who wish to return to in-person instruction in no less than five instructional days. Furthermore, high schools must offer all A-G courses to make students eligible for four-year universities (Johnson, 2021a).

School counselors will continue to be servant leaders in the capacity of Virtual Learning. California has differentiated between distance learning, where some districts had limited live instruction, to now having school districts offer robust virtual learning options for families, which means having live instructions for students. Even in a virtual learning setting, school counselors can be servant leaders in helping their virtual teachers focus on social-emotional concerns that students are having during virtual learning. Each district is figuring out the best way to provide these services, if it is the school counselors, coming into the Zoom once a month to provide lessons to the class, or having a group counseling session in an informal format where students can drop in.

At the current time, one of the challenges school districts face is school attendance. Under current California law, school districts are funded based on their average daily attendance. The state takes into consideration the school's current or prior school year, whichever is higher. The state's daily average attendance calculation includes students physically in classrooms and those enrolled in independent study programs (Johnson, 2021b). The calculations mean students must be present in school for districts to get funding. Therefore, schools need to find strategies and ways to keep students engaged if they participate in a virtual learning program. As servant leaders, now more than before, school counselors should build a strong rapport with students and support their colleagues who might be struggling to make connections with students. Keeping students engaged in their education and creating a learning environment where students feel welcomed, heard, understood, and supported is key to keeping students interested in learning.

American School Counselor Association and School Counselor Leadership

Five characteristics were recommended to build school counselor leadership: resourceful problem-solving, systematic collaboration, interpersonal influence, social justice advocacy, and professional efficacy (Young, 2013). In order to have a strong leadership style, school counselors must have effective communication skills and create systems that hold themselves and others accountable. One of the systems that school counselors can use is timekeeping. School counselors can show data to the administration to demonstrate how they use their time. ASCA recommends that 80% of school counselor time is spent in direct and indirect work for the students, while the other 20% should be spent on planning for programming for students and their families (ASCA, 2019). Technology can be beneficial in this area as school counselors can use Google calendar to track how they use their time. In addition, ASCA provides an Excel template to keep track of time. Using this data, school counselors can engage with their administrators and will be compliant with the ASCA National Model. The ASCA National Model gives school counselors a way to create their school programming encompassing helping ALL students. The current National Model, version 4.0, has the following four steps: Define, Manage, Deliver and Assess. The second step, manage, is where a school counselor uses the time management tool to analyze their time allocation. Using this data will help school counselors advocate to reduce responsibilities that are not directly impacting students. When school counselors share their time allocations with their administrators and school board members, this can begin the conversation about where they should focus their time. Sharing this information can be the first step for a school counselor to lower their caseload numbers to the recommended 250:1 student to counselor ratio. Sharing the data with teachers in a monthly newsletter will also allow the teaching staff to understand how school counselors allocate time and help students. School counselors can share how many students they see each month, how many lessons they provide at the school, and make sure that staff and teachers are informed of what a school counselor's appropriate duties are.

The ASCA National Model highly encourages school counselors to have a planning meeting with the administrator at the beginning of the year to review roles and duties and yearly goals. In 2021, in response to the ongoing pandemic, one of the ideal roles for school counselors would be to consult with teachers to schedule and present school counseling curriculum lessons based on developmental needs and needs identified through data. A needs assessment for the school site will be required. Planning will support the needs assessment results can be overwhelming if the proper support is not in place at the school site. In addition, as a school counselor, this data can create lessons for the entire school (Tier 1 intervention) that teachers can deliver and even create groups (Tier 2 intervention). The following section will go more in-depth on how to support students' social-emotional needs.

Social-Emotional Support

A recommendation is for schools to begin to establish a strong Social-Emotional Learning (SEL) program. Schools across the nation are integrating SEL curriculum and techniques to support students holistically. SEL helps students develop social and personal skills to succeed in their personal lives and their academics. In February 2018, California's State Schools Chief Torlakson announced new SEL Guidelines. The guidelines ensure that students learn the skills needed to succeed in school, their career, and their communities (California Department of Education News Release, 2018). In addition, since the pandemic started in 2020, California's Department of Education updated its SEL website with SEL resources for students during distance learning. SEL is a growing field, and schools that have implemented an SEL program have reported an increase in positive school climate, students improving in academic coursework, and higher graduation rates (DePaoli et al., 2017).

Through SEL, students learn to effectively apply the knowledge, attitudes, and skills necessary to understand other people's emotions and manage their own emotions (Domitrovich et al., 2017). Students also learn to set personal goals, maintain relationships with others, and make responsible decisions (Domitrovich et al., 2017; Weissberg et al., 2017). These skills are vital to know and learn right now since students have been at home during distance learning, and they are relearning how to be at a physical school building and integrate into a social environment.

Schools can begin to research what SEL is and the benefits of having an SEL environment by looking into the Collaborative for Academic, Social, and Emotional Learning (CASEL). CASEL has been a leader in SEL for more than two decades, and they teach these skills to students while focusing on five different competencies: self-awareness, self-management, social awareness, relationship skills, and responsible decision-making (Weissberg et al., 2017). Together the competencies help students improve their social and academic performance, they help create strong student-teacher relationships and peer relationships, and help design a caring school environment (Rimm-Kaufman & Hulleman, 2017; Schonert-Reichl et al., 2017).

Schools can teach students SEL through school-based SEL programs and curricula. These SEL programs can vary depending on the students' needs and the budget at that specific school site or district. Teachers and school counselors can deliver the programs, and they can be used as a Tier 1 support (Zolkoski et al., 2021). They create an overall positive classroom learning environment, and schools can also implement school-wide strategies to help with school climate and culture (Domitrovich et al., 2017; Zolkoski et al., 2021). These skills are vital for students to practice as they get used to their new school routines since some students might have forgotten how to behave at a school campus.

In addition to schools seeing the benefits of SEL, parents who have children that are part of an SEL program also have positive reactions and comments when it comes to SEL. Zolkoski et al. (2021) conducted a study in a K-12 rural school to learn more about the parents' perspectives on SEL. The campus where the study took place used the Jesse Lewis Choose Love Movement (JLCL) program. The parents who participated in the study, from grades 4-12, reported an increase in pro-social behaviors after the students ended their program (Zolkoski et al., 2021). The behaviors included consideration of other people's feelings, kindness to younger children, sharing readily, helpfulness if someone is hurt, and volunteering to help others (Zolkoski et al., 2021). SEL programs are necessary to support students holistically, especially when students are overwhelmed with many different emotions as they transition to in-person learning.

When implementing a robust SEL program, educators have to think of both the micro and macro levels of implementation. Durlak (2015) explains that implementation is complex, as one has to think of the program's cost, evaluate the effectiveness of the SEL program, and critically evaluate the fidelity with which the program will be implemented (capacity); in particular, Durlak underscores the importance of school leadership. Redding and Walberg (2015) state that leadership is essential and invaluable at the school site and district level. One of the keys is to have a school leader who is reflective about their school site and is open to suggestions regarding the SEL program that would most benefit the school. Once they pick a program, school leadership will have to follow through on the actual program implementation. According to Redding and Walberg (2015), leadership should be looking to measure the effectiveness of the SEL program at their site. Patti et al. (2015) provide recommendations for leaders to develop their style. Patti et al. (2015) state that SEL includes promoting learning in a safe environment, building a personal and shared vision with the school community, setting goals for that vision, recognizing and using social-emotional competencies as a leader, and building peer networks and coaching.

The district can also support the school site in implementing an SEL curriculum and programming. Mart et al. (2015) discussed how the systematic support by the site and district level in helping implement the regulations, routines, resources, and culture of an SEL program had an immense impact on their students. Mart et al. (2015) also highlighted that SEL programs should be accessible to all students, no matter the subgroup, and the district must be open to change as a whole system, not only in the classroom setting. Researchers stress that there is little research on the district-wide implementation of SEL programming. Due to the challenges of implementing a district-wide program, all staff in a school district would have to be appropriately trained and onboard with faithfully implementing the curriculum.

The evaluation component of an SEL program can provide leadership data to see if the program is effective. Denham (2015) discussed three primary evaluation methods: formative, interim, and summative. Denham (2015) emphasizes that when examining an SEL program from preschool to adolescents, it is essential to note the bias in the assessment tool. Marzano (2015) reported on formative assessments at the Illinois State Board of Education, which has created SEL standards for educators to use through Kindergarten to high school. Three main goals include five benchmark levels students should be able to reach by each grade level. Goal 1 is to develop self-awareness and self-management skills to achieve school and life success. Goal 2 is to use social awareness and interpersonal skills to establish and maintain positive relationships. The last goal, goal 3, is to demonstrate decision-making skills and responsible behaviors in personal, school, and community contexts (Illinois State Board of Education, 2020).

The pitfall, Marzano (2015) warned, is that teachers must be trained to break down the standards for students and provide concrete examples. The need for training leads to the issue of quality of delivery in SEL instruction. Wanless et al. (2015) discuss the importance of a school community analyzing the leadership's commitment and the capacity of the faculty and partnerships the school has to deliver quality SEL programming to its students. Specifically, Wanless et al. (2015) discuss a model that educators can use to assess whether their organizational system is ready to implement instruction; the organization must consider the history and climate of the organization, leaders' relationship and commitment, and direct service providers' social emotional competence.

Collaboration and Communication With Peers Within the District

There is value when working with peers from different schools within the same district. Returning to in-person instruction has been a challenge. Collaboration and constant communication with district peers can be a form to share strategies, ideas, and it can enable everyone within the school community to better serve students. School counselors, as servant leaders, look for ways that would benefit others.

Having intentional opportunities to network, collaborate, and stay in constant communication with other school counselors that work for the same school district can help alleviate some of the stress school counselors might feel. Lipscombe et al. (2019) explain that these interactions can enable the necessary conditions of members to work effectively together and can produce a meaningful impact on the school organization. School counselors can share effective practices developed at their specific school sites, share community resources and information about activities happening around the community, and create a network of care to prevent stress and burnout.

FUTURE RESEARCH DIRECTIONS

School Counselor Challenges and Future Research

The first challenge school counselors face will be during their graduate school counseling programs. The school counseling graduate programs can improve by training school counselors in MTMDSS and leadership methodology. However, school counseling graduate programs are specialized, and every program is different in California. For example, California State University, Los Angeles (CSULA) has a Marriage and Family Therapist concentration with counseling, while California State University Dominguez Hills (CSUDH) concentrates on school counseling and higher education counseling. As a result, school counseling students do not get the same type of training when they enter the field. In addition, there are specific programs that teach counseling students indirectly about school counseling leadership, while others do not.

While many graduate programs do not have specific leadership courses for school counselors, the Council for Accreditation of Counseling and Related Educational Programs (CACREP) has accredited some schools. CACREP-approved schools are required to include and provide students with instruction on leadership methodologies (CACREP, 2021). The accreditation creates a tiered system of school counselors and professional school counselors (PSCs). One can only be a professional school counselor if the counseling program has a similar accreditation to CACREP.

A second challenge facing school counselors is large caseloads. ASCA recommends that school counselors have a ratio of 250 students per school counselor for the K to 12-grade levels to allow the school counselor to spend at least 80% of their time working directly or indirectly with students (Education Trust, 2019). Unfortunately, this is not the case for many schools across the nation. In California, the average ratio is 622 students to every school counselor (American School Counseling Association, 2019). The large caseload number negatively affects the school counselors' quality of support to students under the MTMDSS framework. School counselors will have more time to provide indirect and direct student support in all three tiers and domains. In addition, school counselors would have an easier time collecting and analyzing data since more people would be helping students.

If the student-to-counselor ratio dropped to the recommended level in the K-12 setting, students would be able to individually meet with the school counselors to review academics and college and career goals (Hoxby & Turner, 2013). At this time, meeting with students individually is difficult because school counselors have placed upon them several administrative responsibilities (Vela-Gude et al., 2009). Therefore, one of the groups that school counselors could support more is first-generation low-income students, who have fewer alternative sources of relevant information and support. Research shows that this group currently lacks information and needs support and information to enroll in post-secondary institutions (Belasco, 2013). Researchers have shown that students who can visit their school counselor regarding college information are more likely to enroll in a 4-year college program (Belasco, 2013). Moreover, school counselors will have more time to provide individualized support for students who need social-emotional support. As servant leaders, school counselors always try to find different ways to care for other people, especially their students.

The third challenge that school counselors face is a complete lack of a formal framework for the servant leadership model. Northouse (2019) stated that one limitation to this leadership model was that the leader could come off as altruistic and utopian. Instead, school counselors want to build a working partnership with all stakeholders to advance the common goal of advocating for all students. The ASCA National Model (2019) states that school counselors use their leadership to design, implement and assess a school counseling program for their school site or district. School counselors as servant leaders are constantly looking for ways and different opportunities to collaborate with stakeholders to ensure they have a comprehensive school counseling program that is effective, inclusive, and will assist all students.

A fourth challenge is that many educators have decided to leave the field, including school counselors. The lack of educators and school counselors has created a need for qualified school counselors. SB130, in California, has allowed for a temporary increase in school counselors. California has provided temporary funding to increase mental health professionals in schools, but what happens when that money is not there? Will school districts be able to fund these positions on their own to maintain mental health professionals on school campuses? A sub-challenge is keeping mental health professionals in school settings even if they make less money than working in other settings such as hospitals or other mental health agencies.

The challenges presented are the four most pressing challenges that K-12 schools counseling programs face at this time. School counselors face challenges in their graduate programs since not all graduate programs offer leadership courses. Also, school counselors have large caseloads. Not all counselors have the recommended 250:1 student-to-school counselor ratio. Another challenge is the lack of a leadership framework which can provide school counselors with leadership tools they can use in their profession. Lastly, there is temporary funding to increase mental health professionals in schools. These are the present areas that other researchers and educational practitioners should further explore. The four areas mentioned provide a good starting point for discussion and future research.

CONCLUSION

Each day school counselors demonstrate servant leadership in their work. School counselors, as mentioned, help with the development of school culture and school faculty and administrators by implementing the MTMDSS framework and rooting their practice in the ASCA Model. As school counselors and servant leaders, their goal is to influence leadership decisions to benefit their students. They advocate for their school counseling program while being student-centered since their goal is to help students be the best possible version of themselves.

REFERENCES

American School Counselor Association. (2018). *The school counselor and multitiered system of supports*. American School Counselor Association (ASCA). https://www.schoolcounselor.org/Standards-Positions/Position-Statements/ASCA-Position-Statements/The-School-Counselor-and-Multitiered-System-of-Sup

Belasco, A. S. (2013). Creating college opportunity: School counselors and their influence on postsecondary enrollment. *Research in Higher Education*, *54*(7), 781–804. doi:10.100711162-013-9297-4

Bemak, F., & Chung, R. C.-Y. (2005). Advocacy as a critical role for urban school counselors: Working toward equity and social justice. *Professional School Counseling*, *8*(3), 196–202.

Betters-Burbon, J., Brunner, T., & Kansteiner, A. (2016). Successful for all? The role of the school counselor in creating and sustaining culturally responsive positive behavior interventions and supports. *The Professional Counselor*, *6*(3), 263–277. doi:10.15241/jbb.6.3.263

Bishop, J., & Noguera, P. (2019). The ecology of educational equity: Implications for policy. *Peabody Journal of Education*, *94*(2), 122–141. doi:10.1080/0161956X.2019.1598108

California Association of School Counselors. (2019). *Covid-19 planning considerations and resources: addressing staff and student mental health for school re-entry*. https://www.schoolcounselor-ca.org/files/Covid-19%20Planning%20Considerations%20and%20Resources-Addressing%20Staff%20and%20Student%20Mental%20Health%20for%20School%20Re-Entry.pdf

California Department of Education News Release. (2018). *State schools chief Tom Torlakson announces new social emotional learning guidelines*. https://www.cde.ca.gov/nr/ne/yr18/yr18rel15.asp

Denham, S. (2015). Assessment of SEL in Educational Contexts. In J. A. Durlak, C. E. Domitrovich, R. P. Weissberg, & T. P. Gullotta (Eds.), *Handbook of social and emotional learning: Research and practice* (pp. 285–300). The Guilford Press.

DePaoli, J. L., Atwell, M., & Bridgeland, J. (2017). *Ready to lead: A national principal survey on how social and emotional learning can prepare children and transform schools*. Civic Enterprises and Hart Research Associates for CASEL.

Domitrovich, C., Durlak, J., Staley, K., & Weissberg, R. (2017). Social-emotional competence: An essential factor for promoting positive adjustment and reducing risk in school children. *Child Development*, *88*(2), 408–416. doi:10.1111/cdev.12739 PMID:28213889

Duquette, K. (2021). "We're powerful too, you know?" A narrative inquiry into elementary school counselors' experiences of the RAMP process. *Professional School Counseling*, *25*(1), 1–15. doi:10.1177/2156759X20985831

Durlak, J. (2015). What everyone should know about implementation. In J. A. Durlak, C. E. Domitrovich, R. P. Weissberg, & T. P. Gullotta (Eds.), *Handbook of social and emotional learning: Research and practice* (pp. 395–405). The Guilford Press.

Fye, H. J., Bergen, S., & Baltrinic, E. R. (2020). Exploring the relationship between school counselors' perceived ASCA national model implementation, supervision satisfaction, and burnout. *Journal of Counseling and Development*, *98*(1), 53–62. doi:10.1002/jcad.12299

Goodman-Scott, E., Betters-Bubon, J., Olsen, J., & Donohue, P. (2020). *An ASCA National Model: Making MTSS Work*. American School Counselor Association Publication.

Hatch, T. (2020). *Multi tiered, multi-domain system of supports*. https://www.hatchingresults.com/blog/2017/3/multi-tiered-multi-domain-system-of-supports-by-trish-hatch-phd

Hatch, T., Duarte, D. R., & De Gregorio, L. K. (2018). *Hatching results for elementary school counseling: implementing core curriculum and other tier one activities* (1st ed.). Corwin. doi:10.4135/9781506389684

Hatch, T., Tripplett, W., Duarte, D., & Gomez, V. (2019). *Hatching results for secondary school counseling: Implementing core curriculum, individual student planning, and other Tier one activities*. Corwin.

Hoxby, C., & Turner, S. (2013). Expanding college opportunities. *Education Next, 13*(4), 66–73.

Johnson, S. (2021a). *California directs districts to offer remote independent study this fall*. EdSource. https://edsource.org/2021/california-directs-districts-to-offer-remote-independent-study-this-fall/657578

Johnson, S. (2021b). *California schools move ahead with fall distance learning plans despite limitations*. EdSource. https://edsource.org/2021/california-schools-move-ahead-with-fall-distance-learning-plans-despite-limitations/655901

Leuwerke, W. C., Walker, J., & Shi, Q. (2009). Informing principals: The impact of different types of information on principals' perceptions of professional school counselors. *Professional School Counseling, 12*(4), 263–271. Advance online publication. doi:10.5330/PSC.n.2010-12.263

Lipscombe, K., Buckley-Walker, K., & McNamara, P. (2020). Understanding collaborative teacher teams as open systems for professional development. *Professional Development in Education, 46*(3), 37–3390. doi:10.1080/19415257.2019.1613256

Mart, A., Weissberg, R., & Kendziora, K. (2015). Systematic support for SEL in school districts. In J. A. Durlak, C. E. Domitrovich, R. P. Weissberg, & T. P. Gullotta (Eds.), *Handbook of social and emotional learning: Research and practice* (pp. 482–499). The Guilford Press.

Marzano, R. (2015). Using formative assessment with SEL skills. In J. A. Durlak, C. E. Domitrovich, R. P. Weissberg, & T. P. Gullotta (Eds.), *Handbook of social and emotional learning: Research and practice* (pp. 336–347). The Guilford Press.

Nelson, J. A., Robles-Pina, R., & Nichter, M. (2008). An analysis of Texas high school counselors' role: Actual and preferred counseling activities. *Journal of Professional Counseling, Practice, Theory, & Research, 36*(1), 30–46. doi:10.1080/15566382.2008.12033842

Northouse, P. (2019). *Leadership: Theory and practice* (8th ed.). SAGE Publications.

Olsen, J., Parikh-Foxx, S., Flowers, C., & Algozzine, B. (2016). An examination of factors that relate to school counselors' knowledge and skills in multi-tiered systems of support. *Professional School Counseling, 20*(1), 159–171. doi:10.5330/1096-2409-20.1.159

Parzych, J., Donohue, P., Gaesser, A., & Chiu, M. M. (2019). *Measuring the Impact of School Counselor Ratios on Student Outcomes.* ASCA Research Report. https://www.schoolcounselor.org/getmedia/5157ef82-d2e8-4b4d-8659-a957f14b7875/Ratios-Student-Outcomes-Research-Report.pdf

Patti, J., Senge, P., Madrazo, C., & Stern, R. (2015). Developing socially, emotionally, and cognitively competent school leaders and learning communities. In J. A. Durlak, C. E. Domitrovich, R. P. Weissberg, & T. P. Gullotta (Eds.), *Handbook of social and emotional learning: Research and practice* (pp. 438–452). The Guilford Press.

Pincus, R., Hannor-Walker, T., Wright, L., & Justice, J. (2020). COVID-19's Effect on students: How school counselors rise to the rescue. *NASSP Bulletin, 104*(4), 241–256. doi:10.1177/0192636520975866

Redding, S., & Walberg, H. (2015). Indicators of effective SEL practice. In J. A. Durlak, C. E. Domitrovich, R. P. Weissberg, & T. P. Gullotta (Eds.), *Handbook of social and emotional learning: Research and practice* (pp. 37–392). The Guilford Press.

Rimm-Kaufman, S., & Hulleman, C. (2017). SEL in elementary school settings: identifying mechanisms that matter. In C. E. Domitrovich, R. P. Weissberg, & T. P. Gullotta (Eds.), *Handbook of Social Emotional Learning Research and Practice* (pp. 151–166). The Guilford Press.

Schonert-Reichl, K. A., Hanson-Peterson, J., & Hymel, S. (2017). SEL and preservice teachers. In C. E. Domitrovich, R. P. Weissberg, & T. P. Gullotta (Eds.), *Handbook of Social Emotional Learning Research and Practice* (pp. 406–421). The Guilford Press.

Vela-Gude, L., Cavazos, J., Johnson, M., Fielding, C., Cavazos, A., Campos, L., & Rodriguez, I. (2009). "My counselors were never there": Perceptions from Latino college students. *Professional School Counseling, 12*(4), 272–279. doi:10.5330/PSC.n.2010-12.272

Wanless, S., Groark, C., & Hatfield, B. (2015). Assessing organizational readiness. In J. A. Durlak, C. E. Domitrovich, R. P. Weissberg, & T. P. Gullotta (Eds.), *Handbook of social and emotional learning: Research and practice* (pp. 360–376). The Guilford Press.

Weissberg, R. P., Durlak, J., Domitrovich, C. E., & Gullota, T. P. (2017). Social and emotional learning: Past, present, and future. In C. E. Domitrovich, R. P. Weissberg, & T. P. Gullota (Eds.), *Handbook of Social Emotional Learning Research and Practice* (pp. 3–19). The Guilford Press.

Wilder, C. (2018). Promoting the role of the school counselor. *Journal of Professional Counseling, Practice, Theory, & Research*, *45*(2), 60–68. doi:10.1080/15566382.2019.1646085

Williamson, A. A., Modecki, K. L., & Guerra, N. G. (2015). SEL programs in high school. In J. A. Durlak, C. E. Domitrovich, R. P. Weissberg, & T. P. Gullotta (Eds.), *Handbook of social and emotional learning: Research and practice* (pp. 181–196). The Guilford Press.

Zalequette, C. P., & Chatters, S. J. (2012). Middle school principals' perceptions of middle school counselors' roles and functions. *American Secondary Education*, *40*(2), 89–103.

Zolkoski, S. M., Holm, J. M., West, E., Ismail, H., Kennedy, B. R., Votaw, A., Miller, G. J., Stocks, E., & Sass, S. M. (2021). Social-emotional learning in rural schools: Parents' perspectives. *Kappa Delta Pi Record*, *57*(1), 43–46. doi:10.1080/00228958.2021.1851587

Chapter 6
Virtual School Counseling

Barbara Christine Wilson
Connections Academy, USA

ABSTRACT

The American School Counselor Association (ASCA) is a national organization that provides frameworks for school counseling programs. ASCA developed a national model that outlines a comprehensive school counseling program. The purpose of the model is to help school counselors do more school counseling, do fewer non-school counseling activities, and provide expert-level tools. This chapter explores the history of virtual schools and the various forms of distance education. Practitioners will learn the benefits and barriers to a virtual school counseling program. Additionally, the chapter presents best practices and highlights special considerations. This chapter is not necessarily an implementation guide; it is a resource for professionals who consider using virtual school counseling and those who already provide a virtual program.

INTRODUCTION

In 2020, the world experienced the beginning of a global pandemic due to Coronavirus Disease 2019 (Covid-19). According to the Centers for Disease Control (CDC), Covid-19 is a respiratory disease caused by SARS-CoV-2, a variation of the coronavirus identified in 2019 (CDC, 2021). The pandemic became a shared traumatic experience with detrimental mental health consequences (Sanchez-Gomez, et al., 2021). The virus spread quickly worldwide, causing a ripple effect of lifestyle changes. One such change was in the education system. When the pandemic hit and schools responded to the needs of their respective communities, ASCA also responded with tools and resources for implementing virtual school counseling into existing

DOI: 10.4018/978-1-7998-9785-9.ch006

programs. The Covid-19 pandemic brought attention to the market and value of virtual school counseling. However, virtual school counseling is not a new concept.

The American School Counselor Association (ASCA) is a national organization that provides frameworks for school counseling programs. ASCA developed a National Model that outlines a comprehensive school counseling program (American School Counselor Association, 2019). The purpose of the model is to help school counselors do more school counseling, do fewer non-school counseling activities, and provide expert-level tools.

This chapter explores the history of virtual schools and the various forms of distance education. School counselors will learn the benefits and barriers to a virtual school counseling program within a virtual school setting. Additionally, the chapter presents best practices for school counselors and highlights special considerations. This chapter is not presented as an implementation guide; it is a resource for professionals who consider using virtual school counseling and those who already provide a virtual program. Virtual school counseling is a valuable option for students and their families. Additionally, the virtual format serves as a trauma-informed practice as well. School counselors and school counselor leadership are advised to explore resources, tools, and techniques to find the most appropriate format for each school district's vision.

Terms and Definitions

There is an array of school formats that come under "virtual." Therefore, it is essential to understand the different terms that identify specific types of programs. The author of this chapter uses "virtual school counseling" to describe technology-based school counseling services. However, the resources cited also use words such as online school counseling and distance school counseling interchangeably. The field of virtual schools and virtual school counseling is quickly advancing; therefore, the vocabulary included in the literature is not yet clearly defined. This chapter informs the reader of the options, formats, and tools related to virtual school counseling.

The www.merriam-webster.com definitions of terms related to virtual school and virtual school counseling are listed below:

Distance Learning- A method of study where teachers and students do not meet in a classroom but use the internet, email, mail, etc., to have class. They are also known as distance education.

Online- Connected to, served by, or available through a system and especially a computer or telecommunications system (such as the internet).

Telehealth- Healthcare provided remotely to patients in a separate location using two-way voice and visual communication (as a computer or cell phone).

Virtual- Being on or simulated on a computer or computer network; occurring primarily online; related to or using virtual memory.

"Virtual school" is not currently listed in the online Merriam-Webster dictionary.

In 2017, the American School Counselor Association (ASCA) published a position statement on virtual school counseling. "Distance school counseling" is equivalent to virtual, online, and eLearning formats in the position statement. In addition, the position statement affirmed that virtual school counseling includes both asynchronous and synchronous communication (*The School Counselor and Virtual School Counseling - American School Counselor Association (ASCA)*, 2020). Synchronous communication occurs in real-time, either through written messages, face-to-face or auditory interactions. Asynchronous communication is still two-way between the student and the teacher, but it does not require live, real-time interactions. For example, in a world language course, students might record themselves speaking in the other language, send the video to their teacher, and view the recording later for assessment and feedback.

As defined by Barbour (2012), virtual schools are "an entity approved by a state or governing body that offers courses through distance delivery- most commonly using the Internet." The definition provided by Barbour also states that virtual schools offer education through independent learning, synchronous learning, and asynchronous learning. School counseling within this context is defined as using the internet to deliver program components.

Understanding the various definitions is helpful when navigating resources related to virtual school counseling. The terms listed above are often interchangeable, depending on the source and audience. So, it is crucial to know there is a difference in words, and those differences lend themselves to various settings. For example, a school counselor who delivers program components from a brick and mortar setting to students in the building and via a video-based platform provides a hybrid model, blending traditional in-person methods with technology-based methods.

For this chapter, the author uses the term "virtual school counseling" to describe the practice of providing school counseling program services through technology. Technology includes telephone, video, email, chat-based services, and online platforms for document sharing and submissions. The list of technology resources is not exhaustive because technological tools change frequently; therefore, a list provided here could quickly become outdated. The National Center for Education Statistics quotes David Dwyer, "Technology is a lot like the rungs on a ladder. Once you reach one level, there's another one higher up to aspire to" (*Technology in Schools*, 2022).

School counselors are encouraged to remain aware of the latest technological advances and options through frequent collaborations with the Information Systems department staff within the school district, periodic review of literature and data in professional journals, such as the School Counselor magazine published by ASCA, and remaining engaged with technology themselves as individuals.

In addition to understanding the vocabulary related to virtual school descriptors, it is helpful to know the difference between formats. For example, public and private schools are different educational settings. Each type of school system uses various funding sources. Public schools have state and federal funding and operate under state guidelines. Private schools receive funding through grants, donations, tuition, and stakeholder resources. The curriculum in private schools is either internally developed or provided through an external curriculum company.

Charters schools are another format for K-12 education. Charter schools often fill a gap within the local school system. An example is a school district that no longer offers a drama program may want a charter school designed for the arts. Charter schools are publicly funded entities where instruction follows the associated state standards.

Some districts offer online courses to supplement the existing curriculum. This option is often helpful for credit recovery courses. The supplemental model may occur within the existing school building, a separate building, or remotely between the student's home and an online platform. Districts that welcome online courses may also have the systems and resources to provide virtual school counseling. The reader is encouraged to advocate for options within their respective districts.

Virtual School Counseling as a Trauma-Informed Practice

As stated earlier, the pandemic created a globally traumatic experience. Schools responded by providing virtual school options, including virtual school counseling. Although virtual school is not a new concept, as discussed later, the purpose and value became magnified through pandemic responses.

School counselors have a unique opportunity to provide trauma-informed practices through comprehensive virtual school counseling programs. A key element of trauma-informed practices is providing safe spaces that encourage hope and normalize reactions to stress (*BUILD TRAUMA-INFORMED PRACTICES*, 2021). When using ASCA Mindsets & Behaviors for research-based standards, school counselors can offer conversations, lessons, activities, and interactive meetings that are trauma-informed.

Bibliocounseling is an example of a trauma-informed practice. A 2020 study investigated the efficacy of biblio[counseling] as a non-pharmaceutical intervention during the Covid-19 pandemic (Monroy-Fraustro et al., 2021). The study's findings indicated that child and adult individuals experience benefits from biblio[counseling]. Additionally, the study stated that providing electronic books is a better option to meet the needs of individuals who cannot receive counseling in a brick-and-mortar setting (Monroy-Fraustro et al., 2021).

For example, a virtual school counselor could invite their students to meet on a video-based platform at a specific time and day. Students log in with cameras on or off, depending on the school's policies and best practices for counseling activities. The counselor would read a book to the students, then follow up with supportive and thought-provoking questions. In this setting, the virtual school counselor provides counseling services to multiple students in a safe, welcoming, and virtual space.

Schools that utilize a Multi-Tiered System of Supports (MTSS) will find trauma-informed practices as a valuable tool in Tier 1 and Tier 2 work (*BUILD TRAUMA-INFORMED PRACTICES*, 2021). MTSS programs, also referred to as Response to Intervention (RTI) and Positive Behavior Intervention System (PBIS), identify students with different needs and provide interventions based on the level of demand (*What is MTSS?*, 2019). Students transition through the tiers as their progress is monitored for either growth or a lack of development. MTSS and similar programs are not federally mandated, so their name and structure may differ according to local and state guidelines (*Issue Brief: Multi-Tier System of Supports/Response to Intervention - NCLD*, 2021).

HISTORY

The chapter began with a review of recent pandemic events related to virtual school counseling and trauma-informed practices. Many professionals in education became aware of virtual options as a direct result of the pandemic and its impact on education. However, virtual schools existed decades before the Covid-19 changes in education. Surprisingly, distance education existed nearly 300 years ago. A review of the literature shows that generations responded to the needs of people, utilizing the tools available at that time.

The earliest example of distance education is a correspondence course that ran as an advertisement in the *Boston Gazette* (jrfreese, 2019). Caleb Phillips ran an ad in 1728 offering to teach shorthand to anyone in the United States via letter correspondence. Interested parties received weekly lessons from Phillips and submitted their completed assignments through the postal service.

Isaac Pitman is recognized as the pioneer of distance education for creating correspondence education in 1840 in Bath, England (College & Kentnor, 2015). His system was based on postcards to submit work and receive corrections.

The Chautauqua Movement of the 1870s is responsible for introducing and accepting distance education, also called correspondence education, in the United States. (College & Kentnor, 2015). Boston was the home of one of the first correspondence schools in the United States to establish The Boston Society to Encourage Studies at Home (jrfreese, 2019). The school opened in 1873 and only admitted women into their program. Unfortunately, the school closed after only 24 years when Anna Eliot Tickner passed away.

In 1878, John Heyl Vincent established the first adult education and correspondence school in the United States, called the Scientific Circle in Chautauqua, New York (College & Kentnor, 2015). In 1889, the Colliery Engineer School of Mines (currently called the *ICS Learn, International Correspondence Schools*) opened its doors in Scranton, Pennsylvania. Again, the school served men only and offered technical and practical education (jfreese, 2019). In addition, the curriculum focused on safety education to reduce the number of accidents in the mines.

In New York state, the Chautauqua Correspondence College opened in 1881. The State of New York authorized the college to offer diplomas and degrees in 1883. Its founder, William Rainey Harper, established a similar program at the University of Chicago. Also, in 1881, the University of Wisconsin (UW) created a correspondence course taught by the existing faculty. This program was the early version of the UW Independent Learning.

In 1915, the National University Extension Association was formed to meet the growing needs for professional development and increase access to university-level education (College & Kentnor, 2015). The desire for college degrees grew in the early 1900s, as did increasing barriers to education (e.g., family obligations, geographic) (College & Kentnor, 2015). The United States was shifting from agricultural to industrial systems, so individuals wanted to increase their skillsets and employment options.

The introduction of radio and household access to radios created the space for educational broadcasting opportunities (College & Kentnor, 2015). Unfortunately, the Great Depression disrupted educational broadcasting. At the start of the Great Depression, there were 176 radio stations at educational institutions. However, only 35 of the radio stations survived. Institutions developed "schools of the air" to offer programs on topics such as science, literature, history, and music (College & Kentnor, 2015). The Ohio State Department of Education developed the Ohio School of the Air in 1928. Interestingly, the National Broadcasting Company (NBC) started the Radio Corporation of America (RCA) Educational Hour, also known as the "Music Appreciation Hour," in 1928 (College & Kentnor, 2015).

Television's invention and home usage allowed for another option to provide distance education. The first use of broadcast television for education originated between 1932 and 1937 at the University of Iowa (College & Kentnor, 2015). However, the Federal Communications Commission (FCC) quickly identified issues related to frequencies and allocation. By 1952, the FCC initially permitted exclusive educational usage to 242 channels, increasing to 632 channels by 1966.

Of the 632 channels, one-third were licensed to state and local educational systems, another third utilized by colleges and universities, and the final third for community organizations (College & Kentnor, 2015).

At this time in history, we see the birth of what we currently know as school counseling programs. In the early 1900s, we see the first "vocational guidance" (Gysbers, n.d.). Secondary schools during this time began to include vocational counseling, although there wasn't an organizational structure. In the 1920s, there was a shift in the United States from vocational guidance to counseling in school settings for personal growth (Gysbers, n.d.). The Vocational Education Act of 1946 and the National Defense Education Act (NDEA) of 1958 helped significantly increase school counselor training and positions. ASCA was established in 1952 (Gysbers, n.d.).

The 20th century brought new technology and innovative tools, such as radio and television, that perfectly met the needs of distance learning programs. Computer technologies existed in the mid-1900s, but primarily within military establishments (College & Kentnor, 2015). By the 1980s, computers were utilized in the corporate world. Then, in 1989, online education programs emerged.

As the internet became a household resource in the 1990s, the opportunity to develop internet-based programs grew. In 1991, the World Wide Web was introduced. The University of Phoenix became one of the first schools to offer online college programs through the internet. The Asynchronous Learning Network (ALN) was developed in 1992 to explore educational options for individuals unable to attend college in person (College & Kentnor, 2015). In 1993, California developed district-based K-12 programs. Approximately one year later, the Utah e-school began.

The Florida Virtual School (FLVS) began in 1997 as a collaborative relationship between the Orange and Alachua County school districts. The initial focus was providing complete high school education. Today, Florida Virtual School offers flexible, full-time, and tuition-free education in grades K-12. Their philosophy is "Anytime, any place, any path, any pace" (Clark, 2021). In 2007, Michigan mandated that high school students complete a non-credit online course or learning experience as a graduation requirement. The addition of the graduation requirement responded to the growing internet use in school, home, and the workplace. Michigan saw the opportunity to become a leader in online academics and reacted accordingly (*The Case for Michigan's Online Learning Mandate, 2011)*. Alabama, Florida, and Idaho followed suit and adopted an online learning component to the curriculum.

Massachusetts opened the first in-state public online school in the 2010-2011 school year. The school began with a 500-student limit. Students with the online school completed the required state assessments, called the Massachusetts Comprehensive Assessment System (MCAS). By 2009, online school enrollment hit an estimated one million students. The trend continued and appeared to keep the growth momentum in the future. A report from GovTech.com in 2021 stated that 20% of schools plan to establish and expand online learning (Paykamian, 2021).

Benefits

Virtual learning offers an educational service without geographical limitations. Teachers could utilize the postal service to reach a larger population of potential students. Students then could learn a new skill from the comfort of their own homes. As the world modernized, communication methods increased, and the world expanded. Educators and schools utilized mailing services, radio stations, and telephones to provide learning opportunities. Generations have discovered the many benefits of distance learning.

The National Education Association (NEA) released a policy statement in February 2020 that states,

The appropriate use of technology in education will improve student learning, quality of instruction, and employee effectiveness and provide opportunities to eradicate educational inequities.

As mentioned above, a benefit of distance learning is expanding the range of learning opportunities for individuals. Before virtual options existed, proximity to the school was often a deciding factor. However, families must consider transportation. Families are not required to send their children to their local schools anymore. The School Choice Act, S.235, expands educational options so that families can choose a school based on their child's needs. A selection process allows for a more substantial buy-in from the family and creates a "best fit" opportunity for the student(s). Each state has its regulations for school choice, so school counselors are encouraged to check with their local state and district guidelines.

Before School Choice, students attended the schools within the district where they lived. It was not uncommon for families to select a home based on the local school system. As a result, people chose their education facilities according to opportunities in the same geographical region. Alternately, the potential student would have to relocate and move closer to their desired school or school district. Unfortunately, moving and transportation resources are not viable options for many people, so the range of opportunities becomes limited.

Schools could also expand their reach by implementing distance learning. School systems could offer programs of interest to people in various locations. By offering in-demand programs, schools can increase enrollment and meet the needs of a more significant number of students. For example, someone interested in engineering might not have the program available in their local district. So, the student could apply for a Science Technology Engineering Arts and Math (STEAM) program outside of their immediate location.

Virtual schools commonly provide education with a flexible schedule. Courses occur either synchronously or asynchronously; therefore, students can find a program that fits their needs. For example, student-athletes have demanding schedules that may include required travel. The online format permits these students to bring their school and study according to their plan. Similarly, students engaged with performing arts, such as professional dance, acting, or music, also find the virtual school option the best for their lifestyle.

A significant percentage of students seek rigorous courses and an accelerated pace. Some online formats allow students to complete courses beyond their local school level. Additionally, virtual schools do not have to follow a traditional school schedule. Therefore, students can complete classes, advance grade levels, and earn credits toward graduation at an accelerated rate.

Students with Disabilities

Some students require a smaller classroom setting than their local district provides. Virtual schools can offer support for students with disabilities, although the available options may differ between schools. Students with disabilities in public schools are protected under the Individuals with Disabilities Education Act. However, school counselors acknowledge adherence to the ASCA recommendations for providing services to students with disabilities, regardless of their school setting (public or private). ASCA states that school counselors recognize their strengths and limitations in their work with students with disabilities (*The School Counselor and Students with Disabilities - American School Counselor Association (ASCA)*, 2020). This statement refers to students with disabilities who may or may not have an Individualized Education Plan (IEP) or a 504 plan.

Although an Individualized Education Plan (IEP) or a Section 504 Plan might include accommodations, an online option is sometimes best for students who need more direct attention or fewer distractions. Similarly, a 2019 study performed by the University of Colorado Boulder found that a higher percentage of students who qualified for special education enrolled in virtual schools than in "brick-and-mortar" settings (National Education Study Center, 2019).

Absenteeism

Mental or physical health will dictate educational needs for some students. Health is often an underlying factor in chronic absenteeism. Students with a history of chronic absenteeism before the second grade are more likely to read below grade level by the third grade. Therefore, chronically absent students are four times as likely to drop out of school than proficient readers (The Relationship Between School Attendance and Health, 2016).

Common causes of physical health limitations are asthma, dental health, visual impairments, diabetes, and obesity. Mental health is a significant factor in absenteeism. Students managing depression, anxiety, and fear might feel more comfortable in online education environments. However, more than 15% of school-aged children are uninsured, so the physical and mental health concerns become increasingly problematic for school attendance (The Relationship Between School Attendance and Health, 2016).

Virtual school options can also address the needs of students from low-income homes. Transportation is a common issue for families who seek online opportunities. Equally troublesome, unstable housing and food insecurities might also influence school selections. These factors are barriers to education that may impact attendance and performance.

It is worth mentioning that when a student has high absenteeism in the brick-and-mortar setting, the absences are typically one of two situations. When students avoid attending school, usually it is because they are either avoiding leaving home or avoiding presence at school. For example, students may have babysitting responsibilities. Or perhaps the student feels the need to protect someone or something at home. When school avoidance is the concern, there might be a history of bullying. School counselors should talk with their students and their caretakers about their reasons for enrolling in virtual schools.

Bullying

Many students in virtual settings experienced bullying in their brick-and-mortar schools. For example, in 2017, the Oklahoma Statewide Virtual Charter School Board surveyed the state's virtual schools. The survey revealed that 41% of their students cited bullying as why students chose to attend virtual school (Felder, 2018). According to the National Center for Education Statistics (NCES), approximately 20% of students report being a victim of bullying. Most bullying occurs in-person, in unsupervised locations, such as the cafeteria or in the hallway. Virtual schools do not have the areas mentioned above, so the online option creates a physically safer school setting.

Virtual school formats reduce or remove the in-person threat of bullying. Victims often fear going to school and experience chronic absenteeism. Merely seeing the aggressor can cause a victim to avoid school. After bullying, incents occur, triggers related to the events still exist, such as where the bullying occurred. However, virtual school is not a panacea to all bullying. Remote learning students can also fall prey to bullying incidents. Cyberbullying is a consideration, and it is discussed later in the chapter.

Virtual School Demographics

According to the National Education Policy Center at the University of Colorado, fewer than 1% of K-12 students attended virtual school full-time before the pandemic. The health crisis that Covid-19 created impacted remote learning enrollment. School districts moved their classrooms online in response to the medical recommendations.

After the initial response to Covid-19, many schools chose to keep the online option for students. As a result, the demand for virtual schools soared, and districts responded. For example, one of the United States' largest school districts, Fulton County Schools in Atlanta, Georgia, planned 1,000 students to enroll in its new online school. Likewise, the number of online schools in Minnesota doubled, from 37 schools before the pandemic to 80 immediately after the pandemic began.

The demographics in virtual schools shifted during the pandemic. Some districts required all students to attend school virtually. Therefore, assessing interest in an online school option is not entirely accurate when looking at the academic years during the pandemic. However, the mandatory virtual setting introduced students and staff to the remote possibility, creating awareness and interest. As a result, new statistical trends might appear in the years following the Covid-19 pandemic.

The National Education Policy Center reviewed the demographics of virtual schools in the U.S. in 2019. The study found that online schools have significantly fewer minority students and fewer low-income students compared to public school enrollment across the U.S. However, in blended schools, those that offered the curriculum in both in-person and online formats, the proportion of low-income students was relative to the national average.

Virtual and blended schools have substantially fewer English Language Learners (ELLs) than U.S. public school enrollment. In addition, binary gender statistics across the U.S. reveal a nearly even split between male and female student enrollment within public and blended schools. However, virtual schools enrolled slightly more females (53.9%) than males.

Classroom size and student-teacher ratios are significantly different in virtual schools compared to public schools in the U.S. The national average in public schools is 16 students per teacher. Blended schools average 34 students per teacher, and virtual schools average 44 students per teacher. Online students might not notice the student-teacher ratios in virtual environments. Sitting in a home or other remote location with 43 other students signed into the same virtual platform does not feel the same as sitting in a physical classroom with the same number of students. It is important to note that these ratios vary from state to state.

ASCA conducted a study in 2020, *State of the Profession*, surveyed school counselors in the United States. The purpose of the study was to collect data regarding student demographics, the impact of Covid-19 on school environments, and counselor-student ratios. ASCA recommends a counselor-student ratio of 250:1. According to the U.S. Department of Education, the national average is 430:1. In addition, the ASCA study disaggregated the data by school level and found the national average for K-8 counselors is 708:1 and 9-12 counselors is 212:1.

Best Practices

The National Education Association (NEA) released a policy statement on digital technology. The NEA states that technology is meant to supplement instruction as an enhancement. Technology should not replace education employees. The NEA emphasizes the importance of considering student maturity and developmental skills when deciding which tools to implement (National Education Association, 2020). School formats and curriculum delivery models fall on a spectrum between 100% online delivery and 100% technology-free.

School Formats

Before discussing best practices further, it is essential to review the different styles of virtual school settings. There is a wide range of systems, though, and this list is not exhaustive. Virtual schools are developing, and a uniform model does not exist. Although some virtual schools existed before the pandemic, there is no "one size fits all" structure.

An all-virtual school provides students with courses and school interactions (i.e., conversations with teachers). The communication is either synchronous or asynchronous. Students do not attend class in person, although face-to-face events may occur as options throughout the school year. The staff at virtual schools typically work from home or in remote locations. All-virtual schools might offer a complete curriculum and operate as the student's full-time school. Alternately, an online school could supplement the student's full-time coursework completed in a different school.

Blended formats use in-person and online platforms to provide educational services. For example, grades K-3 might attend in-person school on the 1st and 3rd week of the month, and grades 4-5 could participate on the 2nd and 4th weeks of the month. When the students are not in-person, they work remotely, accessing online platforms. In addition, the school staff in blended schools often report in-person to the school building, regardless of if their assigned students are present in the establishment or not.

Another example of a blended format is a full-time, face-to-face school setting that offers some courses through online vendors. In these settings, students attend their brick-and-mortar school full-time, Monday through Friday, from the beginning to the end of the school day. However, some of their classes during the day could require the student to log in from a school computer lab to complete assignments from a third-party vendor. This format is often seen in credit recovery situations but is also applicable in other scenarios.

Students approved for Hospital Homebound (HHB) services can sign in, as a video call, into the live classroom to receive their lessons. Hospital Homebound services are temporary instructional programs designed for students experiencing a qualifying physical or mental health condition. The in-person students and teachers engage in classroom lessons while the student receiving HHB services views the teacher and lesson information remotely.

The ASCA *State of the Profession 2020* report found that school counselors consider meeting the needs of students in a virtual setting to be their biggest challenge (ASCA, 2021). It is worth noting that most of the study respondents experienced virtual school as a necessary option during the pandemic. However, 1.2% of the respondents worked in a virtual school before the pandemic.

The pandemic caused a flurry of activity among school districts. Local, state, and federal education experts scrambled to determine appropriate responses to the Covid-19 health crisis. Many virtual programs developed quickly, with short notice, and intended to be short-term. However, a significant number of schools decided to continue offering virtual as the primary source or an additional option for educating their students. As school counselors settled into their new roles as virtual school counselors, some using pre-existing virtual school counseling programs as a model, best practices emerged. Regardless of the grade level(s) served, virtual school counselors must adhere to the same ethical guidelines as non-virtual school counselors. ASCA adopted ethical guidelines for school counselors in 1984, periodically updating the policies, and the most recent version was published in 2020. Section A.15 of the *Ethical Standards* is specifically for virtual school counseling (*ASCA Ethical Standards for School Counselors - American School Counselor Association (ASCA)*, 2020). Legal and ethical issues are discussed in greater detail later in this chapter.

Technology Resources

Virtual school counseling occurs through technology-based platforms. A diverse range of reliable and high-quality modalities is available for virtual school counselors to interact remotely with their students and families. School counselors must consider legal and ethical issues, confidentiality, Family Education Rights and Privacy

Act (FERPA) compliance, and professional liability. ASCA and state counseling associations are valuable resources for current information.

Virtual school counselors should not make decisions regarding technology usage in isolation. School counselors are encouraged to consult with their leadership and information systems department experts. Additionally, if issues indicate a potential issue with district-approved technology, the school counselor should report all problems immediately. The virtual students and their families need training and support for technology usage. The same considerations around privacy are an issue, just as they are for the virtual school counselor. Additionally, families might need orientation to platform options and education related to online safety.

Examples of possible technology formats include internet-based telephone numbers, video-based online meeting spaces, internet, and intranet-based chat platforms, file-sharing spaces, cloud-based calendars, and online schedulers for creating appointments and events. Virtual school counselors interested in learning more about the available options in their district are encouraged to contact their supervisor and district-level counseling coordinators. If technology options are available but are not approved within the district, the virtual school counselor can advocate for the service as appropriate.

Plan for Emergencies, Urgent Situations, and Inappropriate Behavior

One of the priority actions for a virtual school counseling program is developing procedures for critical and emergencies. The policies should outline what to do when the counselor is available and what to do when he/she/they are not available. Knowing a child's location when speaking remotely with a school staff member is essential. Knowing the child's location is crucial if an urgent or emergent situation occurs. Schools should develop the procedures and train the staff on the guidelines.

School counselors providing online services should educate students and their families about the benefits and limitations of virtual counseling. The virtual environment might be new for the students and the staff, so orientation is helpful in the transition. Teach families about what they can expect to experience through virtual school counseling. Prepare to educate them about the technology you desire to use. Imagine the new middle school student afraid on the first day of school because of the potential for getting lost. It is the same with online school.

Educate students about appropriate behavior and atmosphere online. Proper behavior includes proper dress, language, name (in situations where they assign their screen name), peer-to-peer interactions, and attendance. Talk with students about what appears in the background of their video and recommend a blank wall whenever possible.

Appropriate online behavior is the same for the school counselor(s). Dressing appropriately and having a professional appearance in view is critical. Family photos, personal documents, and non-professional items should not be in view while on camera. The school counselor's responsibility is to understand the platforms utilized with their program services. Set up the virtual rooms ahead of time to include safety and privacy features, such as no private chatting. Proper setup can prevent and reduce awkward, embarrassing, and disastrous situations later.

Acknowledge the limitations of confidentiality when working online. Unfortunately, there is no guarantee of privacy, even with the best technology in place. Inform students and their families of the limitations and remain vigilant about protecting privacy. Talk to information technology department representatives, if possible, to ensure the system used is protected.

Follow the district guidelines for virtual programs and good platforms while providing services. Districts might have licensing agreements and teacher accounts for specific programs, so make sure to check with your leadership team(s) before selecting a communication medium.

Grade Level Best Practices

At all grade levels, a comprehensive counseling program is possible. It is worth noting that at least two virtual public charter schools currently hold Recognized ASCA Model Program recognition (RAMP), Indiana Connections Academy and Georgia Connections Academy (*Current RAMP Schools - American School Counselor Association (ASCA)*, 2020). However, do not expect your program to look or feel the same as what you offered in the brick-and-mortar setting. With a few adjustments, individual counseling, small groups, and classroom guidance lessons are possible.

Elementary and Primary grade levels. ASCA has an online toolkit for each school level: elementary, middle, and high school. Use the ASCA National Model as your guide (*ASCA National Model - American School Counselor Association (ASCA)*, 2020). Virtual school counseling may require more involvement from the adults at home at the elementary level. Educate the family and students ahead of time to help them understand what to expect from the counseling program and where they fit in. Understand that students at the primary level might not have long attention spans while online.

Consider the amount of time students engage with their teachers online and schedule your services accordingly. Keep your lessons brief, check with the students frequently for understanding, and find ways to keep the engagement interactive. For example, if cameras are on, ask students to raise their hands or some fingers in response to your questions. Permit microphone use under the facilitator's control.

Ask students to respond in the chat area with a letter or number response when you ask for feedback.

Virtual field trips are valuable to connect with students and their families. Students can learn about various careers and jobs through online visits to workplaces, such as a zoo. In addition, many museums and historical sites offer virtual tours of their facilities. Virtual field trips are also valuable touring local middle schools for rising middle school students. Use the ASCA Mindsets & Behaviors to help plan creative online events with the students.

Middle School grade levels. Virtual middle school counselors acknowledge that students are maturing, so offering advanced material that matches their developmental levels is appropriate. Along with physical developmental changes, middle school students are also likely to have technical knowledge, perhaps beyond the counselor's understanding. Use this skillset to engage with the students on an "edutainment" level. For example, utilize Google forms to collect pre and post-test data. Sites such as Padlet and Nearpod allow students to respond with their names or anonymously to prompted discussion questions.

Again, ASCA has a toolkit available for virtual middle school counseling that includes a list of helpful resources (*Virtual Middle School Counseling - American School Counselor Association (ASCA)*, 2020). Included in the *Toolkit* are suggestions for taking face-to-face counseling lessons to virtual.

Middle school counselors can offer virtual field trips to students as a creative way to deliver program components. The ASCA Mindsets & Behaviors are a helpful tool to help guide your options for online trips. Virtual field trips are a fantastic method for offering a Career Day event. Through technology, counselors can introduce students to college campuses, museums, and historical sites. A virtual tour of the local high schools is a great way to alleviate fears about middle and high school transitions. Additionally, consider coordinating with teachers to provide blended opportunities that connect counseling standards with teaching standards.

High School grade levels. High school counseling via online services provides additional opportunities not necessarily developmentally aligned with younger grades. For example, students can directly manage their interactions with the school counselor(s) at the secondary level. So, counselors can set up scheduling resources, such as Calendly and youcanbook.me, so that students can arrange meetings with their counselor.

Students can visit college websites with their counselor through screen sharing options on many platforms, including Zoom and Google Meet. Real-time interaction with college and career websites is an excellent way for a counselor to help the student locate important information. Additionally, screen sharing is a beautiful technique for troubleshooting, such as if a student has trouble logging into a school account. High school counselors can also walk students through state and national assessment scores while sharing and highlighting tools.

High school students commonly focus on post-high school plans. Virtual field trips are helpful when students are making decisions about colleges. An online university tour allows students to see the campus without travel, time, and transportation limitations. Through vocational tours, students can also learn about military options and various job opportunities.

Delivery of the Comprehensive School Counseling Program

School counselors must consider how they provide their services to the stakeholders, staff, families, and students. Respect and follow the school district and building-level protocols regarding the delivery of services, including necessary parent permission slips. Check for approved platforms and programs and ask for administrative permission before utilizing other resources. Use devices provided by the district and avoid using personal devices for school-related work. The district devices are vetted and secured per the district standards.

Develop work hours, like a school day has a start and a finish. Adhere to the work hours with exceptions for emergencies only. Provide emergency resources as part of the voicemail message and an autoreply on emails. School counseling departments should consider scheduling routine meetings for consultations and case reviews. When school counselors work remotely, the option to talk to the counselor(s) in the office next door is not available.

While on calls, video sessions, or lessons, try to use a room separate from other people, regardless of location in a school building or remote setting. Use quality headphones with a microphone so anyone in the vicinity cannot hear what the students share during the interactions. A noise machine near the counseling space can help cover the counselor's voice during sessions.

Prepare the families and students beforehand when there is a transition to or from a virtual setting. Coordinate with the school administration to disseminate information to the families about the change. For example, families need to know where to find contact information, student grades, student schedules, available platforms for coursework, and important school events.

Legal and Ethical Considerations

Information in this chapter is not a substitute for legal advice or legal consultation. Always consult with your leadership, liability insurance company, available legal representatives, and use professional guidelines.

Potter Stewart, Associate Justice of the US Supreme Court, said, "Ethics is knowing the difference between what you have a right to do and what is right to do." School counselors frequently navigate legal and ethical issues. Usually, urgent situations arise, so school counselors must know their obligations and resources (i.e., the governing board). Counselors who provide virtual counseling in their program must ensure their liability insurance covers tele-counseling. Additionally, and perhaps most importantly, consult with school leadership and the district lawyers when necessary. ASCA published *Ethical Standards for School Counselors* (Cook et al., Adopted 1984, revised 1992, 1998, 2004, and 2010, 2016) as a resource for school counselors. Section A.5.d. states:

Do not use personal social media, email accounts, or personal texts to interact with students unless specifically encouraged and sanctioned by the school district. School counselors adhere to professional boundaries and legal, ethical, and school district guidelines when using technology with students, parents/guardians, or school staff. The technology utilized, including, but not limited to, social networking sites or apps, should be endorsed by the school district and used for professional communication and the distribution of vital information.

Section A.5.d. clearly outlines the proper usage of devices and online resources. Section A.15.a-f. addresses virtual/distance counseling. This section states:
School counselors:

1. Adhere to the same ethical guidelines in a virtual/distance setting as school counselors in face-to-face settings.
2. Recognize and acknowledge the challenges and limitations of virtual/distance school counseling.
3. Implement procedures for students to follow in emergency and non-emergency situations when the school counselor is unavailable.
4. Recognize and mitigate the limitation of virtual/distance school counseling confidentiality, including unintended viewers or recipients.
5. Inform both the student and parent/guardian of the benefits and limitations of virtual/distance counseling.
6. Educate students on participating in the electronic school counseling relationship to minimize and prevent potential misunderstandings due to lack of verbal cues and inability to read body language or other visual cues that provide contextual meaning to the school counseling process and school counseling relationship.

FERPA or HIPAA

A common source of confusion among school counselors is whether they follow the Family Education Rights & Privacy Act of 1974 (FERPA) or the Health Insurance Portability and Accountability Act of 1996 (HIPAA). School counselors should know the privacy policies of their students' platforms. Do not use a tool, device, or platform without district approval. School counselors are advocates, so notify school leaders of a potentially harmful resource, including privacy protection concerns.

ASCA published a helpful article that outlines the FERPA vs. HIPAA debate (*HIPAA or FERPA or Not - American School Counselor Association (ASCA)*, 2021). In addition, the Centers for Disease Control and Prevention (CDC) developed an infographic illustrating the differences between FERPA and HIPAA (*Health Information & Privacy*, 2021). The image contains text that explains what each of the Acts is, who must comply, and the information protected by each Act. Generally, schools that receive federal funds follow FERPA guidelines. HIPAA applies to school counselors in settings where the counselor bills for services. The best practice is understanding the differences and adhering to the guidelines.

Special Considerations

Brick-and-mortar schools serve students with Individualized Education Plans (IEP) and 504 Plans. Virtual schools can offer the same services, although the modifications and accommodations may appear different from brick-and-mortar schools. For example, the total of "Frequent rest breaks" might fall on the individuals working at home with the student rather than the school staff. Coordination between counseling and special education departments is the most appropriate way to provide the best support for students with IEPs and 504 plans.

Virtual school counseling requires counseling skills in addition to technology skills. Counselors should engage in professional development regularly to stay up to date on the most recent trends, technology, and issues facing students they serve. Seeking quality training from credible sources is crucial. If the school district does not offer training opportunities, counselors should advocate for a change. Ultimately, it is the counselor's responsibility to participate in appropriate training.

Limitations

Virtual school counseling is not without limitations. The modality itself may hinder anyone, including the virtual school counselor and student, who is not skilled with technology-based tools. Virtual school counselors should engage in systematic professional development related to virtual school counseling to circumvent this potential issue. Additionally, virtual school counselors should identify or provide orientation and training resources to students and families entering virtual school settings. Educating the families on the format during enrollment can prevent issues.

As discussed earlier, limitations exist with legal and ethical issues. There isn't a guaranteed method to ensure the student follows privacy guidelines. For example, a student attending a virtual small group session on identifying emotional triggers might have other people present in their physical space during the meeting. In the brick-and-mortar setting, that is the equivalent of a student inviting a non-student friend into a group setting to listen to group members' disclosures.

Emergent and urgent situations may arise. Additionally, progress for the student is not guaranteed. Virtual school counselors should establish clear crisis response guidelines before providing services. Further, the students and their guardians must be informed of the crisis response guidelines before any situation arises. Lastly, clear boundaries and expectations should be defined between personal and professional usage of all technology, including all software, devices, and applications. Virtual school counselors must understand and respect the difference between related communication and personal interactions. Virtual school counselors must ensure that their technological resources are not accessible to anyone other than school-district approved individuals.

CONCLUSION

Virtual, distance, and online learning are not new formats for educating students. In this chapter, we learned that distance learning started in the 1700s. Remote learning progressed according to the needs of communities and the available technological tools. However, there is still debate about the effectiveness of online learning compared to brick-and-mortar settings. In 2001, Clark published a study of computer-based education programs that assessed the value of technology in educational settings. According to Clark, computers are the medium that provides instruction to students; computers are not why students learn (Clark, 2001). Clark believes that technology is not a replacement for education; it is a tool meant to deliver services. Conversely, a similar study by Kozma concluded that computers are necessary to create simulated real-life connections to learners (Kozma, 2001). Kozma stated that the medium used for teaching information does influence learning.

Virtual school counseling is a valuable trauma-informed practice. The Covid-19 pandemic forced many schools to utilize virtual learning while other districts offered online education before the health crisis. Covid-19 highlighted concerns related to safety, health, and protection. For some individuals, this danger initiated new feelings of grief and loss (*Trauma-Informed School Strategies during COVID-19*, n.d.). For others, the pandemic reignited preexisting trauma. A trauma-informed approach to school counseling is a responsive and valuable method for providing a comprehensive school counseling program.

As technology advances and becomes more accessible, the learning opportunities potentially grow. Flexibility and a willingness to learn how to integrate online tools is perhaps the best way to meet the needs of students. Of course, the future is unpredictable, but historical trends inform us about potential paths. School counselors in virtual settings provide comprehensive school counseling services to students. The delivery model may differ between schools and districts, such as a full-time virtual or a blended model. Fortunately, school counselors have pioneers in virtual school counseling as guides. Additionally, professional organizations, such as the American School Counselor Association (ASCA), provide excellent virtual school counseling tools and resources for reference.

REFERENCES

ASCA Ethical Standards for School Counselors - American School Counselor Association (ASCA). (2020). https://schoolcounselor.org/About-School-Counseling/Ethical-Legal-Responsibilities/ASCA-Ethical-Standards-for-School-Counselors-(1)?sso=30ba5b4f-cab3-4168-b136-8f1ecad5c7aa

ASCA National Model - American School Counselor Association (ASCA). (2020). https://www.schoolcounselor.org/About-School-Counseling/ASCA-National-Model-for-School-Counseling-Programs

Barbour, M. (n.d.). *Are Virtual Schools More Cost-Effective Compared to Traditional, Brick-and-Mortar Schools?* Retrieved September 11, 2021, from https://digitalcommons.sacredheart.edu/cgi/viewcontent.cgi?article=1103&context=ced_fac

Bergmann, H. (2001). "The Silent University": The Society to Encourage Studies at Home, 1873-1897. *The New England Quarterly*, *74*(3), 447–477. doi:10.2307/3185427

Build Trauma-Informed Practices. (2021). https://www.ascaschoolcounselor-digital.org/ascaschoolcounselor/march_april_2021/MobilePagedArticle.action?articleId=1666564#articleId1666564

Clark, R. E. (2001). A summary of disagreements with the 'mere vehicles' argument. In R. E. Clark (Ed.), *Learning from media: Arguments, analysis, and evidence* (pp. 125–136). Information Age Publishing.

Clark, T. (2021). *Virtual Schools: Trends and Issues. A Study of Virtual Schools in the United States.* http://www.dlrn.org/virtualstudy.pdf. https://eric.ed.gov/?id=ED462923

College, S., & Kentnor, H. (2015). Digital Commons @ DU Distance Education and the Evolution of Online Learning in the United States. *Curriculum and Teaching Dialogue, 17*. https://digitalcommons.du.edu/cgi/viewcontent.cgi?article=1026&context=law_facpub

Cook, J., Rock, W., Steele, T., & Stone, C. (2016). *Ethical Considerations in Virtual School Counseling*. Retrieved October 5, 2021, from https://admin.schoolcounselor.org/getmedia/bf746827-db38-421f-addf-6ffb7e8b52b7/Ethics-and-Virtual-School-Counseling.pdf

COVID-19 Resources - American School Counselor Association (ASCA). (2020). https://www.schoolcounselor.org/Publications-Research/Publications/Free-ASCA-Resources/COVID-19-Resources

Current RAMP Schools - American School Counselor Association (ASCA). (2020). https://www.schoolcounselor.org/Recognition/RAMP/Current-RAMP-Schools?sso=6f7294ff-dc72-49e5-b53b-98e9e48f7925

Ethical Considerations: School Counseling in a Virtual Setting (Part 1). (2020). *American School Counselor Association*. https://videos.schoolcounselor.org/ethics-virtual-school-counseling

Felder, B. (2018, January 10). *Bullying most common reason students choose virtual schools*. Oklahoman.com; Oklahoman. https://www.oklahoman.com/article/5578967/bullying-most-common-reason-students-choose-virtual-schools

FERPA and Virtual Learning | Protecting Student Privacy. (2020). https://studentprivacy.ed.gov/resources/ferpa-and-virtual-learning

First virtual school in Mass. opens Thursday. (2021). http://archive.boston.com/news/education/k_12/articles/2010/08/31/first_virtual_school_in_mass_opens_thursday/

GysbersN. (n.d.). https://www.schoolcounselor.org/getmedia/52aaab9f-39ae-4fd0-8387-1d9c10b9ccb8/History-of-School-Counseling.pdf

Health Information & Privacy. (2021). https://www.cdc.gov/phlp/publications/topic/healthinformationprivacy.html

HIPAA or FERPA or Not - American School Counselor Association (ASCA). (2021). https://www.schoolcounselor.org/Magazines/July-August-2010/HIPAA-or-FERPA-or-Not

Issue Brief: Multi-Tier System of Supports/Response to Intervention - NCLD. (2021, November 23). *NCLD*. https://www.ncld.org/get-involved/understand-the-issues/multi-tier-system-of-supports-response-to-intervention/

K–12 Student Digital Divide Much Larger Than Previously Estimated and Affects Teachers, Too, New Analysis Shows | Common Sense Media. (2020). https://www.commonsensemedia.org/about-us/news/press-releases/k-12-student-digital-divide-much-larger-than-previously-estimated-and

Kolek, T. (2020, October 22). *6 Ethical Considerations for Virtual School Counseling: Region 13's Blog*. Region 13'S Blog. https://blog.esc13.net/6-ethical-considerations-for-virtual-school-counseling/

Kozma, R. B. (2001). Counterpoint theory of 'learning with media. In R. E. Clark (Ed.), *Learning from media: Arguments, analysis, and evidence* (pp. 137–178). Information Age Publishing Inc.

Long, C. (2020). *One-Quarter of U.S. Students Do not Have What They Need for Online Learning*. https://www.nea.org/advocating-for-change/new-from-nea/one-quarter-us-students-dont-have-what-they-need-online-learning

Monroy-Fraustro, D., Maldonado-Castellanos, I., Aboites-Molina, M., Rodríguez, S., Sueiras, P., Altamirano-Bustamante, N. F., de Hoyos-Bermea, A., & Altamirano-Bustamante, M. M. (2021). Bibliotherapy as a Non-pharmaceutical Intervention to Enhance Mental Health in Response to the COVID-19 Pandemic: A Mixed-Methods Systematic Review and Bioethical Meta-Analysis. *Frontiers in Public Health*, *9*, 629872. Advance online publication. doi:10.3389/fpubh.2021.629872 PMID:33796496

National Center for Education Statistics. (2019). *Student reports of bullying: Results from the 2017 school crime supplement to the national crime victimization survey*. https://nces.ed.gov/pubs2019/2019054.pdf

National Education Association. (2020). *NEA Policy Statement on Digital Learning*. https://www.nea.org/advocating-for-change/new-from-nea/nea-policy-statement-digital-learning

National Education Association. (2020). *The Digital Divide and Homework Gap in Your State*. NEA. Nea.org. https://www.nea.org/resource-library/digital-divide-and-homework-gap-your-state

National Education Policy Center. (2019). *Virtual Schools in the U.S. in 2019*. http://nepc.colorado.edu/publication/virtual-schools-annual-2019

New Analysis Shows Students of Color Far More Likely to Be Cut off from Online Learning. (2020). *Alliance for Excellent Education.* https://all4ed.org/press/new-analysis-shows-students-of-color-far-more-likely-to-be-cut-off-from-online-learning/

Online Schools Are Here to Stay, Even After the Pandemic. (2021). *The New York Times.* https://www.nytimes.com/2021/04/11/technology/remote-learning-online-school.html

Osborn, D. S., Peterson, G. W., & Hale, R. R. (2014). Virtual School Counseling. *Professional School Counseling, 18*(1). https://doi.org/doi:10.1177/2156759x0001800114

Pandey, E. (2021, September 22). *Charter schools boomed during the pandemic.* NewsBreak; Axios. https://www.newsbreak.com/news/2380033548629/charter-schools-boomed-during-the-pandemic

Pape, S. J., & Prosser, S. K. (2018). Barriers to technology implementation in community college mathematics classrooms. *Journal of Computing in Higher Education*, *30*(3), 620–636. doi:10.100712528-018-9195-z

Paykamian, B. (2021, March 24). *Virtual Schools to Be Increasingly Common After COVID-19.* GovTech. https://www.govtech.com/education/k-12/virtual-schools-to-be-increasingly-common-after-covid-19.html

Protecting Student Privacy While Using Online Educational Services: Model Terms of Service. Protecting Student Privacy. (2016). https://studentprivacy.ed.gov/resources/protecting-student-privacy-while-using-online-educational-services-model-terms-service

Sanchez-Gomez, M., Giorgi, G., Finstad, G. L., Urbini, F., Foti, G., Mucci, N., Zaffina, S., & León-Perez, J. M. (2021). COVID-19 Pandemic as a Traumatic Event and Its Associations with Fear and Mental Health: A Cognitive-Activation Approach. *International Journal of Environmental Research and Public Health*, *18*(14), 7422. doi:10.3390/ijerph18147422 PMID:34299873

State of the Profession 2020 ascaresearch report. (n.d.). https://www.schoolcounselor.org/getmedia/bb23299b-678d-4bce-8863-cfcb55f7df87/2020-State-of-the-Profession.pdf

Steele, T. M., Jacokes, D. E., & Stone, C. B. (2014). An Examination Of The Role Of Online Technology In School Counseling. *Professional School Counseling*, *18*(1), 125–135. doi:10.1177/2156759X0001800118

Student Discipline in a Virtual Classroom Legal or Board Policy Connection. (n.d.). Retrieved September 26, 2021, from http://thecommons.dpsk12.org/cms/lib/CO01900837/Centricity/Domain/52/SOP%20for%20Student%20Discipline%20in%20a%20Virtual%20Classroom.pdf

Technology in Schools. (2022). *National Center for Education Statistics.* https://nces.ed.gov/pubs2003/tech_schools/chapter4.asp

The Case for Michigan's Online Learning Mandate -- THE Journal. (2011). *THE Journal.* https://thejournal.com/articles/2007/01/24/the-case-for-michigans-online-learning-mandate.aspx

The History of Distance Learning: An Online Education Timeline. (2021, June 18). *World Wide Learn.* https://www.worldwidelearn.com/articles/history-of-distance-learning/

The History Of K-12 Online Education??? (2010, February). *Virtual School Meanderings.* https://virtualschooling.wordpress.com/2010/02/01/the-history-of-k-12-online-education/

The NCES Fast Facts Tool provides quick answers to many education questions (National Center for Education Statistics). (2021). *National Center for Education Statistics.* https://nces.ed.gov/fastfacts/display.asp?id=372

The Relationship Between School Attendance and Health. (2016, September). *The Relationship Between School Attendance and Health.* RWJF. https://www.rwjf.org/en/library/research/2016/09/the-relationship-between-school-attendance-and-health.html

The School Counselor and Students with Disabilities - American School Counselor Association (ASCA). (2020). https://schoolcounselor.org/Standards-Positions/Position-Statements/ASCA-Position-Statements/The-School-Counselor-and-Students-with-Disabilities

The School Counselor and Virtual School Counseling - American School Counselor Association (ASCA). (2020). https://www.schoolcounselor.org/Standards-Positions/Position-Statements/ASCA-Position-Statements/The-School-Counselor-and-Virtual-School-Counseling

Trauma-Informed School Strategies during COVID-19. (n.d.). https://www.nctsn.org/sites/default/files/resources/resource-guide/trauma_informed_school_strategies_during_covid-19.pdf

Virtual Elementary School Counseling - American School Counselor Association (ASCA). (2020). https://www.schoolcounselor.org/Publications-Research/Publications/Free-ASCA-Resources/COVID-19-Resources/Virtual-Elementary-School-Counseling

Virtual High School Counseling - American School Counselor Association (ASCA). (2020). https://www.schoolcounselor.org/Publications-Research/Publications/Free-ASCA-Resources/COVID-19-Resources/Virtual-High-School-Counseling

Voting with Their Feet: A State-level Analysis of Public Charter School and District Public School Enrollment Trends. (2021, September 22). *National Alliance for Public Charter Schools*. https://www.publiccharters.org/our-work/publications/voting-their-feet-state-level-analysis-public-charter-school-and-district

What is MTSS? (2019, February 27). *PBIS Rewards*. https://www.pbisrewards.com/blog/what-is-mtss/

Chapter 7
Gifted and Talented:
Not Always a Gift

Stacey L. Guthrie
Capella University, USA

Corey L. Gurskyj
Knox County Schools, USA

ABSTRACT

In this chapter, the authors will explore the basics of being gifted and talented: what it means, presents, and how best to support. Gifted and talented is associated as a disability and is best served under special education resources. Serving this community requires plans that will encourage and support furthering this exceptional ability. Being gifted does not protect one from experiencing trauma. The giftedness poses a challenge when processing the traumatic event. There is very little research with the combination of gifted and trauma, so more will be discussed to provide this information on how gifted children and adolescents experience trauma and cope. Developing a strong supportive relationship to motivate towards change and healing along with other tools and techniques are discussed for working with the gifted population, wrapping up with a fictional case study as an example.

INTRODUCTION

For an identified gifted and talented student, many things may prove to not be as fortuitous as it sounds. Gifted and Talented students, often called GT kids, are not immune to traumatic stress. The impact of the traumatic stress could potentially lead to traumatization. These gifted individuals excel in their ability to think, reason

DOI: 10.4018/978-1-7998-9785-9.ch007

and judge, making it necessary for them to receive special education services and support to be able to fully develop their potential and talents (Davidson Institute, 2021). Being gifted presents differently and is unique to each individual. There are some common denominators or qualities observed, but in gifted kids, it is best to not assume or group together but support each person uniquely especially when dealing with trauma.

School counselors tend to focus their attention on students who are failing academically, and gifted students are often overlooked until problems escalate (Burke, 2009). It is important to note that gifted students often are reluctant to ask for help and their pain often is invisible to adults (Peterson, 2006). Gifted children have strong critical thinking skills, and particularly the profoundly gifted, are prone to higher levels of anxieties, heightened sensitivities, suicidal tendencies, and depression (Peterson, 2006).

Gifted students possess unique attributes that shape their personalities. These attributes also contribute to their social-emotional characteristics. These personality traits may complicate their response to a trauma, encompassing a wide span of potential concerns ranging from excessive anxiety and depression to profound guilt (Burke, 2009). Emotional sensitivity generally accompanies high cognitive abilities as found in many gifted children (Hébert & Sergent, 2005). Gifted children may understand at a higher level; however, a disparity between what the child understands mentally and what can be managed emotionally should be considered as a child is dealing with trauma.

Gifted children with this increased understanding beyond their years, may struggle with intensified emotions related to trauma (Burke, 2009). With an influx of information and the ease of media, it is common for children to witness calamities across the world leading gifted students to ask the tough questions of life. Depression may accompany a child's ability to question existential issues and theological concerns that can be psychologically overwhelming (Peterson, 2006). Having a greater awareness and understanding potentially affects the gifted student more adversely coupled with the intensity of their social-emotional characteristics can complicate their response to trauma. Dabrowski theorized that gifted individuals with high degrees of emotional intensity would suffer during times of crisis/trauma based upon this intensity, which according to Dabrowski's Theory of Positive Disintegration, is a powerful response to sensory stimuli manifested as abundant physical, sensual, creative, intellectual, and emotional energy (Tiesco, 2007; Silverman, 2000). Times of stress and trauma may exacerbate these emotions, leaving the gifted student feeling particularly vulnerable (Peterson, 2006).

WHAT IS GIFTED AND TALENTED?

Being gifted involves exceptionality with intellectual characteristics specifically, but not limited to academia, creativity, leadership, and artistic capabilities (Parritz and Troy, 2018). GT students pick up new skills with ease. They learn new information quickly and easily. They excel in several, if not most, areas of their lives. Some shine in the classroom setting while some display high curiosity and creativity. Some show strengths in their leadership capabilities while some show strengths in artistic capabilities. However, being gifted can be incredibly difficult and can come with a variety of complications, struggles, and issues that are rarely identified or addressed (Arky, 2021). Therefore, gifted students fall under the Special Education umbrella. Not only are GT kids misunderstood, but many are also stuck in education systems that do not know how to challenge and teach them (Green, 2021). When GT students are not challenged at school, they may become disengaged. They may act out or withdraw altogether. They may bully or be bullied. Some of these kids become marginalized to the point where they are at risk for mental health concerns. In high school or post-secondary education, they may even drop out (Green, 2021).

It is against the Individuals with Disabilities Education Act (IDEA) to not provide accommodations and/or modifications for students with diagnosed learning styles and/or disabilities, yet it does happen to gifted students. When there is no support plan in place, it becomes evident that a discrepancy in the performance manifests. GT students learn rapidly; however, they are expected to sit still and learn nothing more than what their peers can master. Such practice simply does not meet their educational needs. Thus, when they are offered specialized instruction and individualized related services, a written legal document called an Individualized Educational Plan (IEP) attends to those needs. Evidence has shown that GT students are not as frequently served by IEPs and the necessity is just as needed for GT students as it is for all students with disabilities (Kamenetz, 2015).

For kids with neurological or learning disabilities also known as "twice exceptional" (2e), giftedness may be harder to spot. Intelligence is often masked by fundamental cognitive differences or other behavioral characteristics. Potential misdiagnosis is a major concern in gifted kids. A 2e student could struggle in certain areas of the gifted program or not be challenged in the special education program. There needs to be a balance between the two services. Both situations could cause frustration leading to anxiety, depression, a lack of self-esteem, and/or emotional dysregulation (Arky, 2021). Finding balance can prevent this.

Although intellectually gifted students are the most acknowledged and identified, there are other domains of giftedness. The creative characteristics of a GT student may include inventiveness, a keen sense of humor, the ability for fantasy, intuitiveness, flexibility, self-acceptance (without concern for social norms), or an aesthetic or moral commitment to self-selected work. They also utilize abstract, complex, logical, and insightful thinking. These creative students can be seen as risk-takers, defiant, troublemakers, indecisive, and independent. A creative GT student may not be artistically inclined. Artistically gifted students typically exhibit a keen sense of creativity. They are risk-takers who employ innovative methods, use interesting materials, and test artistic boundaries. Often, artistic GT students have a desire to express themselves through their art, and they see their art as an extension of themselves (Brajcic, Kuscevic, Lazeta, 2020).

Several states include the domain of leadership in their definition of children who are gifted and talented. Such students who exhibit high levels of leadership need the opportunity to hone and develop their leadership skills. Real leadership is not taking control and doing all the work but setting a goal and devising a plan to work with others in reaching it. Leadership is about making things happen (Roberts, 2004). All children who are identified as gifted intellectually, in creativity, or in the visual and performing arts, would benefit from leadership development.

Most GT students show perfectionistic tendencies. While many people think perfectionism is a benefit. It can inhibit work production and self-esteem. Through implementing a GT student's IEP, or while working on goal setting and developing leadership skills, one thing to look out for is perfectionistic tendencies. Perfectionism is a personality trait. Those who have this trait tend to be very self-critical, unhappy, and suffer from low self-esteem. They can also be lonely or isolated as their critical nature and their rigidity can push others away. Types of perfectionism tendencies include fear of failure, procrastination, focus on results, unrealistic standards, and being overly critical (Scott, 2020). School counselors and educators can support the GT kid with practical steps to turn the negative into positive, build resilience, and develop optimism (Van Gemert, 2017).

It is erroneous to assume GT students' emotional intelligence matches their high IQ. The emotional quotient (EQ) is the level of a person's emotional intelligence representing self-awareness, self-regulation, motivation, empathy, and social skills (Segal, Smith, Robinson, Shubin, 2021). When there is a deficit in EQ, social skills need to be taught to support the GT kid. It is common for GT students to learn in isolation, and it is typical to see a GT student desiring to work alone rather than in a group setting. Both of which do not allow for emotional growth.

EDUCATING SOCIAL AND EMOTIONAL SKILLS

Gifted education programs vary from state to state with some gifted youth not receiving needed services that would enhance and promote their educational opportunities. Services, such as counseling might be included to coordinate and assist with educational settings. In a school setting, a school counselor may need to consult with other health care providers and refer to outside sources when the mental health needs cannot be met within the school setting. Involving family caregivers may take many forms but should be included so that all parties are aligned and all working together for a common outcome (Studer, 2015).

All children need support, modeling, and direct instruction regarding social and emotional skills. Many GT kids need targeted assistance with peer relationships, perfectionism, asynchronous development, situational stressors, and post-secondary planning. Teaching GT students a handful of social skills can reduce the number of negative experiences they may encounter while in school. The phrasing of questions and comments and perspective-taking are skills that are helpful in teaching GT students to navigate the difficult social waters in school and life. With the inability to interact with their peers, educating GT kids on how to reduce social anxiety and manage stress appropriately is another important skill.

One hallmark of giftedness is asynchrony, which is the mismatch between cognitive, emotional, and physical development. Gifted kids often seem out of sync. Their maturity is at odds with their cognitive abilities. This discrepancy can make it hard for a child to fit in. They need support with social and emotional skills because they cannot converse with grade-level peers the same way they can with other gifted students or adults (Mula, Janus, Palomar, 2022). Gifted and talented students are typically accustomed to talking more with adults than with classmates. Their deep interests and complex ways of looking at ideas can put them at a distance from their peer (Green, 2021).

GT students learn from the behavior of adults just like all children do. Whether it is effective coping strategies, non-threatening communication techniques, or how to relax; teachers, school counselors, and parents often become the models who children follow. Teachers, parents, and/or school counselors can have a significant impact on the minds of gifted children. An initiative-taking counseling program can be invaluable to GT students. Learning about oneself and how to effectively relate to others in school can positively affect the psychological development of gifted students. When this occurs, students are less anxious and more social.

A GT student may lack tolerance, so this is critical to emphasize all people have unique qualities such as intelligence, athleticism, creativity, and/or social skills. Having group work allows a GT student to become more rounded and balanced. In reaching GT students, a counselor/educator can focus on motivating, appealing to a student's leadership abilities by promoting teamwork, and instructing them to perform at their personal best. Motivation is at the heart of learning and taking the time to build a relationship can support the desire to learn and have fun while doing it. Being placed in group work may subject a GT kid to bullying, so it is important to not victimize or retraumatize if the GT student has experienced this in the past.

Therefore, it is critical that the counselor/educator be strategic when involving the student in teamwork.

TRAUMA

As previous chapters have indicated, crises and traumas are experienced by many people, and Gifted and Talented students are no exception. Trauma has been described as markedly distressing, perceived as threatening to life or physical integrity, and associated with feelings of helplessness, fear, horror, and/or disgust (Greenwald, 2005). Many children and adolescents encounter stress in some form or fashion, but for GT students, there are additional challenges that complicate matters (Studer, 2015). When a traumatic event happens, the understanding of the world is questioned. Attempts are made to reduce the ambiguity caused by the imbalance of thoughts. This can prove to be difficult for gifted kids as more questions and deeper thoughts come into play. However, the intellectual ability can help develop strategies for coping with traumatic experiences, make sense of experiences, and learn to self-regulate in response to posttraumatic stress (Peterson, 2014). Despite having high intelligence, there can still be difficulties in thoughts, feelings, and behaviors that may complicate processing and moving through a traumatic experience. Since trauma is based upon a perception, a GT student may not be aware or overly sensitive to the victimization of bullying and isolation (Rhoton, 2013). Certain variables such as previous events, lack of support, personal characteristics, and direct exposure may place some GT kids at a higher risk for a crisis. According to James and Gilliland, a crisis is a situation that happens unexpectedly and overwhelms an individual, preventing the person from coping effectively. Reactions may present differently in individuals as has been previously noted, but these are a few signs that a GT kid is in crisis if having feelings of hopelessness, fear, confusion, nightmares, changes in appetite, and other somatic ailments (James & Gilliland, 2005).

The Adverse Childhood Experiences (ACEs) study posed various questions regarding events that may or may not be perceived to an individual as traumatic. Specific traumas are interpreted uniquely, as extreme mental and emotional intensity bring on complexity for many questions involving the "unanswerable why" of trauma. Traumatic events, whether anticipated or unexpected, serve as a critical juncture in how one views the world and the self as it disrupts the understanding of self and others (Studer, 2015). Depression may be a result of the inability to find answers and cope effectively. When one experiences loneliness and lacks connections with others, it puts one at a greater risk to ponder one's purpose in life, potentially leading to an existential crisis or depression (Webb, 2020). This precipitates suicidal thoughts or ideation (Flom & Hansen, 2006). For some gifted students, isolation is already part of normalcy, so when trauma is experienced, they are more susceptible.

"Gifted Trauma" is a new term coined to describe how a gifted person may feel as they relate with others in their world. "Gifted trauma" is the trauma that gifted people can experience if they feel ridiculed, ignored, rejected, pressured to conform, or misunderstood (Sallin & Eglinton, 2015). Additional emotions such as anxiety can exacerbate traumatic situations, creating more difficulties for the gifted population. Perceived high expectations from self and others could contribute to perfectionistic tendencies. As such, more emotional assistance is needed.

Gifted students obtain a sense of being different from peers. When comments are made about intellectual ability, a gifted student could internalize and have that added to the sense of self, manifesting positively or negatively (Peterson, 2014). A study by McQueen, Reynolds, and Rinn (2011) reported that adolescents who were gifted saw classmates as less supportive than older peers or adults. Lacking this connection with peers introduces a sense of not belonging. When anyone is set apart, it subjects the individual to potential bullying or isolation. Gifted people's interpretations in comparison to other non-gifted individuals may become conflicted, creating a greater misunderstanding with more feelings of seclusion. GT students begin to feel like an outsider and discover quickly they do not think like other peers. A GT kid will ponder deeper meanings to life and are typically met with confused looks and vague responses. These situations leave gifted individuals feeling alone.

When supporting a GT kid who has been traumatized, leaving them alone to process on their own might create a cognitive distortion. Some common cognitive distortions are engaging in catastrophic thinking, discounting the positive, emotional reasoning, jumping to conclusions, overgeneralization, personalization, and polarized thinking (Ackerman, 2021). It has been shown to be beneficial to feel a part of a whole and not alone when trauma arises. Having the social skills to be a part of a team is important for the healing process. It will be hard for them to see at this juncture, "I can learn from others. I do not have to know everything or be the leader in this regard." Increasing the ability to self-reflect, interpret, find meaning, and articulate own thoughts are goals for these groups.

Gifted students must cope with a number of problems. Shame is another feeling often experienced by GT kids. Students who are gifted place high expectations on themselves and feel pressure implicitly and explicitly imposed by themselves and others for high achievement. They feel obligated to achieve excellence in all things which can lead to perfectionism tendencies. If not successful, guilt and shame follow. When assumptions are made by themselves and others for the gifted individual regarding how they should manage certain circumstances, disappointment is felt from the obligation to perform a set way as expected by someone who is gifted. These same assumptions on how a gifted person should perform are experienced when dealing with trauma as well. Expectations are high as they see themselves as more capable than their peers, leaving GT students to feel as if they should not be having any difficulties. Students who are gifted need ongoing support and access to adult role models. This support reassures the student that the thoughts and pressure to perform may be too high and unrealistic to have all the time (Sallin & Eglinton, 2015).

THE THERAPEUTIC RELATIONSHIP

As mentioned previously, there are indisputable reasons for creating healthy relationships with gifted individuals. The gifted student is often alone and feels isolated. When trauma happens, if there is not a strong support system in place, the trauma may develop into further complications. Having a therapeutic relationship in place can prevent a situation from worsening.

The essentials of counseling begin with establishing a trusting foundational relationship and forming relationships with gifted and talented students is no different. It may prove to be more challenging for school counselors/educators to develop relationships with gifted and talented kids due to the asynchronous development. When interacting with GT students, their maturity level is often expected to match their cognitive level which oftentimes is not the case (Kesner, 2005). The barriers faced in developing a healthy relationship need to be addressed and overcome so when a support system is needed, one is in place.

The right fit is extremely important for the counselor/educator and gifted student. If it is not, then solutions for finding a better arrangement prove essential. Challenging behaviors are exhibited at times by the GT kid which could potentially trigger a reaction in the counselor/educator. A feeling of inadequacy may develop knowing the student's IQ may be higher than the school counselors/educators.

A barrier to establishing a trusting relationship is the intelligence factor that might create a dynamic, making it hard to connect. Gifted individuals sometimes have difficulties communicating and expressing thoughts and feelings on a level understood by others. Confusion may take place when gifted individuals are raised, taught, or counseled by non-gifted individuals. GT kids may overthink situations, creating defensive walls. They may remember slights and misconceive intentions. However, GT students can grow and flourish with appropriate social mirroring, learning to fit in with their peers. Yet conversely without social mirroring, not fitting in may cause the GT student to underperform.

With these obstacles, the counselor/educator should seek consultation and supervision to make sure the therapeutic relationship is not in jeopardy. Competent school counselors and educators should be aware of their own values, biases, preconceived notions, and limitations to work toward understanding the student's worldview to provide a foundational groundwork that is needed for this relationship (Henderson & Thompson, 2016).

The therapeutic relationship is crucial for communicating when problems arise, and a needed listener is required. Some GT students lack communication skills and find it challenging to express how they are feeling. Feelings get minimalized, for thoughts usually dictate their intentions. When trauma or victimization enters the picture, an emotional hijacking occurs and thinking is abandoned (Nash, 2015). GT kids may not know what this experience even feels like, so having the relationship in place can safely create a place of comfort for these emotions to be broached.

Qualities of a healthy therapeutic relationship will resemble a gifted student feeling at ease to discuss presenting concerns and actively participate in the conversation. A trusting relationship will equally demonstrate respect for one another. Motivation to change and find a resolution will be seen and growth will happen.

MOTIVATION

A counselor/educator needs to find the right combination to appeal to and motivate further learning. Motivation, both intrinsic and extrinsic, is a key factor in the success of all students, especially GT ones. When GT student is motivated, they find value in their school experience. The motivated GT kid believes what they are doing will produce beneficial outcomes. They trust in their environment and expect to be successful, thus the instruction needs to be purposeful, intentional, and thorough. Most GT students become enthralled by the details, leaving room to fully explore and expand on a topic. When trauma has occurred in a GT kid's life, finding motivation is a great catalyst to move through the trauma and make meaning of it (Simmen-Janevska, Brandstatter & Maercker, 2012).

But what if a GT student is not motivated? This can come across as underachievement, which is frustrating for the parents, teachers, and school counselors because the student can be successful with some effort. Before settling on underachievement and motivational problems, the student should be screened for a wide variety of physical, emotional, and mental difficulties first. Once settled upon motivation as the presenting concern, strategies should be implemented.

Increasing motivation can take some time to develop. Here are five strategies that are proven to show results. The first one is promoting a growth mindset over a fixed one. There are many resources available on this topic. As stated earlier in this chapter, developing a meaningful and respectful relationship with students is key. Thus, the second strategy is building a firm relationship. If the GT student feels respected and valued, reciprocity is shown to the teacher/counselor by completing the task or activity assigned. The third strategy is growing a community of learners in the classroom or in a small group counseling setting. Having clear procedures and roles created sets the stage for a successful environment for all learners. Establishing high expectations and clear goals is the fourth strategy. The final strategy is modeling and being inspirational. There are many great children's books and videos that tie into inspiration and motivation that can be shared with GT students. These five strategies take time to develop and need nurturing throughout the school year and/or counseling goal cycle (Bainbridge, 2020). Utilizing these strategies with a GT student who has experienced trauma would be a great starting point.

There are also some strategies that can be implemented quickly and with ease. Giving a GT student a sense of control is beneficial to increase motivation, such as allowing choice as much as possible. Another strategy is offering varied experiences. Positive competition can also help with motivation for some. Another strategy to support extrinsic motivation is offering rewards. Everyone likes to be rewarded; however, considerations are needed around the personalities of the individual to determine appropriate rewards. Along the lines of rewards is praise. Encouragement is a great form of motivation. Giving praise for a job well done along with sharing exemplary work can go a long way. Making goals high but attainable is crucial. Then, tracking the progress and encouraging self-reflection are the next steps. The above-mentioned strategies can support a GT kid who is working through a trauma.

The Stages of Change model can support a counselor/educator in determining where the GT student is with readiness to move through the trauma (LaMorte, 2019). Meeting the student where they are is the first step in supporting the change. Once the realization happens that change is needed, steps can be taken to move the GT kid through processing the trauma. Seeing the reward in overcoming and finding resilience and growth from the trauma continues to motivate and inspire further changes. Goal setting is necessary to continue the work toward healing.

At the end of the day, a GT student needs to be able to generate intrinsic motivation. Helping students find their own personal reasons for doing classwork, therapy session work, and/or any other activity, whether because they find the material interesting, want to improve and grow, want to go to college, or just love to learn, is one of the most powerful gifts given.

TOOLS AND TECHNIQUES FOR SUPPORT

Counseling has been shown to be helpful in improving mental health and quality of life. It is never easy to seek help when abuse or trauma occurs. As a counselor, the objective is to support the presenting concern for resolution and provide a hands-on learning experience, enabling the GT student to discover or learn coping skills for future situations. If GT students experience an issue, it is typical behavior for them to handle problems on their own, so in the same manner, a crisis or trauma may be dealt with similarly. This is where knowing your GT students and what typical behaviors look like can assist with assessing if something might be troubling them. Out of the normal performance, a manifestation of behavior or lack of engagement might be observed.

To pinpoint and narrow down problematic behaviors, a functional behavioral assessment (FBA) might be used. The FBA is used to understand the purpose of the behavior and guide toward appropriate intervention. Campbell (2003) conducted studies to substantiate the efficacy of functional behavior assessments and found using the FBA guided the reduction of problem behaviors. It is important to note that the FBA includes positive behavior support for effectiveness (Prout & Fedewa, 2015). Once the assessment is complete and has identified specific presenting concerns, it is time to establish strategies to target and increase understanding of the problem and implement healthy coping skills.

From here, a counselor may need to intervene to provide crisis counseling and trust-rebuilding strategies to support and create resiliency. A counseling intervention is most effective if the GT student can be seen whenever and however often as needed. This may not be the easiest or most feasible for the counselor, but it is what is best for the student. School counselors are expected to assist with supporting equilibrium or helping the GT kid in returning to a state of balance in thoughts, feelings, and behaviors (Studer, 2015). The end goal is to resolve the crisis and begin a new normal with freshly acquired coping skills known as post-traumatic growth (Parritz & Troy, 2018). Post-traumatic growth can occur from an unfortunate trauma if supportive people are there to encourage healthy processing of the event. When dealing with a crisis, therapeutic strategies embedded within the session may include grounding and relaxation techniques. These approaches can be taught to serve as a self-monitoring approach as well.

Cognitive techniques have been found effective to manage distress and replace irrational thoughts. Working with gifted individuals may require a counselor to tailor the approach to include their strengths and weaknesses. Best practices in therapy include the individual being part of creating and setting the goals. Having the GT student's viewpoint shared will allow the counselor to interpret and be flexible in the delivery of therapy and individually develop treatment approaches (Prout & Fedewa, 2015).

Restructuring negative thoughts using social stories, cognitive scripts, role-playing, and visualization can decrease discouraging feelings and problematic behaviors. Scaling is another tool that has been a useful technique for measuring how a student is doing in any given session. Scaling is used to express how problematic a situation is by rating on a scale. For example, on a scale from 1-10, with ten being the best and one being the worst, how are you feeling today? (Henderson & Thompson, 2016).

Considering loneliness and isolation are common emotions felt by gifted individuals, group work would be useful. It is important to establish the right fit and consider the GT kids functioning within a small group setting. The skills learned within a small group are transferred to a larger social setting. Group work or group therapy performed by school counselors has proven to be beneficial when the goal of teaching social skills is the topic to create better connections with same-age peers (Prout & Fedewa, 2015).

Understanding that gifted children can be emotionally vulnerable is critical to their healing process (Burke, 2009). It is important to tailor a strategy to match the developmental level of a student to decide what intervention may work best. Societal pressures may influence how gifted boys and girls respond to trauma intervention (Burke, 2009). For example, during challenging times, gifted girls are more likely to want support-seeking strategies over boys (Preuss & Debrow, 2004). Sorting issues in a problem-solution format may be most effective to support boys' needs (Burke, 2009).

Culture plays an influential role in how students may react to a traumatic event. It is important to realize that gifted children come from various backgrounds, and school counselors will want to be sensitive to the diversity of the individual preferences (Rosenblatt, 2008). Regardless of gender or culture, providing a safe environment for children to share concerns is vital to their emotional health. Maintaining routines, allowing for in-depth discussions and questions, and establishing security through supportive adults can help, particularly for the gifted child who may internalize feelings from the trauma (Burke, 2009).

Gifted kids have strong capabilities for solving problems, so giving them the necessary tools to cope with trauma will not only aid them in times of sorrow, but it will also strengthen their resilience for the future (Burke, 2009). Listed are some known strategies to support gifted students in processing intense emotions: Bibliotherapy, Art Therapy/Music Intervention, Journaling/Narrative Therapy, Being in Nature, and Service-Learning Projects.

Bibliotherapy is a creative arts approach by telling a story with a specific purpose for healing. Bibliotherapy can be used as an intervention for anxiety, depression, those struggling with trauma, or those going through grief, a divorce, or other relationship-related challenges (Pehrsson & McMillen, 2007). Because gifted students often are advanced readers and can grasp metaphorical connotations, bibliotherapy is an excellent counseling tool (Silverman, 2000).

Art Therapy/Music Intervention can be especially appealing for gifted students even if they are not identified as creatively gifted. Creating art can aid in one's ability to work through life problems by expressing emotion in which words seem insufficient (Barker, 2006). Music intervention offers similar benefits for trauma by helping to restructure problems while providing an integrated approach to healing (Gallant & Holosko, 2001).

Journaling/Narrative Therapy are both techniques gifted students can explore feelings through writing. Journaling allows students to record events and feelings to process the issues and then analyze their writing for the events in their lives (Burke, 2009). Along with journaling, Narrative Therapy allows the use of imagination to re-write the story of the trauma. The student has a means in which to gain insight as well as control within his or her own life and ending the story positively or however they choose (Thomas & Ray, 2006).

Having a safe place outside for children to explore in nature reconnects a child to the world and promotes healing when they are dealing with trauma. School counselors can help students strengthen their bond with the natural world by giving access to gardens and animals (Sisk, 2008). Consider taking children for walks outside to connect with the healing power of nature. Exercise can increase an individual's energy level and improve mental health after a trauma (Parachin, 1996).

Implementing service-learning projects encourages a student's focus on others instead of dwelling on their trauma and re-directs towards giving back (Sisk, 2008). Service learning can empower students to contribute to solving societal problems, which can turn into transformative experiences (Terry et al., 2008).

It would be negligent to forget the family caregivers and siblings of a gifted student. It can be challenging raising a gifted child and family members may benefit from counseling separately or together in a family therapy approach (Spirito & Kazak, 2006). School counselors can provide resources and information on support groups to improve communication and form connections.

CASE STUDY (FICTIONAL)

Rylea, a third-grade Caucasian female, was identified as gifted and talented since she was reading on a 12th-grade reading level. Rylea did not understand what this meant. She was pulled out of class to be given extra work with another teacher while still expected to do the classwork she was missing which she considered unfair. She remained in the school's GT pull-out program through fifth grade. In middle and high school, she was placed in advanced classes, taking many AP courses to get college credit. All along, she knew she was smart and pushed herself to continue to excel. She had a reputation for being so smart and once was laughed at by other classmates when she missed a problem.

This led Rylea down the path of experiencing anxiety and fear of failure. Perfectionistic tendencies developed as a way to cope, prevent making mistakes, and eliminate ridicule. Rylea found making connections with others difficult. She thought she would not have anything to talk about so became avoidant and isolated from social events. Negative self-talk allowed Rylea to become a victim of her own thoughts. Others saw her as a loner so never included her in conversations creating further seclusion.

One day when Rylea was in the 10th grade, she experienced major life trauma. Her maternal grandmother who raised her most of her life died unexpectedly. She spent months questioning the death, having angry outbursts at everyone around her, then became severely depressed exploring the whole meaning of even why she was alive. This can be termed as having existential depression. Existential depression is a depression that arises when an individual confronts certain basic issues of existence (Webb, 2011).

Rylea was referred for counseling by her aunt and during sessions asked many questions: If I am so smart, why is my life a wreck? I am feeling depressed because no one gets me. Everyone is expecting me to be better, yet I am not. Why am I able to solve the most difficult math equations, but I have no idea how to resolve this situation?

With the admission of depression, it is important to note that assessing for suicide is the first step in supporting Rylea. In this situation it is important to rule out before next steps. After ruling out potential harm, the school counselor can further move to support Rylea by building a trusting relationship and supporting her.

To support Rylea, the counselor began to build a trusting relationship and support her as she was grappling with the meaning of life. Noting Rylea was not alone was essential and at the same time provided a way to cope with the anger felt by life being unfair and finite. Replacing the fear-producing thoughts and stopping the isolation feelings leading to depression were the next steps in offering support and healthier coping strategies. With the appropriate support being demonstrated by the counselor, showing Rylea was valued and understood, she was able to overcome the trauma and experience some post-traumatic growth.

CONCLUSION

This chapter provided explanations of what it means to be gifted, how gifted individuals experience trauma, and for school counselors, ways to support these exceptional students. The authors explored qualities that are seen as strengths yet also present challenges with being gifted. GT kids need support to promote growth as they continue developing this exceptional talent. It is imperative for students who are gifted to understand and appreciate their uniqueness. A sense of realistic expectations for their own abilities and talents has been identified as a need to acquire while distinguishing the difference between pursuing excellence and pursuing perfectionism.

Despite their advanced IQ, their developmental age is the same as their peers. Social skills are needed to be taught so that healthy relationships can be cultivated. School counselors are important team members for the multidisciplinary team for a gifted student to support social-emotional needs. There are many challenges when working with students who are gifted but once the relationship is established, motivation to make other connections begins.

Working with GT students is quite rewarding. They bring unique abilities and ways of thinking outside of the typical thought process, exploring concepts unseen. When faced with a trauma, these exceptional abilities may go into overdrive, spinning unhealthy thoughts and producing unacceptable behaviors if not guided by caring individuals. Julie Skolnick sums it up nicely in her article "Gifted Does Not (only) Mean Smart" by stating, "Create safe environments for these deep thinkers to think, these intense feelers to feel, and perfectionists to take risks." (Skolnick, 2019). This can be done in the classroom, in small groups, individual counseling sessions, and at home. Everyone deserves to have a strong support system.

REFERENCES

Ackerman, C. (2021, December 6). *Cognitive distortions: When your brain lies to you.* Retrieved November 1, 2021, from https://positivepsychology.com/cognitive-distortions/

Arky, B. (2022, April 8). *Twice-exceptional kids: Both gifted and challenged.* Child Mind Institute. Retrieved November 11, 2021, from https://childmind.org/article/twice-exceptional-kids-both-gifted-and-challenged

Bainbridge, C. (2020, May 7). *10 ways to motivate gifted children.* Verywell Family. Retrieved October 28, 2021, from https://www.verywellfamily.com/ways-to-motivate-gifted-children-1449283

Barker, E. (2006). The artist within. *Natural Health, 36*(10), 98–99.

Brajcic, M., Kuscevic, D., & Lazeta, M. (2020). A comparison between competencies of teachers and students of teacher education in recognizing artistically gifted students. *European Journal of Educational Research, 9*(3), 1327–1336. doi:10.12973/eu-jer.9.3.1327

Burke, A. (2009). Gifted and grieving: Why it is critical to offer differential support to gifted kids during times of loss. *Gifted Child Today Magazine*, *32*(4), 30–37. doi:10.1177/107621750903200409

Campbell, J. M. (2003). Efficacy of behavioral interventions for reducing problem behavior in persons with autism: A quantitative synthesis of single-subject research. *Research in Developmental Disabilities*, *24*(2), 120–138. doi:10.1016/S0891-4222(03)00014-3 PMID:12623082

Clark, B. (2008). *Growing up gifted: Developing the potential of children at home and at school*. Pearson/Merrill Prentice Hall.

Davidson. (2021, July 19). *What is giftedness? Gifted definition & meaning*. Davidson Institute. Retrieved April 18, 2022, from https://www.davidsongifted.org/gifted-blog/what-is-giftedness/

Floom, B., & Sundal Hansen, S. (n.d.). *Just don't shut the door on me: Aspirations of adolescents in crisis*. Sage Journals. Retrieved November 1, 2021, from https://journals.sagepub.com/doi/full/10.1177/2156759X0601000103

Gallant, W., & Holosko, M. (2001). Music intervention in grief work with clients experiencing loss and bereavement. *Guidance and Counseling*, *16*, 115–121.

Green, J. M. (2021). *Why being gifted isn't always a gift*. Today's Parent. Retrieved November 18, 2021, from https://www.todaysparent.com/family/how-to-help-your-gifted-kid-thrive/

Greenwald, R. (2005). *Child trauma handbook: A guide for helping trauma-exposed children and adolescents*. Haworth Maltreatment and Trauma Press/The Haworth Press.

Hébert, T., & Sergent, D. (2005). Using movies to guide: Teachers and counselors collaborating to support gifted students. *Gifted Child Today*, *28*(4), 14–24. doi:10.1177/107621750502800405

Henderson, D. A., & Thompson, C. L. (2016). *Counseling children*. Cengage Learning.

James, R. K., & Gilliland, B. E. (2017). *Crisis intervention strategies*. Cengage Learning.

Kamenetz, A. (2015, September 28). *Who are the 'gifted and talented' and what do they need?* NPR. Retrieved April 18, 2022, from https://www.npr.org/sections/ed/2015/09/28/443193523/who-are-the-gifted-and-talented-and-what-do-they-need

Kesner, J. E. (2005). Gifted Children's Relationships with Teachers. *International Education Journal*, *6*(2), 218–223.

LaMorte, W. (2019). *Behavioral change models. The Transtheoretical Model (Stages of Change).* Retrieved November 12, 2021, from https://sphweb.bumc.bu.edu/otlt/MPHModules/SB/BehavioralChangeTheories/BehavioralChangeTheories6.html

Mula, K., Janus, P., & Palomar, D. (2022). *Gifted children and social relationships.* Afg Guidance Center. Retrieved April 20, 2022, from https://afgfamily.com/blog/gifted-children/gifted-children-and-social-relationships/

Nash, J. (2017, November 8). *Emotional hijacking: How connecting to old hurts heals us*. Therapy Blog. Retrieved April 18, 2022, from https://www.goodtherapy.org/blog/emotional-hijacking-how-connecting-to-old-hurts-heals-us-1022155

Parachin, V. M. (1996). Medicine for the mind. *American Fitness*, *14*(3), 64–65.

Parritz, R. H., & Troy, M. F. (2018). *Disorders of childhood development and psychopathology*. Cengage Learning.

Pehrsson, D. E., & McMillen, P. (2007). *Bibliotherapy: Overview and implications for counselors (ACAPCD-02).* American Counseling Association.

Peterson, J. S. (2006). Addressing counseling needs of gifted students. *Professional School Counseling*, *10*(1), 43–51. doi:10.5330/prsc.10.1.b76h32717q632tqn

Peterson, J. S. (2014). Giftedness, trauma, and development: A qualitative, longitudinal case study. *Journal for the Education of the Gifted*, *37*(4), 295–318. doi:10.1177/0162353214552564

Peterson, J. S. (2015). School counselors and gifted kids: Respecting both cognitive and affective. *Journal of Counseling and Development*, *93*(2), 153–162. doi:10.1002/j.1556-6676.2015.00191.x

Peterson, J. S., & Morris, C. W. (2010). Preparing school counselors to address concerns related to giftedness: A study of accredited counselor preparation programs. *Journal for the Education of the Gifted*, *33*(3), 311–336. doi:10.1177/016235321003300302

Peterson, J. S., & Ray, K. E. (2006). Bullying and the gifted: Victims, perpetrators, prevalence, and effects. *Gifted Child Quarterly*, *50*(2), 148–168. doi:10.1177/001698620605000206

Preuss, L. J., & Dubrow, E. F. (2004). A comparison between intellectually gifted and typical children in their coping responses to a school and a peer stressor. *Roeper Review*, *26*(2), 105–111. doi:10.1080/02783190409554250

Prout, H. T., & Brown, D. T. (2012). *Counseling and psychotherapy with children and adolescents theory and practice for school and clinical settings*. Wiley.

Rhoton, R. (2022, March 28). *Childhood trauma can alter reactivity to real or perceived threat*. Arizona Trauma Institute. Retrieved April 18, 2022, from https://aztrauma.org/childhood-trauma-can-alter-reactivity-real-perceived-threat/

Rinn, A. N., Reynolds, M. J., & McQueen, K. S. (2011). Perceived Social Support and the Self-Concepts of Gifted Adolescents. *Journal for the Education of the Gifted*, *34*(3), 367–396. doi:10.1177/016235321103400302

Roberts, J. L. (2004). Leadership is a "Must" for Children Who are Gifted and Talented. *Gifted Child Today*, *27*(1), 5–5. doi:10.1177/107621750402700101

Rosenblatt, P. C. (2008). Recovery following bereavement: Metaphor, phenomenology, and culture. *Death Studies*, *32*(1), 6–16. doi:10.1080/07481180701741228 PMID:18646394

Sallin, J. H., & Eglinton, K. (2021, November 15). *Conversations on gifted trauma podcast*. InterGifted. Retrieved April 17, 2022, from https://intergifted.com/conversations-gifted-trauma/

Scott, E. (2022, January 5). *10 telltale signs you may be a perfectionist*. Verywell Mind. Retrieved April 17, 2022, from https://www.verywellmind.com/signs-you-may-be-a-perfectionist-3145233

Segal, J., Smith, M., Robinson, L., & Shubin, J. (2022, February 8). *Improving emotional intelligence (EQ)*. Retrieved November 18, 2021, from https://www.helpguide.org/articles/mental-health/emotional-intelligence-eq.htm

Silverman, L. K. (2000). *Counseling the gifted and talented*. Love.

Simmen-Janevska, K., Brandstätter, V., & Maercker, A. (2012). The overlooked relationship between motivational abilities and posttraumatic stress: a review. *European Journal of Psychotraumatology, 3*. doi:10.3402/ejpt.v3i0.18560

Sisk, D. (2008). Engaging the spiritual intelligence of gifted students to build global awareness in the classroom. *Roeper Review*, *30*(1), 24–30. doi:10.1080/02783190701836296

Skolnick, J. (2019, October 1). *Gifted does not (only) mean smart*. Gifted Does Not (only) Mean Smart | National Association for Gifted Children. Retrieved October 28, 2021, from https://www.nagc.org/blog/gifted-does-not-only-mean-smart

Spirito, A., & Kazak, A. E. (2006). *Effective and emerging treatments in pediatric psychology*. Oxford Univ. Press.

Studer, J. R. (2015). The Essential School Counselor in a changing society. *Sage (Atlanta, Ga.)*. Advance online publication. doi:10.4135/9781483399881

Terry, A. W., Bohnenberger, J. E., Renzulli, J. S., Cramond, B., & Sisk, D. (2008). Vision with action: Developing sensitivity to societal concerns in gifted youth. *Roeper Review*, *30*(1), 61–67. doi:10.1080/02783190701836478

Thomas, V., & Ray, K. E. (2006). Counseling exceptional individuals and their families: A systems perspective. *Professional School Counseling*, *10*(1), 58–65. doi:10.5330/prsc.10.1.whr69001g7573m75

Tieso, C. L. (2007). Overexcitabilities: A new way to think about talent? *Roeper Review*, *29*(4), 232–239. doi:10.1080/02783190709554417

Van Gemert, L. (2017). *Perfectionism: A practical guide to managing "Never good enough"*. Gifted Guru Publishing.

Vernon, A., & Clemente, R. (2005). *Assessment and intervention with children and adolescents: Developmental and cultural approaches*. American Counseling Association.

Webb, J. T. (2011, September 14). *Existential depression in gifted individuals*. SENG. Retrieved November 18, 2021, from https://www.sengifted.org/post/existential-depression-in-gifted-individuals

Webb, J. T. (2022, February 25). *Dabrowski's theory and existential depression in gifted children and adults*. Davidson Institute. Retrieved April 18, 2022, from https://www.davidsongifted.org/gifted-blog/dabrowskis-theory-and-existential-depression-in-gifted-children-and-adults/

KEY TERMS AND DEFINITIONS

Asynchronous: Cognitive, emotional, and/or physical development of gifted individuals not developing at the same Time.

Emotional Quotient: usually represented by a score in a standardized test to measure the level of a person's emotional intelligence.

Functional Behavioral Assessment: A process utilized to help identify challenging behaviors and form viable solutions.

Gifted Trauma: A trauma that gifted children experience that stems from feeling like you do not belong, are ridiculed, ignored, rejected, misunderstood, and/or are out-of-place.

Individuals With Disabilities Education Act (IDEA): A piece of American legislation that ensures students with a disability are provided with appropriate public education that is free and tailored to their individual needs.

Individualized Educational Plan (IEP): A written education plan developed to ensure that a child with an identified disability receives specialized instruction and related services.

Intelligence Quotient: Represented by a score derived from a set of standardized tests to measure the level of a person's intelligence.

Twice Exceptional (2e): A gifted child who also has one or more disabilities.

Chapter 8
Addressing Social Justice Issues in Schools Utilizing Trauma-Informed Care

Melissa P. Phelan
Abilene Christian University, Dallas, USA

Jennifer T. Butcher
Abilene Christian University, Dallas, USA

ABSTRACT

Trauma affects students in areas of social/behavioral skills and academic performance. This observation is supported with research. Researchers noted that traumatic exposure at home, school, or in the community has been associated with social anxiety, depression, suicidal ideation, and oppositional and aggressive behavior. Goodman et al. reported that trauma can have a negative impact on academic functioning, with higher symptoms of traumatic stress predicting poorer reading, math, and science achievement scores among elementary students. Trauma is indeed a social justice issue. Socioeconomic inequality, low educational level, and living in impoverished neighborhoods are major predisposing factors for exposure to a traumatic event. This chapter will provide recommendations on the utilization of trauma-informed care in addressing social justice issues in schools. Strategies to assist varied student groups will be noted in the chapter.

DOI: 10.4018/978-1-7998-9785-9.ch008

INTRODUCTION

According to Vivrett and Bartlett (2020), trauma is one possible outcome of exposure to adversity. The researchers noted that trauma occurs when a person perceives an event or set of circumstances as extremely frightening, harmful, or threatening, which can be either emotionally, physically, or both. Vivrett and Barlett went on to define adversity as a wide range of circumstances or events that pose a serious threat to physical or psychological well-being. There are numerous school-aged children who have experienced trauma as well as adversities.

Throughout the years, many children encounter sexual, physical, and emotional abuse.

Finkelhor et al. (2013) noted that 41.2% of children experienced physical assault during 2011 and 10.1% of the reported incidents caused physical injury with 6.2% of the incidents involving a weapon. Lynch (2003) noted that traumatic experiences and exposure to community violence can contribute to dysregulation of the hypothalamic-pituitary-adrenal axis, which in turn can manifest as either hypoarousal or hyperarousal in response to different routine or distressing stimuli.

Trauma affects students in areas of social/behavioral skills and academic performance. This observation is supported with research. Researchers noted that traumatic exposure at home, school, or in the community has been associated with social anxiety, depression, suicidal ideation, and oppositional and aggressive behavior (Overstreet & Mathews, 2011). Goodman et al. (2012) reported that trauma can have a negative impact on academic functioning, with higher symptoms of traumatic stress predicting poorer reading, math, and science achievement scores among elementary students. The researchers also noted that traumatic symptoms are associated with a high probability of students experiencing behavior problems.

Social Justice and Trauma Informed Care

During the year 2020, numerous factors impacted students' mental, physical, and social well-being. COVID was prevalent in schools and students were taught in online settings, instead of the traditional classrooms. The year 2020 also was a time that individuals witnessed systemic racism and police brutality. Other factors that impacted families during this time was the loss of jobs, food insecurities, social isolations, death of loved ones and loss of homes. The circumstances created concerns and discussions around the topic of the impact of social justice issues and trauma on the education and mental health of students. Diversity, equity, and inclusion initiatives have been implented in schools to address trauma informed care for students. Programs to provide support to educational agencies to assist with the mental health of students and how to identify and respond to trauma are vital.

Trauma is indeed a social justice issue. Socioeconomic inequality, low educational level, and living in impoverished neighborhoods are major predisposing factors for exposure to a traumatic event (Boyle & Hassett-Walker, 2008; Klest, 2012). This is supported by Copeland et al. (2018) indicating that trauma produces economic and educational difficulties, mental and social problems, or, in other words, inadequate personal, familial, and community resources.

To aid with students, trauma-informed care is a necessity. Educational settings can implement a trauma-informed approach with the guidance of a school counselor. identified the following four aspects of a trauma-informed approach to service delivery.

1. Realize the widespread impact of trauma and understand potential paths for healing.
2. Recognize the signs and symptoms of trauma.
3. Respond by fully integrating knowledge about trauma into policies, procedures, practices, and settings.
4. Actively resist re-traumatization.

Keesler (2013) suggested that a trauma-informed approach can be incorporated in schools using a multi-tier service delivery system for students exposed to trauma. Keesler noted that for a school to adopt a trauma-informed approach, changes need to be made to the culture, policies, and procedures that govern the school community. This chapter will provide information and recommendations on the utilization of trauma-informed care in addressing social justice issues in schools. The specific groups noted in this chapter are Mobile Students, Homeless Students, Students of Incarcerated Parents, and LGBTQ Students.

Mobile Students

According to Baker and Butcher (2022), mobile students are a group that can benefit from additional educational support at school and in the community. During the years 2020-2022, mobile students typically resulted from families being relocated due to loss of income and housings. Baker and Butcher noted that COVID-19 and weather-related factors contributed to the increase of mobile students. Due to the circumstances, many students experienced trauma. The following section will address homeless students and suggested support for these students, which are also applicable to the support that can be provided for trauma informed care for mobile students.

Homeless Students

The consensus among researchers is that homelessness carries with it a continuum of risk for those students and families experiencing it. The U.S. Conference of Mayors' Report on Hunger and Homelessness (2020) reported that in 2016 more than 544,084 people were identified as being homeless in the United States. During the 2019-2020 school year, public schools in the United States identified 1,280,886 students who experienced homelessness. This represents 2.5% of all students enrolled in public schools (National Center for Homeless Education (NCHE), 2021). Yet, Havlik and Bryan (2015) revealed that 40% of the school counselors in their study felt that they had not received adequate training to prepare them to assist homeless students.

These school counselors also noted that they frequently encountered and were tasked with assisting homeless students and their families.
The NCHE (2016) reported that in the United States:

- 75% of homeless children and youth were in families that practiced "doubling up" which is when families share housing with others.
- 7% were living in hotels.
- 4% were reported to be "unsheltered" living outside, in abandoned buildings or cars.

Toro et.al (2007) reported that youth affected by homelessness:

- have high rates of involvement in the juvenile justice system,
- are more likely to engage in substance use and delinquent behavior,
- be teenage parents,
- drop out of school,
- suffer from sexually transmitted diseases,
- and meet the criteria for mental illness.

Legislation for Homeless Youth

The McKinney-Vento Homeless Assistance Act (MVHAA) was established in 1987 as a response to homeless youth. The U.S. Department of Education collects data on homeless students under the MVHAA, law [42 U.S.C.§11432(g)(1)(J)(ii)]. In 2015 the act was reauthorized under the Every Student Succeed Act of 2015. This reauthorization required schools to enroll homeless students within two days without requiring proof of residency or medical immunization records.

The McKinney-Vento Act

- Requires that school districts identify and report on all students who are experiencing homelessness.
- Requires that schools guarantee homeless youth the right to enroll in public schools and access to all available educational opportunities.

The Act's legislation also guarantees homeless youth participation in:

- Tutoring Programs
- Nutritional Programs
- And to have access to available transportation services.

This Act also targets the homeless through programs such as the Education for Homeless

Children and Youth program (EHCY) which provides resources and support to remove barriers that promote academic success for all homeless students, and the Consolidated Runaway and Homeless Youth Programs (CRHYP) which focuses on transitional living for homeless youth where safe and stable living accommodations are made available.

Role of the School Counselor

School counselors must:

- Have a clear understanding of the McKinney-Vento Act.
- Be familiar with ways to work with their school districts and communities to identify homeless children.
- Review policies and practices to ensure the school success of homeless students.
- Create awareness of the needs and rights of homeless children and youth in the school district and the community.

COUNSELOR TOOL-KIT RESOURCES

Listed below are resources that are helpful in assisting and serving those experiencing homelessness:

- American Psychological Association. (2014). Effects of poverty, hunger, and homelessness on children and youth. http://www.apa.org/pi/families/poverty.aspx
- American School Counselor Association. (2010). The professional school counselor and children experiencing homelessness. The School Counselor and Children Experiencing Homelessness - American School Counselor Association (ASCA)
- Bassuk, E., Volk, K., & Olivet, J. (2010). A framework for developing supports and services for families experiencing homelessness. The Open Health Services and Policy Journal, 3, 34–40. doi: 10.2174/1874924001003020034
- Child Trends. (2019). Children and Youth Experiencing Homelessness. Retrieved from Child Trends.
- Education of Homeless Children and Youth. (2007). National coalition for the homeless. http://nationalhomeless.org/publications/facts/education.pdf
- National Association for the Education of Homeless Children and Youth. (2011). Unaccompanied youth toolkit for high school counselors and McKinney Vento Liaisons.
- National Association for the Education of Homeless Children and Youth. (2015). Summary of major amendments on homelessness and foster care in "The Every Student Succeeds Act of 2015." Washington, DC. https://naehcy.org/welcome/
- National Center for Homeless Education, (NCHE). This is a wonderful site. Provides free educational materials. https://nche.ed.gov/
- National Law Center on Homelessness and Poverty. (2019). Alone Without a Home: A National Review of State Laws Affecting Unaccompanied Youth. https://youthtoday.org/2019/02/alone-without-a-home-a-national-review-of-state-laws-affecting-unaccompanied-youth/

Students of Incarcerated Parents

Each day across the United States they can be found within classrooms. Many of them endure their anguish and grief secretly, others exhibit a range of problematical and maladaptive behaviors. They have been referred to in the literature as the hidden victims of the criminal justice system (Moses, 2010), the unseen victims of the prison boom (Petersilia, 2005), and the orphans of justice (Shaw, 1992). They are hidden because in the past their plight has been understudied and relatively neglected. There aren't hundreds or thousands of them, there are millions of them. Frequently misunderstood, unidentified, stigmatized and trapped within a system that is unaware of the myriad of difficulties they confront and attempt to cope with, they are the minor children of incarcerated parents, (COIPS).

During the last quarter of the twentieth century, the incarceration rate within the United States has become a relatively common reality for many of our minor citizens. When a parent goes to jail the children left behind most often experience many changes within their daily lives. Some of them experience few, if any changes, others face a legion of difficult circumstances that affect their psychological and emotional development and, consequently, their academic outcomes and life experiences. Due to the overwhelming and significant number of children that are experiencing the effects of parental incarceration and the vast array of problems associated with them, it is time that all educators and administrators take a proactive stance in serving them.

The National Resource Center on Children and Families of the Incarcerated (2016) reports that on any given day in the United States that:

- 1 in every 40 minor children, or 2.7 million minor children, are affected by parental incarceration. These are staggering statistics especially considering that these statistics are conservative estimates since the criminal justice system, both on the state and federal levels, has no standardized way to track the actual number of minor children affected by parental incarceration (Osborne Association, 2018).
- An additional 10 million children have a parent that has been or is involved in the criminal justice system (Schirmir et al. 2009).

The Public-School System and Students Experiencing Parental Incarceration

School employees can play a key role in the social-emotional and academic development of all children whom they serve; however, research by Chute (2017) established that there is virtually no information, training, or educational strategies provided to counselors, administrators or to in-service and preservice teachers concerning this student population.

Chute reported that Alisha Murdock, program director for Project WHAT, which partners with the San Francisco Unified School District to support students of incarcerated parents, reveals that more than 10 years ago when she was in sixth grade and her mother was incarcerated, she "skipped classes, fought with other students, got suspended and missed so much school she had to repeat the grade" (p. 7). Chute (2017) noted that Murdock stated that "no one at school reached out to help" and that "it would have made a difference if a teacher or someone else in the school had said, "Are you OK?," "Do you want to talk?" "I know something has changed," and I'm here if you want to talk," but no one did (pp. 2-3).

Eric Rossen (2011), a school psychologist and director of professional development standards at the National Association of School Psychologists, explained that in most cases, information about parental incarceration is not shared with the school due to shame and embarrassment or a lack of trust, or fear that the school will somehow treat the students differently or judge them. Rossen contended that "adolescents whose parents are incarcerated may feel significant shame and embarrassment, engage in risk-taking or criminal behavior, and be less likely to adhere to boundaries set within classrooms, the school, or the community at large" (p. 13).

Frequently Identified School Outcomes in Minors Experiencing Parental Incarceration

Researchers affirm that many of the children and adolescents with an incarcerated parent suffer from an array of negative outcomes including:

- Poor mental health and trauma reactive behaviors (Aaron & Dallaire, 2010; Davis & Shlafer, 2017; Mears & Siennick, 2016; Murray et al., 2012).
- Truancy and school failure (Nichols et al., 2016; Wakefield & Wildeman, 2013).
- Dysfunctional relationships and stigmatization (Davis & Shlafer, 2017; Foster & Hagan, 2015; Wildeman et al., 2017).
- Delinquency and involvement with the criminal justice system themselves (Mears & Siennick, 2016; Murray & Farrington, 2005).

Within the school system, these children are frequently identified as at-risk students due to their elevated school drop-out rates and poor academic outcomes (Nichols et al., 2016; Wakefield & Wildeman, 2013). Nichols and Loper (2012) reported that youth experiencing incarceration within the family face many household disruptions and "chaos" that has long-term effects on their academic outcomes, as well as their risk for adverse behaviors and mental stress.

Children Experiencing Parental Incarceration: Living Arrangements, Stigma and Secrecy, and Problematic and Maladaptive Behaviors

Frequently children experiencing parental incarceration:

- Experience disruptions in their living arrangements.
- Are stigmatized and participate in secrecy about the incarceration.
- Exhibit problematic and maladaptive behaviors.

Living Arrangements

Living arrangements for children with an incarcerated parent are usually affected when a parent is incarcerated. Children who live with their parent(s) at the time of arrest or incarceration are frequently placed with a nonparent adult for their care and support (Glaze & Maruschak, 2008). The most current, official data by Glaze and Maruschak gathered for the U.S. Department of Justice detailed the living arrangements, as reported by the incarcerated parent(s). According to Glaze and Maruschak (2008):

- 88% of fathers reported that at least one of their children was in the care of the child's mother, compared to
- 37% of mothers who reported the father as the child's caregiver.
- Mothers in state prison most identified the child's grandmother (42%) as the current caregiver.
- 23% of mothers identified other relatives as the current caregiver
- Mothers (11%) were five times more likely to report that their children were in the care of a foster home, agency, or institution than fathers
- Children of incarcerated mothers experienced more living arrangement disruptions than children with incarcerated fathers.
- Fathers in prison reported that their children were in the care of a grandmother (12%) or other relatives (5%).

Dallaire (2007) suggested that a mother's incarceration, due to the higher percentage of disruptions in living arrangements for these children, would trigger more frequent emotional and behavioral problems than a father's incarceration. Dallaire reported that "because they are more likely to be in nonfamilial care situations, children with incarcerated mothers, more so than children of incarcerated fathers, might be suffering from the anxiety and trauma often associated with disruptions in attachment relationships" (p. 22).

Stigma and Secrecy

Within their daily lives, children of incarcerated parents are often faced with the stigma that society has attached to incarceration (Boswell & Wedge, 2002; Dallaire et al., 2010). Stigma is defined by Link and Phelan (2001) as the labeling, stereotyping, separating, or discriminating of people. Link and Phelan argued that stigma can affect multiple domains of people's lives and has a dramatic bearing on the distribution of life chances in such areas as:

- Earnings
- Housing
- Criminal involvement
- Health, and life itself.

Shlafer and Poehlmann (2010) discovered that teachers, as well as caregivers, attributed many of the behavior problems exhibited by students of the incarcerated to the social stigma experienced by these children. This type of stigma was precisely summed up by a 16-year-old student of an incarcerated parent in the Adalist-Estrin (2006) article when she reported that if anything was stolen from a desk or a locker, "those of us with parents in jail get blamed" (p. 8).

Adalist-Estrin (2006) explained that even in communities heavily affected by incarceration, families of prisoners fear judgment by others. The social stigma associated with parental incarceration has been found to:

- Exacerbate the psychological and emotional difficulties children naturally experience when they are separated from a parent (Young and Smith 2000).
- Altered the educators' expectations of students (Link and Phelan, 2001).

Wildeman et al. (2017) reported that their study, which examined teachers' expectations of students secondary to paternal incarceration, revealed that the stigma associated with paternal incarceration shapes teachers' expectations of students, leading to a 10 to 40% increase in teachers' negative expectations of children's behavioral problems. Dallaire et al. (2010) reported in their study that 10 out of 30 teachers surveyed noted that they have witnessed colleagues being unsupportive, unprofessional, and expecting less from children with incarcerated parents.

Dallaire et al. shared that one teacher noted that for some of her colleagues, knowing that a parent was incarcerated would play a role in how they treated the student. In the same study, another teacher noted that knowledge of a parent's incarceration often translated into lower teacher expectations, stating that some teachers would not expect as much because the incarceration explained it (i.e., the child's behavior).

- Lead to Bullying

Boswell and Wedge (2002) noted that students affected by parental incarceration not only experienced stigma, but they also experienced bullying, verbal abuse, and teasing, and the caregivers interviewed for this study reported that the pressure was so great that the children did not want to go to school.

- Secrecy

Poehlmann (2005) reported that 20% of the caregivers in her study reported they had lied to their children about the location of incarcerated parents to avoid stigma. Shlafer and Poehlmann (2010) reported that some children reported secrecy regarding their relationship with the parent and their incarceration. Poehlmann also noted that some of the children seemed uncomfortable sharing their thoughts and feelings about the incarcerated parent during interviews and the children revealed information about the incarcerated parent, which they were told by their caregivers not to share to avoid the stigma and embarrassment associated with parental incarceration.

Problematic and Maladaptive Behaviors

According to Murray and Murray (2010), the social isolation children experience due to their parents' incarceration may contribute to maladaptive and contumacious behaviors such as:

- Withdrawing emotionally in school
- Truancy
- Pregnancy
- Drug Abuse
- Gang Affiliation or membership
- Diminished academic performance
- Post-Traumatic Stress Disorder (PTSD)
- Disruptive externalized behaviors such as fighting, bullying, arguing, and defiance at school (Shlafer & Poehlman, 2010).

Shlafer and Poehlmann noted that one study participant wrote, "He blows up and gets mad. He is defiant, smoking cigarettes and pot. He's sexually active and stays out late running the streets." Another wrote, "Interactions with peers and adults have been very problematic-rude, dangerous, poor attitude, uncooperative" (p. 8). In addition, Shlafer and Poehlmann reported that teachers and caregivers of children involved with parental incarceration voiced concerns about the challenges observed regarding the friendships and peer relationships that these children attempted to forge. The researchers noted that "these youth appear: needy, distrustful, sad, anxious and moody," and these characteristics often interfere with friendship and relationship building (Shlafer & Poehlmannn, 2010, p. 408). Murray and Murray (2010) reiterated these findings when they noted that these kids have difficulty forming and maintaining relationships.

In a frequently cited and referenced longitudinal cohort study, known as the Cambridge Study, Murray et al. (2007) found that parental incarceration predicted severe antisocial delinquent outcomes in the form of intergenerational incarceration.

These findings are not new as Baunach (1985) found that 70% of the children in her study exhibited social and psychological disorders, such as aggression, hostility, and withdrawal. These identified problem behaviors, associated with this population of students, can have a significant impact on their development, social skills, and ability to learn and remain in school (Mears & Siennick, 2016).

Intervention Ideas

Several interventions have been suggested by numerous researchers to support students involved with the incarceration of a parent.

- First and foremost, building awareness among all school employees as well as the community, family, and caregivers, on the impact incarceration of a parent can have on a student and their families (Adalist-Estrin, 2006; Clopton & East, 2008; Dallaire, 2007; Murray & Farrington, 2005; Shlafer et al., 2017; Timmons, 2006).
- Provide training and professional development each semester for all current and new employees on what Trauma Informed Care consists of.
- Ensure that all staff and employees are aware of what is considered as an Adverse Childhood Event (ACE), e.g., Emotional, sexual, or physical abuse, Violence, Neglect, Discrimination, Poverty, and that these ACE's induce trauma within individuals.
- Examine with employees the number of ACE's (usually 3+) that students experiencing parental incarceration are frequently exposed to.
- Instruct faculty and staff what mindful talk consists of. (People in jail are bad, etc.).
- Providing books, articles, and pamphlets about parental incarceration at your school (Adalist-Estrin, 2006).
- Integrate age-appropriate justice issues within the curriculum.
- Developing support groups.
- Providing access to appropriate therapists, counselors, and mentors (Timmons, 2006).
- With appropriate legal consents in place, the inclusion of incarcerated parents in teacher/parent conference calls or sending report cards to the prison (Adalist-Estrin, 2006; Shlafer et al., 2017).

Counselor Tool-Kit Resources

Over the past few years parental incarceration has been given significant attention. There are many resources available online to assist with the education of school employees and organizations on how to best support students and families experiencing parental incarceration.

The National Resource Center on Children and Families of the Incarcerated (NRCCFI). This organization provides relevant resources and information regarding current research, programs, policies, training and practice on parental incarceration. The National Resource Center on Children and Families of the Incarcerated (rutgers.edu)

Project WHAT! Project WHAT! raises awareness about the impacts of parental incarceration on children, with the long-term goal of improving services and policies that affect these children. www.communityworkswest.org/index.php/project-what

San Francisco Children of Incarcerated Parents Partnership. SFCIPP is a coalition of social service providers, representatives of government bodies, advocates and others who work with or are concerned about children of incarcerated parents and their families. They have created a "Bill of Rights for Children of Incarcerated Parents." www.sfcipp.org

Youth. gov Youth.gov provides information for School Administrators and Teachers and provides information on: Trauma, Exposure to Violence, Exposure to Drugs or Alcohol, Services & Supports, Tools, Guides, & Resources, and various Presentations. Children of Incarcerated Parents | Youth.gov

CONCLUSION

While researchers will continue to study factors associated with social justice issues and trauma informed care for students, it is imperative that school districts provide professional development opportunities and resources to assist school counselors. One strategy cannot address the support needed for students, because students should be provided with the necessary individualized support to address their specific needs. Schools should also provide professional support for teachers and staff members relating to support factors for students impacted by trauma. Parent workshops are also recommended to support families of students who are experience trauma. Researchers have shown that children's exposure to specific traumatic events can impact academic performance, discipline concerns and attendance of students (Duplechain et al., 2008; Schwartz & Gorman, 2003)

REFERENCES

Aaron, L., & Dallaire, D. (2010). Parental incarceration and multiple risk experiences: Effects on family dynamics and children's delinquency. *Journal of Youth and Adolescence, 39*(12), 1471–1484. doi:10.100710964-009-9458-0 PMID:19834796

Adalist-Estrin, A. (2006). Providing support to adolescent children with incarcerated parents. *Prevention Researcher, 13*(2), 7–10.

Baker, W., & Butcher, J. (2022). Demystifying the stigma of transient African American housing dwellers: Recommendations for school and church partnerships. In Butcher & Baker (Eds.), Addressing Issues of Systemic Racism During Turbulent Times. IGI Global Publications.

Baunach, P. (1985). *Mothers in prison.* Transaction Books.

Boswell, G., & Wedge, P. (2002). *Imprisoned Fathers and Their Children.* Jessica Kingsley Publishers. doi:10.1046/j.1365-2206.2002.t01-1-00258.x

Boyle, D., & Hassett-Walker, C. (2008). Individual-level and socio-structural characteristics of violence: An emergency department study. *Journal of Interpersonal Violence, 23*(8), 1011–1026. doi:10.1177/0886260507313966 PMID:18296572

Chute, E. (2017). When parents of school children go to prison. Keep their children on track with mentoring, specialized clubs and other approaches in education. *District Administration, 53*(3), 34–40.

Clopton, K., & East, K. (2008). "Are there other kids like me?" children with a parent in prison. *Early Childhood Education Journal, 36*(2), 195-198. doi:10.1007/s10643-008-0266-z

Copeland, W., Shanahan, L., Hinesley, J., Chan, R., Aberg, K., Fairbank, J., van den Oord, E., & Costello, J. (2018). Association of childhood trauma exposure with adult psychiatric disorders and functional outcomes. *JAMA Network Open, 1*(7), e184493. Advance online publication. doi:10.1001/jamanetworkopen.2018.4493 PMID:30646356

Dallaire, D. H. (2007). Children with incarcerated mothers: Developmental outcomes, special challenges, and recommendations. *Journal of Applied Developmental Psychology, 28*(1), 15–24. doi:10.1016/j.appdev.2006.10.003

Davis, L., & Shlafer, R. (2017). Mental health of adolescents with currently and formerly incarcerated parents. *Journal of Adolescence, 54*(1), 120–134. doi:10.1016/j.adolescence.2016.10.006 PMID:28011442

Duplechain, R., Reigner, R., & Packard, A. (2008). Striking differences: The impact of moderate and high trauma on reading achievement. *Reading Psychology*, *29*(2), 117–136. doi:10.1080/02702710801963845

Foster, H., & Hagan, J. (2015). Punishment regimes and the multi-level effects of parental incarceration: Intergenerational, intersectional, and interinstitutional models of social inequality and systemic exclusion. *Annual Review of Sociology*, *41*(1), 135–158. doi:10.1146/annurev-soc-073014-112437

Glaze, L. E., & Maruschak, L. M. (2008). Parents in prison and their minor children. Washington, DC. *Bureau of Justice Statistics Special Report.*

Havlik, S., & Bryan, J. (2015). Addressing the needs of students experiencing homelessness: School counselor preparation. *The Professional Counselor*, *5*(2), 200–216. doi:10.15241h.5.2.200

Klest, B. (2012). Childhood trauma, poverty, and adult victimization. *Psychological Trauma: Theory, Research, Practice, and Policy*, *4*(3), 245–251. doi:10.1037/a0024468

Link, B., & Phelan, J. (2001). Conceptualizing stigma. *Annual Review of Sociology*, *27*(1), 363–385. doi:10.1146/annurev.soc.27.1.363

Mears, D., & Siennick, S. (2016). Young adult outcomes and the life-course penalties of parental incarceration. *Journal of Research in Crime and Delinquency*, *53*(1), 3–35. doi:10.1177/0022427815592452

Moses, M. (2010). Children of the incarcerated must be studied and responded to comprehensively. *Corrections Today*, *72*(3), 58–60.

Murray, J., Farrington, D., & Sekol, I. (2012). Children's antisocial behavior, mental health, drug use, and educational performance after parental incarceration: A systemic review and meta-analysis. *Psychological Bulletin*, *138*(2), 175–210. doi:10.1037/a0026407 PMID:22229730

Murray, J., & Farrington, D. P. (2005). Parental imprisonment: Effects on boys' antisocial behavior and delinquency through the life-course. *Journal of Child Psychology and Psychiatry, and Allied Disciplines*, *46*(12), 1269–1278. doi:10.1111/j.1469-7610.2005.01433.x PMID:16313427

Murray, J., & Murray, L. (2010). Parental incarceration, attachment and child psychopathology. *Attachment & Human Development*, *12*(4), 289–309. doi:10.1080/14751790903416889 PMID:20582842

National Center for Homeless Education. (2018). *Enrolling Children and Youth Experiencing Homelessness in School*. Author.

National Center for Homeless Education. (2021). *Student Homelessness in America: School Years 2017-18 to 2019-20*. Author.

National Resource Center on Children and Families of the Incarcerated. (2016). *Children of prisoners' library*. http://wwwfcnetwork.org/cpl/cpindex.html

Nichols, E., & Loper, A. (2012). Incarceration in the household: Academic outcomes of adolescents with an incarcerated household member. *Journal of Youth and Adolescence*, *41*(11), 1455–1471. doi:10.100710964-012-9780-9 PMID:22714743

Nichols, E., Loper, A., & Meyer, J. (2016). Promoting educational resiliency in youth with incarcerated parents: The impact of parental incarceration, school characteristics, and connectedness on school outcomes. *Journal of Youth and Adolescence*, *45*(6), 1090–1109. doi:10.100710964-015-0337-6 PMID:26259843

Osburne Association. (2018). *A call to action: Safeguarding New York's children with incarcerated parents*. https://www.osborneny.org/programs-down/strengthening-communities/new-york-initiative-for-children-of-incarcerated-parents/a-call-to-action/

Petersilia, J. (2005). From cell to society: Who is returning home? In J. Travis & C. Visher (Eds.), *Prisoner reentry and crime in America* (pp. 15–49). Cambridge University Press. doi:10.1017/CBO9780511813580.002

Poehlmann, J. (2005). Children of incarcerated mothers: Representations of attachment relationships in children of incarcerated mothers. *Journal of Child Development*, *76*(3), 679–696. doi:10.1111/j.1467-8624.2005.00871.x PMID:15892786

Powers-Costello, B., & Swick, K. J. (2011). Transforming teacher constructs of children and families who are homeless. *Early Childhood Education Journal*, *39*(3), 207–212. doi:10.100710643-011-0455-z

Schwartz, D., & Gorman, A. (2003). Community violence exposure and children's academic functioning. *Journal of Educational Psychology*, *95*(1), 163–173. doi:10.1037/0022-0663.95.1.163

Shlafer, R., & Poehlmann, J. (2010). Attachment and caregiving relationships in families affected by parental incarceration. *Attachment & Human Development*, *12*(4), 395–415. doi:10.1080/14616730903417052 PMID:20582847

Toro, P. A., Dworsky, A., & Fowler, P. J. (2007). *Homeless youth in the United States: Recent research findings and intervention approaches*. Paper presented at the National Symposium on Homeless Research, Washington, DC.

Vivrett, R., & Bartlett, J. (2020). *Trauma-informed strategies for supporting children and youth in the child welfare system during COVID-19*. ChildTrend.

Wakefield, S., & Wildeman, C. (2013). *Children of the prison boom: Mass incarceration and the future of American inequality*. Oxford University Press. doi:10.1093/acprof:oso/9780199989225.001.0001

Young, D., & Smith, C. (2000). When moms are incarcerated: The needs of children, mothers and caregivers. *Families in Society*, *81*(2), 130–141. doi:10.1606/1044-3894.1007

Chapter 9
Trauma-Informed School Counseling Practices to Address COVID-19-Fueled Discrimination and Racial Trauma in Asian-American Youth:
A Multitiered System of Support

Hulya Ermis-Demirtas
https://orcid.org/0000-0001-7247-5038
Northeastern Illinois University, USA

Ye Luo
https://orcid.org/0000-0003-0133-3918
University of North Texas, USA

Jia Rung Wu
Northeastern Illinois University, USA

DOI: 10.4018/978-1-7998-9785-9.ch009

ABSTRACT

Following the COVID-19 outbreak, Asian Americans, more specifically East and Southeast Asian Americans, have become the targets of racism, discrimination, and hate crimes. Mirroring this broader societal problem of COVID-related racism, schools have become a hostile environment for Asian American students with a significant rise in bullying and discriminatory incidents. In addition to experiencing harassment and discrimination in schools, Asian American students have also reported such incidents in online platforms. Both in-person and online COVID-related discrimination experienced by Asian American students have been linked to the PTSD symptoms, racial trauma, in this minoritized population. Therefore, the purpose of this chapter is to serve as a resource for school counselors to implement trauma-informed, culturally-sensitive practices, using the multitiered systems of support (MTSS) as a guide, when working with Asian American youth affected by COVID-19-related racial discrimination.

Yu-Jun is a 16-year-old Korean female high school student attending a White-majority public school. She is one of only a few Asian American students in her high school. After the COVID-19 outbreak, Yu-Jun feels that the school environment has become particularly hostile and unsafe. At school, a group of her classmates started to taunt her with a racist "slanted eyes" gesture. When she confided this incident in one of her teachers, the teacher did not take this seriously, and she felt discouraged and unvalidated. On several occasions, this group of students continued to surround her and pretend to cough on her. They even pushed her and shouted, "Ching chong! You have the Chinese virus! Your insides are full of bats! You should kill yourself because you are dirty dog eaters." Using an anonymous account, the group also created a fake profile with Yu-Jun's photoshopped pictures eating bats and racial slurs on them and spread them on social media sites.

Imagine that you are the school counselor at Yu-Jun's school. She sees a poster on your office wall that is supportive of Asian Americans and approaches you to tell about the harassment and discrimination she has experienced at school. She reports such symptoms as having nightmares, avoiding the classmates, experiencing uncontrolled crying spells in her room for an hour at a time, and feeling "punched in the stomach". After hearing about Yu-Jun's experiences, what would you do?

INTRODUCTION

Across the globe, the coronavirus disease (COVID-19) has been spreading rapidly since its outbreak in December 2019. As of October 8, 2021, about 236,599,025 cases of COVID-19 have been confirmed in more than 150 countries, resulting in 4,831,436 deaths around the world. With the emergence of the virus in Wuhan, China (Wu et al., 2021) and the extensive anxiety surrounding the COVID-19 disease (Lee, 2020), the climate of xenophobia and racism targeting people of Asian descent have soared in the United States (Congressional Asian American Pacific American Caucus [CAPAC], 2020; Litam, 2020). Within one month, for example, Asian Americans reported approximately 1,500 racist attacks with incidents ranging from being yelled at to spit on and physically attacked (Liu & Modir, 2020).

The Anti-Asian sentiments in the broader society have manifested in schools as bullying, harassment, and discrimination. For example, Ermis-Demirtas et al. (in press), in their study, have found that 73.3% of the participants ($n = 116$) experienced COVID-related discrimination in either online or in-person settings, 81.9% witnessed COVID-related discrimination, and 83.6% witnessed anti-Asian sentiments associated with the pandemic. There a growing body of evidence suggesting an adverse impact of COVID-fueled discrimination on the mental health and psychological wellbeing of Asian American students (Akiba, 2020). Although empirical research has not extensively addressed such findings given the recency of the situation, Cheah et al. (2020) have reported worrying outcomes, connecting the experiences of COVID-related discrimination to poor psychological health for Asian American youth. More specifically, Ermis-Demirtas et al. (in press), in their recent study, have reported the relationship of COVID-19 direct and vicarious racial discrimination in online and offline (in-person) settings with the posttraumatic stress disorder (PTSD) symptoms in East and Southeast Asian American high school students. Given the prevalence of racist incidents targeting Asian American students and findings linking COVID-19 fueled racial discrimination to trauma in this population, we urge school counselors to educate themselves and apply the best practices in culturally sensitive, trauma-informed school counseling to address COVID-associated racial trauma in this group of students.

MAIN FOCUS OF THE CHAPTER

Asian American students have been prone to COVID fueled racist attacks and discrimination since the emergence of the virus in China and expressed racial trauma symptoms that require school counselors' attention. The ASCA Ethical Standards (2016a) call school counselors to be systemic change agents and advocates by providing equitable educational systems of support as well as working toward dismantling racism and discrimination in schools to mitigate the impact of such adverse experiences on students social-emotional development. The ASCA Position Statement on Trauma-Informed Practices (2016b) also points out school counselors' unique position to identify students affected by traumatic events and provide support and trauma-informed services to the students in need. Therefore, this chapter will endeavor to give voice to Asian American students and serve as a resource for school counselors to implement trauma-informed practices using the Multitiered Systems of Support (MTSS) as a guide when working with Asian American youth affected by COVID-19 related racial discrimination.

This chapter begins with the characteristics of the Asian American population in the U.S., especially East and Southeast Asian Americans which is the focus of this chapter, to highlight the diversity among this minoritized group, followed by a discussion on the history, stereotypes, and racism targeting Asian American communities and students. After that, this chapter will extensively discuss COVID-fueled discrimination and racial trauma in Asian American youth. Finally, the chapter will conclude with a presentation of trauma-informed strategies in accordance with the MTSS framework with the hope that school counselors will be better equipped to address COVID discrimination and trauma in school settings.

Issues, Controversies, Problems

Racial discrimination has been a lasting battle for racial minorities and a well-documented social problem in the U.S. (Elias & Paradies, 2016). As one of the racial minority groups in the States, despite their underrepresentation in the discrimination literature (Kiang & Bhattacharjee, 2016), Asian Americans have been a frequent target of racism since they first arrived in this country in 1763 (Chang, 2016). Especially following the COVID-19 outbreak in 2019, individuals of Asian descent have become a scapegoat as the source of the outbreak and encountered a surge in xenophobia and discrimination (Chen et al., 2020; Wu et al., 2021). Considering the emergence of the virus in Wuhan, China, stigma and hostility have specifically targeted Chinese Americans; yet, the victims included other Asian Americans with Chinese appearance (Litam, 2020). Stereotypical and misleading media coverage, public and political figures' terminology blaming China for the origin of the virus, and misinformation spread on social media have also contributed to the anti-Asian sentiments and dramatic increase in the rates of racial discrimination, violence, and xenophobic attitudes against Americans with Chinese descent and other individuals with Asian origin (CAPAC, 2020; Litam, 2020). As an example, an analysis of popular social media platforms (e.g., Twitter) from November 2019 to March 2020 revealed a substantial increase in xenophobic slurs, such as "Ching Chong" and "Chink"

(Schild et al., 2020). Moreover, Stop AAPI Hate (2021) reported 2,808 incidents targeting Asian Americans across the country, ranging from verbal harassment, shunning or avoidance to physical assaults. While the most often targeted ethnic group was Chinese, other Asian Americans with Chinese appearances, such as Korean, Vietnamese, and Filipinos, have also faced COVID-related discrimination and assaults. Therefore, this chapter focuses on East and Southeast Asian Americans, composed of people of Chinese descent and other Asians with Chinese appearances, such as Koreans, Vietnamese, Japanese, and Filipinos.

Paralleling the stigma and hostility against individuals of Asian descent in American society, Asian American youth have reported incidents of COVID-related discrimination in schools and online settings (Cheah et al., 2020; Ermis-Demirtas et al., in press). Experiences of COVID-fueled discrimination among this group of students have been linked to various adverse mental health outcomes (Misra et al., 2020), including PTSD symptoms (Ermis-Demirtas et al., in press). More specifically, Ermis-Demirtas et al. (in press) surveyed a group of East and Southeast Asian American high school students and revealed a significant relationship between COVID-fueled online and in-person discrimination and racial trauma in this group. These preliminary results encourage school counselors to learn and implement trauma-informed practices with the goal of addressing COVID discrimination and racial trauma among Asian American youth in schools to promote their wellbeing and positive social-emotional development.

ASIAN AMERICAN POPULATION IN THE UNITED STATES

According to the U.S. Census Bureau population (2020), Asian Americans recorded the fastest growing population among all racial/ethnicity groups in the United States between 2000-2019. The Asian population in the U.S. grew 81% from approximately 10.5 to 18.9 million during this timeframe, and it is projected to rise to 35.8 million by 2060, according to a Pew Research Center (2021). Hispanics were the second -fastest growing population (70%) followed by Native Hawaiians and Pacific Islanders (NHPIs) (61%), the nation's Black population (20%) and White (1%).

Asian and Pacific Islanders are generally grouped by regions, although some can be politically controversial. There is tremendous diversity, with Asia having more than 40 countries and more ethnicities than countries. For example, Hmong are an ethnic group from Laos. Also, Asian diasporas are extremely large, and the oversimplification of ethnic identity is not applicable to the current society. Notions of ethnic and national identity carry political, social, and familial meanings too complex to analyze; however, there is a general understanding that **East Asians** include Chinese, Japanese, Korean, Okinawan, Taiwanese, Tibetan; **Southeast**

Asians include Bruneian, Myanmarese (formerly Burmese), Cambodian, Filipino, Hmong, Indonesian, Laotian, Malaysian, Mien, Singaporean, Timorese, Thai, Vietnamese; **South Asians** include Bangladeshi, Bhutanese, Indian, Maldivians, Nepali, Pakistani, Sri Lankan (Asian Pacific Institute, 2020).

Currently, more than 22 million Asians live in the U.S. and almost all can trace their roots to specific countries from East and Southeast Asia and the Indian subcontinent, according to a Pew Research Center analysis of U.S. Census Bureau data. As of 2019, Chinese, Indian, Filipino, Vietnamese, Korean and Japanese, six origin groups make up 85% of Asian Americans. Among these, Chinese-origin Asians are the largest single Asian in the U.S., making up 24% (5.4 million), followed by Indian Americans 21% (4.6 million), Filipinos 19% (4.2 million), Vietnam 10% (2.2 million), Korea 9% (1.9 million), and Japan 7% (1.5 million). The other 15 Asian origin groups in the Pew Research Center analysis each make up about 2% or less of the nation's Asian population, including Pakistani (2%), Thai (2%), Cambodian (2%), Hmong (1%), Laotian (1%), Taiwanese (1%), Bangladeshi (1%), Indonesian (1%), Sri Lankan (<1%), Malaysian (<1%), Mongolian (<1%), Bhutanese (<1%), and Okinawan (<1%). The largest Asian origin groups in the U.S. differ significantly by income, education, and other characteristics. These differences highlight the wide diversity of the nation's Asian population and provide a counterpoint to the "model minoritized" myth and the description of the population as monolithic.

HISTORY, STEREOTYPES, AND RACISM AGAINST ASIAN AMERICANS

To understand the full experiences of Asian Americans being the target for racism and discrimination during the COVID-19 pandemic, it is essential to also discuss the concept of racism and discrimination as well as examine the racial and discriminatory experiences of Asian Americans in the U.S. society. By definition, racism is grounded in a system that categorizes people into varied population groups. Each group received different societal resources based on their rankings in the system (Bonilla-Silva, 1996). That is to say; racism generates privileged positions for members of certain groups over other groups (Chen et al., 2020). As a by-product of racism, racial prejudice refers to the negative assumption and opinions towards someone based on their race. Racial prejudice further contributes to racial discrimination, referring to the differential (usually unjust and negative) treatment of individuals based on the racial groups they belong to (Williams & Mohammed, 2009). Racism and discrimination not only exist at the individual level but also manifest on a much larger scale, such as institutional and societal structures (Williams & Mohammed, 2009). Putting aside the context of the COVID-19 pandemic, Asian Americans were positioned uniquely in U.S. society regarding their race and ethnicity. On the one hand, members of Asian American communities either experience direct racism and discrimination themselves or witness fellow Asian Americans suffering from racism and discrimination. On the other hand, due to the proximity to the dominant White power, Asian Americans also from time to time contribute to racism against other minoritized groups, such as Black Americans (Chen et al., 2020; Kiang et al., 2016a).

As a concept similar to discrimination, stereotype refers to an oversimplified view of an individual that mainly focuses on the trait. Unlike discrimination which mainly emphasized negative views and treatments towards individuals, stereotypes can be either positive, neutral, or negative on the surface level. However, both discrimination and stereotypes of certain racial groups can cause harm (Kiang et al., 2016b). The stereotype and discrimination of Asian Americans are grounded in the sociopolitical environment and White supremacy and are heavily influenced by historical incidents and immigration waves in the United States.

For the pursuit of wealth and work opportunities, the first wave of Asian immigrants arrived in the U.S. from mainland China in the 19th century (Kiang et al., 2016a). They were originally embraced by the U.S. capitalists as cheap labor and were exploited to work in railroad, farming, and gold mining industries (Kim, 1999). Nonetheless, as their presence grew, Chinese workers were portrayed by mainstream media like the *Yellow Peril*, which was described as "dirty, diseased, sinister, sexually depraved, invasive, and perpetually foreign" (Chen et al., 2020, p. 1625). Followed by this stereotype, a number of unjust and discriminatory policies emerged. In 1882, the Chinese Exclusion Act, a law initially banning Chinese laborers and then all Chinese people from immigrating to the U.S., was passed, making it the first federal law that excluded immigrants solely based on their ethnicity. In 1924, the Immigration Act extended these unreasonable restrictions to all Asian immigrants (Chen et al., 2020). In World War II, with Japan being an enemy against the U.S., American society newspapers started to differentiate Japanese immigrants from other Asian Americans as enemies. In addition, approximately 120,000 Japanese Americans, over 60% of whom were US citizens and half of them were children, were relocated and placed into internment camps followed by the mandatory order of President Franklin Roosevelt (Jensen, 1997).

During the Civil Rights and Black Power Movements in the 1960s, Asian Americans were identified as a homogenous group and were compared to Black Americans as the *model minority*, described as hardworking, perseverant, and accommodating (Suzuki, 2002). This myth is rooted in White supremacy and has been utilized to isolate Asian Americans from the communities of color, to disparage other populations of color as inferior and problematic, to dismiss claims of racism towards non-Asian American racial minoritized groups, and to place Asian Americans as a target racial group to blame for inequalities (Anand & Hsu, 2020; Ho, 2021; Li & Nicholson, 2021). U.S. News and World Report (1996) wrote:

At a time when it is being proposed that hundreds of billions be spent to uplift Negroes and other minorities, the nation's 300,000 Chinese-Americans are moving ahead on their own – with no help from anyone else . . .. applying the virtues of hard work, thrift, and morality (p. 73).

For many Asian Americans, the model minority image serves as a source of ethnic pride and promotes self-esteem (Kiang et al., 2016a; Oyserman & Sakamoto, 1997; Thompson & Kiang, 2010). For instance, research showed that Asian American young adults and children demonstrated better academic performance when the model minority stereotype was activated before taking exams (Ambady et al., 1999, 2001). Nonetheless, like many other stereotypes, the model minority label also restricts the identity of individuals and causes harm to Asian Americans, especially among Asian American youths. To begin with, viewing all Asian Americans as overachievers is simply inaccurate. According to Hune and Takeuchi (2008), in Washington state, Taiwanese Americans reported the highest levels of educational achievement as evidenced by 67% obtaining undergraduate degrees, followed by Indian Americans (58%); on the contrary, only 7% of Cambodian and 5% of Laotian Americans graduated from college. Generalizing all Asian American youths as successful in academics limits the necessary educational resources and support provided for them (Kiang et al., 2016b). Secondly, internalizing the model minority stereotype makes Asian Americans struggle to keep up with unrealistic expectations, causing added distress associated with their performance (Kiang et al., 2016b). Moreover, the model minority stereotype mistakenly communicates that Asian Americans are immune from discrimination and racism because of their cultural values of hardworking and education (Lee, 2009), which could lead to the negligence of the adverse experiences associated with their racial and ethnic identities (Niwa et al., 2011). For Asian American children and adolescents, being perceived as the model students by teachers and students could generate tension with their peers in school. This tension serves as a source of bullying as evidenced by Asian American youths reporting more bullying incidents than Black American and Latinx students (Fisher et al., 2000; Green et al., 2006; Rosenbloom & Way, 2004).

After earlier Chinese settlers, Indians, Hmong people, and Filipinos migrated to the U.S. over the years. Due to government actions (i.e., state laws and court decisions) of protecting labor opportunities for White people, the progress of Indian immigration has been halted until 1965, featuring a strong need for doctors, nurses, and engineers in the labor market (Kiang et al., 2016a; Rangaswamy, 2000). To fulfill this need, groups of Indian professionals immigrated to the U.S. and brought the second wave of Indian immigrants consisting of their relatives and family members who were less educated in the 1980s and 1990s (Wong & Hirschman, 1983). Similar to other ethnic groups, Indian Americans reported anxiety and stress related to their cultural identities divergent from the mainstream society (Mistry & Wu, 2010). Hmong Americans settled in the U.S. as refugees in 1975 followed by the fall of Laos and Saigon (Chuong & Ta, 2003). These individuals previously lived in Southeast Asia, including Laos, south China, and Vietnam. Due to the aftermath of wars, many members of this group experienced violence and personal trauma (Kiang et al., 2016a). Filipino Americans have a unique culture due to the influence of interactions with people from multiple countries (e.g., Span, U.S., Indonesia, China, Malaysia, etc.; Rita, 1996). Although Filipino Americans were the second-largest Asian group in the U.S., research on this population is scarce (Kiang et al., 2016a).

Discrimination against Asian Americans continued in the 1990s, symbolized by the 1992 Los Angeles riots. On April 29, 1992, four Los Angeles Police Department white police officers accused of beating a Black motorist in 1991, received acquittals, which sparked a series of violent and deconstructive incidents (e.g., looting, burning, and theft) that lasted for five days. As a result, the riots caused damage to over 2,000 family-owned businesses, the majority of which were located in Koreatown, the largest residential area for ethnic Koreans outside of Seoul. Before the riot, the tension between Korean Americans and Black Americans in the area was long-standing and intensified by American and Korean media, which laid the foundation for the 1992 riots (Oh, 2010). In 2003, when severe acute respiratory syndrome (SARS) broke out in China, fear, stigma, and discriminations towards potential patients of SARS were widespread in the U.S. Individuals who appeared to be Asian regardless of their nationality and those who traveled to Asian countries during the SARS epidemic were isolated, avoided, and discriminated against by the public (Person et al., 2004). Seventeen years later, similar discrimination emerged during the COVID-19 pandemic towards anyone with an Asian appearance worldwide.

COVID DISCRIMINATION AND RACE-BASED TRAUMA IN ASIAN AMERICAN YOUTH

COVID-Fueled Discrimination

In December 2019, the 2019 novel coronavirus (COVID-19) disease emerged in Wuhan, China, and has been spreading at an exponential rate. In March 2020, the World Health Organization announced that the COVID-19 outbreak has progressed to a pandemic on a global level. In addition to the fear and anxiety of their health, Asians have experienced escalating racial discrimination and have been scapegoated as the cause of the COVID-19 spread in the U.S. Although the stigma and resentment have targeted individuals of Chinese descent, in reality, anyone with an Asian appearance is in danger of being victimized for the discrimination (Litam, 2020). This anti-Asian sentiment has been promoted through the terminology used by political leaders. For example, from March to early April 2020, President Donald Trump openly blamed China for the spread of the virus and consistently used racist terms, such as "yellow alert," "China virus," and "Kung flu" (Chiu, 2020). Coincided with the President's remarks (especially with the term "Chinese virus"), the number of anti-Asian hate crimes rocketed significantly (Cabanatuan, 2020; Kang, 2020) - approximately 1,500 racist harassments and attacks toward Asian Americans have been reported through news media (Liu & Modir, 2020). Anti-Asian racism and discrimination amid the COVID-19 pandemic are a result of a multitude of factors, including not only the presumed origin of COVID-19 in China and xenophobic language used by public figures, but also the historical antecedents linking Asian Americans to communicable disease and stereotypical views of Asian Americans as "perpetual foreigners" (Cheah et al., 2020; Litam, 2020; Wu et al., 2021) and "yellow peril" (i.e., dirty, ill, sinister, and sexually depraved; Wu et al., 2021). As Chen et al. (2020) claimed in their recent article: "In the midst of the COVID-19 pandemic we see not only a rise in anti-Asian sentiment, but also a recapitulation of history" (p. 556).

Following the COVID-19 outbreak, misinformation has been spread through biased mass media coverage and social media, which further exacerbated the stereotypical view, rooted in racism and White supremacy, of Asian Americans (Litam, 2020). As a result, individuals who appear to be Asian (including those of Chinese descent and Asian origin) have gone through an increase of racial discrimination, violence, and sinophobic attitudes against them across the U.S. (Congressional Asian American Pacific American Caucus [CAPAC], 2020). According to CAPAC (2020), content targeted toward Asian Americans on social media involves hate speech, harassment, discriminatory language, and conspiracy theories. For instance, Schild and colleagues (2020) analyzed popular social media platforms including Twitter from November 2019 to March 2020 and discovered a substantial rise in sinophobic slurs, such as "Ching Chong," "asshole," and "Chink." In a recent statement published by the advocacy group Stop AAPI Hate on February 2021, a total of 2,808 racial discriminatory incidents against Asian Americans across the U.S. were reported, including verbal harassment (70.9%), discrimination against businesses (38.1%), shunning or avoidance (21.4%), physical assaults (8.7%), denial of access to services and public spaces (8%), and coughing/spitting (6.4%), with race being cited as the primary source (90.3% of incidents) of discrimination. Specifically, victims reported being discriminated against at work, coughed upon in public, denied access from public transportation, shunned, beaten, stabbed, and insulted as transmitters of the coronavirus (Stop AAPI Hate, 2021; United Nations, 2020). In the same report, female participants reported twice more harassment than males. While the most often targeted ethnic group was Chinese (40.7% of incidents), other Asian Americans have also reported experiencing COVID-19 racism and discrimination, including Koreans (15.1%), Vietnamese (8.2%), Filipinos (7.2%), and others.

Trauma Symptoms in American Youths

Posttraumatic stress disorder (PTSD) is a mental health condition where individuals display debilitation in their daily functioning at work, home, school, and socially, due to persistent reactions to traumatic experiences in the past (Moorhead & Zoldan, 2019). One can develop PTSD after exposure to incidents like physical, sexual, or mental assaults, natural or man-made disasters, accidents and injuries, combat or war, and other forms of violence (National Institute of Mental Health [NIMH], n.d.). According to the *Diagnostic and Statistical Manual of Mental Disorders* (5th ed.; *DSM-5*; American Psychological Association [APA], 2013), PTSD symptoms can be categorized into four groups: (a) intrusion symptoms, such as distressing dreams and involuntary memories associated with traumatic events, (b) negative changes in cognitive and/or affective functioning, including detachment from others, feelings of numbness, and more, (c) active avoidance of stimuli (e.g., objects, people, or places that can remind individuals of the traumatic experiences), and (d) reactivity or enhanced arousals, such as anger bursts and hypervigilance.

According to NIMH (n.d.), approximately 3.6% of American adults are affected by PTSD each year, with women being twice as likely as men to have the disorder. Although professionals estimated PTSD impacted approximately 5% of American adolescents (Merikangas et al., 2010; NIH, n.d.), the prevalence of PTSD among American youth is still hard to predict because parents, guardians, and their adolescent children tend to under-report this condition (Moorhead & Zoldan, 2019) potentially due to negligence of, and stigma associated with the disorder. In the *DSM-5* (APA, 2013), ethnic and racial minoritized groups including Asian Americans were documented as having the lowest prevalence rate of PTSD despite their experiences of cultural risk factors (i.e., low socioeconomic status and minoritized racial/ethnic status) for the disorder. For Asian Americans, one explanation could be the long-standing stigma of mental illness in the Asian culture. When individuals suffer from mental health issues, instead of seeking help from professionals, they tend to turn to their families for support (Sue & Sure, 2019).

Race-Based Discrimination and Trauma

In the past twenty years, research studies showed empirical evidence for the positive relationship between PTSD symptoms and race-based discrimination among racially and ethnically minoritized groups. In a longitudinal study among 110 Mexican Americans whose age ranged from 16 to 20 years, Flores et al. (2010) found that participants with a higher level of perceived racial discrimination also experience more posttraumatic stress symptoms. In another longitudinal study with 152 Black Americans and 139 Latinx adults with anxiety disorders, researchers concluded that participants who experienced discrimination more frequently within a five-year period ended up developing more symptoms related to trauma and meeting more diagnostic criteria of PTSD (Sibrava et al., 2019). Scholars also studied race-based discrimination and trauma among Asian ethnic groups. A survey of 69 Asian American college students revealed that a negative racial climate in school uniquely predicted trauma-related symptoms among participants (Pieterse et al., 2010). Correspondingly, in the study of Wei et al. (2012), perceived racial discrimination positively predicted posttraumatic stress symptoms above and beyond general life stress among Chinese international students in the U.S.

Scholars proposed different theories to understand the correlations between race-based discrimination and trauma-related symptoms. Carter (2007) alleged that race-based discrimination should be viewed as a type of traumatic injury that leads to trauma-related symptoms among racial and ethnically marginalized groups. Hamblen and Barnett (2014) noted that minoritized groups with a higher level of PTSD symptoms might be due to more exposure to trauma. During the COVID-19 pandemic, Asian Americans, including both adults and adolescents, experienced a surge of Anti-Asian online and in-person racism, discrimination, as well as hate crimes in the U.S. This experience becomes a risk factor that can lead to the development of PTSD symptoms. In fact, Ermis-Demirtas et al. (in press) found that East and Southeast Asian high school students reported high levels of posttraumatic stress symptoms that are associated with online and in-person discriminations and bullying based on race. Thus, it is critical that school counselors seek to address discrimination fueled by the COVID-19 pandemic of Asian American youths from a trauma-informed approach.

TRAUMA-INFORMED PRACTICES TO ADDRESS COVID-19 FUELED DISCRIMINATION AND RACIAL TRAUMA IN ASIAN AMERICAN YOUTH: A MULTI-TIERED SYSTEM OF SUPPORT

Given the frequency and association with the racial trauma symptoms of COVID-fueled discrimination in ESEAA youth, it is pivotal for schools to take a proactive approach to preventing and assessing trauma as well as helping students recover from potentially traumatic experiences. At the broader level, it is imperative for schools to collaborate with the community leaders to address COVID-related anti-Asian stigma, harassment, and discrimination and coordinate a powerful response. First, school and community leaders can collaborate to encourage and fund local and school-wide initiatives to provide evidence-based culturally-responsive mental health services (Sue & Sue, 2019), mental health advocacy and stigma campaigns, and school and community outreach to East and Southeast Asian American youth to mitigate the impact of racial trauma in this marginalized group following the outbreak of COVID-19 (Anyon et al., 2014; Wu et al., 2021). Considering empirical evidence that indicates the similar impact of discrimination on Chinese and non-Chinese ESEAA youths' trauma symptoms, such efforts should target both populations.

In schools, school counselors can play a critical role in developing a trauma-informed approach and implementing anti-racist practices (ASCA, 2021) by applying school counseling standards to change the school culture and promote student support (McIntyre et al., 2019). Ieva et al. (2021) emphasizes the acknowledgment of structural racism in education and development of critical consciousness as the core elements of anti-racist practices. Using a multi-tiered systems of support (MTSS), trauma-sensitive school counseling programs should be provided on the school-wide level, and individual level in order to be effective (Sulkowski & Michael, 2014). In a trauma-sensitive framework rooted in MTSS, all students receive Tier 1 services from school counselors and other educational staff in such a way that they are able to gain awareness regarding students in need of more intensive mental health services and that no further psychological trauma is inflicted upon students (Taylor, 2021). Stafford et al. (2008) described these initial steps as *Psychological First Aid* (PFA; p. 20) where the primary goal is to create feelings of safety, connection, self-regulation, and self-help for those who have recently experienced trauma to start working toward recovery. According to Stafford and colleagues, the key principles include *look*, *listen*, and *link*. The first step is to look and assess for needs and concerns. The second step is to listen to individuals without placing pressure on them to talk about the traumatic event or their experiences while also comforting them, validating their feelings and experiences, and helping them calm down. The third step is to link affected students to other community supports to ensure basic needs are being met.

Tier 1 level services can offer students universal prevention programs (Sink, 2016), such as the *Resilience Classroom Curriculum* (Ijadi-Mghsoodi et al., 2017) and school-based trauma-informed interventions, including mindfulness techniques (Dove & Costello, 2016). As a school-wide intervention targeting all students, school counselors can be proactive to advocate for a comprehensive bullying prevention policy that addresses COVID-fueled discrimination (Stop AAPI Hate Youth Campaign, 2020) and deliver classroom lessons that align with the ASCA mindsets and behaviors to educate students o identifying hate and bias and how to disrupt it (Dillard, 2020). Exploring anti-Asian rhetoric around the virus might be worthy of critical conversations in the classroom even when students are not engaging or repeating racist tropes. The class conversations may also involve digital literacy since students become more aware of hateful and biased speech online and report COVID related online discrimination and racial trauma. In addition to the classroom-level interventions, school counselors can conduct school-wide assessments for culturally unique risk factors to identify Asian American students with potential mental health needs related to COVID discrimination and racial trauma by using screening tools, such as Race-Based Traumatic Symptom Stress Scale [RBTSS]; Carter & Muchow, 2017). School counselors may also follow the standard protocols for considering trauma exposure by utilizing the Child Trauma Toolkit for Educators (National Child Traumatic Stress Network [NCTSN]; 2008).

At Tier 1 level, school counselors can gain trauma literacy and further their awareness and knowledgebase about the prevalence of anti-Asian bias and discrimination during the pandemic and its psychological impact on Asian American students by seeking professional development opportunities, engaging in self-reflection, and building collaboration with the AAPI organizations in the community (Grassroots Asians Rising, 2020). School counselors also take on a significant role in providing seminars for teachers, administrators, allied professionals, and partners in the community to create a shared understanding of racial discrimination and trauma within Asian American students (Okazaki et al., 2020) and what is needed to build their coping and protective skills (NCTSN, 2017). This information can further support the foundational knowledge to identify the signs of racial trauma and toxic stress that Asian American youth in schools may experience. These professional development workshops may help challenge the stereotypes associated with Asian Americans, such as model minority myth (Chen et al., 2020). School counselors can also become more intentional and provide psychoeducation to Asian American students about the effects of discrimination and racial trauma, share strategies to develop healthy coping skills for managing stress, encourage associations and activities that nurture healthy peer and family relationships and connections to community organizations, and incorporate practices to enhance youths' resilience and protective skills (Chafouleas et al., 2016). Psychoeducation might empower Asian American youths to seek the school counselors' services when needed.

At Tier 2 and Tier 3 levels, school counselors can conduct more in-depth assessments to better understand the nature of racial trauma in Asian American youth by implementing counselor-administered interview surveys, such as the UConn Racial/Ethnic Stress & Trauma Survey (UnRESTS; Williams et al., 2018). Such tools can be useful for school counselors to uncover racial trauma, develop culturally-informed strategies, and include experiences of racial discrimination in understanding trauma when warranted. When addressing racial trauma in the school system, it is imperative for school counselors to understand all the ways in which students interact with each other, including online. Social media plays a significant role in the interpersonal exchanges among youth, both in and outside of school. For example, Ermis-Demirtas et al. (in press) In addition, Asian American students' discriminatory experiences in online settings have been found to be linked to trauma symptoms (Ermis-Demirtas et al., in press). Therefore, school counselors can integrate questions about social media experiences and online activities when assessing racial trauma (Handford & Marrero, 2022). In this process of assessment, Hanford and Marrero (2022) encourage school counselors to intentionally explore, process, and attend to the students' experiences of others and themselves online as well as what increasing feelings of empowerment would look like for them. Moreover, scholars and researchers have linked the severity of psychological reactions to racism, in part, to how well one copes; that is, when people have the resources to cope effectively, they view stressful situations as a challenge rather than a threat and experience a reduced stress response (Brondolo et al., 2009). Therefore, school counselors can apply assessments to identify the range of specific strategies people of color use to cope with racism, such as the Racism-Related Coping Scale (RRCS; Forsyth & Carter, 2014). Identifying effective strategies to cope with chronic stressors, including race-related stress could provide school counselors with a basis to develop interventions that mitigate the impact of stress reactions by promoting students' coping resources.

Tier 2 practices involve interventions available to some students who need more support (ASCA, 2018). School counselors can examine data, including universal screeners and outcome data in collaboration with school staff to determine which students may need additional support. For Asian American students with racial discrimination and trauma experiences who need additional services, school counselors can apply Check-in/Check-out (CICO) regularly to provide mentoring. Further, since Asian American are often identified with a collectivist culture, engaging these students in social justice oriented support groups where they could be invited to share their COVID related discriminatory experiences and trauma narratives in a braver space (Ieva et al., 2021; "I wonder if you would describe what your experience has been like as an Asian American following the COVID-19 outbreak.").

Otherwise, it may be more difficult for them to initiate this conversation (Chen et al., 2021). Consistent with anti-racist school counseling practices, groups are also viewed as a preferred system of support when working with minoritized students to provide the space for discussions centered on oppression, discrimination, and privilege (Ieva et al., 2021). These support groups can create an important space for Asian American students to promote their critical consciousness by helping them explore the ways internalized racism reveals in their coping strategies and daily life experiences (Chopra, 2021). According to Chopra (2021), such groups may also lead Asian American youth to feel empowered to take action toward social justice together and dismantle oppression. Moreover, in the emotional safety of groups, these students can develop a positive ethnic identity where the school counselor facilitates conversations about the history of Asian Americans in the U.S., including racism, inequalities, and civil rights activists. A strong positive identity could play a protective role against discrimination and adverse mental health outcomes in Asian American students (Chen et al., 2021). Due to Asian American adolescents' higher tendency to internalize the model minority trope, school counselors can incorporate trauma-informed, culturally-sensitive targeted interventions, such as *Cognitive Behavioral Intervention for Trauma in Schools* (CBITS; Stein et al., 2003) and *Creative Arts-Based Wellness Program* (Sitzer & Stockwell, 2015), as well as practices based on mindfulness and self-compassion in particular (e.g., guided imagery exercises) as a culturally relevant approach to healing racial trauma among this population (Litam, 2020; Liu et al., 2020). These practices may be advantageous for Asian American adolescents, as they often prefer self-help approaches to mental health services (Chopra, 2021).

In schools, creative interventions, such as bibliotherapy and play-based strategies, can offer powerful tools when working with Asian American youths in addressing racial trauma (Handford & Marrero, 2022). In their book, Hanford and Marrero (2022) provide a list of play-based creative activities to help youths process struggles related to race, ethnicity, identity, and stress via the use of play, art, and drama. One of the activities they suggest, for example, is *Trauma Trivia*, a psychoeducational game used to introduce the concept of ethno-racial stress and racial trauma to youths indirectly and engagingly. For this game, school counselors create categories and questions for the youth to answer and assign points to each level of questions. Some of the categories may include general information about racial trauma, psychoeducation about post-traumatic symptoms, coping skills, and avenues of support. This game can be a powerful tool to provide information and begin challenging the distortions the youth may have about race and trauma. Another empowering activity Hanford and Marrero suggest to address racial trauma is *I am not My Trauma*. In this experiential activity, youths cover a large picture of themselves with a piece of saran wrap and affix it to a poster board. The school counselor encourages them to look at the picture and name positive traits about themselves and their cultural identity. Then, the school counselor guides them in throwing different colored paints at the picture to symbolize the negative messages or incidents that they have received or experienced because of their racial identity. As they process how they feel about the covered picture and relate it to their positive and negative feelings about their identity, the school counselor removes the wrap to reveal a pristine picture. The group together reflects on how the messages and events do not change their amazing, unique, and authentic core self. Hanford and Marrero (2022) also recommend bibliotherapy to address cultural differences and general trauma as well as provide a list of books, such as *This Book is Anti-Racist: 20 Lessons on How to Wake up, Take Action, and Do the Work by Jewell* (2020) and *Where are you From?* by Mendez (2019). Since Asian Americans are underrepresented in the discrimination literature, we need more books and resources addressing racial trauma in Asian American youth.

At Tier 3 level, school counselors may refer Asian American youth to evidence-based, trauma-informed, culturally sensitive interventions on an as-needed basis when school personnel are unable to meet the student's mental health needs. Facilitating referrals to mental health services can normalize help-seeking behaviors among Asian American students (Cheah et al., 2020). School counselors may also advocate for adopting the co-located mental health model, in which the school provides a space for a clinical counselor to meet with students during the day, and the billing goes through insurance. This practice permits those students and their families with barriers surrounding mental health stigma and transportation an opportunity to receive services consistently and maintain privacy preferences (Martinez et al., 2020). Within trauma-informed Tier 3, school counselors serve in collaborative and consultative roles (ASCA, 2018). School counselors can help their school develop strong relationships with community providers and collaborate with the AAPI organizations in the community to ensure there are supports outside of school. The school counselor can invite community partners to introduce their resources via brief presentations at school staff meetings. Inviting these parties to meetings may also help them learn more about the school's needs related to developing trauma-informed, culturally sensitive practices and about the issues experienced by Asian American youth within their particular school community. Another strategy school counselors can implement is to collaborate with local counseling and psychological services to provide comprehensive and ongoing screening, assessment, and monitoring aligned with interventions for racial trauma in Asian American youth (Hendricks et al., 2011; Zaenah & Humphreys, 2019).

CONCLUSION

Following the COVID-19 outbreak, Asian Americans, more specifically, East and Southeast Asian Americans, have become the targets of racism, discrimination, and hate crimes. Mirroring this broader societal problem of COVID-related racism, schools have become a hostile environment for Asian American students with a significant rise in bullying and discriminatory incidents. In addition to experiencing harassment and discrimination in schools, Asian American students have also reported such incidents in online platforms. Both in-person and online COVID-19 discrimination Asian American students experience have been linked to PTSD symptoms and racial trauma. After reading this chapter, it is hoped that school counselors will be able to identify the history of racism, COVID-19 fueled discrimination, and racial trauma in East and Southeast Asian American youth as well as develop culturally sensitive, trauma-informed, anti-racist practices and interventions to address racial trauma in this student population.

REFERENCES

Akiba, D. (2020). Reopening America's schools during the COVID-19 pandemic: Protecting Asian students from stigma and discrimination. *Frontiers in Sociology*, *5*, 1–6. doi:10.3389/fsoc.2020.588936 PMID:33869517

Ambady, N., Shih, M., Kim, A., & Pittinsky, T. L. (2001). Stereotype susceptibility in children: Effects of identity activation on quantitative performance. *Psychological Science*, *12*(5), 385–390. doi:10.1111/1467-9280.00371 PMID:11554671

Ambady, N., Shih, M., & Pittinsky, T. L. (1999). Stereotype susceptibility: Identity salience and shifts in quantitative performance. *Psychological Science*, *10*(1), 80–83. doi:10.1111/1467-9280.00111

American Psychiatric Association. (2013). *Diagnostic and statistical manual of mental health disorders* (5th ed.). doi:10.1176/appi.books.9780890425596

American School Counselor Association. (2016a). *ASCA ethical standards for school counselors.* https://www.schoolcounselor.org/asca/media/asca/Ethics/EthicalStandards2016.pdf

American School Counselor Association (2016b). *The school counselor and trauma-informed practice.* The School Counselor and Trauma-Informed Practice - American School Counselor Association (ASCA).

American School Counselor Association. (2021). *The school counselor and anti-racist practices.* https://www.schoolcounselor.org/getmedia/12cec1e8-5dab-44e5-acf8-6f10484cbaab/ps-anti-racist-practices-draft.pdf

Anand, D., & Hsu, L. M. (2020). COVID-19 and Black Lives Matter: Examining anti-Asian racism and anti-Blackness in US education. *International Journal of Multidisciplinary Perspectives in Higher Education*, *5*(1), 190–199. doi:10.32674/jimphe.v5i1.2656

Anyon, Y., Ong, S. L., & Whitaker, K. (2014). School-based mental health prevention for Asian American adolescents: Risk behaviors, protective factors, and service use. *Asian American Journal of Psychology*, *5*(2), 134–144. doi:10.1037/a0035300

Asian Pacific Institute on Gender-Based Violence. (2021, October 16). *Census data & API identities.* https://www.api-gbv.org/resources/census-data-api-identities/

Atkin, A. L., Yoo, H. C., & Yeh, C. J. (2019). What types of racial messages protect Asian American adolescents from discrimination? A latent interaction model. *Journal of Counseling Psychology*, *66*(2), 247–254. doi:10.1037/cou0000297 PMID:30035592

Budiman, A., & Ruiz, N. G. (2021, April 29). *Key facts about Asian Americans, a diverse and growing population.* Pew Research Center. https://www.pewresearch.org/fact-tank/2021/04/29/key-facts-about-asian-americans/

Budiman, A., & Ruiz, N. G. (2021, April 9). *Asian Americans are the fastest-growing racial or ethnic group in the U.S.* Pew Research Center. https://www.pewresearch.org/fact-tank/2021/04/09/asian-americans-are-the-fastest-growing-racial-or-ethnic-group-in-the-u-s/

Cabanatuan, M. (2020, March 19). Coronavirus: Asian American groups compile hate crime reports as Trump persists in 'Chinese virus' attacks. *San Francisco Chronicle.* https://www.sfchronicle.com/bayarea/article/Coronavirus-Asian-American-groups-compile-hate-15144295.php

Carter, R. T. (2007). Racism and psychological and emotional injury: Recognizing and assessing race-based traumatic stress. *The Counseling Psychologist*, *35*(1), 13–105. doi:10.1177/0011000006292033

Carter, R. T., & Muchow, C. (2017). Construct validity of the Race-Based Traumatic Stress Symptom Scale and tests of measurement equivalence. *Psychological Trauma: Theory, Research, Practice, and Policy*, *9*(6), 688–695. doi:10.1037/tra0000256 PMID:28165267

Cheah, C. S., Wang, C., Ren, H., Zong, X., Cho, H. S., & Xue, X. (2020). COVID-19 racism and mental health in Chinese American families. *Pediatrics*, *146*(5), e2020021816. Advance online publication. doi:10.1542/peds.2020-021816 PMID:32873719

Chen, J. A., Zhang, E., & Liu, C. H. (2020). Potential Impact of COVID-19-Related Racial Discrimination on the Health of Asian Americans. *American Journal of Public Health*, *110*(11), 1624–1627. doi:10.2105/AJPH.2020.305858 PMID:32941063

Cheng, H. L., & Mallinckrodt, B. (2015). Racial/ethnic discrimination, posttraumatic stress symptoms, and alcohol problems in a longitudinal study of Hispanic/Latino college students. *Journal of Counseling Psychology*, *62*(1), 38–49. doi:10.1037/cou0000052 PMID:25602606

Chiu, A. (2020, March 20). Trump has no qualms about calling the coronavirus the 'Chinese Virus.' That's a dangerous attitude, experts say. *The Washington Post*. https://www.washingtonpost.com/nation/2020/03/20/coronavirus-trump-chinese-virus/

Chopra, S. B. (2021). Healing from internalized racism for Asian Americans. *Professional Psychology, Research and Practice*, *52*(5), 503–512. doi:10.1037/pro0000407

Chuong, C. H., & Ta, M. H. (2003). Vietnamese: Overcoming the past and building a future. In E. Lai & D. Arguelles (Eds.), *The new face of Asian Pacific America: Numbers, diversity & change in the 21st century* (pp. 67–72). Asian Week.

Cohen, J. (1992). A power primer. *Psychological Bulletin*, *112*(1), 155–159. doi:10.1037/0033-2909.112.1.155 PMID:19565683

Congressional Asian American Pacific American Caucus. (2020). *As coronavirus fears incite violence, CAPAC members urge colleagues to not stoke xenophobia.* https://capac-chu.house.gov/press-release/coronavirusfears-incite-violence-capac-members-urge-colleagues-not-stoke-xenophobia

Dillard, C. (2020). Speaking up against racism around the coronavirus. *Teaching Tolerance*. https://www.learningforjustice.org/magazine/speaking-up-against-racism-around-the-coronavirus

Ermis-Demirtas, H., Luo, Y., & Huang, Y. (in press). The trauma of COVID-19 fueled discrimination: Posttraumatic stress in Asian American adolescents. *Professional School Counseling*.

Fisher, C. B., Wallace, S. A., & Fenton, R. E. (2000). Discrimination distress during adolescence. *Journal of Youth and Adolescence, 29*(6), 679–695. doi:10.1023/A:1026455906512

Flores, E., Tschann, J. M., Dimas, J. M., Pasch, L. A., & de Groat, C. L. (2010). Perceived racial/ethnic discrimination, posttraumatic stress symptoms, and health risk behaviors among Mexican American adolescents. *Journal of Counseling Psychology, 57*(3), 264–273. doi:10.1037/a0020026 PMID:21133578

Foa, E. B., Asnaani, A., Zang, Y., Capaldi, S., & Yeh, R. (2018). Psychometrics of the Child PTSD Symptom Scale for *DSM*-5 for trauma-exposed children and adolescents. *Journal of Clinical Child and Adolescent Psychology, 47*(1), 38–46. doi:10.1080/15374416.2017.1350962 PMID:28820616

Forsyth, J. M., & Carter, R. T. (2014). Development and preliminary validation of the Racism-Related Coping Scale. *Psychological Trauma: Theory, Research, Practice, and Policy, 6*(6), 632–643. doi:10.1037/a0036702

Grassroots Asians Rising. (2020). *Asian American racial justice toolkit.* https://www.asianamtoolkit.org/the-toolkit

Greene, M. L., Way, N., & Pahl, K. (2006). Trajectories of perceived adult and peer discrimination among Black, Latino, and Asian American adolescents: Patterns and psychological correlates. *Developmental Psychology, 42*(2), 218–236. doi:10.1037/0012-1649.42.2.218 PMID:16569162

Hamblen, J., & Barnett, E. (2014). *PTSD in children and adolescents.* http://www.georgiadisaster.info/Schools/fs%207%20school/PTSD%20in%20Children%20&%20Adolescents.pdf

Handford, C., & Marrero, A. D. (2021). *Racial trauma in the school system: Naming the Pain* (1st ed.). Routledge. doi:10.4324/9780429029615

Hendricks, A., Conradi, L., & Wilson, C. (2011). Creating trauma-informed child welfare systems using a community assessment process. *Child Welfare, 90*, 187–205. PMID:22533049

Ho, J. (2021). Anti-Asian racism, Black Lives Matter, and COVID-19. *Japan Forum, 33*(1), 148–159. doi:10.1080/09555803.2020.1821749

Hune, S. H., & Takeuchi, D. T. (2008). Asian Americans in Washington State: Closing their hidden achievement gaps. Report submitted to The Washington State Commission on Asian Pacific American Affairs, University of Washington.

Ieva, K. O., Beasley, J., & Steen, S. (2021). Equipping school counselors for anti-racist healing centered groups: A critical examination for preparation, connected curricula, professional practice and oversight. *Teaching and Supervision in Counseling, 3*, 64–78. doi:10.7290/tsc030207

Ijai-Maghsoodi, R., Marlotte, L., Garcia, E., Aralis, H., Lester, P., Escudero, P., & Kataoka, S. (2017). Adapting and implementing a school-based resilience-building curriculum among low-income racial and ethnic minority students. *Racial and Ethnic Minority Students. Contemporary School Psychology, 21*(3), 223–239. doi:10.100740688-017-0134-1 PMID:29686938

Kang, E. (2020, March 31). Asian Americans feel the bite of prejudice during the COVID-19 pandemic. *NPR WBEZ Chicago.* https://www.npr.org/local/309/2020/03/31/824397216/asian-americansfeel-the-bite-of-prejudice-during-the-c-o-v-i-d-19-pandemic

Kaplow, J. B., Rolon-Arroyo, B., Layne, C. M., Rooney, E., Oosterhoff, B., Hill, R., Steinberg, A. M., Lotterman, J., Gallagher, K. A. S., & Pynoos, R. S. (2020). Validation of the UCLA PTSD Reaction Index for *DSM*-5: A developmentally informed assessment tool for youth. *Journal of the American Academy of Child and Adolescent Psychiatry, 59*(1), 186–194. doi:10.1016/j.jaac.2018.10.019 PMID:30953734

Kiang, L., & Bhattacharjee, K. (2016). A narrative-linguistic approach to understanding Asian American adolescents' discrimination experiences. *Asian American Journal of Psychology, 7*(1), 41–51. doi:10.1037/aap0000036

Lee, E. (2015). *The making of Asian American: A history*. Simon & Schuster Paperbacks.

Lee, S., & Waters, S. F. (2021). Asians and Asian Americans' experiences of racial discrimination during the COVID-19 pandemic: Impacts on health outcomes and the buffering role of social support. *Stigma and Health, 6*(1), 70–78. doi:10.1037ah0000275 PMID:35369673

Lee, S. A. (2020). Coronavirus Anxiety Scale: A brief mental health screener for COVID-19 related anxiety. *Death Studies, 44*(7), 393–401. doi:10.1080/07481187.2020.1748481 PMID:32299304

Li, Y., & Nicholson, H. L. Jr. (2021). When "model minorities" become "yellow peril"—Othering and the racialization of Asian Americans in the COVID-19 pandemic. *Sociology Compass, 15*(2). Advance online publication. doi:10.1111oc4.12849 PMID:33786062

Litam, S. D. A. (2020). "Take your kung-flu back to Wuhan": Counseling Asians, Asian Americans, and Pacific Islanders with race-based trauma related to COVID-19. *The Professional Counselor, 10*(2), 144–156. doi:10.15241dal.10.2.144

Litam, S. D. A., & Oh, S. (2020). Ethnic identity and coping strategies as moderators of COVID-19 racial discrimination experiences among Chinese Americans. *Counseling Outcome Research and Evaluation*, 1–15. Advance online publication. doi:10.1080/21501378.2020.1814138

Liu, S. R., & Modir, S. (2020). The outbreak that way always here: Racial trauma in the context of COVID-19 and implications for mental health providers. *Psychological Trauma: Theory, Research, Practice, and Policy, 12*(5), 439–442. doi:10.1037/tra0000784 PMID:32551756

Lowe, S. R., Tineo, P., & Young, M. N. (2019). Perceived Discrimination and Major Depression and Generalized Anxiety Symptoms: In Muslim American College Students. *Journal of Religion and Health, 58*(4), 1136–1145. doi:10.100710943-018-0684-1 PMID:30094677

Martinez, R. R., Williams, R. G., & Green, J. (2019). The role of school counselors delivering a trauma-informed care approach to supporting youth in foster care. *Professional School Counseling, 23*(1), 1–10. doi:10.1177/2156759X20947747

Merikangas, K. R., He, J. P., Burstein, M., Swanson, S. A., Avenevoli, S., Cui, L., Benjet, C., Georgiades, K., & Swendsen, J. (2010). Lifetime prevalence of mental disorders in US adolescents: Results from the National Comorbidity Survey Replication–Adolescent Supplement (NCS-A). *Journal of the American Academy of Child and Adolescent Psychiatry, 49*(10), 980–989. doi:10.1016/j.jaac.2010.05.017 PMID:20855043

Mistry, J., & Wu, J. (2010). Navigating cultural worlds and negotiating identities: A conceptual model. *Human Development, 53*(1), 5–25. doi:10.1159/000268136

Moorhead, H. H., & Zoldan, C. A. (2019). Trauma- and stressor-related disorders. In V. E. Kress & M. J. Paylo (Eds.), *Treating those with mental disorders: A comprehensive approach to case conceptualization and treatment* (2nd ed., pp. 209–238). Pearson.

National Child Traumatic Stress Network. (2008). *Child trauma toolkit for educators.* https://www.nctsn.org/resources/child-trauma-toolkit-educators

National Child Traumatic Stress Network. (2017). *Creating, supporting, and sustaining trauma-informed schools: A system framework.* https://www.nctsn.org/resources/creating-supporting-and-sustaining-trauma-informed-schools-system-framework

Niwa, E. Y., Way, N., & Hughes, D. L. (2014). Trajectories of ethnic-racial discrimination among ethnically diverse early adolescents: Associations with psychological and social adjustment. *Child Development, 85*, 2339–2354. doi:10.1111/cdev.12310 PMID:25345480

Oh, A. E. (2009). An issue of time and place: The truth behind Korean Americans' connection to the 1992 Los Angeles riots. *Asian American Policy Review, 19*, 39–48.

Okazaki, S., Shea, M., Thakore-Dunlap, U., & Wang, C. (2020). *Bullying prevention, intervention, and resource guide for parents.* Asian American Psychological Association. https://aapaonline.org/resources/bullying-awareness-campaign/

Oyserman, D., & Sakamoto, I. (1997). Being Asian American: Identity, cultural constructs, and stereotype perception. *The Journal of Applied Behavioral Science, 33*(4), 435–453. doi:10.1177/0021886397334002

Person, B., Sy, F., Holton, K., Govert, B., Liang, A., Garza, B., Gould, D., Hickson, M., McDonald, M., Meijer, C., Smith, J., Veto, L., Williams, W., & Zauderer, L. (2004). Fear and stigma: The epidemic within the SARS outbreak. *Emerging Infectious Diseases, 10*(2), 358–363. doi:10.3201/eid1002.030750 PMID:15030713

Pieterse, A. L., Carter, R. T., Evans, S. A., & Walter, R. A. (2010). An exploratory examination of the associations among racial and ethnic discrimination, racial climate, and trauma-related symptoms in a college student population. *Journal of Counseling Psychology, 57*(3), 255–263. doi:10.1037/a0020040 PMID:21133577

Rangaswamy, P. (2000). *Namaste America: Indian immigrants in an American metropolis*. Pennsylvania State University Press.

Rolon-Arroyo, B., Oosterhoff, B., Layne, C. M., Steinberg, A. M., Pynoos, R. S., & Kaplow, J. B. (2020). The UCLA PTSD Reaction Index for *DSM*-5 Brief Form: A screening tool for trauma-exposed youths. *Journal of the American Academy of Child and Adolescent Psychiatry, 59*(3), 434–443. doi:10.1016/j.jaac.2019.06.015 PMID:31376502

Rosenbloom, S. R., & Way, N. (2004). Experiences of Discrimination among African American, Asian American, and Latino Adolescents in an Urban High School. *Youth & Society, 35*(4), 420–451. doi:10.1177/0044118X03261479

Schild, L., Ling, C., Blackburn, J., Stringhini, G., Zhang, Y., & Zannettou, S. (2020). "Go eat a bat, Chang!" An early look on the emergence of sinophobic behavior on web communities in the face of COVID-19. *Computers & Society*, 1–16. https://arxiv.org/pdf/2004.04046.pdf

Seaton, E. K., Neblett, E. W. Jr, Cole, D. J., & Prinstein, M. J. (2013). Perceived Discrimination and Peer Victimization Among African American and Latino Youth. *Journal of Youth and Adolescence*, *42*(3), 342–350. doi:10.100710964-012-9848-6 PMID:23124713

Sibrava, N. J., Bjornsson, A. S., Pérez Benítez, A. C. I., Moitra, E., Weisberg, R. B., & Keller, M. B. (2019). Posttraumatic stress disorder in African American and Latinx adults: Clinical course and the role of racial and ethnic discrimination. *The American Psychologist*, *74*(1), 101–116. doi:10.1037/amp0000339 PMID:30652903

Sibrava, N. J., Bjornsson, A. S., Pérez Benítez, A. C. I., Moitra, E., Weisberg, R. B., & Keller, M. B. (2019). Posttraumatic stress disorder in African American and Latinx adults: Clinical course and the role of racial and ethnic discrimination. *The American Psychologist*, *74*(1), 101–116. doi:10.1037/amp0000339 PMID:30652903

Sink, C. (2016). Incorporating a multi-tiered system of support into school counselor preparation. *The Professional Counselor*, *6*(3), 203–219. doi:10.15241/cs.6.3.203

Stein, B. D., Jaycox, L. H., Kataoka, S. H., & Wong, W. T., Elliott, W. M. N., & Fink, A. (2003). A mental health intervention for school-aged children exposed to violence: A randomized controlled trial. *Journal of the American Medical Association*, *290*, 603–611. doi:10.1001/jama.290.5.603 PMID:12902363

Stop AAPI Hate. (2021, February 9). *New data on anti-Asian hate incidents against elderly and total national incidents in 2020.* https://secureservercdn.net/104.238.69.231/a1w.90d.myftpupload.com/wp-content/uploads/2021/02/Press-Statement-re_-Bay-Area-Elderly-Incidents-2.9.2021-1.pdf

Stop AAPI Hate Youth Campaign. (2020). *They blamed me because I am Asian: Findings from youth-reported incidents of anti-AAPI hate.* http://www.asianpacificpolicyandplanningcouncil.org/wp-content/uploads/Stop-AAPI-Hate-Youth-Campaign-Report-9.11.20.pdf

Sue, D. W., Sue, D., Neville, H. A., & Smith, L. (2019). *Counseling the culturally diverse: Theory and practice*. John Wiley & Sons.

Sulkowski, M. L., & Michael, K. (2014). Meeting the mental health needs of homeless students in schools: A multi-tiered system of support framework. *Children and Youth Services Review*, *44*, 145–151. doi:10.1016/j.childyouth.2014.06.014

Suzuki, B. H. (2002). Revisiting the model minority stereotype: Implications for student affairs practice and higher education. *New Directions for Student Services*, *97*(97), 21–32. doi:10.1002s.36

Taylor, S. S. (2021). Trauma-informed care in schools: A Necessity in the time of COVID-19. *Beyond Behavior, 30*(3), 124–134. Advance online publication. doi:10.1177/10742956211020841

Teaching Tolerance. (2017). *Responding to hate and bias at school: A guide for administrators, counselors, and teachers.* https://www.learningforjustice.org/sites/default/files/2017-07/Responding%20to%20Hate%20at%20School%202017.pdf

Teaching Tolerance. (2019). *Speak up at school: How to respond to everyday prejudice, biases, and stereotypes.* https://www.learningforjustice.org/magazine/publications/speak-up-at-school

Thompson, T. L., & Kiang, L. (2010). The model minority stereotype: Adolescent experiences and links with adjustment. *Asian American Journal of Psychology, 1*(2), 119–128. https://doi.org/10.1037/a0019966

Tynes, B. M., Rose, C. A., & Williams, D. R. (2010). The development and validation of the online victimization scale for adolescents. *Cyberpsychology (Brno), 4*(2). https://cyberpsychology.eu/article/view/4237

United Nations, Human Rights, Office of the High Commissioner. (2020, March 23). *States should take action against COVID-19-related expressions of xenophobia, says UN expert.* https://www.ohchr.org/EN/NewsEvents/Pages/DisplayNews.aspx?NewsID=25739&LangID=

United States Census Bureau. (2021, October 4). *State population by characteristic:2010-2019.* https://www.census.gov/data/tables/time-series/demo/popest/2010s-state-detail.html

U.S. News and World Report. (1966). *Success story of one minority group in the U.S.* Author.

Wei, M., Wang, K. T., Heppner, P. P., & Du, Y. (2012). Ethnic and mainstream social connectedness, perceived racial discrimination, and posttraumatic stress symptoms. *Journal of Counseling Psychology, 59*, 486–493. https://dx.doi.org/10.1037/a0028000

Williams, M. T., Metzger, I. W., Liens, C., & DeLapp, C. (2018). Assessing racial trauma within a DSM-5 framework: The UConn Racial/Ethnic Stress and Trauma Survey. *Practice Innovations (Washington, D.C.), 3*, 242–260. https://dx.doi.org/10.1037/pri0000076

Wong, M. G., & Hirschman, C. (1983). The new Asian immigrants. In W. C. McCready (Ed.), *Culture, ethnicity, and identity: Current issues in research* (pp. 381–403). Academic Press.

Woo, B., & Jun, J. (2021). COVID-19 racial discrimination and depressive symptoms among Asians Americans: Does communication about the incident matter? *Journal of Immigrant and Minority Health.* doi:10.1007/s10903-021-01167-x

Wu, C., Qian, Y., & Wilkes, R. (2021). Anti-Asian discrimination and the Asian-white mental health gap during COVID-19. *Ethnic and Racial Studies, 44*(5), 819–835. https://doi.org/10.1080/01419870.2020.1851739

Yoo, H. C., Steger, M. F., & Lee, R. M. (2010). Validation of the Subtle and Blatant Racism Scale for Asian American college students (SABRA (2)). *Cultural Diversity & Ethnic Minority Psychology, 16*, 323–334. https://dx.doi.org/10.1037/a0018674

Zeenah, C. H., & Humphreys, K. L. (2019). Child abuse and neglect. *Journal of the American Academy of Child and Adolescent Psychiatry, 57*, 637–644. https://doi.org/10.1016/j.jaac.2018.06.007

ADDITIONAL READING

Act to Change. (2020). *The racism is a virus toolkit: Strategies on how to stand against bullying, racism, and xenophobia in the face of COVID-19.* https://acttochange.org/resources/educational-resources-toolkit/

Act to Change. (2021). *Homeroom anti-bullying workshop.* https://acttochange.org/wp-content/uploads/2021/02/Homeroom-Curriculum.pdf

Act to Change. (n.d.). *COVID-19 resources to fight bullying and hate.* https://acttochange.org/covid-19/

Alegria, M., Baum, R., McCabe, M. A., & Williams, J. L. (2021). *School-based strategies for addressing the mental health and well-being of youth in the wake of COVID-19.* The National Academic Press. https://www.nap.edu/read/26262/chapter/1

American School Counselor Association. (n.d.). *Anti-racism resources.* https://www.schoolcounselor.org/Publications-Research/Publications/Free-ASCA-Resources/Anti-Racism-Resources

Asian Americans Advancing Justice. (n.d.). *Resources.* https://www.standagainsthatred.org/resources

Edutopia (2021, April 9). *Addressing anti-Asian racism with students.* https://www.edutopia.org/video/addressing-anti-asian-racism-students

Grassroots Asians Rising. (2020). *Asian American racial justice toolkit.* https://www.asianamtoolkit.org/the-toolkit

Handford, C., & Marrero, A. D. (2021). *Racial trauma in the school system: Naming the Pain* (1st ed.). Routledge. doi:10.4324/9780429029615

National Association of School Psychologists (2020). *Countering COVID-19 stigma and racism: Tips for parents and caregivers.*

National Child Traumatic Stress Network. (2008). *Child trauma toolkit for educators.* https://www.nctsn.org/resources/child-trauma-toolkit-educators

National Child Traumatic Stress Network. (2017). *Creating, supporting, and sustaining trauma-informed schools: A system framework.* https://www.nctsn.org/resources/creating-supporting-and-sustaining-trauma-informed-schools-system-framework

Sibbald, L., & Phifer, L. W. (2020). *Trauma-informed social-emotional toolbox for children & adolescents: 116 worksheets & skill-building exercises to support safety, connection & empowerment.* Pesi.

Stop AAPI Hate. (2021, February 9). *New data on anti-Asian hate incidents against elderly and total national incidents in 2020.* https://secureservercdn.net/104.238.69.231/a1w.90d.myftpupload.com/wp-content/uploads/2021/02/Press-Statement-re_-Bay-Area-Elderly-Incidents-2.9.2021-1.pdf

Stop AAPI Hate Youth Campaign. (2020). *They blamed me because I am Asian: Findings from youth-reported incidents of anti-AAPI hate.* http://www.asianpacificpolicyandplanningcouncil.org/wp-content/uploads/Stop-AAPI-Hate-Youth-Campaign-Report-9.11.20.pdf

Substance Abuse and Mental Health Services Administration. (2014). *SAMSHA's concept and guidance for a trauma-informed approach.* https://store.samhsa.gov/product/SAMHSA-s-Concept-of-Trauma-and-Guidance-for-a-Trauma-Informed-Approach/SMA14-4884

Teaching Tolerance (2019). *Speak up at school: How to respond to everyday prejudice, biases, and stereotypes.* https://www.learningforjustice.org/magazine/publications/speak-up-at-school

Urban Youth Trauma Center. (n.d.). *Issues of race, equity, and social justice: Addressing the impact of racial trauma and inequality on ethnic minority families.* Institute for Juvenile Research, University of Illinois at Chicago. https://www.psych.uic.edu/research/urban-youth-trauma-center

Wakabayashi, T., Cheah, C. S. L., Chang, T. F., Lai, G., Subrahmanyam, K., Chaudhary, N., Hyun, S., & Patel, P. (2020). *Addressing inequalities ineducation: ConsiderationsforAsianAmerican children and youth in the era ofCOVID-19.* Society for Research in Child Development.https://www.srcd.org/research/addressing-inequities-education-during-covid-19-pandemic-how-education-policy-and-schools

Chapter 10
Reporting Child Abuse and Neglect on K-12 Campuses

Samantha Klassen
Texas A&M University, Commerce, USA

Donna L. Hickman
Texas A&M University, Commerce, USA

ABSTRACT

The purpose of this chapter is to provide students with a primer for assessing for and reporting child abuse and neglect on K-12 campuses. The authors highlight physical abuse, emotional abuse, sexual abuse, and neglect, which may manifest in a variety of different forms. Prevalence rates of abuse and neglect in the United States are reviewed, along with statistics reflecting the most common types of abuse as well as specific groups at greater risk for victimization. Guidelines for assessing and reporting allegations to Child Protective Services are presented, along with a case study to support students in the application of chapter constructs and procedures. The chapter ends with a discussion of specific post-reporting self-care strategies that may be implemented by school counselors.

INTRODUCTION

This chapter will encompass the practice of recognizing and reporting child abuse on K-12 campuses. First, the authors begin by defining child abuse and neglect and highlighting the four primary forms it takes: physical abuse, sexual abuse, emotional abuse, and neglect. Warning signs of abuse and neglect, which may vary depending on the child's age and developmental stage, are explored. Next, the authors situate

DOI: 10.4018/978-1-7998-9785-9.ch010

experiences of abuse and neglect within the broader literature about traumatic experiences in childhood and adolescence, particularly the lasting adverse effects on mental health outcomes for those who experience it. Then, the authors explore the prevalence of child abuse and neglect in the United States, along with the challenge of recognizing and reporting it in light of the COVID-19 pandemic and subsequent transition to remote or hybrid learning environments.

After this foundational discussion, the authors describe the school counselor's role in assessing for abuse and neglect on K-12 campuses. Next, best practices for reporting abuse and neglect are reviewed, including where and how to submit a report; when a school counselor might choose to phone in a report versus submitting one online; language the school counselor should include in the report, including how to request an escalation of priority; and potential post-reporting outcomes. The chapter also includes a handy reporting checklist which the school counselor may follow to structure and streamline this process and recommendations for continuing to work with students and families post-reporting. To round out the discussion, readers will explore an abuse/neglect case study and discuss post-reporting self-care strategies for school counselors, such as mindfulness and self-compassion.

Abuse and Neglect Reporting as a Function of Trauma-Informed School Counseling

Prior to defining these constructs, it is imperative that school counselors understand how working with child abuse and neglect is a natural extension of a trauma-informed approach. SAMHSA (2014) notes the four "r's" of trauma-informed care as 1) a basic **realization** about trauma and its effects on individuals, families, groups, organizations, and communities, such as schools; 2) an ability to **recognize** the signs of trauma within the population served; 3) knowing how to **respond** effectively to individuals who have experienced trauma; and 4) **resisting re-traumatization** through the creation of systems and environments which support recovery.

Within the context of child abuse and neglect reporting/intervention, school counselors must have a **realization** of the ways trauma manifests and be trained to **recognize** when the students they serve are experiencing physical, emotional, and sexual abuse and/or neglect. They must also be trained to **respond** with sensitivity to students in traumatic and/or abusive situations, which encompasses both reporting abuse and neglect to Child Protective Services *and* continuing to provide post-reporting care to children and families. Lastly, by understanding how to **resist re-traumatization**, school counselors prepare themselves to advocate for students and work thoughtfully with teachers and administrators to support young people who have experienced the trauma of childhood abuse and neglect.

Defining Child Abuse and Neglect

The Child Abuse Prevention and Treatment Act (CAPTA) defines child abuse and neglect as "any recent act or failure to act on the part of a parent or caretaker which results in death, serious physical or emotional harm, sexual abuse, or exploitation" or as an "act or failure to act, which presents an imminent risk of serious harm" (U.S. Department of Health and Human Services [U.S. HHS], 2019, pg. 11). More simply put, child abuse and neglect could involve acts of omission, commission, or both: a failure to care for the child or protect them from harm; the act of hurting the child physically, sexually, or emotionally; or some combination of the two. It is important to note that child abuse and neglect are defined at both the state and federal level and codified in criminal and civil statutes; to that end, there are some variations in what constitutes child abuse and neglect depending on location, though significant overlap does exist. A general definition of each appears next, including examples of abusive or neglectful behaviors with children and adolescents and some important warning signs to look for when assessing for abuse and neglect.

Physical Abuse

Physical abuse is typically defined as "any nonaccidental physical injury to the child," which could include behaviors such as striking, punching, kicking, burning, and biting the child, or trafficking the child for labor or involuntary servitude (Child Welfare Information Gateway [CWIG], 2019a, pg. 2). It is important to consider the difference between physical abuse and disciplinary practices such as spanking. School counselors should remember that some physical disciplinary practices are culture-bound and specific to factors like ethnicity, national origin, and spiritual or religious identification. Some helpful guidelines for determining whether physical discipline is excessive include physical injury to the child (e.g., bruising, broken skin, swelling, or a situation that requires medical attention); the punishment's purpose (e.g., instillation of fear vs. education); whether the caretaker loses control of his or her actions during the punishment; whether the action is age-appropriate for the child's developmental level; and whether the action results from what may constitute unreasonable demands or expectations on the caregiver's behalf (Hamilton County Jobs & Family Services, 2012).

Physical abuse can be simpler than other forms of abuse to identify, particularly if the student frequently presents to campus with bruises, bite marks, burns, scalds, stitches, broken bones, or other evidence of physical trauma or injury. However, students who are physically abused do not always have visible injuries and may attempt to hide or otherwise explain away injuries to the school counselor (e.g., "I fell," "It happened in football practice," and so on). To that end, the school counselor must be aware of warning signs that physical abuse may be occurring and assess accordingly. Physically abused students may manifest a variety of mental health issues, including anxiety, behavioral concerns in the classroom, angry outbursts, depression, drug and alcohol problems, disordered eating, running away from home, and suicidal thoughts or attempts (National Society for the Prevention of Cruelty to Children [NSPCC], n.d.b).

Sexual Abuse

Sexual abuse occurs when a child is subjected to sexual offenses, which can include acts such as indecent exposure, molestation, rape, sexual assault, sex trafficking, and prostitution; permitting or subjecting the child to engage in obscene photographing or filming; and soliciting or luring a child for sexually exploitative purposes in person or over the Internet (CWIG, 2019a). Some examples of sexually explicit contact (either actual or simulated) include acts such as vaginal or anal penetration; sexual stimulation or gratification using a child's clothed or unclothed body parts; masturbation in the presence of a child or with the child; and lewd or lascivious exhibition of the breasts, genitals, anus, or pubic area in the child's presence.

Sexual abuse can be challenging for school counselors to identify, as some students may not understand what's happening to them or realize the behavior is wrong; students may also be hesitant to speak out, either because they have been threatened by their perpetrator or have a complicated relationship with their abuser. Some important emotional and behavioral signs of sexual abuse include being afraid to be alone, especially with the abuser; sexually-oriented language or behaviors that the school counselor would not expect the student to know; having nightmares or wetting the bed; using alcohol and other drugs; self-harming behaviors or suicidal ideation; changes in eating habits; engaging in promiscuous or otherwise risky sexual behaviors online, on campus, or in the community; and unexplained mood changes, such as depression, anxiety, irritability, or angry outbursts (NPSCC, n.d.d.).

Emotional Abuse

Emotional abuse, sometimes called "mental injury to a child," occurs when intellectual, emotional, or psychological development is impaired as a result of emotional maltreatment. After experiencing emotionally abusive interactions with a parent or caregiver, the child may exhibit an "observable or substantial change in behavior, emotional response, or cognition" and "injury as evidenced by anxiety, depression, withdrawal, or aggressive behavior" (CWIG, 2019a, pg. 3). Some examples of emotionally abusive behaviors include chronic or recurrent ridiculing, demeaning, cursing, or making derogatory remarks to or about the child. Signs of emotional abuse can manifest differently depending on the child's age, gender, and developmental level, though some general warning signs could include a lack of self-confidence or self-assurance; difficulties with emotional regulation; struggles to form or maintain interpersonal relationships; a lack of social skills; difficulty accepting feedback or constructive criticism from peers or school personnel; aggressive or cruel behaviors towards peers; and isolating behaviors (NPSCC, n.d.a.).

Neglect

Neglect is defined as the failure of a parent or caregiver to provide food, clothing, shelter, medical care, or supervision to the extent that the child's health, safety, and well-being are impacted (CWIG, 2019a). Abandonment, or the failure to maintain contact with the child or provide reasonable support to the child over a specified period of time, is a particular type of neglect. For school counselors, one especially relevant neglect-related consideration is **failure to educate**, which is codified as neglect in approximately half of all States, the District of Columbia, and other American territories. Educational neglect can involve the caregiver's failure to enroll a child in school or provide homeschooling, or a failure to facilitate school attendance to the extent that the child's education has been impaired or harmed (e.g., missing so many days of school that the child cannot be promoted to the next grade level).

Because neglect can include a variety of behaviors and situations, signs of neglect can vary considerably depending on the child's living situation. Some warning signs of neglect can include poor hygiene and dirty clothing; insufficient clothing (e.g., having no jacket or coat in cold weather); medical issues such as low body weight, poor dental hygiene, and lack of access to needed medication; unstable or unsuitable living environments (e.g., having no electricity or running water at home); being left alone for long periods of time; and serving as the primary caregiver to younger siblings or adult family members with mental health or addiction issues (NSPCC, n.d.c.).

School counselors who work with lower-income students and families may struggle to determine whether a child's living situation is due to caregiver neglect or the inevitable result of high stress, low resource home environments. Because this can be tricky to distinguish, a helpful litmus test can be to observe how the caregiver responds to the school counselor's efforts to provide resources to the family. If parents are dismissive of concerns or refuse referrals for social services like Medicaid or food assistance despite evidence that the family would benefit from these resources, that may be an indicator that neglect is present. When in doubt, the authors recommend a preemptive report to Child Protective Services highlighting the family's resource issues and articulating the counselor's concerns about food or housing insecurity or the lack of basic necessities.

Abuse and Neglect as Traumatic Experiences

Children and adolescents who experience abuse or neglect may suffer lifelong and even intergenerational consequences as a result of their experiences. School counselors who serve children who have been abused or neglected should understand the lasting adverse effects that this form of trauma may have on physical health and psychological/behavioral functioning.

The physical health consequences of abuse may be immediately obvious (e.g., brain damage resulting in intellectual disability due to head trauma), but an array of long-term health problems may occur as well. One particularly salient impact for school counselors to consider is reduced volume in brain size, which can impact functioning of the amygdala, hippocampus, orbitofrontal cortex, cerebellum, and corpus callosum; these are key brain structures responsible for processing emotions, learning and remembering, reinforcement-based decision-making, executive functioning, and left/right brain communication, which regulate arousal and enable complex cognitive processes such as higher-order thinking (CWIG, 2019b). Children and teens who have endured physical abuse may have a harder time with academics and emotion regulation, and there may be a neurological basis behind these struggles outside the student's conscious control. The recognition of this fact should necessarily inform treatment planning, particularly for students who do not seem to benefit from behavioral intervention plans, coaching, or modeling to improve emotional and social functioning.

There can be vast psychological consequences for children and adolescents who experience abuse and neglect as well; children may feel isolated, fearful, and mistrustful of others, which can manifest as low self-esteem, depression, anxiety, and disrupted social relationships with peers and adults (CWIG, 2019b). Beyond these psychological outcomes, researchers have also identified links between childhood abuse and neglect with diminished executive functioning and cognitive skills (Kavanaugh et al., 2016; Bick & Nelson, 2016); poor mental and emotional health, including a higher prevalence of attempted and completed suicide (Choi et al., 2017); attachment and social difficulties which manifest in challenges forming peer, social, and romantic relationships later in life (Doyle & Cicchetti, 2017); and posttraumatic stress disorder, which can lead to depression, suicidal behavior, substance use, and oppositional or defiant behaviors which perpetuate into adulthood (CWIG, 2019b).

Finally, children and teens who experience abuse or neglect often exhibit behavioral challenges, some of which persist beyond the duration of the maltreatment. One of the most common adverse behavioral correlates with childhood abuse and neglect is juvenile delinquency leading to adult criminality, especially in boys and young men, who are more prone to exhibiting externalizing behaviors such as bullying, aggression, and hostility towards others in school and within the broader community

(Herrenkohl et al., 2017). Other common behavioral challenges include unhealthy sexual practices and sexually risky behaviors, including earlier initiation of sexual activity and transactional sex practices, and an increased likelihood of perpetuating maltreatment against their own children (CWIG, 2019b).

Prevalence Rates of Abuse and Neglect

The National Child Abuse and Neglect Data System (NCANDS) collects and analyzes data submitted voluntarily by all 50 states in the United States, the District of Columbia, and the Commonwealth of Puerto Rico. In 2019, there were 4,378,000 reports of abuse or neglect reported to Child Protective Services representing the alleged maltreatment of approximately 7.9 million children. Of these reports, 2,368,325 were "screened-in" for response by Child Protective Services (CPS), indicating the allegations were credible and warranted investigation (U.S. HHS, 2019). The U.S. Department of Health and Human Services (2019) noted a steady increase in the number of referrals received, with a 12.6 percent increase in reports submitted from 2015 to 2019, to which the agency attributed an "increased public awareness of child abuse and neglect due to media coverage of child deaths, a centralized and publicly promoted child abuse and neglect hotline, improvements to existing child abuse and neglect definitions, and improvements in the ability to collect and report maltreatment allegations" (pg. 8).

Prevalence Rates by Demographics and Maltreatment Category

In the United States, victims of abuse or neglect are distributed fairly evenly across genders (48.3% boys, 51.4% girls), with victimization rates for girls at 9.4 per 1,000 girls and 8.4 per 1,000 boys. Racial distributions vary considerably, however, with most victimized children belonging to one of three races or ethnicities: White (43.5%), Hispanic (23.5%), or African American (20.9%). In terms of victimization rates, American-Indian or Alaskan Native children have the highest rate (14.8 per 1,000 children), whereas African American children have the second-highest rate at 13.8 per 1,000 children (U.S. HHS, 2019). When considering the ages of victimized children, the youngest children are frequently the most vulnerable to abuse and maltreatment, with 28.1% of victims between birth and 2 years of age and victimization rates steadily declining as children grow older (U.S. HHS, 2019).

The U.S. Department of Health and Human Services (2019) also collects data about the most prevalent types of maltreatment reported to Child Protective Services. In 2019, the most prominent form of maltreatment was neglect (74.9%), followed by physical abuse (17.5%), sexual abuse (9.3%), and other forms of abuse such as drug and alcohol addiction or a lack of supervision at home (6.8%). When accounting for maltreatment type, 84.5% of substantiated reports reflected a single type of abuse per incident (e.g., a child exclusively experiencing neglect), with the remaining 15.5% of victims experiencing two or more forms of maltreatment (e.g., a neglected child who was also sexually abused; U.S. HHS, 2019).

Caregiver Risk Factors

Although caregiver risk factors for the perpetration of abuse and neglect can be difficult to accurately assess and measure, the U.S. Department of Health and Human Services (2019) notes seven specific risk factors that may increase the likelihood of victimization:

1. Caregiver alcohol abuse, especially when drinking is compulsive;
2. Domestic violence among family members, which includes abusive, violent, coercive, forceful, or threatening acts or words among individuals in the same household;
3. Caregiver drug abuse, especially when drug use is compulsive;
4. Financial problems, or the family's inability to provide sufficient financial resources to meet minimum needs;
5. Inadequate housing, which could be substandard, overcrowded, or unsafe, or reflect families who are experiencing homelessness;
6. Receipt of public assistance, such as Temporary Assistance for Needy Families (TANF, also known colloquially as food stamps), Special Supplemental Nutrition Program for Women, Infants, and Children (WIC), or Medicaid;
7. Caregiver disabilities, which could include an intellectual disability, emotional disturbance, visual or hearing impairment, physical disability, or other medical condition (U.S. HHS, 2019, pg. 39).

Exploring Discrepancies in Child Abuse Reporting and Substantiation of Reports

As highlighted in the previous section, discrepancies exist in both child abuse reporting and in the substantiation of reports, specifically for non-White and Hispanic/Latinx-identified children and adolescents. Luken et al. (2021) conducted an exploratory mapping study to provide insight regarding the overrepresentation of non-White communities in reports to CPS. Their findings indicated that Black communities were the most overrepresented for all types of maltreatment; the authors suggested that these disparities are reflective of economic insecurity due to a "structural system of racial oppression in the U.S. that has…disenfranchised non-White and Latinx communities…and increased their susceptibility to the risk factors associated with child maltreatment," such as food insecurity, reduced access to resources, and higher rates of substance abuse, mental illness, and general life stress (pg. 274).

Hispanic/Latinx-identified children and adolescents also experience high reporting rates across maltreatment type in some states. Where high rates exist, provider bias and a misunderstanding of cultural practices such as coining and cupping could be contributors, and where low rates exist, language barriers, strong familial support networks, and moral dilemmas toward reporting undocumented perpetrators have been speculated (Dakil et al., 2011; Luken et al., 2021). Some confusion exists around prevalence rates for Native American-identified children as well; where low rates exist, there may be a true low incident rate or because of referrals to tribal healthcare systems or jurisdictions, and where higher prevalence rates exist, they may reflect economic disadvantages and difficulties allocating resources to affected communities, particularly in vast states with high NA populations, such as Alaska (Luken et al., 2021). Lastly, Asian American and Pacific Islander-identified children experience low referrals to CPS, which could reflect a true low incident rate or the underreporting of maltreatment due to a lack of cultural sensitivity for detecting cases (e.g., the "model minority effect" limiting detection by mandated reporters), a mistrust of child welfare services among AA or PI families, or the collectivist belief that society's perceptions of the family outweigh the harm that may be inflicted on a child (Luken et al., 2021).

In summary, minoritized students and families may experience additional challenges and/or risk factors which could increase the likelihood of abuse and neglect, *and* they may also be at risk for discrimination within the school and the child welfare systems. In light of these statistics and the disproportionately high involvement of non-White populations with Child Protective Services, school counselors must take a sensitive, mindful approach to reporting child abuse and neglect. Counselors must protect the welfare of children but also not unduly involve families in the child welfare system.

Therefore, it is important that school counselors understand the difference between a situation which requires protective intervention and one which requires thoughtful resourcing on the part of the counselor. For example, if a school counselor suspects a lack of supervision and food insecurity for a student who is being raised by a single Black mother working multiple jobs to keep the family afloat, it may be more prudent to begin by respectfully connecting the family with community referrals to meet those needs, rather than by immediately making a report to CPS because of suspected neglect. While it can be challenging to determine when resourcing should be considered over reporting, it can be helpful for the school counselor to consider the way a parent or caregiver responds to the counselor's attempts to help supply an unmet need. If a school counselor receives a hostile or aggressive response from a parent after an attempt to connect occurs, that response may serve as an impetus for choosing to involve CPS to ensure the need is met and that the child or adolescent in their care remains safe.

Abuse and Neglect During the COVID-19 Pandemic

Last but not least, school counselors should take the effects of the COVID-19 pandemic into consideration within the context of assessing for and reporting of child abuse and neglect. The COVID-19 pandemic beginning in late 2019-early 2020 created significant challenges for educational systems in the United States and abroad. The United Nations Educational, Scientific, and Cultural Organization (UNESCO; 2021b) noted that most world governments "temporarily closed educational institutions in an attempt to contain the spread of the COVID-19 pandemic…impacting over 60% of the world's student population" (para. 1). These school closures negatively impacted learning communities, particularly for vulnerable and disadvantaged communities, and forced many parents to rapidly shift to homeschooling their children to mitigate the spread of the virus. At the same time, parents were attempting to continue to work and/or care for younger children who had not yet entered school or daycare. In some cases, parents who transitioned to remote working assignments were tasked with reimagining their homes as workplaces; other parents, especially those who served as essential workers such as healthcare professionals or grocery store employees, had to figure out how to support homebound learners while still showing up for work. These circumstances led to significant stress for families with children, many of whom were already vulnerable to stress from factors such as underemployment and poverty. Beyond the educational impact, school closures carried other social and economic costs for individuals across communities, including:

- Poor nutrition for children and youth who rely on free or discounted meals at school;
- Gaps in childcare for working parents who had no choice but to leave children alone, or else face high economic costs and wage losses;
- Unintended strains on healthcare systems as workers had to stay home to care for children or monitor homebound learners;
- A rise in dropout rates related to protracted school closures;
- Economic pressures for teens in financially distressed families to work to generate income;
- Increased exposure to violence and exploitation, especially for girls and young women; and
- Lack of social contact necessary for learning and development (UNESCO, 2021a).

Conger and Elder's (1994) family stress model illustrates that external factors such as economic instability, job loss, unemployment, debt, and the receipt of income transfers (such as food stamps) place significant strain on family relationships. The social and economic upheaval resulting from the COVID-19 health crisis had the potential to exacerbate parenting stress, financial stress, substance use, social isolation, and negative interactions with children, which are well-documented risk factors for the perpetration of child abuse (Kang & Jain, 2020). The experience of parental job loss, in particular, significantly increased the risk of physical abuse and psychological maltreatment in families with children during the pandemic. In fact, "children of parents who experienced job loss related to the COVID-19 pandemic were nearly five times as likely to be psychologically maltreated during the pandemic compared with children of parents who did not lose their jobs," and parents who self-reported fewer positive coping strategies such as reframing, acquiring social support, and seeking spiritual support were more likely to physically abuse their children as well (Lawson et al., 2020, pg. 7).

These patterns are even more troubling when considering the impact of virtual education and quarantining on the likelihood that children would have the opportunity to share their concerns or be physically observed by mandatory reporters of abuse and neglect (e.g., teachers, coaches, school counselors; Lawson et al., 2020). Kang and Jain (2020) identified that nearly two-thirds of reports made to Child Protective Services were submitted by professionals with work-related contact with children, such as educators, law enforcement personnel, social services workers, and healthcare providers, with the remaining third of reports coming from friends, neighbors, and extended family members. These findings are corroborated by the U.S. Department of Health and Human Services (2019) as well, which indicates that almost 70% of reports are submitted by professionals. When social distancing, virtual education, and quarantining measures limit a child's access to these professional and nonprofessional groups, many cases of child maltreatment go unobserved and underreported.

Assessing for Abuse and Neglect on K-12 Campuses: The School Counselor's Role

While all 50 states, the District of Columbia, and the U.S. Territories have different methods for reporting child abuse and neglect, each one has laws that designate specific professionals (e.g., teachers, school counselors, etc.) and institutions (e.g., public or private schools) as **mandatory reporters** of any suspected maltreatment of minor children (U.S. HHS, 2019). Beyond the legal duty that school counselors have as mandatory reporters, the American School Counselor Association (ASCA) also holds that it is "the school counselor's legal, ethical, and moral responsibility to report suspected cases of child abuse and neglect to the proper authorities" and to assess for the "behavioral, academic, and social/emotional impact of abuse and neglect on students" (ASCA, 2021, para. 1).

While specific reporting guidelines vary from state to state, typically, a report should be submitted when an individual either *suspects* or *has reason to believe* that a child has been abused or neglected. This extends to knowledge or observation of a child being subjected to conditions that could result in harm to the child, such as witnessing physical harm to the child or learning about a child living in unsafe conditions (e.g., having no electricity or running water at home; CWIG, 2019b).

School Counselor Responsibilities

As discussed, school counselors are mandated to report suspected child abuse and neglect to Child Protective Services. It is important to emphasize that it is the school counselor's responsibility to **report**, and it is the responsibility of CPS to **investigate** suspicions or allegations of abuse or neglect. As frontline mental health workers who provide direct and indirect services to students at school, it is imperative for school counselors to understand the ethical standards and reporting requirements related to this responsibility. Laws and policies pertaining to child abuse and neglect vary by state, and school counselors must understand and comply with the guidelines that apply to their work setting. Although it can be very difficult to make these reports, school counselors should err on the side of caution to protect the students they serve.

In addition to reporting suspected cases of child abuse and neglect, ASCA (2021) recommends that school counselors should:

- Understand the impact of child abuse and neglect on a student's academic and social/emotional development;
- Educate students on healthy communication, boundaries, and personal safety;
- Provide referrals to outside agencies when needed;
- Involve families in the school environment and community;
- Provide professional development on child abuse and neglect to teachers and school staff; and
- Provide consultation to teachers and school staff who are concerned about possible cases of child abuse and neglect (ASCA, 2021).

One of the most important roles of a school counselor is to be an **advocate** for all students. According to the ASCA Ethical Standards for School Counselors, an advocate is someone who "speaks, writes, or acts to promote the well-being of students" (ASCA, 2016, p. 9). Section A.11.b of the ASCA Ethical Standards (2016) states that school counselors should "report suspected cases of child abuse and neglect to the proper authorities and take reasonable precautions to protect the privacy of the student for whom abuse or neglect is suspected when alerting the proper authorities" (ASCA, 2016, p. 5). Although trust and confidentiality are the cornerstones of an effective counseling relationship, confidentiality must be breached in cases of suspected child abuse and neglect. Above all else, school counselors have a primary obligation to protect the welfare of their students (ASCA, 2016).

Assessment Recommendations for School Counselors

Sometimes mandatory reporters are hesitant to submit a report because they do not know for certain that a child is being abused or neglected. It is imperative to remember that mandatory reporters do **NOT** have the burden of providing proof that a child is experiencing abuse or neglect; rather, their responsibility is to report the facts and circumstances which led to their suspicion (CWIG, 2019b). Essentially: it is not the school counselor's job to determine whether abuse or neglect occurred (that's what the CPS investigator does!). The school counselor's job is to describe the circumstances which led to their concern for the child, organize that information into a phone or online report to Child Protective Services, and then allow the investigation to unfold, providing additional information to support the investigation if needed.

When organizing information to submit a report to CPS, the school counselor should be prepared to provide basic information about the child and their family system, such as the name, age, and home address of the child; the name(s) of caregiver(s); and information about other children who live in the home, if applicable. School counselors should also be encouraged to submit a report of suspected abuse or neglect *even if* they are missing some of this information; the school counselor's primary ethical and legal responsibility is to notify the proper authorities, who can "fill in the blanks" once they make contact with the child and their family system. School counselors should also not shy away from submitting multiple reports reflecting concern for a single child at different periods in time, or as new information about allegations of abuse or neglect come to light.

Responding to Allegations of Abuse and Neglect

When students reveal that abuse or neglect may be occurring, it is important to respond in a way that does not inadvertently compound trauma the child may be experiencing. School counselors should rely on their basic counseling skills, such as active listening, paraphrasing, reflecting feelings, and providing an empathic, nonjudgmental space for the student to articulate their concerns. Beyond these basic counseling skills, other best practices for responding to allegations of abuse and neglect include remaining calm, showing interest and concern for the child, believing the child and supporting their feelings, allowing the child to speak at length without interruption, and being prepared to take immediate action on the child's behalf by sharing the information with Child Protective Services (Children's Advocacy Centers of Texas, n.d.). Just as important, the school counselor should not panic or overreact, overwhelm the child with questions, press the child to talk or provide more detail than necessary, promise things that they cannot control, confront the alleged offender, or minimize or dismiss the child's concerns or feelings (Children's Advocacy Centers of Texas, n.d.).

Some counselors may be tempted to forgo a report if they experience hesitation or doubt about the information shared by the student. If a school counselor is unclear as to whether a concern revealed by a child constitutes abuse or neglect, consultation with a more experienced peer may be helpful for clarifying next steps. In the event that consultation with another professional is not possible in a reasonable time frame (i.e., during the same day that the concerns come to light), school counselors should preemptively submit a report and allow Child Protective Services to reach their own conclusions about the issues at hand.

Best Practices for Reporting Abuse and Neglect

As previously mentioned, professional reporters, or individuals who encounter the child as part of their occupation, submit 68.6 percent of reports to Child Protective Services, with 21% of professional reporters identifying themselves as education personnel (e.g., teachers, school counselors; U.S. HHS, 2019). To that end, it is not a matter of *if* a professional school counselor will have to make a report about alleged abuse or neglect, but *when*. In this section, the Child Protective Services reporting system is reviewed, along with the process of submitting a report, a checklist for gathering the information required to make a comprehensive report, and the actions that may be taken post-submission.

Understanding the CPS Reporting System

When reports are submitted to Child Protective Services and screened-in for investigation, the assigned caseworker makes a determination (also known as a disposition) about the alleged incident of child maltreatment. The two most prevalent investigation determinations are **substantiated** and **unsubstantiated**, though they may also be classified as indicated, intentionally false, closed with no finding, or no alleged maltreatment (U.S. HHS, 2019). Substantiated reports are those which typically lead to additional investigation and intervention by Child Protective Services, and the outcomes that may follow a substantiated report are described at the end of this section. First, the authors review the reporting process from beginning to end and provide a reporting checklist to facilitate that endeavor.

Submitting a Report

Each state or specific territory of the United States has a dedicated Child Protective Services hotline through which a report can be made. State child abuse and neglect reporting numbers are available online through Child Welfare Information Gateway (n.d.); they are also typically the first results to appear when searching for the phrases "child protective services" or "reporting child abuse" in an online search engine. Another option for reporting abuse and neglect is to contact local law enforcement agencies or the Child Protective Services office for instructions on submitting a report. Reporters may also call or text the Childhelp National Abuse Hotline at 1.800.4.A.CHILD (1-800-422-4453) to speak with a professional crisis counselor at any time of day or night. The hotline offers crisis intervention, information, and referrals to thousands of emergency, social service, and support resources (CWIG, n. d.).

While reporting processes vary depending on the school counselor's state of employment, reporters typically have the option to submit a report online or over the telephone through an abuse hotline. When choosing an avenue to make a report, a good rule of thumb is to consider the immediacy of the need and the severity of the risk. For more emergent needs, school counselors should make phone contact with Child Protective Services, as reporters have the ability to request an escalation of priority from the caseworker; they also have the opportunity to stress the importance of immediate contact with the child and their family in a way that online reporting portals may not support. For example, if the school counselor suspects that a child may have sporadic access to basic necessities at home or inadequate after-school supervision, an online report might suffice, whereas concerns about physical or sexual abuse should be reported over the phone so the school counselor has the opportunity to stress the severity of the concern and immediacy of the risk to the hotline worker.

Reporting Checklist

- What are the child's basic demographics, including their name, age, gender, ethnicity, disability status, and primary language?
- What is the child's physical address and the phone number for his or her guardian?
- Who is the alleged perpetrator of the abuse or neglect, and how are they connected to the primary alleged victim?
- Who lives in the home with the child? Are other children at risk for abuse or neglect as well? If so, what are their names and ages?
- What are the primary concerns about the child or their living situation?

- Is this report part of a pattern of behavior or a singular incident?
- Are there other safety concerns, such as weaponry in the home, gang affiliation, or people, pets, or conditions that could put the child in danger?
- Is it safe for this child to go home today?

Post-Submission Processes

Although the report will be documented by CPS, it is important for the school counselor to notate the submission of a report internally as well. School counselors should keep a record of the hotline worker's identification number, the report's identification number (if available), and the date and time of submission. These records should be notated separately from the student's individual permanent record, which may be accessed by any school personnel with a legitimate educational interest. To that end, the authors recommend keeping a separate file to notate all interactions with Child Protective Services, including the aforementioned post-submission documentation and any contact with a CPS worker that follows, such as a phone call requesting additional information, an investigator's visit to the school campus, or an individual meeting with an investigator.

Beyond keeping timely, accurate documentation surrounding a report, school counselors may also need to inform and/or collaborate with other stakeholders about the case. It is imperative that the school counselor maintain student confidentiality, while also recognizing that other educators with a legitimate educational interest may need to be apprised of a child or teen's situation. For example, some school districts may have policies in place which require limited communication with district lawyers after reports to Child Protective Services have been submitted. Principals and school resource officers may also need to be apprised of the specifics of an abusive or neglectful situation, particularly where safety issues exist (e.g., in high-risk situations, a school resource officer might need to be alerted about an angry or violent parent who may wish to retaliate against school personnel after CPS has contacted the family).

After a counselor submits a report to CPS, it may take some time to learn about the outcome of the report. A caseworker may contact the counselor or other knowledgeable individuals for more information prior to making contact with the child and their family, or the counselor may not hear anything until the agency has made one of the determinations mentioned above. If follow-up with the report's originator occurs, it may be done via telephone, an in-person visit to the school counselor's campus, or through an official letter sent by Child Protective Services to the reporter's business address, especially if the initial report was submitted through an online reporting portal.

While the counselor may not have additional contact with CPS following their report, it can be helpful to understand the steps that Child Protective Services may take after receiving information about alleged child abuse or neglect. After receiving a report, CPS conducts an initial assessment or investigation to determine whether maltreatment occurred, if there are immediate safety concerns, if there is a risk of future maltreatment, and whether agency services are needed to address the effects of child maltreatment or to reduce the risk of future abusive or neglectful behaviors (DePanfilis & Salus, 2003). If the initial assessment yields a determination that abuse or neglect has occurred, the assigned caseworker then conducts a family assessment and creates a plan for the family, which may include a **safety plan** to reduce imminent harm to the child, a **case plan** identifying family goals, outcomes, and interventions needed to achieve them, and a **permanency plan**, which describes alternatives to the child's permanent residency with the family and the circumstances under which reunification might be possible (DePanfilis & Salus, 2003).

Following the planning process, CPS will arrange, provide, and coordinate the delivery of services to the child and their family, which could include interventions such as individual or family therapy, parent training and education, domestic violence intervention, and substance abuse treatment, to name a few (Texas Department of Family and Protective Services, n.d.). Throughout the intervention process, the caseworker assesses for family progress, focusing on "ensuring the child's safety; reducing the risk of maltreatment; addressing successfully any of the effects of maltreatment on the child and family; achieving the goals and tasks in the case plan; and achieving family-level outcomes," which are identified through the aforementioned planning process (DePanfilis & Salus, 2003, pg. 27).

Optimally, CPS closes a family's case once their goals have been achieved and the risk of abuse or neglect has been reduced or eliminated, although some closures do occur because families refuse or discontinue services.

Recommendations for Continuing to Work With Students Post-Reporting

The work of a trauma-informed school counselor does not come to an end after they have referred a family to Child Protective Services. These students and families will often require continuing services and follow-up care. However, providing this support can be extremely challenging when the student or family suspects or knows that the counselor has made a report because of something shared in a counseling session. Below, the authors provide some general guidelines for continuing the therapeutic relationship post-submission:

1. *Recognize—and respect—possible damage to the therapeutic alliance.* The student and family may be not be aware that the report originated with the school counselor. However, in some cases, the family may suspect or know that the school counselor made the report. As a trauma-informed school counselor, understand that the student's reaction to reporting often represents a complex relationship with their parent or guardian. Students may logically know that the situation they are in is unsafe or wrong, but feel compelled to protect their abuser due to family loyalty, a responsibility for keeping younger siblings safe, or fear that contact with CPS or removal from the home could result in an even more dangerous situation. Try not to take the student's anger or frustration personally, and do remind the student that the school counselor will always be available to talk through complex emotions and uncertain situations in the future.
2. *Be honest about the school counselor's role in reporting abuse or neglect.* Outside their work with individual students, school counselors should be intentional about communicating their role as the campus mental health professional to the entire student body. Every student should know who the school counselor is and what their job entails, including that one of those jobs is keeping students safe. If a student asks directly about CPS, the school counselor can respond by saying: "Remember that as a school counselor, one of my jobs is to keep students safe. Sometimes that job means contacting others with the ability to help students once they leave campus." If students are fearful about what contact with CPS entails, the school counselor should be prepared to walk them through possible outcomes using the foundational information in this chapter.
3. *Be prepared to respond to parents who may confront the school counselor about their role in abuse/neglect reporting.* While the school counselor may never have follow-up contact with a parent or guardian after submitting a CPS report, it is not unusual for parents to seek a meeting with the school counselor or other administrators after being contacted by child welfare services. In the event that a parent confronts the school counselor or wants information about a report, possible language to use includes, "It is the school district's policy that we cannot discuss any past or present report to Child Protective Services." Other recommendations include school-wide training in de-escalation techniques and alternatives for managing aggressive behavior, such as those provided by Satori Alternatives to Managing Aggression (SAMA; Satori Learning, 2022).
4. *Continue to remind students about the limits to confidentiality.* Discussions about confidentiality are crucial when building trust with students, but they shouldn't just occur in the first counseling session. School counselors should revisit this conversation often. With K-5 students, the counselor can say,

"Remember when we talked about confidentiality? That's a big word that means that everything we talk about in here stays in here. However, if you tell me that someone is hurting you or that you're going to hurt someone else, it's my job to tell someone that can help you." If the counselor is working with a middle or high school student, the counselor can remind students that they have an ethical obligation to keep information disclosed in counseling sessions confidential whenever possible, and that harm to a student is one situation where confidentiality is not possible.

5. *students that the school counselor's office is always a safe place for them, especially in times of dysregulation or distress.* A trauma-informed approach to school counseling recognizes that students may need a safe place at school to dysregulate or calm down when experiencing difficult emotions. School counselors can regularly remind students that their office is always available to them if they need a quiet moment to themselves during the day or need someone to talk to. Students can even create a list of coping skills with their school counselor to keep in their binder or their desk in times of distress.
6. *Continue to check in with students post-report.* Even if students don't have a need for follow-up services, a trauma-informed school counselor can be purposeful about following up with students after a report has been made. School counselors can put a reminder on their calendars to check in with students formally or informally after a week, a month, or a even a semester. Being purposeful about follow-up care is especially important for students who are experiencing ongoing abuse or neglect. If school counselors are working with students who share new information or continue to experience abuse or neglect, the school counselor may need to make another report and/or add information to an existing report.

Abuse and Neglect Case Study

This section describes the case of Karina, an eight-year-old girl in an abusive and neglectful home environment. Following a description of her case, there are follow-up questions for individual reflection or group discussion.

The Case of Karina

Olita is an early-career elementary school (K-5th grade) counselor who works in the southwestern United States on a mid-sized campus serving approximately 600 students. Karina is an 8-year-old Mexican American girl being raised by her maternal grandparents, Maria and Oscar, who are also caring for her two younger siblings, Yuliana (2) and Xavier (4). Karina's third-grade teacher, Ms. Robertson, approached

Olita with concerns about Karina's well-being. Ms. Robertson described Karina as "emotionally volatile" in the classroom, indicating that she cries very easily when given simple redirection, resorts to name-calling or physical aggression when her peers do something she does not like, has gotten in trouble for stealing food out of her classmates' lunchboxes, and occasionally comes to school in unwashed clothing or reuses the same soiled shirts and pants throughout the week. Ms. Robertson asks Olita to visit with Karina after an especially disruptive outburst and subsequent "nervous breakdown" on Karina's behalf after Ms. Robertson told her she planned to call Karina's grandparents to discuss her behavior.

Questions for Self-Reflection or Group Discussion

1. Are there concerns that Karina may be experiencing abuse or neglect at home? What questions should Olita have for Karina when she meets with her one-on-one?
2. Does a report to Child Protective Services need to be submitted? How would Olita make this determination?
3. If a report does need to be submitted, how should Olita handle it? Online? Over the phone? Reference the **Submitting a Report** section above to support the decision.
4. Use the **Reporting Checklist** to craft an outline for the report using the information in the case study. If Olita is missing some of the information described in the **Reporting Checklist**, how should she handle it?

Bonus Role-Play Exercise: In groups of three students, use the information in the case study as a "jumping off" point for a role-play exercise. Instructions for three separate character roles are presented next:

- *Karina*: Using the information provided about Karina's situation at home and interpersonal orientation with peers and Ms. Robertson, meet with the school counselor to discuss her recent behaviors in class.
- *Olita*: Using the guidelines presented throughout the chapter, assess Karina for the presence of abuse and neglect. The **Responding to Allegations of Abuse and Neglect** section and **Reporting Checklist** should be helpful in this endeavor.
- *CPS Worker*: After the school counselor has finished her conversation with Karina, roleplay the process of gathering the information from the school counselor for the report. Inform the school counselor of the next steps that may be taken using the information contained in the **Post-Submission Processes** section.

POST-REPORTING SCHOOL COUNSELOR SELF-CARE

Reporting suspected child abuse and neglect can be difficult and stressful for school counselors. Beginning school counselors are particularly susceptible to experiencing distress due to a lack of structured reporting guidelines, fear of consequences or retaliation, and a limited amount of training (Tuttle et al., 2019). Furthermore, school counselors often develop close, trusting relationships with the students they serve, which may lead to a higher number of reports. The weight of this responsibility and the high stakes involved may leave school counselors feeling physically and emotionally spent. Therefore, school counselors should have self-care strategies in place to buffer against the emotional toll of supporting students who may be experiencing abuse and neglect.

According to Bradley and colleagues (2013), **self-care** can be described as any activity that enhances or maintains wellness, such as eating a healthy diet, exercising, getting a sufficient amount of sleep, maintaining a work-life balance, and seeking support from other professionals. Corey et al. (2018) define self-care as a collection of practices that promote wellness and effective coping. Barlow and Phelan (2007) define self-care as the integration of mental, emotional, physical, and spiritual wellness. According to Thomas and Morris (2017), counselors should (1) regularly engage in mentally, emotionally, physically and spiritually nourishing activities, (2) schedule restorative activities when anticipating stress, (3) prepare a list of coping skills, (4) meet regularly with colleagues for support, (5) evaluate personal and professional challenges to self-care, and (6) record and reflect on successes. However self-care is defined, keep in mind that school counselors cannot adequately care for their students if they do not take care of themselves first.

The ASCA Ethical Standards also require school counselors to "monitor their emotional and physical health and practice wellness to ensure optimal professional effectiveness" (ASCA, 2016, p. 7). In addition, school counselors should "seek physical or mental health support when needed to ensure professional competence" (ASCA, 2016, p. 7). Counselors who understand the importance of their own wellness and intentionally practice self-care strategies will be better prepared to meet the needs of the students they serve.

Self-Compassion as Self-Care

Although graduate programs address self-care and the concept has been discussed extensively in the literature, many counselors struggle to regularly and intentionally engage in wellness practices (Coaston, 2017). Although counselors naturally excel at taking care of others, they sometimes fail to treat themselves with the same level of compassion and kindness. Self-compassion as a self-care practice provides a helpful structure for maintaining wellness as a school counselor, and it is especially relevant for school counselors who may experience emotional dysregulation after involving the students they serve with Child Protective Services. School counselors may worry if they have done the right thing after making a report to CPS and whether they may have inadvertently made the child's situation worse; they may also wonder if they have irrevocably damaged their therapeutic alliance with a young person who is already in an unsafe, isolating, and/or traumatic situation. Self-care through self-compassion can provide the school counselor with a much-needed buffer against these worries.

Neff (2021) defines **self-compassion** as intentionally treating oneself with kindness when struggles arise. Rather than ignoring or minimizing pain, school counselors should acknowledge the difficulties they are facing and identify strategies to care for themselves in the moment. For example, Stephan is in his first year as a school counselor. He just had to make a particularly difficult CPS report. He might find himself feeling sad, angry, guilty, anxious, or scared (or all of the above!). Instead of ignoring his feelings, Stephen could reach for self-compassion by taking a few minutes to check in with himself and acknowledge that he is in a difficult moment. Whether calling a supportive friend or colleague or making space for a quick two-minute meditation, taking a moment to pause, reflect, and recharge can help support school counselors in working through these difficult moments.

Neff's model of self-compassion (2003) has three components: self-kindness, common humanity, and mindfulness. **Self-kindness** refers to the ability to be gentle and understanding with oneself, especially when experiencing turmoil. **Common humanity** involves recognizing failings and sufferings as part of the human experience. When school counselors remind themselves of this principle, they can see pain, inadequacies, and failures as part of a shared human experience. Instead of feeling like there is something wrong, they understand that all humans struggle and that they are not alone. Finally, **mindfulness** refers to the ability to have an awareness of feelings without avoiding them or ruminating over them. Mindfulness is a nonjudgmental state where one simply observes what is going on internally. Instead of engaging in activities to temporarily numb feelings, the practice of mindfulness involves gently acknowledging those feelings and holding space for them.

How can school counselors integrate self-compassion into their self-care plans? A regular self-compassion practice can help restore a sense of calm, balance, and acceptance in difficult moments. As discussed throughout this chapter, reporting suspected child abuse and neglect is an important responsibility for school counselors. However, the authors acknowledge how difficult it can be to fulfill that role. As the chapter comes to a close, take a few minutes to reflect on how school counselors can care for themselves while caring for their students and school community.

Summary

In this chapter, the authors examined the concepts of abuse and neglect, which encompass a myriad of acts or failures to act that range from physical or emotional harm to sexual exploitation and the failure to provide necessary conditions for children to be safe and healthy. The chapter also explored specific examples of abusive and neglectful behaviors; identified the school counselor's legal and ethical responsibility for reporting abuse and neglect; reviewed methods for submitting a report and potential post-reporting outcomes; practiced reporting abuse and neglect through a case study example; and ended with a discussion of post-reporting self-care practices for school counselors, with a special focus on self-compassion as an important form of school counselor self-care.

REFERENCES

American School Counselor Association. (2021). *The school counselor and child abuse and neglect prevention*. https://www.schoolcounselor.org/Standards-Positions/Position-Statements/ASCA-Position-Statements/The-School-Counselor-and-Child-Abuse-and-Neglect-P

Barlow, C. A., & Phelan, A. M. (2007). Peer collaboration: A model to support counsellor self-care. *Canadian Journal of Counselling*, *41*, 3–15.

Bick, J., & Nelson, C. A. (2016). Early adverse experiences and the developing brain. *Neuropsychopharmacology*, *41*(1), 177–196. doi:10.1038/npp.2015.252 PMID:26334107

Bradley, N., Whisenhunt, J., Adamson, N., & Kress, V. E. (2013). Creative approaches for promoting counselor self-care. *Journal of Creativity in Mental Health*, *8*(4), 456–469. doi:10.1080/15401383.2013.844656

Child Welfare Information Gateway. (2019a). *Definitions of child abuse and neglect*. U.S. Department of Health and Human Services, Children's Bureau.

Child Welfare Information Gateway. (2019b). *Long-term consequences of child abuse and neglect*. U.S. Department of Health and Human Services, Children's Bureau.

Child Welfare Information Gateway. (2019c). *Mandatory reporters of child abuse and neglect*. U.S. Department of Health and Human Services, Children's Bureau.

Child Welfare Information Gateway. (n.d.). *State child abuse and neglect reporting numbers*. https://www.childwelfare.gov/organizations/?CWIGFunctionsaction=rols:main.dspList&rolType=custom&rs_id=5

Children's Advocacy Centers of Texas. (n.d.). *A Texas school employee's guide to reporting suspected abuse and neglect.* https://tea.texas.gov/sites/default/files/Educators-Guide-2020-English.pdf

Choi, N. G., DiNitto, D. M., Marti, C. N., & Segal, S. P. (2017). Adverse childhood experiences and suicide attempts among those with mental and substance use disorders. *Child Abuse & Neglect*, *69*, 252–262. doi:10.1016/j.chiabu.2017.04.024 PMID:28500922

Coaston, S. (2017). Self-care through self-compassion: A balm for burnout. *The Professional Counselor*, *7*(3), 285–297. doi:10.15241cc.7.3.285

Conger, R. D., & Elder, G. H. (1994). *Families in troubled times*. Aldine de Guyter.

Corey, G., Muratori, M., Austin, J. T., & Austin, J. A. (2018). *Counselor self-care*. American Counseling Association.

Dakil, S., Cox, M., Lin, H., & Flores, G. (2011). Racial and ethnic disparities in physical abuse reporting and Child Protective Services interventions in the United States. *Journal of the National Medical Association*, *103*(9-10), 926–931. doi:10.1016/S0027-9684(15)30449-1 PMID:22364062

DePanfilis, D., & Salus, M. K. (2003). *Child Protective Services: A guide for caseworkers*. U.S. Department of Health and Human Services, Children's Bureau.

Doyle, C., & Cicchetti, D. (2017). From the cradle to the grave: The effect of adverse caregiving environments on attachment and relationships throughout the lifespan. *Clinical Psychology: Science and Practice*, *24*(2), 203–217. doi:10.1111/cpsp.12192 PMID:28924334

Hamilton County Job & Family Services. (2012). *The difference between discipline and abuse*. https://www.hcjfs.org/services/child-protection/know-the-difference-between-discipline-and-abuse/

Herrenkohl, T. I., Jung, H., Lee, J. O., & Kim, M.-H. (2017). *Effects of child maltreatment, cumulative victimization experiences, and proximal life stress on adult crime and antisocial behavior*. https://www.ncjrs.gov/ pdffiles1/nij/grants/250506.pdf

Kang, K. T., & Jain, N. (2020). Child abuse and neglect in the COVID-19 era: A primer for front-line physicians in British Columbia. *BC Medical Journal*, *62*, 238–240.

Kavanaugh, B. C., Dupont-Frechette, J. A., Jerskey, B. A., & Holler, K. A. (2016). Neurocognitive deficits in children and adolescents following maltreatment: Neurodevelopmental consequences and neuropsychological implications of traumatic stress. *Applied Neuropsychology. Child*, *6*(1), 64–78. doi:10.1080/21622965.2015.1079712 PMID:27050166

Lawson, M., Piel, M. H., & Simon, M. (2020). Child maltreatment during the COVID-19 pandemic: Consequences of parental job loss on psychological and physical abuse towards children. *Child Abuse & Neglect*, *110*, 1–11. doi:10.1016/j.chiabu.2020.104709 PMID:32893003

Luken, A., Nair, R., & Fix, R. L. (2021). On racial disparities in child abuse reports: Exploratory mapping the 2018 NCANDS. *Child Maltreatment*, *26*(3), 267–281. doi:10.1177/10775595211001926 PMID:33729016

National Society for the Prevention of Cruelty to Children. (n.d.a). *Signs of emotional abuse*. https://www.nspcc.org.uk/what-is-child-abuse/types-of-abuse/emotional-abuse/

National Society for the Prevention of Cruelty to Children. (n.d.b). *Signs of physical abuse*. https://www.nspcc.org.uk/what-is-child-abuse/types-of-abuse/physical-abuse/

National Society for the Prevention of Cruelty to Children. (n.d.c). *Signs of neglect*. https://www.nspcc.org.uk/what-is-child-abuse/types-of-abuse/neglect/

National Society for the Prevention of Cruelty to Children. (n.d.d). *Signs of sexual abuse*. https://www.nspcc.org.uk/what-is-child-abuse/types-of-abuse/child-sexual-abuse/

Oloumi-Johnson, R. (2016). *The lived experiences of middle school counselors in reporting abuse and neglect to Child Protective Services: A phenomenological study* (Publication No. 10307713) [Doctoral dissertation, Sam Houston State University]. ProQuest Dissertations and Theses Global.

Satori Learning. (2022). *Satori Alternatives to Managing Aggression (SAMA)*. https://satorilearning.com/courses/

Substance Abuse and Mental Health Services Administration. (2014). *SAMHSA's concept of trauma and guidance for a trauma-informed approach*. https://ncsacw.acf.hhs.gov/userfiles/files/SAMHSA_Trauma.pdf

Sylvester-Nwosu, P. (2020). *Self-care practices, work experience, educational setting, and burnout among school counselors* (Publication No. 28157204) [Doctoral dissertation, Walden University]. ProQuest Dissertations and Theses Global.

Texas Department of Family and Protective Services. (n.d.). *Family-based support programs*. https://www.dfps.state.tx.us/Child_Protection/Family_Support/default.asp

Tuttle, M., Ricks, L., & Taylor, M. (2021). *A child abuse reporting framework for early career school counselors*. https://tpcjournal.nbcc.org/a-child-abuse-reporting-framework-for-early-career-school-counselors/

United Nations Educational, Scientific, and Cultural Organization. (2021a). *Adverse consequences of school closures*. https://en.unesco.org/covid19/educationresponse/consequences

United Nations Educational, Scientific, and Cultural Organization. (2021b). *Education: From disruption to recovery*. https://en.unesco.org/covid19/educationresponse

U.S. Department of Health and Human Services. (2019). *Child Maltreatment 2019*. https://www.acf.hhs.gov/sites/default/files/documents/cb/cm2019.pdf

Chapter 11
School Counseling for Children of Incarcerated Parents

Emily C. Brown
https://orcid.org/0000-0002-2376-0497
University of Missouri, St. Louis, USA

Malti Tuttle
Auburn University, USA

Dylan Hebert
Auburn University, USA

ABSTRACT

Children of incarcerated parents may have traumatic experiences that correlate with negative educational and mental health outcomes. School counselors are ideally suited to provide trauma-informed school counseling for children of incarcerated parents through individual, group, or classroom counseling interventions while also collaborating with stakeholders. This chapter provides school counselors an overview of the possible trauma of parental incarceration while describing approaches to help meet the needs of students. The authors describe the importance of collaborating with caregivers, administrators, school nurses, and teachers to help promote a positive school climate, offer support, and reduce the possible stigma connected to parental incarceration. The authors recommend advocacy practices and future research areas to continue to promote trauma-informed school counseling for children of incarcerated parents.

DOI: 10.4018/978-1-7998-9785-9.ch011

INTRODUCTION

More than five million children will experience parental incarceration by the time they complete high school (Murphey & Cooper, 2015). These children are disproportionately children of color and children who live in poverty. The authors acknowledge the need for system reform and an end to mass incarceration that contributes to this problem. Counselors must also recognize the current stress and trauma experienced by children of incarcerated parents (CIP) and be able to recognize and respond to pressing needs. Therefore, this chapter describes some of the needs of CIP with special attention to educational outcomes and describes ways school counselors can provide services.

CIP are more likely to experience multiple childhood adversities (Turney, 2018), which can increase toxic stress and may lead to lasting harm for brain development, well-being, and health risks. Scholars have noted correlations between parental incarceration and mental health or educational outcomes. For example, CIP may demonstrate behavior problems, including aggressive behaviors and attention problems (Geller et al., 2012). Physical and mental health problems associated with parental incarceration include depression and anxiety (Lee et al., 2013). CIP may also have problems at school, including lower school engagement or school connectedness, early grade retention, absenteeism, disciplinary action, and academic achievement difficulties (Murphey & Cooper, 2015; Nichols et al., 2016). Altogether, this data points to the need for intervention and support for CIP.

School counselors regularly work with students experiencing traumatic events (Rumsey et al., 2020). As the first and sometimes only counseling professional providing student support, school counselors are ideally suited to provide counseling interventions and system support for the academic and mental health needs of CIP. However, they may need more training and preparation on trauma-informed counseling (Rumsey et al., 2020; Rumsey & Milsom, 2019). Therefore, in order to help school counselors become more familiar with best practices for trauma-informed counseling services that promote well-being and school success, this book and more specifically this chapter provides information to increase awareness and understanding of the traumatic experiences faced by CIP and provides recommendations to help school counselors support children and families experiencing incarceration through various counseling modalities: individual counseling, group counseling, classroom and school-wide counseling, and system supports.

ADDRESSING THE TRAUMA OF PARENTAL INCARCERATION

Adverse childhood experiences (ACEs), which include physical, emotional, or sexual abuse; physical or emotional neglect; or experiences of household dysfunction (parental divorce, substance abuse, mental illness, domestic violence, or incarceration) have the potential to cause trauma (Anda et al., 2006; Felitti et al., 1998). Multiple and cumulative ACEs can have lasting harm to children's well-being and brain development and increase health risks for adults (e.g., substance abuse, suicide attempts, heart disease) (Anda et al., 2006; Felitti et al., 1998). Trauma has been defined as the result of "an event … or set of circumstances that is experienced by an individual as physically or emotionally harmful or life threatening and that has lasting adverse effects on the individual's functioning and mental, physical, social, emotional, or spiritual well-being" (Substance Abuse and Mental Health Services Administration [SAMHSA], 2014, p. 7). Therefore, school counselors may note these three primary criteria for trauma (i.e., event, experience of event, and effects) among CIP.

First, children have the event or circumstances of parental incarceration, including any preceding substance abuse, violence, and family instability. According to Murphey and Cooper (2015), CIP were more likely than other children to have lived with someone with a substance abuse problem (54.7% vs. 7.4%), to be victim or witness to domestic abuse (36.9% vs. 5.1%) or neighborhood violence (32.7% vs. 6.8%), and to have lived with someone who was mentally ill or suicidal (27.8% vs. 7.2%). CIP were more likely to experience parental divorce or separation (57% vs. 17.3%) and even parental death (9.8% vs. 2.6%). Although scholars believe numbers are underreported, seven percent of children entered foster care in 2019 due to parental incarceration (Adoption and Foster Care Analysis and Reporting System, 2020; de Hann et al., 2019). A study of incarcerated parents ($n = 95$) reported high recidivism rates (75%) and noted some CIP were exposed to parental criminal activity (37%), arrest (26%), and sentencing (11%) (Dallaire & Wilson, 2010). This research suggests CIP may have complex traumatic experiences of parental incarceration and household instability.

The second criteria for trauma is the individual's experience of the event(s) as physically or emotionally harmful. By this definition, not all children may perceive parental incarceration to be traumatic. Some children may feel a sense of relief if an abusive parent is removed from the home, and other children may not have a relationship with the incarcerated parent to be emotionally harmed by parental absence. SAMHSA's (2014) concept of trauma suggests trauma occurs when an individual's experience is shaped by powerlessness, questioning, and feelings of shame, betrayal, or silencing. For CIP, the sense of powerlessness may be acute as parents are imprisoned within the criminal justice system, which is critiqued as not child-friendly or family focused (Arditti, 2012). Contact and relationships between children and imprisoned parents may change during this time given barriers such as prison locations, visitation policies, and caregiver gatekeeping to imprisoned parents (Rubenstein et al., 2021). Caregivers may have acrimonious relationships with incarcerated parents or believe prison visits are harmful to children and limit child-parent contact. Additionally, the emotional responses accompanying parental incarceration are salient for children who perceive this as traumatic. Previous research described emotional turmoil for CIP who reported feeling isolated, lonely, embarrassed, sad, or angry (Kautz, 2017; Nesmith & Ruhland, 2008). The stigma and secrecy of parental incarceration may increase the disenfranchisement of these emotions and CIP's grief responses (Doka, 2009; Kautz, 2017). Altogether, this research demonstrates children may perceive parental incarceration as emotionally harmful, which is in line with the definition of trauma.

Finally, trauma has lasting effects on functioning and domains of well-being (SAMHSA, 2014). CIP are more likely than other children to have multiple ACEs (Turney, 2018). This is important since multiple and cumulative ACEs lead to an increased potential for toxic stress and trauma (Anda et al., 2006). Research on parental incarceration suggests many CIP experience these lasting effects as they may have physical and mental health or educational needs. For example, caregivers of youth were more likely to report attention and behavior problems among youth who were exposed to parental incarceration (Boch et al., 2019). Lee et al. (2013) reported a statistically significant prevalence of health problems in a sample of young adults who had experienced parental incarceration including anxiety, depression, posttraumatic stress disorder (PTSD), asthma, high cholesterol, HIV/AIDS, migraines, and self-reported fair/poor health. In educational settings, scholars have reported CIP are more likely than peers to experience school problems, lower school engagement, and grade retention (Murphey & Cooper, 2015). Furthermore, CIP are more likely to be suspended or expelled from school (Johnson, 2009), and they are less likely than peers to complete college (Hagan & Foster, 2012). Social well-being is affected as CIP navigate the stigma and secrecy of parental incarceration among peers and from educators (Dallaire et al., 2010; Kautz, 2017). Although this body of research does not claim parental incarceration causes these difficulties, these findings do suggest lasting effects of childhood trauma are prevalent among CIP.

School Counseling Services for CIP

To meet the needs of individuals who have experienced trauma, SAMHSA (2014) recommends public institutions and service systems use a trauma-informed care approach in which stakeholders: 1) *realize* the prevalence and impact of trauma, 2) *recognize* signs of trauma, 3) *respond* using best-practices for promoting recovery and resilience, and 4) *resist re-traumatization* of individuals. Trauma-informed schools are an educational approach to recognizing and responding to student needs with an emphasis on awareness and sensitivity. These efforts require a whole system approach and commitment to changing school culture and providing a trauma-informed and culturally responsive curriculum and climate. To provide this approach, educators are encouraged to shift perspectives, respond to students with empathy and understanding, and conceptualize student emotions and behaviors as symptomology of trauma experiences (Thomas et al., 2019). This shift in perspective can counter deficit-centered thinking by acknowledging the impact of trauma and allowing for compassionate rather than punitive responses to students' dysregulation.

School counselors are integral service providers in trauma-informed schools. As school counselors deliver comprehensive school counseling programs to meet the academic, career, and social/emotional needs of all students, they are attuned to the needs of students who have experienced trauma. School counselors provide leadership and resources as they help stakeholders realize the impact of parental incarceration and recognize signs of trauma for CIP. Additionally, school counselors continually advocate for trauma-informed policies and systems change to meet the needs of students (Rumsey & Milsom, 2019). The response element of trauma-informed care is particularly relevant for school counselors who are providing responsive services. Broadly, school counselors provide trauma responsive services by building supportive relationships, helping students acknowledge experiences and emotions, providing interventions to help physiologically regulate activated stress responses, and processing experiences and needs.

The ASCA National Model (American School Counselor Association, 2019) provides a framework for school counselors to address the needs of CIP in trauma-informed comprehensive school counseling programs. The ASCA National Model (2019) advises school counselors to develop programs for student success by intentionally defining, managing, delivering, and assessing components. First, comprehensive school counseling programs are defined by professional standards. School counselors are ethically obligated to consider the impact of family circumstances (including parental incarceration) and to promote equitable opportunities for CIP (ASCA, 2016). Next, school counselors manage their comprehensive programs and can use data to recognize the needs of CIP. School counselors may use needs assessments to help identify CIP and their academic, career, and social-emotional needs. Then, school counselors provide direct and indirect student services for CIP, including individual, group, and school-wide counseling and system supports. This may be provided using a multitier system of supports (MTSS) approach to provide targeted prevention and intervention services. Finally, school counselors assess their programs using data to demonstrate accountability and program effectiveness for the services they provide. Across all components of the program, school counselors are advocates for CIP and work for systemic change. The following sections describe ways school counselors can deliver trauma-informed counseling services to support the needs of CIP.

Individual Counseling

School counselors may provide individual counseling for CIP who are experiencing difficulties in school. According to a MTSS approach, these individualized services are provided to a select group of students who are having numerous trauma-related symptoms (Rumsey & Milsom, 2019). As school counselors provide individual counseling for CIP, they offer support and interventions to promote student success and likely include attention to parental incarceration as a component of counseling sessions. School counselors providing individual counseling to CIP have reported these students were also often struggling with other social-emotional or academic challenges that led to initial counseling referrals (Brown & Barrio Minton, 2018). Overall, trauma-informed individual school counseling services for CIP can focus on helping students process emotions and experiences, increase coping skills for psychological regulation, and build resiliency.

There is a duty for school counselors to be knowledgeable and prepared for their counseling sessions to be effective. School counselors may need to do additional study of the criminal justice system to better address the experiences of their students. Furthermore, when working with CIP, school counselors must understand how past trauma is present in student's lived experiences and how to best address it with appropriate counseling techniques. School counselors may need to incorporate a grief and loss counseling approach given children's experiences with parental absence and separation (Brown, 2020). School counselors with an evidenced-based theoretical orientation may provide more ethically sound and appropriate interventions. Additionally, school counselors must work within time constraints given their caseloads and to avoid having students out of the classroom for extended time. Recognizing this limited time, school counselors utilize targeted brief and solution-focused approaches with CIP to meet their needs, with a focus on goals and problem solving (ASCA, 2019).

School counselors use theoretically sound and evidence-based approaches to provide individual counseling and meet the needs of students. One theoretical approach described in the school counseling literature with CIP is Choice Therapy (Shillingford & Edwards, 2008). This approach can empower CIP with a sense of control and create real solutions that allow for positive choices. Shillingford and Edward's (2008) single case study showed their fifth grade student had a significant decrease in negative behaviors and peer conflicts as well as an increase in completed assignments through the use of this approach. Motivational interviewing (MI) is another time sensitive and evidence-based approach that school counselors may consider when working with CIP (North, 2017). Although there is no specific literature linking MI and school counseling with CIP, MI has been proven to increase motivation in a client-centered manner which leads to changes in behavior (Frey et al., 2011). With the use of empathy and change talk, school counselors may use MI as a tool to help CIP create positive changes (North, 2017).

Ultimately, school counselors should focus on building therapeutic relationships with CIP to validate emotions and experiences and to provide support and coping skills for reducing stress. In a study of resilience among college-aged students who were CIP, Luther (2015) emphasized the importance of CIP having social and emotional support from caring adults. These adults, including school counselors, helped CIP by providing comfort, stability, and a new vision of possibilities that helped to buffer the impact of parental incarceration and build educational resilience (Luther, 2015). In addition to serving as emotional and social support for CIP, school counselors can help CIP increase coping skills for psychological regulation given the understanding of possible trauma symptoms among these students. Collins et al. (2014) described how coping skills help reduce the risk of excessive anxiety by increasing an individual's ability to manage stressful situations. School counselors may focus on teaching healthy coping skills during counseling sessions to increase health and lower the negative impact of stressors (Thomsen et al., 2015). Providing psychoeducation in individual counseling sessions about trauma and the brain-body connection may also be an impactful way to help CIP.

When left untreated, stressors and trauma for CIP can greatly affect areas such as academics, social interactions, and emotional regulation. Focusing on these topics in individual counseling sessions allows school counselors to help CIP process the meaning and effect of their parental incarceration and past trauma. School counselors should continue to seek tools and best practices for individual trauma-informed school counseling practices to most effectively help CIP, and recommendations are provided for strategies to use in elementary or secondary settings.

Elementary Setting

Using developmentally appropriate techniques allows for more effective counseling when working with CIP in elementary and early middle school. As previously stated, CIP have increased rates of trauma exposure and behavior problems (Geller et al., 2012; Turney, 2018). Play therapy is an appropriate school counseling intervention for these and other concerns such as abuse, neglect, grief, divorce, and depression (Vernon, 2009). School counselors can use child-centered play therapy (CCPT) with CIP to allow children to freely express their emotions, experience a sense of control, and receive unconditional acceptance (Brown & Gibbons, 2018). School counselors would want to include police cars, handcuffs, toy phones, and other toys to help represent CIP's experiences in play. Also, CCPT is an effective approach with students from diverse backgrounds and should be considered for culturally responsive counseling (Brown & Gibbons, 2018). Having an understanding of the emotional, mental, and social concerns of CIP, school counselors can incorporate play therapy to provide needed support and offer a space that allows CIP to feel welcomed, happy, and safe.

While also used in secondary settings, expressive interventions can be incredibly effective tools in counseling sessions with young children. These types of interventions offer a powerful approach during counseling sessions since child clients may have some resistance or challenges in expressing themselves verbally (Vernon, 2009). Expressive interventions such as art, games, or drama can all allow CIP to become more relaxed during counseling. Bibliotherapy is one expressive intervention that has been recommended for helping CIP recognize that others have had similar experiences in a way that is emotionally safe (Walker et al., 2020). Walker and colleagues (2020) provided a list of developmentally appropriate books about parental incarceration that can be used to foster resilience. School counselors can indicate their empathy and openness to discussing issues of parental incarceration by having such books on display in their offices. Art therapy is another helpful intervention that has proven beneficial with children who have had complex traumatic experiences of family separation (Kozlowska & Hanney, 2001). School counselors are encouraged to use expressive interventions with CIP to allow for freedom of expression, relief, and change based on the therapeutic powers of play (Schaefer & Drewes, 2014).

Secondary Setting

When working with CIP, school counselors in middle and high school settings are more likely to have deeper conversations about the realities of parental imprisonment. There are some important considerations for counselors when working with CIP. School counselors should be ready to discuss sensitive subject areas such as traumatic experiences, prison visitation, court processes, intergenerational trends, the impact on the child, and more (Reed & Reed, 1997). Similar to grief counseling, processing and making meaning of these experiences can help CIP's mental and emotional health. School counselors need to be competent and culturally sensitive during these conversations. School counselors should recognize benefits and barriers to prison visitation, such as transportation and caregiver gatekeeping, while allowing CIP to discover their feelings, thoughts, and readiness for such visitation (Reed & Reed, 1997). CIP's feelings and behaviors regarding their incarcerated parents are complex, and secondary school counselors have described the difficulty for CIP of acknowledging parent's criminal behaviors while "navigating family love and loyalty" (Brown, 2020, p. 5).

Some creative approaches may be incorporated into individual sessions with older students. For example, sandtray, letter writing, and art can also be used with adolescents who have experienced trauma (Desmond et al., 2015). Youth might choose to write a letter to their incarcerated parent or be prompted to create a scene in the sandtray to help process their experiences. Additionally, music can be incredibly helpful to adolescents. Music can be adapted for use in individual counseling and allow for a decrease in negative self-talk, increase in self-disclosure, and enhance positive mood (Jenson, 2001). Youth may create music or connect with music or lyrics that help them express their feelings and experiences. Regardless of techniques used, school counselors providing individual counseling to CIP should build resilience by focusing on strengths and adaptivity and offering support for their goals and hopes for the future.

Group Counseling

School counselors are in a unique position to provide small group counseling services to CIP. *The School Counselor and Group Counseling* position statement conveys "group counseling is a vital direct service to students and is an effective part of a school counseling program" (ASCA, 2020, para. 1). Group approaches with children and adolescents generate a sense of universality as each person recognizes they are not alone in facing the situation. Previous literature (Gerlach, 2020; Lopez & Bhatt, 2007) describes small group interventions with elementary school aged and secondary aged CIP students. Small groups provide children and adolescents of incarcerated parents opportunities for structure and social support while focusing on areas such as self-esteem and academics (Gerlach, 2020; Lopez & Bhatt, 2007). School counselors at the elementary level generally have more opportunities to provide direct services focusing on the social-emotional domain in comparison to secondary level school counselors; however, there is a significant need for social-emotional direct services at the secondary level for CIP (Gerlach, 2020). As previous literature about conducting small groups indicates, it is imperative to create a safe space for all students involved in the intervention (Warren et al., 2019). The availability of a safe space is an example of the incorporation of trauma informed care in working with CIP.

It is vital that school counselors are aware and cognizant of the ethical mandates surrounding group work (ASCA, 2016a), especially when working with CIP. In the ASCA (2016a) ethical code, Section A.7. Group Work outlines ten (a-j) ethical steps for school counselors to follow when considering, planning, and conducting small group counseling. The first three steps specifically indicate that small groups should be short-term in nature, information about the small group should be communicated to the parents and/or guardians, and a screening process should be conducted to determine whether small group counseling would be appropriate for the student (ASCA, 2016a). These steps are imperative to follow when determining the scope of the group and honoring the wishes of the family in deciding whether the student would have permission to participate in the group. The incarceration of a parent is recognized as a delicate family matter, and therefore, as social justice agents, school counselors must maintain confidentiality and request the privacy of families when seeking to invite students to participate in small groups (ASCA, 2016a; Lopez & Bhatt, 2007). CIP have expressed their strong desire for privacy in schools about their parent's incarceration (Nesmith & Ruhland, 2008). Furthermore, school counselors are to discuss informed consent, disclose the purpose of the group, address the limits and aspirations of confidentiality, identify appropriate topics for the school setting in order to "take precautions to protect members from harm as a result of interactions with the group" (ASCA, 2016a, p. 4), and recognize that student participation is voluntary (ASCA, 2020).

Through intentional practices of promoting a trauma sensitive environment, school counselors are in the position to protect students from harm by selecting appropriate practices so that students are not re-traumatized (ASCA, 2016a, 2016b). In summary, it is imperative for school counselors who facilitate small groups with CIP at the elementary, middle, and high school levels to ethically and appropriately plan, coordinate, and facilitate small group counseling sessions with the focus on not causing harm and re-traumatizing the students. Specific considerations and recommendations include screening, maintaining confidentiality, creating a trusting environment, maintaining cultural competence and social justice awareness, and following ethical guidelines to protect students' privacy and identify appropriate fit for the intervention (ASCA, 2016a; Lopez & Bhatt, 2007). For example, it is vital a thorough audit has been conducted on the skills and knowledge of the group facilitators to ensure that the intervention is appropriately planned for the school setting and students. Prior to conducting small groups, group facilitators should receive trauma-informed training to prevent traumatizing or retraumatizing the students (Lopez & Bhatt, 2007). School counselors working with CIP should approach individual and group work cautiously to ensure confidentiality is maintained (Warren et al., 2019). This can be done by not mentioning parental incarceration of the students during small group sessions, but allowing for a safe space and environment to be organically created to allow for the student to self-disclose on their own (Warren et al., 2019). This aligns with a study conducted by Brown and Barrio Minton (2018) where school counselor participants indicated the focus of the groups for CIP were not on parental incarceration, but instead focused on loss, friendship, and socialization. Additionally, school counselors should frequently consult with colleagues to ensure they are working within their scope of practice and professional competencies (Lopez & Bhatt, 2007).

Elementary Setting

School counselors in an elementary setting may consider conducting small group counseling sessions with CIP since the structure of an elementary setting provides opportunities for small groups to be scheduled more frequently than at the secondary level (Gerlach, 2020). Lopez and Bhatt (2007) describe a group intervention conducted with elementary students which included 8 sessions and addressed the prescreening, theoretical consideration, and leadership recommendations and steps. Other evidence-based small group interventions may help address trauma symptoms for CIP by enhancing coping skills of children. Although not specific to parental incarceration, these curricula often use cognitive-behavioral techniques such as relaxation, psychoeducation, social problem solving, and cognitive restructuring. School counselors can include CIP in small groups using the Bounce Back (Langley et al., 2015) or Support for Students Exposed to Trauma (SSET; Jaycox et al., 2009) curricula. A more intensive clinical group and individual counseling intervention that has been used in school settings is the Cognitive Behavioral Intervention for Trauma in Schools (CBITS; Jaycox et al., 2018).

Secondary Setting

Teenagers with incarcerated parents are one student group identified as having limited access to mental health support; therefore, school counselors are in the position to provide support for students through a comprehensive school counseling program (Gerlach, 2020). Small group counseling is a recommended targeted intervention in trauma-informed high schools (Rumsey & Milsom, 2019). Current literature indicates that "parental incarceration is a risk factor for elevated trauma symptoms" (Gerlach, 2020, p. 4). While high school counselors may not conduct and facilitate small group counseling as frequently as elementary school counselors, it is important to recognize the benefits of small group counseling for CIP in the high school setting (Gerlach, 2020). As previously mentioned, CIP face multiple challenges, such as lack of sense of belonging, sadness, anxiety, depression, lower school engagement, PTSD, and grade retention (Arditti & Salva, 2015; Gerlach, 2020; Lee et al., 2013; Murphey & Cooper, 2015). Therefore, small group counseling could help address these challenges and symptoms by creating an environment for students to build a sense of universality and instillation of hope (Gerlach, 2020; Yalom, 1995). Furthermore, school counselors as social justice advocates ensure they are working from a culturally competent and unbiased lens (Holcomb-McCoy, 2007). Gerlach (2020) reiterates this by stating, school counselors "must be cognizant of the cultural contexts of imprisonment, race and systemic barriers to best counsel and advocate" (p. 7) when working with African American teenagers.

Classroom and School-Wide Counseling

School counselors facilitate and deliver school-wide programs to support CIP. Problems exist when CIP do not receive needed support because educators do not know which students have incarcerated parents or when teachers' knowledge of parental incarceration leads to preconceived notions or lower expectations of students (Brown, 2020; Dallaire et al., 2010; Warren et al., 2019). Therefore, CIP may feel stigmatized or disconnected from others, which affects academic performance (Warren et al., 2019). School-wide initiatives are important to foster a sense of belongingness and connectivity in trauma-informed schools. School counselors as advocates and leaders can promote school-wide initiatives to create a supportive school climate for CIP (Brown, 2020). Such initiatives include classroom lessons, mentoring programs, college and career advising, and referrals and resources.

Classroom Lessons

Facilitating classroom lessons for all students focused on empathy and equity for others can help build coping skills and foster peer support for CIP. During classroom lessons school counselors can help all students build social emotional skills, such as recognizing and regulating emotions, empathizing with others from diverse backgrounds, and communicating with others. Providing this instruction to all students ensures CIP will receive intervention and support since CIP are not always identified by school personnel. Classroom lessons are an important component of trauma-informed schools to provide a foundational knowledge of self-regulation skills, which are often negatively affected by trauma experiences (Rumsey & Milsom, 2019). School counselors might use evidence-based programs and curricula to support CIP at a school-wide level. For example, Second Step (Committee for Children, 2021) and Student Success Skills (Lemberger et al., 2015) are curricula that may help build coping skills for CIP who have experienced trauma.

School counselors or other educators may include mention of parental incarceration during classroom lessons. For example, parental incarceration could be specifically mentioned as a circumstance that might lead children to feel sad, mad, or scared. Lloyd (2019) suggested teachers and librarians include developmentally appropriate reading materials focusing on parental incarceration, which would further initiate and develop awareness for students. Lists of books featuring characters experiencing parental incarceration are available online, and school counselors may use these books within their classroom lessons to remove some of the stigma and silence around parental incarceration. School counselors can provide suggested readings and resources to classroom teachers who may incorporate materials about the criminal justice system into English/language arts or social studies courses. For example, Learning for Justice (2021) published a series of ten lesson plans designed for high school teachers about mass incarceration, race, and justice. School counselors and teachers discussing parental incarceration in the classroom should be prepared in case students are triggered and in need of additional support.

Mentoring Programs

Mentoring programs are recognized as an intervention with positive outcomes for CIP (Laakso & Nygaard, 2012). Stump and colleagues (2018) reported mentoring programs for CIP correlated with "reduced symptoms of depression and improved social, academic, and behavioral adjustment" (p. 163). Mentoring programs have been recommended given some concerns about CIP developing behaviors and attitudes which align to their parents and the possible risk of future incarceration (Warren et al., 2019). Therefore, mentoring programs may provide skills for CIP to enhance their opportunities for long-term success (Laakso & Nygaard, 2012). Mentoring programs can foster relationships, build positive behavior skills, and have a positive impact on academic performance (Laakso & Nygaard, 2012). Various mentoring programs which include CIP currently exist across the nation. School counselors can seek opportunities to connect CIP with mentoring programs, such as Prison Fellowship, Big Brothers Big Sisters, Angel Tree, and Amachi Mentoring.

College and Career Advising

School counselors provide college and career advising to all students in a comprehensive school counseling program (ASCA, 2019). Since CIP have reportedly low rates of postsecondary completion (Hagan & Foster, 2012), school counselors should prepare and guide CIP through the college and scholarship planning process through intentional school counseling practices. This includes assisting CIP by identifying supportive campuses with resources, navigating the financial aid and scholarship planning process, identifying social supports, and monitoring academic progress. For example, high school counselors may support students who choose to disclose experiences of parental incarceration in their college or scholarship essays (Brown & Barrio Minton, 2018). School counselors may provide services through individual counseling, small group counseling, classroom instruction, and/or school-wide initiatives to address college and scholarship advising. The cost of attending college can be a barrier for CIP due to severe financial challenges. Therefore, it is important for school counselors to support CIP by identifying available scholarship opportunities. The National Resource Center on Children and Families of the

Incarcerated (NRCCFI) at Rutgers University recognizes these challenges and provides information for scholarships and programs available to CIP (see Appendix).

Referrals and Resources

School counselors gain awareness of resources and supports available for CIP through partnerships with community agencies (Warren et al., 2019). These partnerships help school counselors build awareness and knowledge to conceptualize and understand the student and have skills to effectively identify resources to address student and family needs (Brown & Barrio Minton, 2018). It is particularly important for school counselors to offer necessary assistance to meet basic needs to families as this has been identified as a priority by adolescent CIP (Johnson, 2012). Several organizations and nonprofits, such as Child Welfare Information Gateway, The Osborne Association, and Youth.gov, provide resources and information which may benefit parents, caregivers, school counselors, and school personnel (see Appendix). For example, school counselors could provide caregivers of elementary school students with resources such as Sesame Street's guide for families experiencing parental incarceration. This guide offers tools and suggestions for caregivers to help children feel secure and supported when dealing with parental incarceration. Additionally, Project Avary (https://www.projectavary.org), hosts a national online program featuring support groups for CIP as well as camps and recreational activities for youth in the Bay Area focusing on reduction of stigma and development of coping skills for CIP. School counselors should seek information from community partners to determine if additional local resources are available for CIP and families.

System Supports

School counselors collaborate with school stakeholders for supporting CIP's school performance and mental health in ways that are respectful, culturally-informed, and sensitive to privacy. Stakeholders in trauma-informed schools recognize the need for collaborative partnership to provide preventative and responsive services. This may be accomplished through consultation and collaboration about the academic, career, and social-emotional needs of children and through providing information about available resources. This allows school counselors to advocate for CIP (ASCA, 2019).

Advocacy is an ethical mandate for school counselors (ASCA, 2016a), and school counselors can advocate for CIP in various ways to create system change. These advocacy efforts allow school counselors to bring awareness of the academic and social-emotional needs of CIP within school settings and seek policy and legislative changes to better support CIP. This includes promoting better mental health care in school settings to meet the psychological needs of CIP. Additionally, advocating for

CIP includes training staff to increase awareness of needed classroom accommodations and interventions, changing discipline policies to be trauma-informed, or examining attendance policies to support parental visitation (Brown, 2020). Previous scholars have noted the need for staff training about incarceration and social justice (Dallaire et al., 2010; Mason et al., 2021); therefore, recommendations and guidelines for staff training and creating school policies for more equitable school experiences for CIP are included in this chapter.

Collaboration

School counselors utilize a collaborative approach to support the well-being of students through various partnerships (ASCA, 2019). Such partnerships include collaboration with administrators (Turney, 2019), school nurses (Mason et al., 2021; Tuttle et al., 2018), teachers (Brown & Barrio Minton, 2018; Warren et al., 2019), and social workers (Drew & Gonzalez, 2021; Skinner-Osei & Levenson, 2018). The vital role of collaboration is recognized as the vehicle to galvanize resources to best support students in the academic, social-emotional, and career development domains (ASCA, 2019). CIP can particularly benefit from these types of collaborations.

School Counselor and Administrator Collaboration

School counselor and administrator collaboration is critical when supporting and working with CIP. School counselors understand the concerns faced by administrators in promoting the school's mission and focus on learning and school climate (ASCA, 2019). Therefore, together school counselors and administrators are able to collaborate to address barriers to CIP's academic and behavioral success. For example, as school counselors collect data about student needs, they can inform administrators about the implications and impact of parental incarceration on students (e.g., adverse experiences) and the prevalence of it within the school setting (ASCA, 2019; Turney, 2019). Furthermore, this discussion can be seen as a conduit to explore and implement policies, practices, and interventions to support positive behavioral interventions, social emotional learning, and positive school climate (ASCA, 2016b). One particular policy and systemic change school counselors can consult with administrators involves parental access to student information and involvement in educational decisions. School counselors and administrators may collaborate to ensure incarcerated parents have access to student report cards and have opportunities to participate virtually in school meetings, such as parent-teacher conferences (Warren et al., 2019).

To advocate for systemic change, school counselors engage administrators in discussions focusing on the school-to-prison pipeline and the implications punishments such as suspensions and expulsions may have on students (Welfare et al., 2021). Discipline policy reform is necessary in all trauma-focused schools. School counselors as social justice advocates are able to educate administrators about the challenges CIP face and promote changes in discipline methods for behavioral concerns away from a punitive lens (Brown et al., 2019; Welfare et al., 2021). School counselors and administrators can collaborate to bring restorative practices into schools for a more trauma-informed approach to supporting dysregulated student behaviors (Rumsey & Milsom, 2019). School counselors and administrators work together in these efforts to encourage educator buy-in for trauma-informed schools through educating others about the impact of trauma and the need for new responses to student behaviors and needs.

School Counselor and School Nurse Collaboration

School counselors and school nurses can collaborate to address barriers to students' attainment of positive mental and physical well-being and health (Tuttle et al., 2018). This collaborative partnership is vital since both groups of professionals have access to sensitive, private, and confidential information about students which impact their mental and physical health and since school counselors and school nurses are often recognized as the first point of contact when a student experiences a crisis (Grubbs et al., 2016; Tuttle et al., 2018). Additionally, school counselors and school nurses can further collaborate to provide training to teachers and staff focusing on "physical and mental health issues that disproportionately impact students and families of color" (Mason et al., 2021, p. 11), especially since statistically a large percentage of CIP are identified as racial or ethnic minorities (Aaron & Dallaire, 2010; Murphey & Cooper, 2015; Turney, 2019; Warren et al., 2019). Such training would further address viewpoints of how various cultures consider mental health and how psychological symptoms might be indicators of possible mental health issues (Mason et al., 2021). Furthermore, specific symptoms such as psychosomatic concerns and frequent visits to the school counselor and school nurse offices may also be indicators of trauma (Tuttle et al., 2018).

School Counselor and Teacher Collaboration

Teachers have the most frequent interaction with CIP and are often able to notice changes in student performance, emotional dispositions, and habits (Warren et al., 2019). Such changes or concerns include absenteeism, grade retention, low test scores, changes in behavior, anxiety, depression, PTSD, attention and behavior problems, sadness, and low rates of high school graduation and college enrollment (Boch et al., 2019; Lee et al., 2013; Turney, 2019). Consulting and collaborating with teachers about the impact of parental incarceration would strengthen the support provided to

CIP and build a more robust trauma-informed school environment (ASCA, 2016b). Teachers have reported feeling unprepared to best support CIP (Dallaire et al., 2010). Therefore, school counselors can provide training to help teachers realize and recognize trauma and loss experienced by CIP (Brown & Barrio Minton, 2018). This training would empower teachers working with CIP to respond with empathy for CIP, provide additional academic resources when needed, and consider dysregulated classroom behaviors within a trauma-informed lens. However, school counselors should emphasize the importance of confidentiality and limitations around what may be disclosed to teachers given CIP and family concerns around privacy (ASCA, 2016a; Brown & Barrio Minton, 2018). Advocating for CIP includes helping teachers and staff recognize and address biases about prisoners since these stigmatize and disenfranchise CIP. School counselors can specifically help teachers identify effects of trauma, learn when they should make referrals to school counselors, and avoid making negative statements that label CIP or about individuals in the criminal justice system (ASCA, 2016b; Lloyd, 2019). Both teachers and school counselors in trauma-informed schools build positive and caring relationships with students and recognize the resilience of CIP.

School Counselor and Social Worker Collaboration

Social workers are recognized as the connecting liaison between schools, families, communities, resources, and agencies (Drew & Gonzalez, 2021). This connection and collaboration between school counselors and social workers is vital when working to support and advocate for CIP. Some districts with school social workers are able to utilize them in the capacity of identifying resources, supports, and agencies to help build a network to further enhance the social-emotional and academic development of CIP. For example, a school social worker can collaborate with the school counselor to identify needs of CIP, connect with community partners for resources, and connect with stakeholders or agencies involved in holistic care (e.g., Department of Family and Children's Services, prison social workers, mentors). Adolescent CIP highly value resources that help meet basic household needs (Johnson, 2012), and social workers and school counselors can work closely to address this services priority. Furthermore, school counselors may refer CIP for therapeutic services provided by social workers in some districts. Social workers can provide trauma-informed services for CIP by validating their experiences and feelings and can mentor students with empathy and compassion (Skinner-Osei & Levenson, 2018).

IMPLICATIONS AND FUTURE RESEARCH

School counselors support CIP by using trauma-informed approaches throughout a comprehensive school counseling program. As school counselors recognize the needs of CIP, they can use a MTSS framework to provide targeted direct or indirect services, including individual or group counseling, classroom lessons, advising, referrals, and consultation and collaboration with stakeholders. These efforts promote the academic, career, and social emotional development and success of CIP. School counselors should remain mindful that not all CIP have trauma, and most CIP demonstrate great resilience. Therefore, some CIP will only receive support from school counselors through school-wide initiatives such as classroom lessons, college and career advising, and collaboration with stakeholders. An important aspect of trauma-informed school counseling for CIP includes advocating in schools and communities for policies and procedures that reduce stigma and bias against families experiencing incarceration. School counselors understand that advocating for a more just society helps students, families, and society have better relationships, mental health, and educational outcomes.

School counselors as leaders and advocates in trauma-informed school environments seek to foster a positive school climate (ASCA, 2019b). Additional research is needed to better understand the ways stigma impacts the social and academic experiences of CIP. This research could help school counselors develop policies and procedures that would improve the school climate, school connectedness, and resilience of CIP. Scholars have recommended reform of school discipline to better support children experiencing trauma and avoid re-traumatization (Rumsey & Milsom, 2019; Welfare et al., 20201); however, more research is needed to better help school leaders translate these recommendations into practice. Furthermore, previous scholars have recommended teacher training about the needs of CIP as a way to increase support for students (Dallaire et al., 2010; Brown & Barrio Minton, 2018); however, research is needed to support the efficacy of any training components or models.

The research about trauma-informed schools is limited by differences in defining and understanding the components of such schools across the nation (SAMHSA, 2014; Thomas et al., 2019). Scholars should better define the parameters of trauma-informed schools and offer more empirical research about effective school-based interventions for students experiencing trauma. The research describing best practices for trauma-informed interventions for CIP, particularly in school settings, is particularly scarce. There are limitations with identifying and researching CIP in schools, including the aforementioned concerns about privacy and confidentiality. However, more research is needed about evidence-based interventions for school counselors working with CIP. For now, school counselors can use these best practices for trauma-informed school counseling when working with CIP to provide necessary support to this group of students.

CONCLUSION

School counselors understand the potential for trauma connected to parental incarceration. With this awareness and knowledge, they provide trauma-informed school counseling to support the academic and mental health needs of students through counseling, collaboration, and advocacy. Using various culturally responsive delivery approaches, school counselors help CIP process emotions and experiences and increase coping skills. They encourage relationships to help CIP experience school connectedness and belonging and offer encouragement and hope for CIP to build resilience. School counselors are advocates for CIP in trauma-informed schools.

REFERENCES

Aaron, L., & Dallaire, D. H. (2010). Parental incarceration and multiple risk experiences: Effects on family dynamics and children's delinquency. *Journal of Youth and Adolescence*, *39*(12), 1471–1484. doi:10.100710964-009-9458-0 PMID:19834796

Adoption and Foster Care Analysis and Reporting System. (2020). *The AFCARS Report preliminary FY 2019 estimates as of June 23, 2020 - No. 27*. US Department of Health and Human Services Children's Bureau. https://www.acf.hhs.gov/cb/report/afcars-report-27

American School Counselor Association. (2016a). *ASCA ethical standards for school counselors*. https://www.schoolcounselor.org/asca/media/asca/Ethics/EthicalStandards2016.pdf

American School Counselor Association. (2016b.) *The school counselor and trauma informed practice* [Position Statement]. https://www.schoolcounselor.org/Standards-Positions/Position-Statements/ASCA-Position-Statements/The-School-Counselor-and-Trauma-Informed-Practice

American School Counselor Association. (2019). *The ASCA national model: A framework for school counseling programs* (4th ed.). Author.

American School Counselor Association. (2020). *The school counselor and group counseling* [Position Statement]. https://www.schoolcounselor.org/Standards-Positions/Position-Statements/ASCA-Position-Statements/The-School-Counselor-and-Group-Counseling

Anda, R. F., Felitti, V. J., Bremner, J. D., Walker, J. D., Whitfield, C., Perry, B. D., Dube, S. R., & Giles, W. H. (2006). The enduring effects of abuse and related adverse experiences in childhood: A confluence of evidence from neurobiology and epidemiology. *European Archives of Psychiatry and Clinical Neuroscience, 256*(3), 174–186. doi:10.100700406-005-0624-4 PMID:16311898

Arditti, J. (2012). *Parental incarceration and the family: Psychological and social effects of imprisonment on children, parents, and caregivers*. NYU Press.

Arditti, J., & Salva, J. (2015). Parental incarceration and child trauma symptoms in single caregiver homes. *Journal of Child and Family Studies, 24*(3), 551–561. https://doi.org/10.1007/s10826-013-9867-2

Boch, S. J., Warren, B. J., & Ford, J. L. (2019). Attention, externalizing, and internalizing problems of youth exposed to parental incarceration. *Issues in Mental Health Nursing, 40*(6), 466–475. https://doi.org/10.1080/01612840.2019.1565872

Brown, E. C. (2020). School counselor conceptualizations of the needs of children of incarcerated parents. *Children and Youth Services Review, 112*, 1–9. doi:10.1016/j.childyouth.2020.104936

Brown, E. C., & Barrio Minton, C. A. (2018). Serving children of incarcerated parents: A case study of school counselors' experiences. *Professional School Counseling, 21*(1), 1–11. doi:10.5330/prsc.9.1.a5j5051x1025t767

Brown, E. C., & Gibbons, M. M. (2018). Addressing needs of children of incarcerated parents with child-centered play therapy. *Journal of Child and Adolescent Counseling, 4*(2), 134–145. doi:10.1080/23727810.2017.1381931

Brown, M., Lenares-Solomon, D., & Deaner, R. (2019). Every Student Succeeds Act: A call to action for school counselors. *Journal of Counselor Leadership and Advocacy, 6*(1), 86–96. https://doi.org/10.1080/2326716X.2018.1557574

Collins, S., Woolfson, L. M., & Durkin, K. (2014). Effects on coping skills and anxiety of a universal school-based mental health intervention delivered in Scottish primary schools. *School Psychology International, 35*(1), 85–100. https://doi.org/10.1177/0143034312469157

Committee for Children. (2021). *Second Step*. http://www.secondstep.org

Dallaire, D., & Wilson, H. (2010). The relation of exposure to parental criminal activity, arrest, and sentencing to children's maladjustment. *Journal of Child and Family Studies, 19*, 404–418. https://doi.org/10.1007/s10826-009-9311-9

Dallaire, D. H., Ciccone, A., & Wilson, L. C. (2010). Teachers' experiences with and expectations of children with incarcerated parents. *Journal of Applied Developmental Psychology, 31*(4), 281–290. https://doi.org/10.1016/j.appdev.2010.04.001

de Haan, B., Mienko, J. A., & Eddy, J. M. (2019). The interface of child welfare and parental criminal justice involvement: Policy and practice implications for the children of incarcerated parents. In J. M. Eddy & J. Poehlmann-Tynan (Eds.), Handbook on children with incarcerated parents: Research, policy, and practice (2nd ed., pp. 279–294). Springer. https://doi.org/10.1007/978-3-030-16707-3_19.

Desmond, K. J., Kindsvatter, A., Stahl, S., & Smith, H. (2015). Using creative techniques with children who have experienced trauma. *Journal of Creativity in Mental Health, 10*(4), 439–455. https://doi.org/10.1080/15401383.2015.1040938

Doka, K. J. (2009). Disenfranchised grief. In C. D. Bryant & D. L. Peck (Eds.), Encyclopedia of death and the human experience (pp. 378–381). Sage. https://doi.org/10.4135/9781412972031.n122.

Drew, M., & Gonzalez, M. (2021). Making the time: Relationships among school specialists. *School Community Journal, 31*(1), 171–204. https://www.schoolcommunitynetwork.org/SCJ.aspx

Felitti, V. J., Anda, R. F., Nordenberg, D., Williamson, D. F., Spitz, A. M., & Edwards, V. … Marks, J. S. (1998). Relationship of childhood abuse and household dysfunction to many of the leading causes of death in adults. *American Journal of Preventive Medicine, 14*(4), 245–258. doi:10.1016/S0749-3797(98)00017-8

Frey, A., Cloud, R., Lee, J., Small, J., Seeley, J., Feil, E., Walker, H., & Golly, A. (2011). The promise of motivational interviewing in school mental health. *School Mental Health, 3*, 1–12. https://doi.org/10.1007/s12310-010-9048-z

Geller, A., Cooper, C. E., Garfinkel, I., Schwartz-Soicher, O., & Mincy, R. B. (2012). Beyond absenteeism: Father incarceration and child development. *Demography, 49*(1), 49–76. https://doi.org/10.1007/s13524-011-0081-9

Gerlach, J. (2020). Teens of incarcerated parents: A group counseling intervention for high school counselors. *Journal of School Counseling, 18*(16). http://www.jsc.montana.edu/articles/v18n16.pdf

Grubbs, L., Muro, J. H., & Clements, K. (2016). School counselors and nurses: Collaborative best practices for maintaining confidentiality with pregnant adolescents. *The Practitioner Scholar: Journal of Counseling & Professional Psychology, 5*(1), 20-29. https://www.thepractitionerscholar.com/issue/view/1263

Hagan, J., & Foster, H. (2012). Children of the American prison generation: Student and school spillover effects of incarcerating mothers. *Law & Society Review*, *46*(1), 37–69. https://doi.org/10.1111/j.1540-5893.2012.00472.x

Holcomb-McCoy, C. (2007). *School counseling to close the achievement gap: A social justice framework for success*. Corwin Press.

Jaycox, L. H., Langley, A. K., & Hoover, S. A. (2018). *Cognitive behavioral intervention for trauma in schools (CBITS)* (2nd ed.). RAND Corporation. https://www.rand.org/pubs/tools/TL272.html

Jaycox, L. H., Langley, A. K., Stein, B. D., Wong, M., Sharma, P., Scott, M., & Schonlau, M. (2009). Support for students exposed to trauma: A pilot study. *School Mental Health*, *1*(2), 49–60. https://doi.org/10.1007/s12310-009-9007-8

Jensen, K. L. (2001). The effects of selected classical music on self-disclosure. *Journal of Music Therapy*, *38*(1), 2–27. https://doi.org/10.1093/jmt/38.1.2

Johnson, R. C. (2009). Ever-increasing levels of parental incarceration and the consequences for children. In S. Raphael & M. Stoll (Eds.), *Do prisons make us safer? The benefits and costs of the prison boom* (pp. 177–206). Russell Sage Foundation.

Johnson, T. (2012). Mapping the critical service needs of adolescent children of prisoners. *Social Work in Public Health*, *27*(1-2), 45–68. https://doi.org/10.1080/19371918.2012.629905

Kautz, S. V. (2017). Adolescent adaptation to parental incarceration. *Child & Adolescent Social Work Journal*, *34*(6), 557–572. https://doi.org/10.1007/s10560-017-0493-5

Kozlowska, K., & Hanney, L. (2001). An art therapy group for children traumatized by parental violence and separation. *Clinical Child Psychology and Psychiatry*, *6*(1), 49–78. https://doi.org/10.1177/1359104501006001006

Laakso, J., & Nygaard, J. (2012). Children of incarcerated parents: How a mentoring program can make a difference. *Social Work in Public Health*, *27*(1-2), 12–28. https://doi.org/10.1080/19371918.2012.629892

Langley, A. K., Gonzalez, A., Sugar, C. A., Solis, D., & Jaycox, L. (2015). Bounce back: Effectiveness of an elementary school-based intervention for multicultural children exposed to traumatic events. *Journal of Consulting and Clinical Psychology, 83*(5), 853–865. https://doi.org/10.1037/ccp0000051

Learning for Justice. (2021). *Teaching 'The New Jim Crow.'* https://www.learningforjustice.org/magazine/publications/teaching-the-new-jim-crow

Lee, R. D., Fang, X., & Luo, F. (2013). The impact of parental incarceration on the physical and mental health of young adults. *Pediatrics, 131*, e1188–e1195. https://doi.org/10.1542/peds.2012-0627

Lemberger, M., Selig, J., Bowers, H., & Rogers, J. (2015). Effects of the student success skills program on the executive functioning skills, feelings of connectedness, and academic achievement in a predominantly Hispanic, low-income middle school district. *Journal of Counseling and Development, 93*(1), 25–36. https://doi.org/10.1002/j.1556-6676.2015.00178.x

Lloyd, T. S. (2019). Teaching students of incarcerated parents. *American Educator, 43*(2), 24–28. https://www.aft.org/ae/summer2019/lloyd

Lopez, C., & Bhatt, C. S. (2007). Supporting students with incarcerated parents in schools: A group intervention. *Journal for Specialists in Group Work, 32*(2), 139–153. https://doi.org/10.1080/01933920701227125

Luther, K. (2015). Examining social support among adult children of incarcerated parents. *Family Relations, 64*(4), 505–518. https://www.jstor.org/stable/43695516

Mason, E., Robertson, A., Gay, J., Clarke, N., & Holcomb-McCoy, C. (2021). Antiracist school counselor preparation: Expanding on the five tenets of the transforming school counseling initiative. *Teaching and Supervision in Counseling, 3*(2), 3-14. https://trace.tennessee.edu/tsc/vol13/iss2/2Mentalhealth

Murphey, D., & Cooper, P. M. (2015). *Parents behind bars: What happens to their children*. Child Trends. http://www.childtrends.org/wp-content/uploads/2015/10/2015-42ParentsBehindBars.pdf

Nesmith, A., & Ruhland, E. (2008). Children of incarcerated parents: Challenges and resiliency, in their own words. *Children and Youth Services Review, 30*(10), 1119–1130. https://doi.org/10.1016/j.childyouth.2008.02.006

Nichols, E. B., Loper, A. B., & Meyer, J. P. (2016). Promoting educational resiliency in youth with incarcerated parents: The impact of parental incarceration, school characteristics, and connectedness on school outcomes. *Journal of Youth and Adolescence, 45*, 1090–1109. https://doi.org/10.1007/s10964-015-0337-6

North, R. (2017). *Motivational interviewing for school counselors*. Author.

Reed, D., & Reed, E. (1997). Children of incarcerated parents. *Social Justice (San Francisco, Calif.), 24*(3), 152–169. https://www.jstor.org/stable/29767028

Rubenstein, B. Y., Toman, E. L., & Cochran, J. C. (2021). Socioeconomic barriers to child contact with incarcerated parents. *Justice Quarterly, 38*(4), 725–751. https://doi.org/10.1080/07418825.2019.1606270

Rumsey, A. D., McCullough, R., & Chang, C. Y. (2020). Understanding the secondary exposure to trauma and professional quality of life of school counselors. *Professional School Counseling, 24*(1), 1–11. https://doi.org/10.1177/2156759X20973643

Rumsey, A. D., & Milsom, A. (2019). Supporting school engagement and high school completion through trauma-informed school counseling. *Professional School Counseling, 22*(1), 1–10. https://doi.org/10.1177/2156759X19867254

Schaefer, C. E., & Drewes, A. A. (Eds.). (2014). *The therapeutic powers of play: 20 core agents of change* (2nd ed.). Wiley.

Shillingford, M., & Edwards, O. (2008). Professional school counselors using choice theory to meet the needs of children of prisoners. *Professional School Counseling, 12*(1), 62–65. https://www.jstor.org/stable/42732864

Skinner-Osei & Levenson. (2018). Trauma-informed services for children with incarcerated parents. *Journal of Family Social Work, 21*(4/5). 421-437. doi:10.1080/10522158.2018.1499064

Stump, K. N., Kupersmidt, J. B., Stelter, R. L., & Rhodes, J. E. (2018). Mentoring program enhancements supporting effective mentoring of children of incarcerated parents. *American Journal of Community Psychology, 62*(1-2), 163–174. https://doi.org/10.1002/ajcp.12250

Substance Abuse and Mental Health Services Administration. (2014). *SAMHSA's concept of trauma and guidance for a trauma-informed approach*. HHS Publication No. (SMA) 14-4884. Substance Abuse and Mental Health Services Administration. https://ncsacw.samhsa.gov/userfiles/files/SAMHSA_Trauma.pdf

Thomas, M. S., Crosby, S., & Vanderhaar, J. (2019). Trauma-informed practices in schools across two decades: An interdisciplinary review of research. *Review of Research in Education, 43*(1), 422–452. https://doi.org/10.3102/0091732X18821123

Thomsen, T., Fritz, V., Mößle, R., & Greve, W. (2015). The impact of accommodative coping on well-being in childhood and adolescence: Longitudinal findings. *International Journal of Behavioral Development, 39*(5), 467–476. https://doi.org/10.1177/0165025414551762

Turney, K. (2018). Adverse childhood experiences among children of incarcerated parents. *Children and Youth Services Review, 89*, 218–225. https://doi.org/10.1016/j.childyouth.2018.04.033

Turney, K. (2019). Understanding the needs of children with incarcerated parents: What educators should know. *American Educator, 43*(2), 22–28. https://www.aft.org/ae/summer2019/turney

Tuttle, M., Yordy, M., Appling, B., & Hanley, E. (2018). School counselor and school nurse collaboration: Partnering for K-12 student success. *Journal of School Counseling, 16*(4). http://www.jsc.montana.edu/articles/v16n4.pdf

Vernon, A. (2009). *Counseling children and adolescents* (4th ed.). Love.

Walker, S. L., Connery, C., Blackson, G. N., Divine, T. F., Walker, T. D., Williams, B., Finke, J. A., & Bartel, K. (2020). Developing resilience in youth with incarcerated parents: A bibliotherapeutic blueprint with tween and young adult literature chapter books. *Journal of Correctional Education, 71*(2), 37–56.

Warren, J. M., Coker, G. L., & Collins, M. L. (2019). Children of incarcerated parents: Considerations for professional school counselors. *The Professional Counselor, 9*(3), 185–199. https://doi.org/10.15241/jmw.9.3.185

Welfare, L. E., Grimes, T. O., Lawson, G., Hori, K., & Asadi, G. (2021). The school to prison pipeline: Quantitative evidence to guide school counselor advocacy. *Journal of Counselor Leadership and Advocacy, 8*(1), 16–29. https://doi.org/10.1080/2326716X.2020.1861490

Yalom, I. D. (1995). *Theory and practice of group psychotherapy* (4th ed.). Basic Books.

ADDITIONAL READING

Arditti, J. A. (2012). Child trauma within the context of parental incarceration: A family process perspective. *Journal of Family Theory & Review*, *4*(3), 181–219. doi:10.1111/j.1756-2589.2012.00128.x

Johnson, E. I., & Easterling, B. A. (2015). Navigating discrepancy: Youth perspectives on parental reentry from prison. *Journal of Offender Rehabilitation*, *54*(1), 60–83. doi:10.1080/10509674.2014.972604

Kautz, S. V. (2018). The emotional experience of parental incarceration from the African-American adolescent perspective. *Journal of Child & Adolescent Trauma*, *12*(2), 187–199. doi:10.100740653-018-0232-x PMID:32318191

Kilgore, J. (2015). *Understanding mass incarceration: A people's guide to the key civil rights struggle of our time*. The New Press.

King, K. M., & Delgado, H. (2021). Losing a family member to incarceration: Grief and resilience. *Journal of Loss and Trauma*, *26*(5), 436–450. doi:10.1080/15325024.2020.1816753

Luther, K. (2016). Stigma management among children of incarcerated parents. *Deviant Behavior*, *37*(11), 1264–1275. doi:10.1080/01639625.2016.1170551

Petsch, P., & Rochlen, A. B. (2009). Children of incarcerated parents: Implications for school counselors. *Journal of School Counseling*, *7*(40). http://www.jsc.montana.edu/articles/v7n40.pdf

Turney, K., & Goodsell, R. (2018). Parental incarceration and children's wellbeing. *The Future of Children*, *28*(1), 147–164. doi:10.1353/foc.2018.0007

KEY TERMS AND DEFINITIONS

Children of Incarcerated Parents: Minors under the age of 18 with a father and/or mother who is in jail or state or federal prison.

Collaboration: The partnership and engagement between stakeholders to support the development of all students within a school setting by creating an environment for all students to succeed.

Comprehensive School Counseling Programs: Efforts led by school counselors to promote student achievement by attending to the academic, career, and personal/social needs of all students in the school.

Group Counseling: A direct service provided by school counselors with a group of students to address academic, career, and social/emotional needs where students work together to build trust, relationships, and support while working on a particular issue or concern.

Mentoring: An intentional relationship between two individuals with one person in a role to support the other in the development of positive characteristics, skills, and attitudes.

School Climate: The social and behavioral factors that influence the school environment.

Stakeholders: Adults who are invested in the success of all students. A few examples within the school setting include administrators, school counselors, school nurses, teachers, parents, and social workers.

Trauma: An event perceived as harmful with lasting effects on well-being.

Trauma-Informed Schools: The intentional focus and approach of implementing practices and policies to create a school environment for students to feel supported and safe.

APPENDIX

School Counseling for CIP Resource Guide

Bibliotherapy:

- *What Do I Say About That?* by Julia Cook
- *My Daddy is in Jail* by Janet Bender (includes small group discussion guide)
- *The Night Dad Went to Jail: What to Expect When Someone You Love Goes to Jail* by Melissa Higgins
- *Visiting Day* by Jacqueline Woodson
- *Wish You Were Here: Teens Write about Parents in Prison* by Youth Communication (compilation of essays for middle/high school students with discussion guide)

Individual and Small Group Counseling Materials:

- *Empowering Children of Incarcerated Parents* by Burgess, Caselman & Carsey
- Sesame Street's Little Children, Big Challenges: Incarceration https://sesamestreetincommunities.org/topics/incarceration/
- Animated Virtual Prison Tour for Children http://ctcip.org/main-childrens-page/
- Tip Sheet for Teens https://youth.gov/sites/default/files/COIP_TipSheet_Youth_Final.pdf
- College Scholarships https://nrccfi.camden.rutgers.edu/resources/college-and-coip-info/
- Echoes of Incarceration Videos https://www.echoesofincarceration.org/docs

Awareness and Advocacy Resources for Educators and Caregivers:

- *A Shared Sentence* from the Annie E. Casey Foundation https://www.aecf.org/resources/a-shared-sentence/
- Children of the Incarcerated Video https://www.youtube.com/watch?v=6I6vL_OyNmA
- Top 10 Things You Should Know https://www.projectavary.org/top-ten/
- *The Children of Incarcerated Parents Bill of Rights* https://www.projectavary.org/bill-of-rights

- Preparing for Prison Visits https://nrccfi.camden.rutgers.edu/files/cipl106-jailandprisonprocedures.pdf
- *Stronger Together* handbooks from The Osborne Association https://www.osborneny.org/stronger-together-handbooks
- Tip Sheet for Teachers Supporting CIP https://youth.gov/sites/default/files/COIP_TipSheet-Teachers_508.pdf

Support Programs for CIP:

- Project Avary Online Support Groups https://www.projectavary.org/onlineprogram
- Amachi Mentoring www.amachimentoring.org

Chapter 12
The Elephant in the Room:
Using AAI in a School Counseling Program

Lois T. Curry-Catanese
https://orcid.org/0000-0001-8076-6855
Walden University, USA

ABSTRACT

This chapter will provide a brief overview of the history and counseling theories associated with animal-assisted interventions and how school counselors can incorporate the use of animal-assisted interventions into their school's trauma-informed counseling program while examining the benefits of using animal-assisted interventions to promote trust, rapport, and healing for students experiencing any type of direct or indirect trauma. This chapter will also review potential problems, issues, and controversies that may arise in using animal-assisted interventions in the school setting. Finally, the author will offer strategies and ideas for encompassing living and other alternative modalities of animal-assisted interventions within an elementary school counseling program.

INTRODUCTION

The colloquialism of "the elephant in the room" is a metaphorical idiom that refers to the problems or issues that are presented in context but avoided because the issues are uncomfortable to confront. School counselors are responsible for designing, implementing, managing, and assessing their school's counseling program to ensure that students thrive socially, emotionally, and academically. The American School

DOI: 10.4018/978-1-7998-9785-9.ch012

Counseling Association (ASCA, 2019) National Model provides the framework for school counselors to develop a comprehensive school counseling program to meet the diverse needs of a school's community. School counselors are tasked with being creative in their approach to meeting the needs of the students in the most beneficial of ways.

There are three types of animal-assisted interventions (AAI) that integrate various species of animals. Stewart et al. (2016) defined those three interventions as:

"*Animal-assisted Interventions* (AAI): Goal-oriented interventions incorporating animals, designed to improve client functioning and delivered by a practitioner with special expertise and training within his/ her scope of practice.

Animal-assisted therapy in counseling (AAT-C): The incorporation of specially trained and evaluated animals as therapeutic agents in the counseling process.

Animal-assisted crisis response (AACR): Trained human-canine response teams that provides comfort, stress relief, and emotional support to those affected by crisis and disasters."

In this chapter, the author will only be addressing animal-assisted interventions which are goal-oriented and structured interventions that intentionally include animals in a human's health, education, and service. Incorporating animal-assisted interventions (AAI) into a school counseling program creatively addresses and potentially meets students' emotional and behavioral needs when they arrive at school with a backpack of trauma.

BACKGROUND

History of Animal-Assisted Interventions

Since the late 1700's animals have been used with the intended purpose of providing therapeutic support for humans. William Tuke provided one of the first documented animal-assisted interventions in 1792 when he used farm animals to enhance the well-being of the emotionally ill. (Jenkins et al., 2014) Then in 1942, at an Army Air Force hospital, a soldier in recovery asked that a dog keep him company while he recuperated from his injuries. (Davis, 1988; as cited by Trivedi & Peri, 1995)

In 1953, child psychologist Boris Levison and his dog, *Jingles*, gained recognition for their work with a young autistic boy Dr. Levinson was treating. Dr. Levison, in 1969, went on to author a book about his work with *Jingles* and the young child in what is now known as the first recorded work with animal-assisted interventions (Levison, 1997). Although a variety of animals (such as dogs, cats, horses, birds, fish, rabbits, and other small animals) have been used over the years in animal-assisted interventions, education, and activities (Dimitrijevic, 2009), dogs continue to be the most popular in today's milieu of intervention and treatment. (Nebbe, 1991; Trivedi and Peri, 1995; Friesen, 2010)

In 2014 the American Counseling Association's *Code of Ethics* adopted competencies that clearly defined that appropriate education, training, and supervision were needed by professional counselors to practice animal-assisted therapy. The competencies were developed by Dr. Leslie Stewart (2016) and adopted by the ACA and American School counselor Association (ASCA, 2012). Individuals such as Dr. Leslie Stewart, Dr. Aubrey Fine, Dr. Cynthia Chandler, Dr. Nancy Parish-Plass, James Serpell, and a host of other prominent individuals in the field of animal-assisted therapy have contributed to developing AAT (Animal Assisted Therapy) into a specialty within the counseling field.

BENEFITS OF USING ANIMAL-ASSISTED INTERVENTIONS (AAI)

Biopsychosocial Model: Physiological, Emotional, and Social Benefits

The biopsychosocial model was first introduced by Chapa et al. (2014) as a model of integration among three contributing factors to health and disease. (Cited in Serpell et al., 2016) These contributing factors are biological (e.g., genetics), psychological (e.g., personality traits, mood disorders, beliefs), and social (e.g., culture, family, peers) in a person. Serpell et al. (2016) suggest that using this comprehensive biopsychosocial model allows for the effectiveness of animal-assisted interventions (AAI) in various settings. The research in the human-animal bond continues to offer insight into AAI's effectiveness. The National Institute of Health (2018) demonstrated that animals have a direct physiological effect on reducing the stress hormone levels known as cortisol and reducing blood pressure in adults through biofeedback.

Folse et al. (1994) showed in their research study that children experienced a reduction in their mood and depression; Anderson and Olson (2006) found that children demonstrated increased academic, social, and behavioral skills in the classroom when introduced to animal-assisted interventions (AAI). The physiological reactions caused by the hyperarousal state can be measured in rapid heart and respiratory rates based on blood flow being diverted from the major internal organs thereby preventing the ability to regulate emotions. And we know through research that the presence of an animal can increase the oxytocin or "feel good" hormones that cause a sense of calm and decrease heart rate.

One of the most interesting research works in the field of psychophysiology has been conducted by Stephen Porges (2001). Porges (2001) developed a theoretical platform for the polyvagal theory that explains how neurophysiology affects social behavior. His research included examining the autonomic nervous system as it is triggered by perceived threats to life and intervention strategies to reduce or reprogram the psychophysiological response. Nancy Parish-Plass (2020) concurred that for neurobiological trauma to be addressed in therapy it must take place in the context of relationships and AAI is conducted in a relational environment.

Many clinicians revealed that animal-assisted interventions yielded positive results in disclosure (Serpell, 2020) and emotional regulation when an animal was present in the counseling session. (Kogan et al., 1999, as cited in Friesen, 2010) Flynn et al. (2020) indicated that AAI incorporated as an adjunct to traditional therapeutic modalities, at-risk youth exhibited higher levels of motivation, increased self-esteem, self-efficacy, and improved boundaries. Additionally, Friesen (2010) addressed the benefits of school counselors using animal-assisted interventions in their counseling programs to interact with students both in therapeutic and non-therapeutic ways.

Theoretical Orientations

One of the components that researchers can agree on is that AAI is compatible with various counseling theories, whether the approach is psychoanalytical, behavioral, cognitive, humanistic, or integrative (Chandler et al.,2010; Bruneau and Johnson, 2011). The use of play therapy, art therapy, bibliotherapy, and simple activities such as walking and talking paired with animal-assisted interventions can be beneficial due to the various theoretical approaches. (Fine, 2015) Several researchers (Chandler et al.,2010; Bruneau and Johnson, 2011) took a closer look at specific theories and AAT interventions. This author will also examine four theories (Person-Centered, Cognitive-Behavioral, Attachment, Integrative) that a school counselor would implement in their program.

1. Person Centered

Carl Rogers (1957, 1961, 1980) believed that there needed to be congruence, empathy, and show unconditional positive regard in the therapeutic relationship to affect personal change. And as the theory suggests, person-centered counseling is non-directive allowing the counselor to reflect and clarify what the client is communicating. The inclusion of an animal in a triadic relationship acquiesces all those qualities.

The school counselor who is versed in person-centered theory and certified in animal-assisted interventions would allow the therapy animal to interact with the student in a natural and spontaneous way. Then the counselor might reflect or comment on the student's relationship with the therapy animal. (Chandler et al., 2010)

Dr. Cynthia Chandler, Ph.D. would call those interactions "Human-Animal Relational Moments (HARM)" in a theory she developed called Human-Animal Relational Theory (HART). (Chandler, 2018) Those relational moments could be animal initiated with the client; other times the relational moments are by the client with the therapy animal; and then there are the times when the relational moments happen simultaneously between the animal, client, and counselor (Chandler, 2018) but all interactions are person-centered.

2. Cognitive-Behavioral and Behavioral

Aaron Beck was considered seminal in contemporary psychology to develop cognitive-behavioral theory in the 1960s. While he spent his career studying psychoanalysis, his work was focused on the distorted thoughts and beliefs that perpetuated negative thought patterns. By developing methods that assist in identifying irrational beliefs and distorted thoughts, cognitive-behavioral theory (CBT) can be used with AAI to build rapport and trust with a client. (Chandler et al., 2010)

The complementary theory that goes along with CBT is the behavioral piece. John Watson originally developed behaviorism, but it was B.F. Skinner who bought the concept of focusing on observable behavior into, then providing opportunities to learn and practice those skills. (Wilson et al., 2001 as cited by Chandler et al., 2010)

One of the primary roles of a school counselor is to work collaboratively with a behavior specialist to support teachers and students who may have a behavior intervention plan (BIP). The school counselor could intervene with using a therapy dog to positively reward a student's compliance with an opportunity to walk, play ball with or teach a trick to the therapy dog. These structured activities between the student and therapy dog could be re-enforced by the school counselor's observation and dialog of the interaction.

Case Example

A young man has been exhibiting self-injurious behaviors such as banging his hand with his hands and calling himself "stupid." A behavioral specialist is called in to observe the student and develop a behavior intervention plan (BIP). If the student can go two days without an incident, then he earns time with the school's therapy dog, Athena. After one week the student has earned time with the therapy dog.

The school counselor is watching the student try to teach Athena how to "shake." After several failed attempts by the therapy dog, the student sighs, and states, "She just isn't getting it." The school counselor then interjects by saying, "Do you think Athena might be feeling dumb that she can't shake her paw with your hand?" The student immediately says, "No, she just doesn't understand and needs to practice."

The school counselor goes on to state, "So, Athena possibly thinking that she is dumb would not be correct but rather she just needs to time to learn something new? Just like you?" The student is quiet for a moment and then says, "Yeah, I guess."

3. Attachment

John Bowlby, Melanie Klein, Mary Ainsworth, and many others joined together to develop the attachment theory back in the 1930s through the1960s. (Brisch, 1999) According to the attachment theory, humans have an inherent and biological desire to be connected and feel secure in their relationships with others. And how we are attached as children to our primary caretaking figures determines our ability to regulate emotions, feel confident and reconcile our self-worth.

Geist (2011) wrote that Schore's research, which was conducted from 2001 to 2009, revealed that the right side of the brain fails to mature when insecure attachments are made. This is due to the triggering of adrenaline and noradrenaline being released in the brain causing a hyperarousal response to an emotionally intense situation. This "fight or flight" reaction creates what is referred to as "an unorganized" or "disorganized" brain. (Bowlby 1969)

In a text written by Karl Brisch (1999) on *Treating Attachment Disorders*, in the first section, he reviews the four classifications of childhood attachment styles of "secure, avoidant, ambivalent, and insecure-disorganized" drawing a clear correspondence between a parent's attachment style of "secure-autonomous, dismissing, preoccupied, and unresolved". He points out in the second section the progression of attachment disorders and the subsequent typology of emotional dysregulation and psychic disorders. (Karl Brisch,1999)

Nancy Parish-Plass discussed how chronic maltreatment and attachment disorders could cause neurobiological damage that contributes to children's difficulties connecting to self and others. (Parish-Plass, 2021) The disconnection between students was magnified by the pandemic shutdown and isolation. And school counselors have observed the increase of emotional dysregulation and psychotic disorders manifested in anxiety, school avoidance, depression, self-harm, suicidal ideations, and suicide. (Parish-Plass, 2021) The children's emotional bonds that were maintained through their attachment with their pets during the pandemic shutdown (Nieforth & O'Haire, 2020) can be utilized in a classroom setting.

4. Integrative

Integrative psychotherapy is the blending of client-centered, cognitive-behavioral, object-relations, gestalt, and body therapy developed by Richard Erskine, Ph.D. in 1972. These core concepts from each theory represent a holistic view of interventions allowing for the treatment of individuals in both a psychological and physical way of healing. Wilhelm Reich (1930) introduced the concept of "body psychotherapy" when he coined the term "body amour" to illustrate what happens to a person's muscle tension when they hold repressed emotions and memories. The use of mindfulness techniques can begin to relax a person's body enough to process what is emotionally taking place.

School counselors incorporate a variety of integrative techniques with students experiencing anxiety. Some of those methods include deep breathing exercises, mindfulness activities, and visualizations. When the student uses breathing methods with a therapy animal, they can sit with one hand placed on the animal, close their eyes, and try to pace their breathing with that of the animal. The student experiencing the sensation of the animal's body moves them out of their fight, flight, or freeze body tension.

In summary of this section, school counselors who use various interventions in their school counseling programs will discover that AAI can establish instant rapport, trust, and mutual respect when an animal is introduced into the therapeutic relationship. The use of an animal can help facilitate obtaining more information (verbal or non-verbal) from a child. (George, 1988, as cited by Trivedi and Perl, 1995) The activities can be directive or non-directive (Fine, 2015) in implementing a student's emotional regulation, behavioral, or educational goals in school.

USING AAI IN A SCHOOL COUNSELING PROGRAM

The American School Counseling Association (ASCA, 2019) provides school counselors with professional standards and competencies for kindergarten to twelfth-grade levels. School counselors understand human development and implement a school program that promotes and enhances a student's academic, career, and social/emotional outcomes. (ASCA, 2019) Recently, ASCA (2021) revised its student standards to include mindsets and behaviors for student success. By addressing the skills needed by a student for self-management and social interaction, a school counselor must identify a need, collect information on the student, create pre-/post-assessment, develop, select, and deliver activities or interventions that assist in student improvement. (ASCA, 2021)

Today, students are experiencing additional trauma brought on by COVID-19, political, and racial tensions that have increased their anxiety, absenteeism, school avoidance and significantly impacted their social skills. (Chaturvedi et al. 2021) This pandemic-induced trauma has had a debilitating effect on students and adults. Students were left home alone to try and deal with the uncertainty of health, education, and relationships; for a student, their pets were present to provide stability, comfort, and security. (Nieforth and O'Haire, 2020)

Covid-related changes forced students to make sense of what was safe or not safe in their environment; as a result, there grew a disconnection between most relationships within a child's life. (Flynn et al., 2020) Those underlying post-traumatic behaviors manifested into anger, depression, anxiety, and underachievement. A positive therapeutic relationship between a school counselor and students can decrease trauma symptoms and increase connection through the triadic work of therapy animals, students, and the counselor.

An article authored by Barbara Holifield (2020) spoke eloquently about the pandemic, the rise of consciousness to Black Lives Matter, and the killing of George Floyd, she likened this change to the quintessential metaphor of "taking the breath of life away." As school counselors, we teach our students the coping skills that they need to reconnect and bring breath back to their lives. Holifield went on to introduce the work of neuroscientist, Stephen Porges, and his *polyvagal theory of emotions*. (Porges, 2001 as cited by Holifield, 2020) When an event is perceived as life-threatening humans transition into a state of hyperarousal thereby leading to immobilization of fight, flight, or freeze.

Many animals have the same hyperarousal response when they feel threatened, and this subsystem only exists in mammals. (Levine, 2010) Humans are among the mammal species that "are unique in that they need other mammals to regulate their emotional and bodily states to survive." (Holifield, 2020) Further supporting the benefits of the human-animal bond and use of animal-assisted interventions.

By developing and delivering a school-based animal-assisted program, students can feel a sense of connection when contributing to an animal's care, nurturing, and safety. Bachi and Parish-Plass (2017) suggested that animals represent reality in a child's life that allows them to verbally or non-verbally work through their trauma. School counselors that deliver animal-assisted intervention for the positive mindset and improved behavior goals for student success can assist in healing a student suffering from trauma. (Herman, 1997; Perry, 2009; as cited by Bachi and Parish-Plass, 2017) It makes sense to incorporate animal-assisted interventions (AAI) in a school's counseling program to continue the natural connection between child and pet (Sable, 2013; Wanser et al., 2019) as they transition back into the educational setting.

Where Do I Begin?

The first step is always the biggest one to take in moving forward with a new program. There are many issues and concerns to take into consideration like student safety, allergies, fears, cultural perceptions, zoonosis, space for the animal(s), animal welfare, intention of the use of AAI, and the list goes on. (Fine, 2015) However, one of the most critical questions is, *"What is the intention of incorporating AAI in the school counseling program?"* Another question to ask is, *"Do I want to implement a volunteer model or a comprehensive model?"*

Jennifer Von Lintel and Laura Bruneau (2021) authored an article addressing two models for implementing a school therapy dog program. The first model is a volunteer model where the school counselor monitors and manages a volunteer handler-dog team to come into the school to provide (a) social-emotional interventions, (b) literacy, (c) special events, and (d) crisis response. (Von Lintel and Bruneau, 2021) The second provision are a comprehensive model in contrast to the first where the school counselor is the handler and brings their own dog. This model provides more specific, goal-directed interventions (Von Lintel and Bruneau, 2021) and activities that are incentives or therapeutic for the student.

The school counselor's integration of animals into therapy requires a complete understanding of the human-animal bond to advance the counseling process. (Bachi and Parish-Plass, 2017) In her master's thesis, Erin Shultz (2006) cautioned that AAI is not about involving the therapy animal whenever there is an on-demand request for contact with an animal by a student, teacher, or administrator. The intervention needs to be purposeful and therapeutically beneficial.

Case Example

A student is struggling in class; he is disruptive and argumentative with his teacher. The principal is called to the classroom to remove the student. The principal states to the agitated student that he needs to calm down and brings the student to the school counselor's office because she has a therapy dog. The student, in his heightened state of agitation, is cursing loudly about not wanting to visit the school counselor. The therapy dog views the student's behavior as aggressive and begins to bark. The principal then scolds the therapy dog, and the school counselor needs to make a split decision as to whose needs take precedence.

A school counselor not trained in animal-assisted therapy would be faced with the dilemma of whose welfare takes precedence (Shultz, 2016). The school counselor must possess the confidence in their ability to be effective with or without an animal (Nebbe, 1991).

The commitment to advocate for an AAI program needs to be a passion and belief in the human-animal bond. It is vital for the school counselor to be the primary person responsible for the therapy animal's well-being and not to designate that responsibility to anyone else. It is essential to understand that the therapy animal(s) need scheduled breaks, days off, and protection from an overabundance of physical and emotional stimuli. There needs to be an acknowledgment that if the program is dissolved, there will be animals dependent on human care for the duration of their lives.

What Animal Is Suitable for my Program?

Now that a few of the advantages and disadvantages have been examined, it is time to decide what species of animal you want to assist you in your school's counseling program. The top choice of many counselors and educators for animal assistance is dogs. A research study conducted by van den Berg et al. (2010) determined that certain breeds of dogs are better suited for AAI than others based on the history of what type of work a breed of dog is bred for. However, most important is the dog's personality and temperament; therefore, that needs to be part of the equation when considering a choice of breed.

Another determining factor is your student population. In a high school, a therapy dog is an excellent choice for AAI; however, dogs can be incorporated across all grade levels for assorted reasons. A dog's response to a human is instantaneous in acknowledging, accepting, and reacting to the student's presence. A dog has often been referred to as a "social lubricant" (Thigpen, Ellis & Smith, 2005) due to its instant rapport-building capabilities between individuals.

Other animals that have been incorporated into AAI are equines, cats, fish, elephants, dolphins, reptiles, birds, rabbits, and guinea pigs. (Tedavi et al., 2019; Flom, 2005) While it is true that cats are the next popular species for pet ownership. Unfortunately, the plan for incorporating a cat and their litter box would be difficult to manage in a school setting, and cat dandruff allergies are among the top listed allergens. (NIEHS, n.d.) Flom (2005) suggested that "small pocket animals" such as hamsters, gerbils, and guinea pigs are good animals to use in AAI, especially in an elementary school setting. Other researchers (O'Haire et al., 2013) have recorded increased social functioning with children in primary school.

This author has incorporated guinea pigs in a middle school counseling program due to the diversity and variety of guinea pig breeds. They have wonderful personalities and are incredibly sociable. In fact, in some Scandanavian countries, it is not humane to own just one guinea pig; pet owners must buy at least two same-sex piggies so that they are never alone. (Chiesa, 2021) Finally, many students have guinea pigs as pets, and they are a great topic of conversation and sharing of information about their discriminating palates!

The effects of the interventions have proven to be a success for the instant rapport and bonding with the guinea pigs. The following is a case example as to the instant connection and bonding that occurred during a school counseling session when a disclosure was made by a student who otherwise would have said extraordinarily little in the session.

Case Example

A student was referred to the school counselor to conduct a threat assessment for a statement made by her the day before towards some boys in her class. The teacher reported that the boys had been very loud and disruptive during class, the student had asked them to be quiet, and they did not comply with her request. After several attempts at pleading with the boys to stop, the student shouted out, "I should just bring a gun to school to shoot you if you don't shut up!"

When the student arrived at the school counselor's office, she was sullen and quiet, refusing to make eye contact. As the school counselor began to inquire about the incident, the student sat there silently. The school counselor putting the issue aside, invited the student to come over to look at the guinea pigs playing in their pen. The student looked at the two guinea pigs chasing each other and then asked their names. The counselor stated, "Their names are Sir Rodney and Sir Timothy." The student smiled and asked if she could pet them. The counselor nodded her head in the affirmative and asked the student if she had guinea pigs. The student stated that she once had seven guinea pigs and four dogs, but they were left behind when she and her family had to move out of her grandparent's home.

At that moment, the student expressed concern about the safety of her dogs. The school counselor then inquired if there was a plan to have the animals join her and her family. The student continued to pet the guinea pigs as they scampered around and tried to hide. The student said aloud, "I won't hurt you." The school counselor repeated, "That's right, Timothy and Rodney, she won't hurt you." Then the student quietly, inaudibly said, "I won't hurt you like granddad."

This case example illustrates what can happen when animal-assisted interventions set the stage for a safe environment within the triadic relationship. The distraction of an animal can open the space for communication (Zents et al., 2016) between the student and school counselor.

This intervention works well in an elementary setting when younger children usually do not have the communication skills to express their inner thoughts and feelings. (Tuma, 2018) Children tend to identify with animals (Bellak, 1975), and the animal's presence opens the counseling space for self-expression. (Parish-Plass, 2013) The school counselor who uses an animal to talk with a student can take the direct focus off that child and eventually elicit disclosure that would not be made by a student.

Obtaining Permission and Providing Documentation

Now that you have decided on what species of animal to use in your school counseling program, the next step is reaching out to your school's principal, superintendent, and school board. All school boards dictate policies involving animals in school; they may be concerned with issues ranging from student safety, zoonosis, liability costs, care, and training of the therapy animal. If required, the school counselor will need to demonstrate full disclosure of insurance coverage, veterinarian records, and therapy animal training.

And while short-term interventions guide the school counselor's interaction with students instead of extended and ongoing therapeutic interventions, parent permission or at least notification of an animal's presence needs to be made known. Transparency in a school's counseling process is necessary to establish trust and rapport within the school's community. (ASCA, 2019)

Individual or Group AAI?

Since school counselors are charged with providing short-term student support during times of transition, stress, anxiety, and other trauma-related incidents with short-term individual and group interventions. (ASCA, 2019) Whether the school counselor chooses to implement AAI in an individual or group setting, there are benefits either way. This writer has already illustrated the power of AAI in a unique environment by establishing instant rapport and disclosure from a student. Let us examine a few examples of AAI in a group setting.

Research is constantly being published on how AAI can benefit groups of children in residential and educational settings. (Chandler, 2001; Fynn et al. 2020) In Germany, a group of researchers (Wohlfarth et al., 2013) designed an AAI program for children diagnosed as being obese. They used the Freiburg Intervention Trial for Obese Children (FITOC)as an interdisciplinary program to collect data and then utilized that data to design an exercise curriculum. (Wohlfarth et al., 2013) The activities developed used a therapy dog for the children to walk with, play fetch, or even compete against in agility competitions for a minimum of 20 to 25 minutes per day. As a result, the children in the group lost weight.

The school counselor can also use AAI to address teamwork and cooperation in a group setting. One such example is to have a small group of students form a circle and, in the center, have the therapy dog sit or stand while students take turns rolling a "feelings" thumb ball to the dog. Whichever feeling word the dog places its paw on, the students describe what that would look like in the dog's behavior and how that may affect a human. The school counselor would then facilitate further discussion about how that same feeling could appear to others around them.

The benefits associated with animal-assisted interventions through direct or in-direct activities in individual or group settings can be observed when used by professional school counselors. (Jenkins et al., 2014) A school counselor in the hallways with a therapy dog greeting students getting on and off the bus or transitioning between classes can reduce the anxiety and stress experienced by a student throughout the day. Chandler (2001) suggested that animal-assisted therapy could also potentially curb violence in a school. The congruence of unconditional regard, acceptance, and warm, enthusiastic wet kisses by a dog can communicate authentic and genuine love.

CHALLENGES IN USING ANIMAL-ASSISTED INTERVENTIONS (AAI)

In this next section, this author will introduce the issues, problems, concerns, and controversies associated with AAI in schools. A research survey conducted by Sara Morrow (2009) surveyed school counselors concerning their attitudes and beliefs about animal-assisted interventions. The results identified several school counselors' benefits and challenges about incorporating AAI into a school counseling program. One of the key issues identified the most by Morrow (2009) in the survey was how little therapeutic work happens within the school counseling setting at the upper-grade levels. They revealed that they are short of time because they are called upon to schedule classes, participate in educational planning, and perform other administrative duties. (Morrow, 2009)

Issues, Problems, Concerns, and Controversies

All school boards dictate policies involving animals in school. And aside from the obvious issues surrounding children's fear of dogs, allergies, and sanitation concerns with animal hygiene that can lend themselves to possible zoonotic diseases like ringworms, many school districts are afraid of legal liability. School administrations are focused on the cost that may be required in paying for the therapy animal training, care of the animal, and the educational training of the school counselor in obtaining certification in animal-assisted therapy (AAT). Then that places the burden of carrying extra insurance directly in the hands of school counselors, a concern for which there is no reimbursement for the school counselor.

And while animals are increasingly becoming part of the daily thread of social content (such as service animals), there needs to be more research to assist in changing policies that exclude animals from the educational setting. (Gee et al., 2017) A study conducted by Jenkins et al. (2014) revealed that data collected provided empirical evidence that school districts could use in deciding whether to implement AAI in their school counseling program. However, with the current concern over Covid transference and contract tracing among students and faculty, the request for animal-assisted programs has taken a back burner.

Alternatives to Living Animal-Assisted Interventions

If the concern is not being able to introduce a live animal into an elementary school counseling program, then bibliotherapy, animal puppets, or an animal-inspired curriculum can facilitate the same social-emotional intervention that can encourage self-actualization by a student. Listed below are a few examples of alternatives to living animal-assisted interventions.

A few years ago, this author came across a social-emotional curriculum entitled, "*Mutt-I-Gress*", which promotes the social and emotional well-being of students paired with educating them about animal shelters. Students learn about compassion and resiliency while understanding the journey of a rescue dog's suffering and vulnerability. This allows students to develop their own coping skills and responsibility. Older students can learn to be ambassadors for a local animal shelter.

Another example of alternatives to living animal-assisted interventions is Fred Rogers from the iconic television show "*Mister Roger's Neighborhood.*" Fred Roger's used animal puppets such as Daniel the Tiger to elicit each child's potential. His approach to establishing rapport, acceptance, expression of one's feelings, and just being yourself came out in every episode. Palmer and Carr (1991), made a theoretical comparison between Carl Rogers and Fred Rogers in a phenomenological approach to understanding unconditional positive regard (C. Rogers, 1951). Roger's core components of positive regard, empathy, and congruence were created and fostered through social, emotional, and educational programming.

In summary, while nothing encourages unconditional positive regard like the wet kiss from a dog; the stories, puppets, stuffed animals, or animal-inspired activities introduced by a school counselor can create a safe space for healing to take place.

CONCLUSION

The American School Counseling Association (ASCA, 2019) provides school counselors with professional standards and competencies for grade levels from kindergarten to twelfth grade that promotes and enhances student academic, career, and social/ emotional outcomes. (ASCA, 2019) Incorporating animal-assisted interventions (AAI) in a school's counseling program supports the natural connection between child and pet. (Sable, 2013; Wanser et al., 2019) Animal-assisted interventions (AAI) woven into an elementary school counseling program creatively addresses and potentially meet students' emotional and behavioral needs who arrive at school with a backpack of trauma.

While the research work conducted by Morrow (2009) with school counselors revealed how little therapeutic work happens within school counseling programs at upper-grade levels. School counselors shared that they are short of time because they are called upon to schedule classes, participate in educational planning, and perform other administrative duties.

Also, many school districts are afraid of legal liability, and therefore that places the burden of carrying extra insurance on the school counselors. The financial costs of maintaining the therapy animal's veterinarian care, food, and habitat are also a concern for which there is no reimbursement for the school counselor.

Another controversy that is showing up in research is the effects of human interaction in AAI on an animal's welfare. (Gut et al., 2018; Palestrini et al., 2016; and Corsetti et al., 2019) While that is not directly correlated with school counseling programs, it is a topic of interest to consider as more educators bring therapy dogs to school without AAT certification or training. And in a school setting, when counselors jump from one crisis to another, animals can become a built-in self-care module. Zents et al. (2016) also suggested that the therapy animal can also help the counselor destress between students.

Future

During the last decade, researchers have stated a potential lack of empirically theoretical evidence to explain or support the effectiveness of animal-assisted interventions (Serpell et al. 2010, 2016). So, then the question that arises is "cui bono?" to whose benefit does AAI contribute? In incorporating animal-assisted interventions, the practitioners of AAI may have to take a step back to re-evaluate the actual benefit of animal-assisted interventions in the educational, medical, and counseling professions.

However, research also supports the evidence that animal-assisted interventions, when conducted in an ethical and responsible manner can elicit healing. AAI is increasingly being used as an adjunct to traditional therapy with success in significantly reducing depression, increasing attention, and developing strong social skills, self-regulation, and motivation in youth.

REFERENCES

American School Counseling Association. (2019). *ASCA National Model*. https://www.schoolcounselor.org/About-School-Counseling/ASCA-National-Model-for-School-Counseling-Programs

American School Counselor Association. (2019). *ASCA School Counselor Professional Standards & Competencies.* Alexandria, VA: Author. https://www.schoolcounselor.org/getmedia/a8d59c2c-51de-4ec3-a565-a3235f3b93c3/SC-Competencies.pdf

American School Counselor Association. (2021). *ASCA Student Standards: Mindsets & Behaviors for Student Success.* Alexandria, VA: Author.https://www.schoolcounselor.org/getmedia/7428a787-a452-4abb-afec-d78ec77870cd/Mindsets-Behaviors.pdf

Anderson, K. L., & Olson, M. R. (2006). The value of a dog in a classroom of children with severe emotional disorders. *Anthrozoos, 19*(1), 35–49. doi:10.2752/089279306785593919

Bachi, K., & Parish-Plass, N. (2017). Animal-assisted psychotherapy: A unique relational therapy for children and adolescents. *Clinical Child Psychotherapy, 22*(1), 3–8. doi:10.1177/1359104516672549 PMID:27742758

Bellak, L. (1975). *The T.A.T., C.A.T., and S.A.T. in clinical use.* Grune and Stratton.

Brisch, K. H. (1999). *Treating attachment disorders: from theory to therapy.* Guilford Press.

Bruneau, L., & Johnson, A. (2011, March 27). *Fido and Freud meet: Integrating animal-assisted therapy into traditional counseling theories* [Paper Presentation]. *American Counseling Association Conference & Exposition,* New Orleans, LA, United States.

Chandler, C. (2001). *Animal-assisted therapy in counseling and school settings* (Report No. EDO-CG-01-05). Greensboro, NC: ERIC Clearinghouse on Counseling and Student Services. (ERIC Document Reproduction Service No. ED459404)

Chandler, C. K., Portrie-Bethke, T. L., Barrio Minton, C. A., Fernando, D. M., & O'Callaghan, D. M. (2010). Matching animal-assisted therapy techniques with counseling guiding theories. *Journal of Mental Health Counseling, 32*(4), 354–374. doi:10.17744/mehc.32.4.u72lt21740103538

Chaturvedi, K., Kumar, D., & Nidhi, S. (2020). COVID-19 and its impact on education, social life, and mental health of students: A survey. *Children and Youth Services Review.* Advance online publication. doi:10.1016/j.childyouth.2020.105866 PMID:33390636

Corsetti, S., Ferrara, M., & Natoli, E. (2019). Evaluating stress in dogs involved in animal-assisted interventions. *Animals*, Vol. 9. *Article*, *833*(10), 1–19. doi:10.3390/ani9100833 PMID:31635094

Dimitrijevic, I. (2009). Animal-assisted therapy- a new trend in the treatment of children and adults. *Psychiatria Danubina*, *21*(2), 236–241. PMID:19556955

Erskine, R. (1972) *Integrative Psychotherapy*. Institute of Integrative Psychotherapy. https://www.integrativetherapy.com/

Fine, A. H. (2015). *Handbook on animal-assisted therapy: Foundations and guidelines for animal-assisted interventions* (5th ed.). Elsevier Academic Press.

Flom, B. (2005). Counseling with pocket pets: Using small animals in elementary counseling programs. *Professional School Counseling*, *8*(5), 469–471.

Flynn, E., Gandenberger, J., Mueller, M. K., & Morris, K. N. (2020). Animal–assisted interventions as an adjunct to therapy for youth: Clinician perspectives. *Child & Adolescent Social Work Journal*, *2020*(37), 631–647. doi:10.100710560-020-00695-z

Friesen, L. (2010). Exploring animal-assisted programs with children in school and therapeutic contexts. *Early Childhood Education Journal*, *37*(4), 261–267. doi:10.100710643-009-0349-5

Gee, N. R., Griffin, J. A., & McCardle, P. (2017, July-September). Human-animal interaction research in school settings: Current knowledge and future directions. *AERA Open*, *3*(3), 1–9. doi:10.1177/2332858417724346

Geist, T. (2011). Conceptual Framework for Animal Assisted Therapy. *Child and Adolescent Social Work*, *28*(3), 243–256. doi:10.100710560-011-0231-3

Gut, W., Crump, L., Zinsstag, J., Hattendorf, J., & Hediger, K. (2018). The effect of human interaction on guinea pig behavior in animal-assisted therapy. *Journal of Veterinary Behavior*, *25*, 56–64. doi:10.1016/j.jveb.2018.02.004

Holifield, B. (2020). Trauma, soul, and the body in jungian analysis. *Jung Journal*, *14*(4), 72–85. doi:10.1080/19342039.2020.1822121

Jenkins, C. D., Laux, J. M., Ritchie, M. H., & Tucker-Gail, K. (2014). Animal-assisted therapy and roger's core components among middle school students receiving counseling services: A descriptive study. *Journal of Creativity in Mental Health*, *9*(2), 174–187. doi:10.1080/15401383.2014.899939

Kruger, K. A., & Serpell, J. A. (2010). Animal-assisted interventions in mental health: definitions and theoretical foundations. In Handbook on Animal-Assisted Therapy (3rd ed.). Academic Press

Levine, P. A. (2001). *In an Unspoken Voice: How the Body Releases Trauma and Restores Goodness*. Routledge.

Levinson, B. M. (1969). *Pet-oriented child psychotherapy*. Charles C. Thomas, Publisher, Ltd.

Marrow, S. (2009) *A survey of school counselor attitudes regarding animal-assisted interventions* [Master's Thesis]. University of New Hampshire.

Mutt-i-Gress Social-Emotional Program. (n.d.). *The Mutt-i-Gress Curriculum.* https://education.muttigrees.org/

National Institute of Environmental Health Science. (n.d.). *Pet Allergens*. https://www.niehs.nih.gov/health/topics/agents/allergens/pets/index.cfm

Nebbe, L. L. (1991). The human-animal bond and the elementary school counselor. *The School Counselor*, *38*, 362-371. http://www.jstor.org/ stable/23900728

Nieforth, L. O., & O'Haire, M. E. (2020). The role of pets in managing uncertainty from covid-19, *Psychological Rauma: Theory, Research, Practices, and Policy*, *12*(1), S245-S246. doi:10.1037/tra0000678

O'Haire, M. E., McKenzie, S. J., McCune, S., & Slaughter, V. (2013). Effects of animal-assisted activities with guinea pigs in the primary school classroom. *Anthroos*, *26*(3), 445-458, http://dx.doi.org.ezp.waldenulibrary.org/10.2752/175303713X13697429463835

Palestrini, C., Calcaterra, V., Cannas, S., Talamonti, Z., Papotti, F., Buttram, D., & Pelizzo, G. (2016). Stress level evaluation in a dog during animal-assisted therapy in pediatric surgery. *Journal of Veterinary Behavior*, *17*, 44–49. https://dx.doi.org/10.1016/j.jveb.2016.09.003

Palmer, E. L., & Carr, K. (1991). Dr. rogers, meet mr. rogers: The similarities between carl and fred rogers. *Social Behavior and Personality*, *19*(1), 39–44.

Parish-Plass, N. (2013). *Animal-assisted psychotherapy: theory, issues, and practice*. Perdue University Press.

Parish-Plass, N. (2020) Animal-assisted psychotherapy for developmental trauma through the lens of interpersonal neurobiology of trauma: Creating connection with self and others. *Journal of Psychotherapy Integration, 31*(3), 302-325. doi:10.1037/int0000253

Porges, S. (2001). The polyvagal theory: Phylogenetic substrates of a social nervous system. *International Journal of Psychophysiology, 42*(2), 123–146. https://doi.org/10.1016/S0167-8760(01)00162-3

Reich, W. (n.d.). *Body Psychotherapy*. Retrieved from Good Therapy. https://www.goodtherapy.org/learn-about-therapy/types/body-psychotherapy

Rogers, C. (1951). *Client-centered therapy: Its current practices, implications, and theory*. Houghton Mifflin.

Sable, P. (2013). The pet connection: An attachment perspective. *Clinical Social Work Journal, 41*, 93–99. doi:10.100710615-012-0405-2

Serpell, J. A., McCune, S., Gee, N., & Griffin, J. A. (2016). Current challenges to research on animal-assisted interventions. *Applied Developmental Science*. Advance online publication. doi:10.1080/10888691.2016.1262775

Shultz, E. (2006) *Furry therapist: The advantages and disadvantages of implementing animal therapy in schools* [Master's Thesis]. University of Wisconsin-Stout.

Stewart, L.A., Bruneau, L., & Elliott, A. (2016). *The role of animal-assisted interventions in addressing trauma-informed care.* ACA (American Counseling Association) Knowledge Center, VISTA.

Stewart, L. A., Chang, C. Y., Parker, L. K., & Grubbs, N. (2016). *Animal-assisted therapy in counseling competencies*. American Counseling Association, Animal-Assisted Therapy in Mental Health Interest Network.

Tedeshi, P., & Jenkins, M. (2019). *Transforming Trauma: Resilience and Healing through Our Connection with Animals*. Purdue University Press.

Thigpen, S., Ellis, S., & Smith, R. (2005). Special education in juvenile residential facilities: Can animals help? *Essays in Education, 14*(20), 1-16. https://openriver.winona.edu/eie/vol14/iss1/20?utm_source=openriver.winona.edu%2Feie%2Fvol14%2Fiss1%2F20&utm_medium=PDF&utm_campaign=PDFCoverPages

Trivedi, L., & Peri, J. (1995) Animal facilitated counseling in the elementary school: A literature review and practical considerations. *Elementary School Guidance & Counseling, 29*, 223-234. http://www.jstor.org/ stable/42871169

Tuma, N. (2018). *The impact of animal-assisted therapy in elementary schools* [Capstone]. Winona State University-Open River. https://openriver.winona.edu/counseloreducationcapstones/74

Von Lintel, J., & Bruneau, L. (2021). Pathways for implementing a school therapy dog program: Steps for success and best practices. *Journal of School Counseling*, *19*(14), 2021. www.jsc.montana.edu/articles/v19n14.pdf

Wanser, S. H., Vitale, K. R., Thielke, L. E., Brubaker, L., & Udell, M. (2019). Spotlight on the psychological basis of childhood pet attachment and its implications. *Psychology Research and Behavior Management*, *2019*(12), 469–479. https://doi.org/10.2147/PRBM.S158998

Wohlfarth, R., Mutschler, B., Beetz, A., Kreuser, F., & Korsten-Reck, U. (2013). Dogs motivate obese children for physical activity: key elements of a motivational theory of animal-assisted interventions. *Frontiers in Psychology*, *4*, 1-7. www.frontiersin.org

Zents, C. E., Fisk, A. K., & Lauback, C. W. (2017). Paws for intervention: Perceptions about the use of dogs in schools. *Journal of Creativity in Mental Health*, *21*(1), 82–98. http://dx.doi.org.ezp.waldenulibrary.org/10.1080/15401383.2016.1189371

Conclusion

Best Practices for Trauma-Informed School Counseling presented an introduction to the concept of trauma-informed school counseling, and offers some insight into providing more quality counseling services to school-aged children and adolescents. The authors have explored and discussed various topics that are within the scope of school counselors.

While there are many areas of school counseling that may seem ambiguous; however, it is important to understand the main idea of advocating for yourself as a school counselor. Advocating for your role provides the opportunity to develop a comprehensive campus-wide trauma-informed program that leads to the wellness of student mental health and academic growth. The authors of this book have examined the perceptions school counselors and responded by offering best-practices to assist in developing a more trauma-informed program.

Written for school counselors, counselors in training, counselor educators, and professional counselors, and those in other related disciplines, *Best Practices for Trauma-Informed School Counseling* illustrates the importance of trauma-informed practices and offers suggestions on how to carry such an important and vital feat. It should serve as a valuable tool with practical, professional resource with easily accessible ideas and strategies. With such ideas and strategies at hand, novice and veteran school counselors will be able to collaborate with administrators to incorporate best practices in implementing an effective comprehensive school counseling program.

Compilation of References

Aaron, L., & Dallaire, D. (2010). Parental incarceration and multiple risk experiences: Effects on family dynamics and children's delinquency. *Journal of Youth and Adolescence, 39*(12), 1471–1484. doi:10.100710964-009-9458-0 PMID:19834796

Ackerman, C. (2021, December 6). *Cognitive distortions: When your brain lies to you.* Retrieved November 1, 2021, from https://positivepsychology.com/cognitive-distortions/

Adalist-Estrin, A. (2006). Providing support to adolescent children with incarcerated parents. *Prevention Researcher, 13*(2), 7–10.

Adoption and Foster Care Analysis and Reporting System. (2020). *The AFCARS Report preliminary FY 2019 estimates as of June 23, 2020 - No. 27.* US Department of Health and Human Services Children's Bureau. https://www.acf.hhs.gov/cb/report/afcars-report-27

Akiba, D. (2020). Reopening America's schools during the COVID-19 pandemic: Protecting Asian students from stigma and discrimination. *Frontiers in Sociology, 5*, 1–6. doi:10.3389/fsoc.2020.588936 PMID:33869517

Amatea, E. S., & Clark, M. A. (2005). Changing schools, changing counselors: A qualitative study of school administrators' conceptions of the school counselor role. *Professional School Counseling, 9*(1), 16–27. doi:10.5330/prsc.9.1.w6357vn62n5328vp

Ambady, N., Shih, M., Kim, A., & Pittinsky, T. L. (2001). Stereotype susceptibility in children: Effects of identity activation on quantitative performance. *Psychological Science, 12*(5), 385–390. doi:10.1111/1467-9280.00371 PMID:11554671

Ambady, N., Shih, M., & Pittinsky, T. L. (1999). Stereotype susceptibility: Identity salience and shifts in quantitative performance. *Psychological Science, 10*(1), 80–83. doi:10.1111/1467-9280.00111

American Psychiatric Association. (2013). *Diagnostic and statistical manual of mental disorders* (5th ed.)., doi:10.1176/appi.books.9780890425596

American School Counseling Association. (2019). *ASCA National Model.* https://www.schoolcounselor.org/About-School-Counseling/ASCA-National-Model-for-School-Counseling-Programs

American School Counselor Association (2016b). *The school counselor and trauma-informed practice.* The School Counselor and Trauma-Informed Practice - American School Counselor Association (ASCA).

American School Counselor Association. (2012). *ASCA national model: A framework for school counseling programs* (3rd ed.). Author.

American School Counselor Association. (2016). *ASCA ethical standards for school counselors.* Schoolcounselor.Org. https://www.schoolcounselor.org/getmedia/f041cbd0-7004-47a5-ba01-3a5d657c6743/Ethical-Standards.pdf

American School Counselor Association. (2016). *The school counselor and trauma-informed Practice.* https://schoolcounselor.org/Standards-Positions/Position-Statements/ASCA-Position-Statements/The-School-Counselor-and-Trauma-Informed-Practice

American School Counselor Association. (2016). *The school counselor and trauma-informed school practice.* Author.

American School Counselor Association. (2016a). *ASCA ethical standards for school counselors.* https://www.schoolcounselor.org/asca/media/asca/Ethics/EthicalStandards2016.pdf

American School Counselor Association. (2016b.) *The school counselor and trauma informed practice* [Position Statement]. https://www.schoolcounselor.org/Standards-Positions/Position-Statements/ASCA-Position-Statements/The-School-Counselor-and-Trauma-Informed-Practice

American School Counselor Association. (2018). *The school counselor and multitiered system of supports.* American School Counselor Association (ASCA). https://www.schoolcounselor.org/Standards-Positions/Position-Statements/ASCA-Position-Statements/The-School-Counselor-and-Multitiered-System-of-Sup

American School Counselor Association. (2019). *ASCA School Counselor Professional Standards & Competencies.* Alexandria, VA: Author. https://www.schoolcounselor.org/getmedia/a8d59c2c-51de-4ec3-a565-a3235f3b93c3/SC-Competencies.pdf

American School Counselor Association. (2019). *ASCA school counselor professional standards & competencies.* https://www.schoolcounselor.org/asca/media/asca/home/SCCompetencies.pdf

American School Counselor Association. (2019). *The school counselor and safe schools and crisis response.* Schoolcounselor.Org. https://schoolcounselor.org/Standards-Positions/Position-Statements/ASCA-Position-Statements/The-School-Counselor-and-Safe-Schools-and-Crisis-R

American School Counselor Association. (2019a). *ASCA school counselor professional standards & competencies.* Author.

American School Counselor Association. (2019b). *The ASCA national model: A framework for school counseling programs* (4th ed.). Author.

American School Counselor Association. (2020). *The school counselor and group counseling* [Position Statement]. https://www.schoolcounselor.org/Standards-Positions/Position-Statements/ASCA-Position-Statements/The-School-Counselor-and-Group-Counseling

American School Counselor Association. (2021). *ASCA Student Standards: Mindsets & Behaviors for Student Success.* Alexandria, VA: Author.https://www.schoolcounselor.org/getmedia/7428a787-a452-4abb-afec-d78ec77870cd/Mindsets-Behaviors.pdf

American School Counselor Association. (2021). *The school counselor and anti-racist practices.* https://www.schoolcounselor.org/getmedia/12cec1e8-5dab-44e5-acf8-6f10484cbaab/ps-anti-racist-practices-draft.pdf

American School Counselor Association. (2021). *The school counselor and child abuse and neglect prevention.* https://www.schoolcounselor.org/Standards-Positions/Position-Statements/ASCA-Position-Statements/The-School-Counselor-and-Child-Abuse-and-Neglect-P

American School Counselor Association. (n.d.). *Appropriate and inappropriate activities for school counselors.* https://www.schoolcounselor.org/getmedia/8fe536c2-7a32-4102-8ce7-42e9b0683b3b/appropriate-activities-of-school-counselors.pdf

Anand, D., & Hsu, L. M. (2020). COVID-19 and Black Lives Matter: Examining anti-Asian racism and anti-Blackness in US education. *International Journal of Multidisciplinary Perspectives in Higher Education*, *5*(1), 190–199. doi:10.32674/jimphe.v5i1.2656

Anda, R. F., Felitti, V. J., Bremner, J. D., Walker, J. D., Whitfield, C., Perry, B. D., Dube, S. R., & Giles, W. H. (2006). The enduring effects of abuse and related adverse experiences in childhood: A confluence of evidence from neurobiology and epidemiology. *European Archives of Psychiatry and Clinical Neuroscience*, *256*(3), 174–186. doi:10.100700406-005-0624-4 PMID:16311898

Anderson, D. C. (1998). Curriculum, culture and community: The challenge of school violence. In M. Tonry & M. Moore (Eds.), *Youth violence* (pp. 317–363). University of Chicago Press.

Anderson, K. L., & Olson, M. R. (2006). The value of a dog in a classroom of children with severe emotional disorders. *Anthrozoos*, *19*(1), 35–49. doi:10.2752/089279306785593919

Ano, G. G., & Vasconcelles, E. B. (2005). Religious coping and psychological adjustment to stress: A meta-analysis. *Journal of Clinical Psychology*, *61*(4), 461–480. doi:10.1002/jclp.20049 PMID:15503316

Anyon, Y., Ong, S. L., & Whitaker, K. (2014). School-based mental health prevention for Asian American adolescents: Risk behaviors, protective factors, and service use. *Asian American Journal of Psychology*, *5*(2), 134–144. doi:10.1037/a0035300

Arditti, J. (2012). *Parental incarceration and the family: Psychological and social effects of imprisonment on children, parents, and caregivers.* NYU Press.

Arditti, J., & Salva, J. (2015). Parental incarceration and child trauma symptoms in single caregiver homes. *Journal of Child and Family Studies*, *24*(3), 551–561. https://doi.org/10.1007/s10826-013-9867-2

Arky, B. (2022, April 8). *Twice-exceptional kids: Both gifted and challenged.* Child Mind Institute. Retrieved November 11, 2021, from https://childmind.org/article/twice-exceptional-kids-both-gifted-and-challenged

Armstrong, S. A., MacDonald, J. H., & Stillo, S. (2010). School counselors and principals: Different perceptions of relationship, leadership, and training. *Journal of School Counseling*, *8*(15), 1–27. http://jsc.montana.edu/articles/v8n15.pdf

ASCA Ethical Standards for School Counselors - American School Counselor Association (ASCA). (2020). https://schoolcounselor.org/About-School-Counseling/Ethical-Legal-Responsibilities/ASCA-Ethical-Standards-for-School-Counselors-(1)?sso=30ba5b4f-cab3-4168-b136-8f1ecad5c7aa

ASCA National Model - American School Counselor Association (ASCA). (2020). https://www.schoolcounselor.org/About-School-Counseling/ASCA-National-Model-for-School-Counseling-Programs

Asian Pacific Institute on Gender-Based Violence. (2021, October 16). *Census data & API identities*. https://www.api-gbv.org/resources/census-data-api-identities/

Atkin, A. L., Yoo, H. C., & Yeh, C. J. (2019). What types of racial messages protect Asian American adolescents from discrimination? A latent interaction model. *Journal of Counseling Psychology*, *66*(2), 247–254. doi:10.1037/cou0000297 PMID:30035592

Aydin, C. (2017). How to forget the unforgettable? On collective trauma, cultural identity, and mnemotechnologies. *Identity*, *17*(3), 125–137. doi:10.1080/15283488.2017.1340160

Bachi, K., & Parish-Plass, N. (2017). Animal-assisted psychotherapy: A unique relational therapy for children and adolescents. *Clinical Child Psychotherapy*, *22*(1), 3–8. doi:10.1177/1359104516672549 PMID:27742758

Bainbridge, C. (2020, May 7). *10 ways to motivate gifted children.* Verywell Family. Retrieved October 28, 2021, from https://www.verywellfamily.com/ways-to-motivate-gifted-children-1449283

Baker, W., & Butcher, J. (2022). Demystifying the stigma of transient African American housing dwellers: Recommendations for school and church partnerships. In Butcher & Baker (Eds.), Addressing Issues of Systemic Racism During Turbulent Times. IGI Global Publications.

Baker, E., Zyromski, B., & Granello, D. H. (2021). School or guidance counselor: How the title influences public perception. *Professional School Counseling*, *25*(1), 1–8. doi:10.1177/2156759X20981034

Barbour, M. (n.d.). *Are Virtual Schools More Cost-Effective Compared to Traditional, Brick-and-Mortar Schools?* Retrieved September 11, 2021, from https://digitalcommons.sacredheart.edu/cgi/viewcontent.cgi?article=1103&context=ced_fac

Barker, E. (2006). The artist within. *Natural Health*, *36*(10), 98–99.

Barlow, C. A., & Phelan, A. M. (2007). Peer collaboration: A model to support counsellor self-care. *Canadian Journal of Counselling*, *41*, 3–15.

Basch, C. E. (2010). *Healthier students are better learners: A missing link in school reforms to close the achievement gap*. http://www.equitycampaign.org/i/a/document/12557_Equitymatters vol6web03082010.pdf

Basch, C. E. (2011). Healthier students are better learners: A missing link in school reforms to close the achievement gap. *The Journal of School Health*, *81*(10), 593–598. doi:10.1111/j.1746-1561.2011.00632.x PMID:21923870

Baunach, P. (1985). *Mothers in prison*. Transaction Books.

Belasco, A. S. (2013). Creating college opportunity: School counselors and their influence on postsecondary enrollment. *Research in Higher Education*, *54*(7), 781–804. doi:10.100711162-013-9297-4

Bellak, L. (1975). *The T.A.T., C.A.T., and S.A.T. in clinical use*. Grune and Stratton.

Bell, V., Robinson, B., Katona, C., Fett, A.-K., & Shergill, S. (2019). When trust is lost: The impact of interpersonal trauma on social interactions. *Psychological Medicine*, *49*(6), 1041–1046. doi:10.1017/S0033291718001800 PMID:30043717

Bemak, F., & Chung, R. C.-Y. (2005). Advocacy as a critical role for urban school counselors: Working toward equity and social justice. *Professional School Counseling*, *8*(3), 196–202.

Bendall, S., Eastwood, O., Cox, G., Farrelly-Rosch, A., Nicoll, H., Peters, W., Bailey, A. P., McGorry, P. D., & Scanlan, F. (2021). A systematic review and synthesis of trauma-informed care within outpatient and counseling health settings for young people. *Child Maltreatment*, *26*(3), 313–324. doi:10.1177/1077559520927468 PMID:32536207

Bergmann, H. (2001). "The Silent University": The Society to Encourage Studies at Home, 1873-1897. *The New England Quarterly*, *74*(3), 447–477. doi:10.2307/3185427

Bergren, M. D. (2021). Post-COVID-19: Trauma-informed care for the school community. *The Journal of School Nursing: the Official Publication of the National Association of School Nurses*, *37*(3), 145. doi:10.1177/10598405211004709 PMID:33969768

Berliner, L., & Kolko, D. J. (2016). Trauma informed care: A commentary and critique. *Child Maltreatment*, *21*(2), 168–172. doi:10.1177/1077559516643785 PMID:27152025

Betters-Burbon, J., Brunner, T., & Kansteiner, A. (2016). Successful for all? The role of the school counselor in creating and sustaining culturally responsive positive behavior interventions and supports. *The Professional Counselor*, *6*(3), 263–277. doi:10.15241/jbb.6.3.263

Bick, J., & Nelson, C. A. (2016). Early adverse experiences and the developing brain. *Neuropsychopharmacology*, *41*(1), 177–196. doi:10.1038/npp.2015.252 PMID:26334107

Bishop, J., & Noguera, P. (2019). The ecology of educational equity: Implications for policy. *Peabody Journal of Education*, *94*(2), 122–141. doi:10.1080/0161956X.2019.1598108

Bloom, S. L. (1995). Creating sanctuary in the school. *Journal for a Just and Caring Education*, *1*(4), 403.

Boch, S. J., Warren, B. J., & Ford, J. L. (2019). Attention, externalizing, and internalizing problems of youth exposed to parental incarceration. *Issues in Mental Health Nursing*, *40*(6), 466–475. https://doi.org/10.1080/01612840.2019.1565872

Boswell, G., & Wedge, P. (2002). *Imprisoned Fathers and Their Children.* Jessica Kingsley Publishers. doi:10.1046/j.1365-2206.2002.t01-1-00258.x

Boyle, D., & Hassett-Walker, C. (2008). Individual-level and socio-structural characteristics of violence: An emergency department study. *Journal of Interpersonal Violence*, *23*(8), 1011–1026. doi:10.1177/0886260507313966 PMID:18296572

Bradley, N., Whisenhunt, J., Adamson, N., & Kress, V. E. (2013). Creative approaches for promoting counselor self-care. *Journal of Creativity in Mental Health*, *8*(4), 456–469. doi:10.1080/15401383.2013.844656

Brajcic, M., Kuscevic, D., & Lazeta, M. (2020). A comparison between competencies of teachers and students of teacher education in recognizing artistically gifted students. *European Journal of Educational Research*, *9*(3), 1327–1336. doi:10.12973/eu-jer.9.3.1327

Briere, J., & Scott, C. (2015). *Principles of trauma therapy: A guide to symptoms, evaluation, and treatment* (2nd ed.). Sage.

Brisch, K. H. (1999). *Treating attachment disorders: from theory to therapy.* Guilford Press.

Brooks, J. (2014). *The process of parenting*. McGraw Hill.

Brown, E. C. (2020). School counselor conceptualizations of the needs of children of incarcerated parents. *Children and Youth Services Review*, *112*, 1–9. doi:10.1016/j.childyouth.2020.104936

Brown, E. C., & Barrio Minton, C. A. (2018). Serving children of incarcerated parents: A case study of school counselors' experiences. *Professional School Counseling*, *21*(1), 1–11. doi:10.5330/prsc.9.1.a5j5051x1025t767

Brown, E. C., & Gibbons, M. M. (2018). Addressing needs of children of incarcerated parents with child-centered play therapy. *Journal of Child and Adolescent Counseling*, *4*(2), 134–145. doi:10.1080/23727810.2017.1381931

Brown, M., Lenares-Solomon, D., & Deaner, R. (2019). Every Student Succeeds Act: A call to action for school counselors. *Journal of Counselor Leadership and Advocacy*, *6*(1), 86–96. https://doi.org/10.1080/2326716X.2018.1557574

Brown, S. D., Brack, G., & Mullis, F. D. (2008). Traumatic symptoms in sexually abused children: Implications for school counselors. *Professional School Counseling Journal, 11*(6), 368–379. doi:10.5330/PSC.n.2010-11.368

Bruneau, L., & Johnson, A. (2011, March 27). *Fido and Freud meet: Integrating animal-assisted therapy into traditional counseling theories* [Paper Presentation]. *American Counseling Association Conference & Exposition*, New Orleans, LA, United States.

Bücker, J., Kapczinski, F., Post, R., Cereser, K. M., Szobot, C., Yatham, L. N., Kapczinski, N. S., & Kauer-Sant'Anna, M. (2012). Cognitive impairment in school-aged children with early trauma. *Comprehensive Psychiatry, 53*, 758-764. doi:10.1016/j.comppsych.2011.12.006

Budiman, A., & Ruiz, N. G. (2021, April 29). *Key facts about Asian Americans, a diverse and growing population.* Pew Research Center. https://www.pewresearch.org/fact-tank/2021/04/29/key-facts-about-asian-americans/

Budiman, A., & Ruiz, N. G. (2021, April 9). *Asian Americans are the fastest-growing racial or ethnic group in the U.S.* Pew Research Center. https://www.pewresearch.org/fact-tank/2021/04/09/asian-americans-are-the-fastest-growing-racial-or-ethnic-group-in-the-u-s/

Build Trauma-Informed Practices. (2021). https://www.ascaschoolcounselor-digital.org/ascaschoolcounselor/march_april_2021/MobilePagedArticle.action?articleId=1666564#articleId1666564

Burke, A. (2009). Gifted and grieving: Why it is critical to offer differential support to gifted kids during times of loss. *Gifted Child Today Magazine, 32*(4), 30–37. doi:10.1177/107621750903200409

Butler, L. D., Critelli, F. M., & Rinfrette, E. S. (2011). Trauma-informed care and mental health. *Directions in Psychiatry, 31*, 197–210.

Cabanatuan, M. (2020, March 19). Coronavirus: Asian American groups compile hate crime reports as Trump persists in 'Chinese virus' attacks. *San Francisco Chronicle*. https://www.sfchronicle.com/bayarea/article/Coronavirus-Asian-American-groups-compile-hate-15144295.php

California Association of School Counselors. (2019). *Covid-19 planning considerations and resources: addressing staff and student mental health for school re-entry.* https://www.schoolcounselor-ca.org/files/Covid-19%20Planning%20Considerations%20and%20Resources-Addressing%20Staff%20and%20Student%20Mental%20Health%20for%20School%20Re-Entry.pdf

California Department of Education News Release. (2018). *State schools chief Tom Torlakson announces new social emotional learning guidelines.* https://www.cde.ca.gov/nr/ne/yr18/yr18rel15.asp

Cambell, A. M. (2020). *An increasing risk of family violence during the Covid-19 pandemic: Strengthening community collaborations to save lives.* doi:10.1016/j.fsir.2020.100089

Campbell, J. M. (2003). Efficacy of behavioral interventions for reducing problem behavior in persons with autism: A quantitative synthesis of single-subject research. *Research in Developmental Disabilities*, *24*(2), 120–138. doi:10.1016/S0891-4222(03)00014-3 PMID:12623082

Carter, R. T. (2007). Racism and psychological and emotional injury: Recognizing and assessing race-based traumatic stress. *The Counseling Psychologist*, *35*(1), 13–105. doi:10.1177/0011000006292033

Carter, R. T., & Muchow, C. (2017). Construct validity of the Race-Based Traumatic Stress Symptom Scale and tests of measurement equivalence. *Psychological Trauma: Theory, Research, Practice, and Policy*, *9*(6), 688–695. doi:10.1037/tra0000256 PMID:28165267

Cavanaugh, B. (2016). Trauma-informed classrooms and schools. *Beyond Behavior*, *25*(2), 41–46. doi:10.1177/107429561602500206

Center for Disease Control and Prevention. (2020). *Six guiding principles to a trauma-informed care approach.* https://www.cdc.gov/cpr/infographics/6_principles_trauma_info.htm

Chafouleas, S. M., Johnson, A. H., Overstreet, S., & Santos, N. M. (2015). toward a blueprint for trauma-informed service delivery in schools. *School Mental Health*, *8*(1), 144–162. doi:10.100712310-015-9166-8

Chandler, C. (2001). *Animal-assisted therapy in counseling and school settings* (Report No. EDO-CG-01-05). Greensboro, NC: ERIC Clearinghouse on Counseling and Student Services. (ERIC Document Reproduction Service No. ED459404)

Chandler, C. K., Portrie-Bethke, T. L., Barrio Minton, C. A., Fernando, D. M., & O'Callaghan, D. M. (2010). Matching animal-assisted therapy techniques with counseling guiding theories. *Journal of Mental Health Counseling*, *32*(4), 354–374. doi:10.17744/mehc.32.4.u72lt21740103538

Chaturvedi, K., Kumar, D., & Nidhi, S. (2020). COVID-19 and its impact on education, social life, and mental health of students: A survey. *Children and Youth Services Review*. Advance online publication. doi:10.1016/j.childyouth.2020.105866 PMID:33390636

Cheah, C. S., Wang, C., Ren, H., Zong, X., Cho, H. S., & Xue, X. (2020). COVID-19 racism and mental health in Chinese American families. *Pediatrics*, *146*(5), e2020021816. Advance online publication. doi:10.1542/peds.2020-021816 PMID:32873719

Cheng, H. L., & Mallinckrodt, B. (2015). Racial/cthnic discrimination, posttraumatic stress symptoms, and alcohol problems in a longitudinal study of Hispanic/Latino college students. *Journal of Counseling Psychology*, *62*(1), 38–49. doi:10.1037/cou0000052 PMID:25602606

Chen, J. A., Zhang, E., & Liu, C. H. (2020). Potential Impact of COVID-19-Related Racial Discrimination on the Health of Asian Americans. *American Journal of Public Health*, *110*(11), 1624–1627. doi:10.2105/AJPH.2020.305858 PMID:32941063

Child Welfare Information Gateway. (2019a). *Definitions of child abuse and neglect*. U.S. Department of Health and Human Services, Children's Bureau.

Child Welfare Information Gateway. (2019b). *Long-term consequences of child abuse and neglect*. U.S. Department of Health and Human Services, Children's Bureau.

Child Welfare Information Gateway. (2019c). *Mandatory reporters of child abuse and neglect*. U.S. Department of Health and Human Services, Children's Bureau.

Child Welfare Information Gateway. (n.d.). *State child abuse and neglect reporting numbers*. https://www.childwelfare.gov/organizations/?CWIGFunctionsaction=rols:main.dspList&rolType=custom&rs_id=5

Children's Advocacy Centers of Texas. (n.d.). *A Texas school employee's guide to reporting suspected abuse and neglect*. https://tea.texas.gov/sites/default/files/Educators-Guide-2020-English.pdf

Chiu, A. (2020, March 20). Trump has no qualms about calling the coronavirus the 'Chinese Virus.' That's a dangerous attitude, experts say. *The Washington Post*. https://www.washingtonpost.com/nation/2020/03/20/coronavirus-trump-chinese-virus/

Choi, N. G., DiNitto, D. M., Marti, C. N., & Segal, S. P. (2017). Adverse childhood experiences and suicide attempts among those with mental and substance use disorders. *Child Abuse & Neglect*, *69*, 252–262. doi:10.1016/j.chiabu.2017.04.024 PMID:28500922

Chopra, S. B. (2021). Healing from internalized racism for Asian Americans. *Professional Psychology, Research and Practice*, *52*(5), 503–512. doi:10.1037/pro0000407

Chuong, C. H., & Ta, M. H. (2003). Vietnamese: Overcoming the past and building a future. In E. Lai & D. Arguelles (Eds.), *The new face of Asian Pacific America: Numbers, diversity & change in the 21st century* (pp. 67–72). Asian Week.

Chute, E. (2017). When parents of school children go to prison. Keep their children on track with mentoring, specialized clubs and other approaches in education. *District Administration*, *53*(3), 34–40.

Clark, B. (2008). *Growing up gifted: Developing the potential of children at home and at school*. Pearson/Merrill Prentice Hall.

Clark, T. (2021). *Virtual Schools: Trends and Issues. A Study of Virtual Schools in the United States*. http://www.dlrn.org/virtualstudy.pdf. https://eric.ed.gov/?id=ED462923

Clark, R. E. (2001). A summary of disagreements with the 'mere vehicles' argument. In R. E. Clark (Ed.), *Learning from media: Arguments, analysis, and evidence* (pp. 125–136). Information Age Publishing.

Clopton, K., & East, K. (2008). "Are there other kids like me?" children with a parent in prison. *Early Childhood Education Journal, 36*(2), 195-198. doi:10.1007/s10643-008-0266-z

Coaston, S. (2017). Self-care through self-compassion: A balm for burnout. *The Professional Counselor*, *7*(3), 285–297. doi:10.15241cc.7.3.285

Cohen, J. (1992). A power primer. *Psychological Bulletin, 112*(1), 155–159. doi:10.1037/0033-2909.112.1.155 PMID:19565683

Cohen, J. A., Berliner, L., & Mannarino, A. (2010). Trauma focused CBT for children with co-occurring trauma and behavior problems. *Child Abuse & Neglect, 34*(4), 215–224. doi:10.1016/j.chiabu.2009.12.003 PMID:20304489

Cohen, J. A., Mannarino, A. P., & Deblinger, E. (2012). *Trauma-focused CBT for children and adolescents: Treatment Applications*. Guilford Press.

Cole, S. F., Eisner, A., Gregory, M., & Risuccia, J. (2013). *Helping traumatized children learn: Creating and advocating for trauma-sensitive schools, safe, supportive learning environments that benefit all children* (Vol. 2). Massachusetts Advocates for Children.

Cole, S. F., Greenwald O'Brien, J., Gadd, G., Ristuccia, J., Wallace, L., & Gregory, M. (2005). *Helping traumatized children learn*. Massachusetts Advocates for Children.

College, S., & Kentnor, H. (2015). Digital Commons @ DU Distance Education and the Evolution of Online Learning in the United States. *Curriculum and Teaching Dialogue, 17*. https://digitalcommons.du.edu/cgi/viewcontent.cgi?article=1026&context=law_facpub

Collins, S., Woolfson, L. M., & Durkin, K. (2014). Effects on coping skills and anxiety of a universal school-based mental health intervention delivered in Scottish primary schools. *School Psychology International, 35*(1), 85–100. https://doi.org/10.1177/0143034312469157

Committee for Children. (2021). *Second Step*. http://www.secondstep.org

Conger, R. D., & Elder, G. H. (1994). *Families in troubled times*. Aldine de Guyter.

Congressional Asian American Pacific American Caucus. (2020). *As coronavirus fears incite violence, CAPAC members urge colleagues to not stoke xenophobia*. https://capac-chu.house.gov/press-release/coronavirusfears-incite-violence-capac-members-urge-colleagues-not-stoke-xenophobia

Conradi, L., & Wilson, C. (2010). Managing traumatized children: A trauma systems perspective. *Current Opinion in Pediatrics, 22*(5), 621–625. doi:10.1097/MOP.0b013e32833e0766 PMID:20717037

Cook, J., Rock, W., Steele, T., & Stone, C. (2016). *Ethical Considerations in Virtual School Counseling*. Retrieved October 5, 2021, from https://admin.schoolcounselor.org/getmedia/bf746827-db38-421f-addf-6ffb7e8b52b7/Ethics-and-Virtual-School-Counseling.pdf

Copeland, W., Shanahan, L., Hinesley, J., Chan, R., Aberg, K., Fairbank, J., van den Oord, E., & Costello, J. (2018). Association of childhood trauma exposure with adult psychiatric disorders and functional outcomes. *JAMA Network Open, 1*(7), e184493. Advance online publication. doi:10.1001/jamanetworkopen.2018.4493 PMID:30646356

Corey, G. (2013). *Theory and practice of counseling and psychotherapy* (9th ed.). Cengage Learning.

Corey, G., Muratori, M., Austin, J. T., & Austin, J. A. (2018). *Counselor self-care*. American Counseling Association.

Corsetti, S., Ferrara, M., & Natoli, E. (2019). Evaluating stress in dogs involved in animal-assisted interventions. *Animals*, Vol. 9. *Article*, *833*(10), 1–19. doi:10.3390/ani9100833 PMID:31635094

Council for Accreditation of Counseling & Related Educational Programs. (2016). *2016 CACREP standards*. Retrieved from https://www.cacrep.org/section-5-entry-level-specialty-areas-school-counseling/

COVID-19 Resources - American School Counselor Association (ASCA). (2020). https://www.schoolcounselor.org/Publications-Research/Publications/Free-ASCA-Resources/COVID-19-Resources

Creswell, J. W. (2013). *Qualitative inquiry and research design: Choosing among five traditions* (3rd ed.). Sage.

Crozier, J. C., & Barth, R. P. (2005). Cognitive and academic functioning in maltreated children. *Children & Schools*, *27*(4), 197–206. doi:10.1093/cs/27.4.197

Current RAMP Schools - American School Counselor Association (ASCA). (2020). https://www.schoolcounselor.org/Recognition/RAMP/Current-RAMP-Schools?sso=6f7294ff-dc72-49e5-b53b-98e9e48f7925

Dahir, C. A. (2004). Supporting a nation of learners: The role of school counseling in educational reform. *Journal of Counseling and Development*, *82*(3), 344–353. doi:10.1002/j.1556-6678.2004.tb00320.x

Dakil, S., Cox, M., Lin, H., & Flores, G. (2011). Racial and ethnic disparities in physical abuse reporting and Child Protective Services interventions in the United States. *Journal of the National Medical Association*, *103*(9-10), 926–931. doi:10.1016/S0027-9684(15)30449-1 PMID:22364062

Dallaire, D. H. (2007). Children with incarcerated mothers: Developmental outcomes, special challenges, and recommendations. *Journal of Applied Developmental Psychology*, *28*(1), 15–24. doi:10.1016/j.appdev.2006.10.003

Dallaire, D. H., Ciccone, A., & Wilson, L. C. (2010). Teachers' experiences with and expectations of children with incarcerated parents. *Journal of Applied Developmental Psychology*, *31*(4), 281–290. https://doi.org/10.1016/j.appdev.2010.04.001

Dallaire, D., & Wilson, H. (2010). The relation of exposure to parental criminal activity, arrest, and sentencing to children's maladjustment. *Journal of Child and Family Studies*, *19*, 404–418. https://doi.org/10.1007/s10826-009-9311-9

Davidson. (2021, July 19). *What is giftedness? Gifted definition & meaning*. Davidson Institute. Retrieved April 18, 2022, from https://www.davidsongifted.org/gifted-blog/what-is-giftedness/

Davis, L., & Shlafer, R. (2017). Mental health of adolescents with currently and formerly incarcerated parents. *Journal of Adolescence*, *54*(1), 120–134. doi:10.1016/j.adolescence.2016.10.006 PMID:28011442

de Haan, B., Mienko, J. A., & Eddy, J. M. (2019). The interface of child welfare and parental criminal justice involvement: Policy and practice implications for the children of incarcerated parents. In J. M. Eddy & J. Poehlmann-Tynan (Eds.), Handbook on children with incarcerated parents: Research, policy, and practice (2nd ed., pp. 279–294). Springer. https://doi.org/10.1007/978-3-030-16707-3_19.

Denham, S. (2015). Assessment of SEL in Educational Contexts. In J. A. Durlak, C. E. Domitrovich, R. P. Weissberg, & T. P. Gullotta (Eds.), *Handbook of social and emotional learning: Research and practice* (pp. 285–300). The Guilford Press.

DePanfilis, D., & Salus, M. K. (2003). *Child Protective Services: A guide for caseworkers*. U.S. Department of Health and Human Services, Children's Bureau.

DePaoli, J. L., Atwell, M., & Bridgeland, J. (2017). *Ready to lead: A national principal survey on how social and emotional learning can prepare children and transform schools*. Civic Enterprises and Hart Research Associates for CASEL.

Desmond, K. J., Kindsvatter, A., Stahl, S., & Smith, H. (2015). Using creative techniques with children who have experienced trauma. *Journal of Creativity in Mental Health*, *10*(4), 439–455. https://doi.org/10.1080/15401383.2015.1040938

Dillard, C. (2020). Speaking up against racism around the coronavirus. *Teaching Tolerance*. https://www.learningforjustice.org/magazine/speaking-up-against-racism-around-the-coronavirus

Dimitrijevic, I. (2009). Animal-assisted therapy- a new trend in the treatment of children and adults. *Psychiatria Danubina*, *21*(2), 236–241. PMID:19556955

Doka, K. J. (2009). Disenfranchised grief. In C. D. Bryant & D. L. Peck (Eds.), Encyclopedia of death and the human experience (pp. 378–381). Sage. https://doi.org/10.4135/9781412972031.n122.

Dollarhide, C. T., Smith, A. T., & Lemberger, M. E. (2007). Critical incidents in the development of supportive principals: Facilitating school counselor-principal relationships. *Professional School Counseling*, *10*(4), 360–369. doi:10.5330/prsc.10.4.k111116677917913

Domitrovich, C., Durlak, J., Staley, K., & Weissberg, R. (2017). Social-emotional competence: An essential factor for promoting positive adjustment and reducing risk in school children. *Child Development*, *88*(2), 408–416. doi:10.1111/cdev.12739 PMID:28213889

Dorado, J. S., Martinez, M., McArthur, L. E., & Leibovitz, T. (2016). Healthy environments and response to trauma in schools (HEARTS): A whole-school, multi-level, prevention and intervention program for creating trauma-informed, safe and supportive schools. *School Mental Health*, *8*(1), 163–176. doi:10.100712310-016-9177-0

Doyle, C., & Cicchetti, D. (2017). From the cradle to the grave: The effect of adverse caregiving environments on attachment and relationships throughout the lifespan. *Clinical Psychology: Science and Practice*, *24*(2), 203–217. doi:10.1111/cpsp.12192 PMID:28924334

Drew, M., & Gonzalez, M. (2021). Making the time: Relationships among school specialists. *School Community Journal*, *31*(1), 171–204. https://www.schoolcommunitynetwork.org/SCJ.aspx

Duplechain, R., Reigner, R., & Packard, A. (2008). Striking differences: The impact of moderate and high trauma on reading achievement. *Reading Psychology*, *29*(2), 117–136. doi:10.1080/02702710801963845

Duquette, K. (2021). "We're powerful too, you know?" A narrative inquiry into elementary school counselors' experiences of the RAMP process. *Professional School Counseling*, *25*(1), 1–15. doi:10.1177/2156759X20985831

Durlak, J. (2015). What everyone should know about implementation. In J. A. Durlak, C. E. Domitrovich, R. P. Weissberg, & T. P. Gullotta (Eds.), *Handbook of social and emotional learning: Research and practice* (pp. 395–405). The Guilford Press.

Duslak, M., & Geier, B. (2016). Communication factors as predictors of relationship quality: A national study of principals and school counselors. *Professional School Counseling*, *20*(1), 115–126. doi:10.5330/1096-2409-20.1.115

Elbedour, S., Alsubie, F., Al'Uqdah, S. N., & Bawalsah, J. A. (2020). School crisis management planning. *Children & Schools*, *42*(4), 208–215. doi:10.1093/cs/cdaa021

Elliott, D. E., Bjelajac, P., Fallot, R. D., Markoff, L. S., & Reed, B. G. (2005). Trauma-informed or trauma-denied: Principles and implementation of trauma-informed services for women. *Journal of Community Psychology*, *33*(4), 461–477. doi:10.1002/jcop.20063

Erbacher, T. A., Singer, J. B., & Poland, S. (2015). *Suicide in schools: A practitioner's guide to multi-level prevention, assessment, intervention, and postvention (School-Based Practice in Action)* (1st ed.). Routledge.

Erikson, K. (1976). *Everything in its path*. Simon and Schuster Paperbacks.

Ermis-Demirtas, H., Luo, Y., & Huang, Y. (in press). The trauma of COVID-19 fueled discrimination: Posttraumatic stress in Asian American adolescents. *Professional School Counseling*.

Erskine, R. (1972) *Integrative Psychotherapy*. Institute of Integrative Psychotherapy. https://www.integrativetherapy.com/

Esquith, D. (2013, November 1). *Plans, processes, and procedures*. Schoolcounselor.Org. https://www.schoolcounselor.org/Magazines/November-December-2013/Plans,-Processes-and-Procedures

Ethical Considerations: School Counseling in a Virtual Setting (Part 1). (2020). *American School Counselor Association*. https://videos.schoolcounselor.org/ethics-virtual-school-counseling

Evans, A., & Coccoma, P. (2014). *Trauma-informed care: How neuroscience influences practice*. Taylor and Francis. doi:10.4324/9781315815572

Evans, S. W., Stephan, S. H., & Sugai, G. (2014). Advancing research in school mental health: Introduction of a special issue on key issues in research. *School Mental Health, 6*(2), 63–67. doi:10.100712310-014-9126-8 PMID:25067959

Federal Emergency Management Agency. (2013). *Guide for Developing High-Quality School Emergency Operations Plans*. https://www.fema.gov/sites/default/files/2020-07/guide-developing-school-emergency-operations-plans.pdf

Felder, B. (2018, January 10). *Bullying most common reason students choose virtual schools*. Oklahoman.com; Oklahoman. https://www.oklahoman.com/article/5578967/bullying-most-common-reason-students-choose-virtual-schools

Felitti, V. J., Anda, R. F., Nordenberg, D., Williamson, D. F., Spitz, A. M., & Edwards, V. … Marks, J. S. (1998). Relationship of childhood abuse and household dysfunction to many of the leading causes of death in adults. *American Journal of Preventive Medicine, 14*(4), 245–258. doi:10.1016/S0749-3797(98)00017-8

Felitti, V. J., Anda, R. F., Nordenberg, D., Williamson, D. F., Spitz, A. M., Edwards, V., Koss, M. P., & Marks, J. S. (2019). REPRINT OF: Relationship of childhood abuse and household dysfunction to many of the leading causes of death in adults: The Adverse Childhood Experiences (ACE) Study. *American Journal of Preventive Medicine, 56*(6), 774–786. doi:10.1016/j.amepre.2019.04.001 PMID:31104722

FERPA and Virtual Learning | Protecting Student Privacy. (2020). https://studentprivacy.ed.gov/resources/ferpa-and-virtual-learning

Filson, B. (2013). *Self-injury: The attempt to cope, connect and communicate* [Webinar]. MA Department of Public Health. https://www.youtube.com/watch?v=JfapTE0R6g0

Filson, B. (2016). The haunting can end: Trauma-informed approaches in healing from abuse and adversity. In J. Russo & A. Sweeney (Eds.), *Searching for a rose garden: Challenging psychiatry, fostering mad studies* (pp. 20–24). PCCS Books.

Fine, A. H. (2015). *Handbook on animal-assisted therapy: Foundations and guidelines for animal-assisted interventions* (5th ed.). Elsevier Academic Press.

Finkelhor, D., Turner, H. A., Shattuck, A., & Hamby, S. L. (2015). Prevalence of childhood exposure to violence, crime, and abuse: Results from the national survey of children's exposure to violence. *Journal of the American Medical Association, 169*(8), 746–754. PMID:26121291

First virtual school in Mass. opens Thursday. (2021). http://archive.boston.com/news/education/k_12/articles/2010/08/31/first_virtual_school_in_mass_opens_thursday/

Fisher, C. B., Wallace, S. A., & Fenton, R. E. (2000). Discrimination distress during adolescence. *Journal of Youth and Adolescence, 29*(6), 679–695. doi:10.1023/A:1026455906512

Fitzgerald, E. (2013). *Perceptions of counselors-in-training regarding preparation and level of confidence when counseling children who have experienced interpersonal trauma* (Doctoral dissertation). Retrieved from ProQuest. (3575109)

Flom, B. (2005). Counseling with pocket pets: Using small animals in elementary counseling programs. *Professional School Counseling, 8*(5), 469–471.

Floom, B., & Sundal Hansen, S. (n.d.). *Just don't shut the door on me: Aspirations of adolescents in crisis.* Sage Journals. Retrieved November 1, 2021, from https://journals.sagepub.com/doi/full/10.1177/2156759X0601000103

Flores, E., Tschann, J. M., Dimas, J. M., Pasch, L. A., & de Groat, C. L. (2010). Perceived racial/ethnic discrimination, posttraumatic stress symptoms, and health risk behaviors among Mexican American adolescents. *Journal of Counseling Psychology, 57*(3), 264–273. doi:10.1037/a0020026 PMID:21133578

Flynn, E., Gandenberger, J., Mueller, M. K., & Morris, K. N. (2020). Animal–assisted interventions as an adjunct to therapy for youth: Clinician perspectives. *Child & Adolescent Social Work Journal, 2020*(37), 631–647. doi:10.100710560-020-00695-z

Foa, E. B., Asnaani, A., Zang, Y., Capaldi, S., & Yeh, R. (2018). Psychometrics of the Child PTSD Symptom Scale for *DSM*-5 for trauma-exposed children and adolescents. *Journal of Clinical Child and Adolescent Psychology, 47*(1), 38–46. doi:10.1080/15374416.2017.1350962 PMID:28820616

Ford, J. D. (2013). *Treatment of complex trauma: A sequenced, relationship-based approach.* Guilford Press.

Forsyth, J. M., & Carter, R. T. (2014). Development and preliminary validation of the Racism-Related Coping Scale. *Psychological Trauma: Theory, Research, Practice, and Policy, 6*(6), 632–643. doi:10.1037/a0036702

Foster, H., & Hagan, J. (2015). Punishment regimes and the multi-level effects of parental incarceration: Intergenerational, intersectional, and interinstitutional models of social inequality and systemic exclusion. *Annual Review of Sociology, 41*(1), 135–158. doi:10.1146/annurev-soc-073014-112437

Frey, A., Cloud, R., Lee, J., Small, J., Seeley, J., Feil, E., Walker, H., & Golly, A. (2011). The promise of motivational interviewing in school mental health. *School Mental Health, 3*, 1–12. https://doi.org/10.1007/s12310-010-9048-z

Friesen, L. (2010). Exploring animal-assisted programs with children in school and therapeutic contexts. *Early Childhood Education Journal, 37*(4), 261–267. doi:10.100710643-009-0349-5

Fye, H. J., Bergen, S., & Baltrinic, E. R. (2020). Exploring the relationship between school counselors' perceived ASCA national model implementation, supervision satisfaction, and burnout. *Journal of Counseling and Development, 98*(1), 53–62. doi:10.1002/jcad.12299

Gallant, W., & Holosko, M. (2001). Music intervention in grief work with clients experiencing loss and bereavement. *Guidance and Counseling*, *16*, 115–121.

Garrison, E. G., Roy, I. S., & Azar, V. (1999). Responding to the mental health needs of Latino children and families through school-based services. *Clinical Psychology Review*, *19*(2), 199–219. doi:10.1016/S0272-7358(98)00070-1 PMID:10078420

Gee, N. R., Griffin, J. A., & McCardle, P. (2017, July-September). Human-animal interaction research in school settings: Current knowledge and future directions. *AERA Open*, *3*(3), 1–9. doi:10.1177/2332858417724346

Geist, T. (2011). Conceptual Framework for Animal Assisted Therapy. *Child and Adolescent Social Work*, *28*(3), 243–256. doi:10.100710560-011-0231-3

Geller, A., Cooper, C. E., Garfinkel, I., Schwartz-Soicher, O., & Mincy, R. B. (2012). Beyond absenteeism: Father incarceration and child development. *Demography*, *49*(1), 49–76. https://doi.org/10.1007/s13524-011-0081-9

Gerlach, J. (2020). Teens of incarcerated parents: A group counseling intervention for high school counselors. *Journal of School Counseling*, *18*(16). http://www.jsc.montana.edu/articles/v18n16.pdf

Gerrity, E., & Folcarelli, C. (2008). *Child traumatic stress: What every policymaker should know*. https://www.nctsn.org/sites/default/files/resources/child_traumatic_stress_what_policymakers_should_know.pdf

Gherardi, S. A., Flinn, R. E., & Jaure, V. B. (2020). Trauma-sensitive schools and social justice: A critical analysis. *The Urban Review*, *52*(3), 482–504. doi:10.100711256-020-00553-3

Giboney Wall, C. R. (2021). What hurt and what helped: How one school's trauma-informed approach provided support during the pandemic. *Journal of Loss and Trauma*, 1–14. doi:10.1080/15325024.2021.1943127

Glaze, L. E., & Maruschak, L. M. (2008). Parents in prison and their minor children. Washington, DC. *Bureau of Justice Statistics Special Report*.

Goodman, R. (1997). The Strengths and Difficulties Questionnaire: A research note. *Journal of Child Psychology and Psychiatry, and Allied Disciplines*, *38*(5), 581–586. doi:10.1111/j.1469-7610.1997.tb01545.x PMID:9255702

Goodman, R. D. (2014). A liberatory approach to trauma counseling: Decolonizing our trauma-informed practices. In R. D. Goodman & P. C. Gorski (Eds.), *Decolonizing "multicultural" counseling through social justice* (pp. 55–72). Springer.

Goodman-Scott, E., Betters-Bubon, J., Olsen, J., & Donohue, P. (2020). *An ASCA National Model: Making MTSS Work*. American School Counselor Association Publication.

Grassroots Asians Rising. (2020). *Asian American racial justice toolkit*. https://www.asianamtoolkit.org/the-toolkit

Green, J. M. (2021). *Why being gifted isn't always a gift.* Today's Parent. Retrieved November 18, 2021, from https://www.todaysparent.com/family/how-to-help-your-gifted-kid-thrive/

Greene, M. L., Way, N., & Pahl, K. (2006). Trajectories of perceived adult and peer discrimination among Black, Latino, and Asian American adolescents: Patterns and psychological correlates. *Developmental Psychology, 42*(2), 218–236. doi:10.1037/0012-1649.42.2.218 PMID:16569162

Greenwald, R. (2005). *Child trauma handbook: A guide for helping trauma-exposed children and adolescents.* Haworth Maltreatment and Trauma Press/The Haworth Press.

Grief.com. (2021, March 31). *Five stages of grief by Elisabeth Kubler Ross & David Kessler.* https://grief.com/the-five-stages-of-grief/

Grubbs, L. (2015). *Texas school counselors' perceptions of job preparedness based on their graduate training programs* (Doctoral dissertation). Retrieved from ProQuest. (3664337)

Grubbs, L., Muro, J. H., & Clements, K. (2016). School counselors and nurses: Collaborative best practices for maintaining confidentiality with pregnant adolescents. *The Practitioner Scholar: Journal of Counseling & Professional Psychology, 5*(1), 20-29. https://www.thepractitionerscholar.com/issue/view/1263

Gündüz, B. (2012). Self-efficacy and burn out in professional school counselors. *Educational Sciences: Theory and Practice, 12*(3), 1761–1767.

Gut, W., Crump, L., Zinsstag, J., Hattendorf, J., & Hediger, K. (2018). The effect of human interaction on guinea pig behavior in animal-assisted therapy. *Journal of Veterinary Behavior, 25*, 56–64. doi:10.1016/j.jveb.2018.02.004

GysbersN. (n.d.). https://www.schoolcounselor.org/getmedia/52aaab9f-39ae-4fd0-8387-1d9c10b9ccb8/History-of-School-Counseling.pdf

Gysbers, N. C. (2010). *Remembering the past, shaping the future: A history of school counseling.* American School Counselor Association.

Hagan, J., & Foster, H. (2012). Children of the American prison generation: Student and school spillover effects of incarcerating mothers. *Law & Society Review, 46*(1), 37–69. https://doi.org/10.1111/j.1540-5893.2012.00472.x

Hall, M. (2017 November). *Advocating for your school counseling program using ASCA resources.* MASCA News. https://www.schoolcounselor.org/Newsletters/December-2017/Advocating-for-Your-School-Counseling-Program-Usin?st=ma

Hamblen, J., & Barnett, E. (2014). *PTSD in children and adolescents.* http://www.georgiadisaster.info/Schools/fs%207%20school/PTSD%20in%20Children%20&%20Adolescents.pdf

Hamilton County Job & Family Services. (2012). *The difference between discipline and abuse.* https://www.hcjfs.org/services/child-protection/know-the-difference-between-discipline-and-abuse/

Handford, C., & Marrero, A. D. (2021). *Racial trauma in the school system: Naming the Pain* (1st ed.). Routledge. doi:10.4324/9780429029615

Harper, A. J., & Singh, A. A. (2013). Counselor agency and action in developing safe schools: Six directions for systemic change. *Journal of LGBT Issues in Counseling*, *7*(4), 405–415. doi:10.1080/15538605.2013.839346

Harris, M., & Fallot, R. D. (2001). *Using trauma theory to design service systems*. Jossey-Bass.

Hatch, T. (2020). *Multi tiered, multi-domain system of supports*. https://www.hatchingresults.com/blog/2017/3/multi-tiered-multi-domain-system-of-supports-by-trish-hatch-phd

Hatch, T., Duarte, D. R., & De Gregorio, L. K. (2018). *Hatching results for elementary school counseling: implementing core curriculum and other tier one activities* (1st ed.). Corwin. doi:10.4135/9781506389684

Hatch, T., Tripplett, W., Duarte, D., & Gomez, V. (2019). *Hatching results for secondary school counseling: Implementing core curriculum, individual student planning, and other Tier one activities*. Corwin.

Haviland, S. (2017). A districtwide effort. *ASCA School Counselor, 54*(3), 14-18. https://asca-prod.azurewebsites.net/asca/media/asca/ASCAU/Trauma-Crisis-Management-Specialist/DistrictwideEffort.pdf

Havlik, S., & Bryan, J. (2015). Addressing the needs of students experiencing homelessness: School counselor preparation. *The Professional Counselor*, *5*(2), 200–216. doi:10.15241h.5.2.200

Health Information & Privacy. (2021). https://www.cdc.gov/phlp/publications/topic/healthinformationprivacy.html

Hébert, T., & Sergent, D. (2005). Using movies to guide: Teachers and counselors collaborating to support gifted students. *Gifted Child Today*, *28*(4), 14–24. doi:10.1177/107621750502800405

Henderson, D. A., & Thompson, C. L. (2016). *Counseling children*. Cengage Learning.

Hendricks, A., Conradi, L., & Wilson, C. (2011). Creating trauma-informed child welfare systems using a community assessment process. *Child Welfare*, *90*, 187–205. PMID:22533049

Herman, J. L. (1992). *Trauma and recovery*. Basic Books.

Hernandez, T. J., & Seem, S. R. (2004). A safe school climate: A systemic approach and the school counselor. *Professional School Counseling*, *7*(4), 256–262.

Herrenkohl, T. I., Jung, H., Lee, J. O., & Kim, M.-H. (2017). *Effects of child maltreatment, cumulative victimization experiences, and proximal life stress on adult crime and antisocial behavior*. https://www.ncjrs.gov/ pdffiles1/nij/grants/250506.pdf

Hickman, D. (2020). *The impact of role ambiguity, stress, and burnout on professional elementary school counselors* (Publication No. 28029586) [Doctoral dissertation, Texas A&M University-Commerce]. Proquest Dissertations & Theses Global.

HIPAA or FERPA or Not - American School Counselor Association (ASCA). (2021). https://www.schoolcounselor.org/Magazines/July-August-2010/HIPAA-or-FERPA-or-Not

Ho, J. (2021). Anti-Asian racism, Black Lives Matter, and COVID-19. *Japan Forum*, *33*(1), 148–159. doi:10.1080/09555803.2020.1821749

Holcomb-McCoy, C. (2007). *School counseling to close the achievement gap: A social justice framework for success*. Corwin Press.

Holifield, B. (2020). Trauma, soul, and the body in jungian analysis. *Jung Journal*, *14*(4), 72–85. doi:10.1080/19342039.2020.1822121

Howell, P. B., Thomas, S., Sweeney, D., & Vanderhaar, J. (2019). Moving beyond schedules, testing and other duties as deemed necessary by the principal: The school counselor's role in trauma informed practices. *Middle School Journal*, *50*(4), 26–34. doi:10.1080/00940771.2019.1650548

Hoxby, C., & Turner, S. (2013). Expanding college opportunities. *Education Next*, *13*(4), 66–73.

Hune, S. H., & Takeuchi, D. T. (2008). Asian Americans in Washington State: Closing their hidden achievement gaps. Report submitted to The Washington State Commission on Asian Pacific American Affairs, University of Washington.

Ieva, K. O., Beasley, J., & Steen, S. (2021). Equipping school counselors for anti-racist healing centered groups: A critical examination for preparation, connected curricula, professional practice and oversight. *Teaching and Supervision in Counseling*, *3*, 64–78. doi:10.7290/tsc030207

Ijai-Maghsoodi, R., Marlotte, L., Garcia, E., Aralis, H., Lester, P., Escudero, P., & Kataoka, S. (2017). Adapting and implementing a school-based resilience-building curriculum among low-income racial and ethnic minority students. *Racial and Ethnic Minority Students. Contemporary School Psychology*, *21*(3), 223–239. doi:10.100740688-017-0134-1 PMID:29686938

Institute on Trauma and Trauma Informed Care. (n.d.). *What is trauma-informed care?* https://socialwork.buffalo.edu/social-research/institutes-centers/institute-on-trauma-and-trauma-informed-care/what-is-trauma-informed-care.html

Issue Brief: Multi-Tier System of Supports/Response to Intervention - NCLD. (2021, November 23). *NCLD*. https://www.ncld.org/get-involved/understand-the-issues/multi-tier-system-of-supports-response-to-intervention/

Jackson, V. (2002). In our own voice: African-American stories of oppression, survival and recovery in mental health systems. *International Journal of Narrative Therapy and Community Work*, *2002*(2), 11–31.

James, R. K., & Gilliland, B. E. (2017). *Crisis intervention strategies*. Cengage Learning.

Jaycox, L. H., Langley, A. K., & Hoover, S. A. (2018). *Cognitive behavioral intervention for trauma in schools (CBITS)* (2nd ed.). RAND Corporation. https://www.rand.org/pubs/tools/TL272.html

Jaycox, L. H., Langley, A. K., Stein, B. D., Wong, M., Sharma, P., Scott, M., & Schonlau, M. (2009). Support for students exposed to trauma: A pilot study. *School Mental Health, 1*(2), 49–60. https://doi.org/10.1007/s12310-009-9007-8

Jenkins, C. D., Laux, J. M., Ritchie, M. H., & Tucker-Gail, K. (2014). Animal-assisted therapy and roger's core components among middle school students receiving counseling services: A descriptive study. *Journal of Creativity in Mental Health, 9*(2), 174–187. doi:10.1080/15401383.2014.899939

Jensen, K. L. (2001). The effects of selected classical music on self-disclosure. *Journal of Music Therapy, 38*(1), 2–27. https://doi.org/10.1093/jmt/38.1.2

Jeon, H. J., Park, J.-I., Fava, M., Mischoulon, D., Sohn, J. H., Seong, S., Park, J. E., Yoo, I., & Cho, M. J. (2014). Feelings of worthlessness, traumatic experience, and their comorbidity in relation to lifetime suicide attempt in community adults with major depressive disorder. *Journal of Affective Disorders, 166*, 206–212. doi:10.1016/j.jad.2014.05.010 PMID:25012433

Johnson, S. (2021a). *California directs districts to offer remote independent study this fall.* EdSource. https://edsource.org/2021/california-directs-districts-to-offer-remote-independent-study-this-fall/657578

Johnson, S. (2021b). *California schools move ahead with fall distance learning plans despite limitations.* EdSource. https://edsource.org/2021/california-schools-move-ahead-with-fall-distance-learning-plans-despite-limitations/655901

Johnson, R. C. (2009). Ever-increasing levels of parental incarceration and the consequences for children. In S. Raphael & M. Stoll (Eds.), *Do prisons make us safer? The benefits and costs of the prison boom* (pp. 177–206). Russell Sage Foundation.

Johnson, T. (2012). Mapping the critical service needs of adolescent children of prisoners. *Social Work in Public Health, 27*(1-2), 45–68. https://doi.org/10.1080/19371918.2012.629905

K–12 Student Digital Divide Much Larger Than Previously Estimated and Affects Teachers, Too, New Analysis Shows | Common Sense Media. (2020). https://www.commonsensemedia.org/about-us/news/press-releases/k-12-student-digital-divide-much-larger-than-previously-estimated-and

Kamenetz, A. (2015, September 28). *Who are the 'gifted and talented' and what do they need?* NPR. Retrieved April 18, 2022, from https://www.npr.org/sections/ed/2015/09/28/443193523/who-are-the-gifted-and-talented-and-what-do-they-need

Kang, E. (2020, March 31). Asian Americans feel the bite of prejudice during the COVID-19 pandemic. *NPR WBEZ Chicago.* https://www.npr.org/local/309/2020/03/31/824397216/asian-americansfeel-the-bite-of-prejudice-during-the-c-o-v-i-d-19-pandemic

Kang, K. T., & Jain, N. (2020). Child abuse and neglect in the COVID-19 era: A primer for front-line physicians in British Columbia. *BC Medical Journal, 62*, 238–240.

Kaplow, J. B., Rolon-Arroyo, B., Layne, C. M., Rooney, E., Oosterhoff, B., Hill, R., Steinberg, A. M., Lotterman, J., Gallagher, K. A. S., & Pynoos, R. S. (2020). Validation of the UCLA PTSD Reaction Index for *DSM*-5: A developmentally informed assessment tool for youth. *Journal of the American Academy of Child and Adolescent Psychiatry*, *59*(1), 186–194. doi:10.1016/j.jaac.2018.10.019 PMID:30953734

Kautz, S. V. (2017). Adolescent adaptation to parental incarceration. *Child & Adolescent Social Work Journal*, *34*(6), 557–572. https://doi.org/10.1007/s10560-017-0493-5

Kavanaugh, B. C., Dupont-Frechette, J. A., Jerskey, B. A., & Holler, K. A. (2016). Neurocognitive deficits in children and adolescents following maltreatment: Neurodevelopmental consequences and neuropsychological implications of traumatic stress. *Applied Neuropsychology. Child*, *6*(1), 64–78. doi:10.1080/21622965.2015.1079712 PMID:27050166

Kesner, J. E. (2005). Gifted Children's Relationships with Teachers. *International Education Journal*, *6*(2), 218–223.

Kiang, L., & Bhattacharjee, K. (2016). A narrative-linguistic approach to understanding Asian American adolescents' discrimination experiences. *Asian American Journal of Psychology*, *7*(1), 41–51. doi:10.1037/aap0000036

Kilgus, S. P., Eklund, K., von der Embse, N. P., Taylor, C. N., & Sims, W. A. (2016). Psychometric defensibility of the Social, Academic, and Emotional Behavior Risk Screener (SAEBRS) Teacher Rating Scale and multiple gating procedure within elementary and middle school samples. *Journal of School Psychology*, *58*, 21–39. doi:10.1016/j.jsp.2016.07.001 PMID:27586068

Kim, N., & Lambie, G. W. (2018). Burnout and implications for professional school counselors. *The Professional Counselor*, *8*(3), 277–294. Advance online publication. doi:10.15241/nk.8.3.277

Kinsler, J. (2011). Understanding the Black–White school discipline gap. *Economics of Education Review*, *30*(6), 1370–1383. doi:10.1016/j.econedurev.2011.07.004

Klest, B. (2012). Childhood trauma, poverty, and adult victimization. *Psychological Trauma: Theory, Research, Practice, and Policy*, *4*(3), 245–251. doi:10.1037/a0024468

Koeller, J. R., & Bertel, J. M. (2006). Responding to today's mental health needs of children, families and schools: Revisiting the preservice training and preparation of school-based personnel. *Education & Treatment of Children*, *29*(2), 197–217.

Kolek, T. (2020, October 22). *6 Ethical Considerations for Virtual School Counseling: Region 13's Blog*. Region 13'S Blog. https://blog.esc13.net/6-ethical-considerations-for-virtual-school-counseling/

Kovler, M. L., Ziegfeld, S., Ryan, L. M., Goldstein, M. A., Gardner, R., Garcia, A. V., & Nasr, I. W. (2021). Increased proportion of physical child abuse injuries at a level I pediatric trauma center during the Covid-19 pandemic. *Child Abuse & Neglect*, *116*(2), 104756. Advance online publication. doi:10.1016/j.chiabu.2020.104756 PMID:33004213

Kozlowska, K., & Hanney, L. (2001). An art therapy group for children traumatized by parental violence and separation. *Clinical Child Psychology and Psychiatry*, *6*(1), 49–78. https://doi.org/10.1177/1359104501006001006

Kozma, R. B. (2001). Counterpoint theory of 'learning with media. In R. E. Clark (Ed.), *Learning from media: Arguments, analysis, and evidence* (pp. 137–178). Information Age Publishing Inc.

Kruger, K. A., & Serpell, J. A. (2010). Animal-assisted interventions in mental health: definitions and theoretical foundations. In Handbook on Animal-Assisted Therapy (3rd ed.). Academic Press

Laakso, J., & Nygaard, J. (2012). Children of incarcerated parents: How a mentoring program can make a difference. *Social Work in Public Health*, *27*(1-2), 12–28. https://doi.org/10.1080/19371918.2012.629892

LaMorte, W. (2019). *Behavioral change models. The Transtheoretical Model (Stages of Change).* Retrieved November 12, 2021, from https://sphweb.bumc.bu.edu/otlt/MPHModules/SB/BehavioralChangeTheories/BehavioralChangeTheories6.html

Lane, J. J., Bohner, G. L., Hinck, A. M., & Kircher, R. L. (2020). Current administrative perceptions of school counselors: Kansas' administrators' perceptions of school counselor duties. *Journal of School Counseling*, *18*(2). http:/www.jsc.montana.edu/articles/v18n2.pdf

Langley, A. K., Gonzalez, A., Sugar, C. A., Solis, D., & Jaycox, L. (2015). Bounce back: Effectiveness of an elementary school-based intervention for multicultural children exposed to traumatic events. *Journal of Consulting and Clinical Psychology*, *83*(5), 853–865. https://doi.org/10.1037/ccp0000051

Lansford, J. E., Dodge, K. A., Pettit, G. S., Bates, J. E., Crozier, J., & Kaplow, J. (2002). A 12-year prospective study of the long-term effects of early child physical maltreatment on psychological, behavioral, and academic problems in adolescence. *Archives of Pediatrics & Adolescent Medicine*, *156*(8), 824–830. doi:10.1001/archpedi.156.8.824 PMID:12144375

Lawrence, J. A. (2014). Managing dissonance: Implications for therapeutic practice with partner violence. *Partner Abuse*, *5*(2), 119–151. doi:10.1891/1946-6560.5.2.119

Lawson, M., Piel, M. H., & Simon, M. (2020). Child maltreatment during the COVID-19 pandemic: Consequences of parental job loss on psychological and physical abuse towards children. *Child Abuse & Neglect*, *110*, 1–11. doi:10.1016/j.chiabu.2020.104709 PMID:32893003

Learning for Justice. (2021). *Teaching 'The New Jim Crow.'* https://www.learningforjustice.org/magazine/publications/teaching-the-new-jim-crow

Lee, E. (2015). *The making of Asian American: A history*. Simon & Schuster Paperbacks.

Lee, R. D., Fang, X., & Luo, F. (2013). The impact of parental incarceration on the physical and mental health of young adults. *Pediatrics*, *131*, e1188–e1195. https://doi.org/10.1542/peds.2012-0627

Lee, S. A. (2020). Coronavirus Anxiety Scale: A brief mental health screener for COVID-19 related anxiety. *Death Studies*, *44*(7), 393–401. doi:10.1080/07481187.2020.1748481 PMID:32299304

Lee, S., & Waters, S. F. (2021). Asians and Asian Americans' experiences of racial discrimination during the COVID-19 pandemic: Impacts on health outcomes and the buffering role of social support. *Stigma and Health*, *6*(1), 70–78. doi:10.1037ah0000275 PMID:35369673

Lemberger, M., Selig, J., Bowers, H., & Rogers, J. (2015). Effects of the student success skills program on the executive functioning skills, feelings of connectedness, and academic achievement in a predominantly Hispanic, low-income middle school district. *Journal of Counseling and Development*, *93*(1), 25–36. https://doi.org/10.1002/j.1556-6676.2015.00178.x

Leuwerke, W. C., Walker, J., & Shi, Q. (2009). Informing principals: The impact of different types of information on principals' perceptions of professional school counselors. *Professional School Counseling*, *12*(4), 263–271. Advance online publication. doi:10.5330/PSC.n.2010-12.263

Levine, P. A. (2001). *In an Unspoken Voice: How the Body Releases Trauma and Restores Goodness*. Routledge.

Levinson, B. M. (1969). *Pet-oriented child psychotherapy*. Charles C. Thomas, Publisher, Ltd.

Link, B., & Phelan, J. (2001). Conceptualizing stigma. *Annual Review of Sociology*, *27*(1), 363–385. doi:10.1146/annurev.soc.27.1.363

Lipscombe, K., Buckley-Walker, K., & McNamara, P. (2020). Understanding collaborative teacher teams as open systems for professional development. *Professional Development in Education*, *46*(3), 37–3390. doi:10.1080/19415257.2019.1613256

Litam, S. D. A. (2020). "Take your kung-flu back to Wuhan": Counseling Asians, Asian Americans, and Pacific Islanders with race-based trauma related to COVID-19. *The Professional Counselor*, *10*(2), 144–156. doi:10.15241dal.10.2.144

Litam, S. D. A., & Oh, S. (2020). Ethnic identity and coping strategies as moderators of COVID-19 racial discrimination experiences among Chinese Americans. *Counseling Outcome Research and Evaluation*, 1–15. Advance online publication. doi:10.1080/21501378.2020.1814138

Liu, S. R., & Modir, S. (2020). The outbreak that way always here: Racial trauma in the context of COVID-19 and implications for mental health providers. *Psychological Trauma: Theory, Research, Practice, and Policy*, *12*(5), 439–442. doi:10.1037/tra0000784 PMID:32551756

Li, Y., & Nicholson, H. L. Jr. (2021). When "model minorities" become "yellow peril"—Othering and the racialization of Asian Americans in the COVID-19 pandemic. *Sociology Compass*, *15*(2). Advance online publication. doi:10.1111oc4.12849 PMID:33786062

Lloyd, T. S. (2019). Teaching students of incarcerated parents. *American Educator*, *43*(2), 24–28. https://www.aft.org/ae/summer2019/lloyd

Long, C. (2020). *One-Quarter of U.S. Students Do not Have What They Need for Online Learning*. https://www.nea.org/advocating-for-change/new-from-nea/one-quarter-us-students-dont-have-what-they-need-online-learning

Lopez, C., & Bhatt, C. S. (2007). Supporting students with incarcerated parents in schools: A group intervention. *Journal for Specialists in Group Work, 32*(2), 139–153. https://doi.org/10.1080/01933920701227125

Lowe, S. R., Tineo, P., & Young, M. N. (2019). Perceived Discrimination and Major Depression and Generalized Anxiety Symptoms: In Muslim American College Students. *Journal of Religion and Health, 58*(4), 1136–1145. doi:10.100710943-018-0684-1 PMID:30094677

Luken, A., Nair, R., & Fix, R. L. (2021). On racial disparities in child abuse reports: Exploratory mapping the 2018 NCANDS. *Child Maltreatment, 26*(3), 267–281. doi:10.1177/10775595211001926 PMID:33729016

Luther, K. (2015). Examining social support among adult children of incarcerated parents. *Family Relations, 64*(4), 505–518. https://www.jstor.org/stable/43695516

Mann, S. (2019, January). *Critical incident response training* [Workshop]. East Central Bexar County Regional Crisis Team Cluster Training, San Antonio, TX.

Marrow, S. (2009) *A survey of school counselor attitudes regarding animal-assisted interventions* [Master's Thesis]. University of New Hampshire.

Mart, A., Weissberg, R., & Kendziora, K. (2015). Systematic support for SEL in school districts. In J. A. Durlak, C. E. Domitrovich, R. P. Weissberg, & T. P. Gullotta (Eds.), *Handbook of social and emotional learning: Research and practice* (pp. 482–499). The Guilford Press.

Martinez, R. R., Gavin Williams, R., & Green, J. (2020). The role of school counselors delivering a trauma-informed care approach to supporting youth in foster care. *Professional School Counseling, 23*(1), 2156759.

Martin, S. L., Ashley, O. S., White, L., Axelson, S., Clark, M., & Burrus, B. (2017). Incorporating trauma-informed care into school-based programs. *The Journal of School Health, 87*(12), 958–967. doi:10.1111/josh.12568 PMID:29096416

Marzano, R. (2015). Using formative assessment with SEL skills. In J. A. Durlak, C. E. Domitrovich, R. P. Weissberg, & T. P. Gullotta (Eds.), *Handbook of social and emotional learning: Research and practice* (pp. 336–347). The Guilford Press.

Mason, E., Robertson, A., Gay, J., Clarke, N., & Holcomb-McCoy, C. (2021). Antiracist school counselor preparation: Expanding on the five tenets of the transforming school counseling initiative. *Teaching and Supervision in Counseling, 3*(2), 3-14. https://trace.tennessee.edu/tsc/vol13/iss2/2Mentalhealth

Maxwell, J. A. (2013). *Qualitative research design: An interactive approach* (3rd ed.). Sage.

McInerney, M., & McKlindon, A. (2014). *Unlocking the door to learning: Trauma-informed classrooms & transformational schools*. Education Law Center. https://www.elc-pa.org/wp-content/uploads/2015/06/Trauma-Informed-in-Schools-Classrooms-FINAL-December2014-2.pdf

Mears, D., & Siennick, S. (2016). Young adult outcomes and the life-course penalties of parental incarceration. *Journal of Research in Crime and Delinquency*, *53*(1), 3–35. doi:10.1177/0022427815592452

Merikangas, K. R., He, J. P., Burstein, M., Swanson, S. A., Avenevoli, S., Cui, L., Benjet, C., Georgiades, K., & Swendsen, J. (2010). Lifetime prevalence of mental disorders in US adolescents: Results from the National Comorbidity Survey Replication–Adolescent Supplement (NCS-A). *Journal of the American Academy of Child and Adolescent Psychiatry*, *49*(10), 980–989. doi:10.1016/j.jaac.2010.05.017 PMID:20855043

Miles, M. B., Huberman, A. M., & Saldana, J. (2014). *Qualitative data analysis: A methods sourcebook*. Sage.

Miller, E. (2019). Trauma-informed approaches to adolescent relationship abuse and sexual violence prevention. *Pediatric Annals*, *48*(7), e274–e279. doi:10.3928/19382359-20190617-01 PMID:31305945

Mistry, J., & Wu, J. (2010). Navigating cultural worlds and negotiating identities: A conceptual model. *Human Development*, *53*(1), 5–25. doi:10.1159/000268136

Mitchell, J. (n.d.a). *Crisis incident stress debriefing*. Info-Trauma.Org/En/e-Library. http://www.info-trauma.org/flash/media-f/mitchellCriticalIncidentStressDebriefing.pdf

Mitchell, J. (n.d.b). *Crisis incident stress management*. Info-Trauma.Org/En/e-Library. http://www.info-trauma.org/flash/media-e/mtichellCriticalIncidentStressManagement.pdf

Monroy-Fraustro, D., Maldonado-Castellanos, I., Aboites-Molina, M., Rodríguez, S., Sueiras, P., Altamirano-Bustamante, N. F., de Hoyos-Bermea, A., & Altamirano-Bustamante, M. M. (2021). Bibliotherapy as a Non-pharmaceutical Intervention to Enhance Mental Health in Response to the COVID-19 Pandemic: A Mixed-Methods Systematic Review and Bioethical Meta-Analysis. *Frontiers in Public Health*, *9*, 629872. Advance online publication. doi:10.3389/fpubh.2021.629872 PMID:33796496

Moorhead, H. H., & Zoldan, C. A. (2019). Trauma- and stressor-related disorders. In V. E. Kress & M. J. Paylo (Eds.), *Treating those with mental disorders: A comprehensive approach to case conceptualization and treatment* (2nd ed., pp. 209–238). Pearson.

Morgan, E., Salomon, N., Plotkin, M., & Cohen, R. (2014). *The school discipline consensus report: Strategies for the field to keep students engaged in school and out of the juvenile justice system*. The Council of State Governments Justice Center.

Morton, B. M., & Berardi, A. A. (2018). Trauma-informed school programing: Applications for mental health professionals and educator partnerships. *Journal of Child & Adolescent Trauma*, *11*(4), 487–493. doi:10.100740653-017-0160-1 PMID:32318170

Moses, M. (2010). Children of the incarcerated must be studied and responded to comprehensively. *Corrections Today*, *72*(3), 58–60.

Moustakas, C. E. (1994). *Phenomenological research methods*. Sage. doi:10.4135/9781412995658

Mula, K., Janus, P., & Palomar, D. (2022). *Gifted children and social relationships*. Afg Guidance Center. Retrieved April 20, 2022, from https://afgfamily.com/blog/gifted-children/gifted-children-and-social-relationships/

Mullen, P. R., & Gutierrez, D. (2016). Burnout, stress, and direct student services among school counselors. *The Professional Counselor*, *6*(4), 344–359. doi:10.15241/pm.6.4.344

Murphey, D., & Cooper, P. M. (2015). *Parents behind bars: What happens to their children*. Child Trends. http://www.childtrends.org/wp-content/uploads/2015/10/2015-42ParentsBehindBars.pdf

Murray, J., & Farrington, D. P. (2005). Parental imprisonment: Effects on boys' antisocial behavior and delinquency through the life-course. *Journal of Child Psychology and Psychiatry, and Allied Disciplines*, *46*(12), 1269–1278. doi:10.1111/j.1469-7610.2005.01433.x PMID:16313427

Murray, J., Farrington, D., & Sekol, I. (2012). Children's antisocial behavior, mental health, drug use, and educational performance after parental incarceration: A systemic review and meta-analysis. *Psychological Bulletin*, *138*(2), 175–210. doi:10.1037/a0026407 PMID:22229730

Murray, J., & Murray, L. (2010). Parental incarceration, attachment and child psychopathology. *Attachment & Human Development*, *12*(4), 289–309. doi:10.1080/14751790903416889 PMID:20582842

Mutt-i-Gress Social-Emotional Program. (n.d.). *The Mutt-i-Gress Curriculum*. https://education.muttigrees.org/

Nash, J. (2017, November 8). *Emotional hijacking: How connecting to old hurts heals us*. Therapy Blog. Retrieved April 18, 2022, from https://www.goodtherapy.org/blog/emotional-hijacking-how-connecting-to-old-hurts-heals-us-1022155

National Center for Education Statistics. (2019). *Student reports of bullying: Results from the 2017 school crime supplement to the national crime victimization survey*. https://nces.ed.gov/pubs2019/2019054.pdf

National Center for Homeless Education. (2018). *Enrolling Children and Youth Experiencing Homelessness in School*. Author.

National Center for Homeless Education. (2021). *Student Homelessness in America: School Years 2017-18 to 2019-20*. Author.

National Child Traumatic Stress Network. (2008). *Child trauma toolkit for educators*. https://www.nctsn.org/resources/child-trauma-toolkit-educators

National Child Traumatic Stress Network. (2017). *Creating, supporting, and sustaining trauma-informed schools: A system framework.* https://www.nctsn.org/resources/creating-supporting-and-sustaining-trauma-informed-schools-system-framework

National Education Association. (2018). *NEA's school crisis guide*. https://www.nea.org/resource-library/neas-school-crisis-guide

National Education Association. (2020). *NEA Policy Statement on Digital Learning*. https://www.nea.org/advocating-for-change/new-from-nea/nea-policy-statement-digital-learning

National Education Association. (2020). *The Digital Divide and Homework Gap in Your State.* NEA. Nea.org. https://www.nea.org/resource-library/digital-divide-and-homework-gap-your-state

National Education Policy Center. (2019). *Virtual Schools in the U.S. in 2019*. http://nepc.colorado.edu/publication/virtual-schools-annual-2019

National Institute of Environmental Health Science. (n.d.). *Pet Allergens*. https://www.niehs.nih.gov/health/topics/agents/allergens/pets/index.cfm

National Policy Board for Educational Administration. (2015). *Professional standards for educational leaders*. Author.

National Resource Center on Children and Families of the Incarcerated. (2016). *Children of prisoners' library*. http://wwwfcnetwork.org/cpl/cpindex.html

National Society for the Prevention of Cruelty to Children. (n.d.a). *Signs of emotional abuse*. https://www.nspcc.org.uk/what-is-child-abuse/types-of-abuse/emotional-abuse/

National Society for the Prevention of Cruelty to Children. (n.d.b). *Signs of physical abuse*. https://www.nspcc.org.uk/what-is-child-abuse/types-of-abuse/physical-abuse/

National Society for the Prevention of Cruelty to Children. (n.d.c). *Signs of neglect*. https://www.nspcc.org.uk/what-is-child-abuse/types-of-abuse/neglect/

National Society for the Prevention of Cruelty to Children. (n.d.d). *Signs of sexual abuse*. https://www.nspcc.org.uk/what-is-child-abuse/types-of-abuse/child-sexual-abuse/

Nebbe, L. L. (1991). The human-animal bond and the elementary school counselor. *The School Counselor*, *38*, 362-371. http://www.jstor.org/ stable/23900728

Nelson, J. A., Robles-Pina, R., & Nichter, M. (2008). An analysis of Texas high school counselors' role: Actual and preferred counseling activities. *Journal of Professional Counseling, Practice, Theory, & Research*, *36*(1), 30–46. doi:10.1080/15566382.2008.12033842

Nesmith, A., & Ruhland, E. (2008). Children of incarcerated parents: Challenges and resiliency, in their own words. *Children and Youth Services Review*, *30*(10), 1119–1130. https://doi.org/10.1016/j.childyouth.2008.02.006

New Analysis Shows Students of Color Far More Likely to Be Cut off from Online Learning. (2020). *Alliance for Excellent Education*. https://all4ed.org/press/new-analysis-shows-students-of-color-far-more-likely-to-be-cut-off-from-online-learning/

Nichols, E., & Loper, A. (2012). Incarceration in the household: Academic outcomes of adolescents with an incarcerated household member. *Journal of Youth and Adolescence*, *41*(11), 1455–1471. doi:10.100710964-012-9780-9 PMID:22714743

Nichols, E., Loper, A., & Meyer, J. (2016). Promoting educational resiliency in youth with incarcerated parents: The impact of parental incarceration, school characteristics, and connectedness on school outcomes. *Journal of Youth and Adolescence*, *45*(6), 1090–1109. doi:10.100710964-015-0337-6 PMID:26259843

Nieforth, L. O., & O'Haire, M. E. (2020). The role of pets in managing uncertainty from covid-19, *Psychological Rauma: Theory, Research, Practices, and Policy*, *12*(1), S245-S246. doi:10.1037/tra0000678

Niwa, E. Y., Way, N., & Hughes, D. L. (2014). Trajectories of ethnic-racial discrimination among ethnically diverse early adolescents: Associations with psychological and social adjustment. *Child Development*, *85*, 2339–2354. doi:10.1111/cdev.12310 PMID:25345480

Northouse, P. (2019). *Leadership: Theory and practice* (8th ed.). SAGE Publications.

North, R. (2017). *Motivational interviewing for school counselors*. Author.

O'Haire, M. E., McKenzie, S. J., McCune, S., & Slaughter, V. (2013). Effects of animal-assisted activities with guinea pigs in the primary school classroom. *Anthroos*, *26*(3), 445-458, http://dx.doi.org.ezp.waldenulibrary.org/10.2752/175303713X13697429463835

Oakes, W. P., Lane, K. L., Cox, M. L., & Messenger, M. (2014). Logistics of behavior screenings: How and why do we conduct behavior screenings at our school. *Preventing School Failure*, *58*(3), 159–170. doi:10.1080/1045988X.2014.895572

Oh, A. E. (2009). An issue of time and place: The truth behind Korean Americans' connection to the 1992 Los Angeles riots. *Asian American Policy Review*, *19*, 39–48.

Okazaki, S., Shea, M., Thakore-Dunlap, U., & Wang, C. (2020). *Bullying prevention, intervention, and resource guide for parents*. Asian American Psychological Association. https://aapaonline.org/resources/bullying-awareness-campaign/

Okonofua, J. A., Walton, G. M., & Eberhardt, J. L. (2016). A vicious cycle: A social–psychological account of extreme racial disparities in school discipline. *Perspectives on Psychological Science*, *11*(3), 381–398. doi:10.1177/1745691616635592 PMID:27217251

Oloumi-Johnson, R. (2016). *The lived experiences of middle school counselors in reporting abuse and neglect to Child Protective Services: A phenomenological study* (Publication No. 10307713) [Doctoral dissertation, Sam Houston State University]. ProQuest Dissertations and Theses Global.

Olsen, J., Parikh-Foxx, S., Flowers, C., & Algozzine, B. (2016). An examination of factors that relate to school counselors' knowledge and skills in multi-tiered systems of support. *Professional School Counseling, 20*(1), 159–171. doi:10.5330/1096-2409-20.1.159

Online Schools Are Here to Stay, Even After the Pandemic. (2021). *The New York Times*. https://www.nytimes.com/2021/04/11/technology/remote-learning-online-school.html

Osborn, D. S., Peterson, G. W., & Hale, R. R. (2014). Virtual School Counseling. *Professional School Counseling, 18*(1). https://doi.org/ doi:10.1177/2156759x0001800114

Osburne Association. (2018). *A call to action: Safeguarding New York's children with incarcerated parents*. https://www.osborneny.org/programs-down/strengthening-communities/new-york-initiative-for-children-of-incarcerated-parents/a-call-to-action/

Osher, D. (2018). *Trauma and Learning Policy Initiative (TLPI): Trauma-sensitive schools descriptive study*. American Institute for Research. https://traumasensitiveschools. org/wp-content/uploads/2019/02/TLPI-Final-Report_Full-Report-002-2-1. pdf

Oyserman, D., & Sakamoto, I. (1997). Being Asian American: Identity, cultural constructs, and stereotype perception. *The Journal of Applied Behavioral Science, 33*(4), 435–453. doi:10.1177/0021886397334002

Padden, J. V. (2021). *Urban trauma: Mental health clinicians' perception of trauma informed care, trauma responsive practice, and trauma resilience* [Doctoral dissertation, Morgan State University]. ProQuest Dissertations and Theses Global.

Palestrini, C., Calcaterra, V., Cannas, S., Talamonti, Z., Papotti, F., Buttram, D., & Pelizzo, G. (2016). Stress level evaluation in a dog during animal-assisted therapy in pediatric surgery. *Journal of Veterinary Behavior, 17*, 44–49. https://dx.doi.org/10.1016/j.jveb.2016.09.003

Palmer, E. L., & Carr, K. (1991). Dr. rogers, meet mr. rogers: The similarities between carl and fred rogers. *Social Behavior and Personality, 19*(1), 39–44.

Pandey, E. (2021, September 22). *Charter schools boomed during the pandemic*. NewsBreak; Axios. https://www.newsbreak.com/news/2380033548629/charter-schools-boomed-during-the-pandemic

Pape, S. J., & Prosser, S. K. (2018). Barriers to technology implementation in community college mathematics classrooms. *Journal of Computing in Higher Education, 30*(3), 620–636. doi:10.100712528-018-9195-z

Parachin, V. M. (1996). Medicine for the mind. *American Fitness, 14*(3), 64–65.

Parish-Plass, N. (2020) Animal-assisted psychotherapy for developmental trauma through the lens of interpersonal neurobiology of trauma: Creating connection with self and others. *Journal of Psychotherapy Integration, 31*(3), 302-325. doi:10.1037/int0000253

Parish-Plass, N. (2013). *Animal-assisted psychotherapy: theory, issues, and practice*. Perdue University Press.

Parritz, R. H., & Troy, M. F. (2018). *Disorders of childhood development and psychopathology*. Cengage Learning.

Parzych, J., Donohue, P., Gaesser, A., & Chiu, M. M. (2019). *Measuring the Impact of School Counselor Ratios on Student Outcomes*. ASCA Research Report. https://www.schoolcounselor.org/getmedia/5157ef82-d2e8-4b4d-8659-a957f14b7875/Ratios-Student-Outcomes-Research-Report.pdf

Patti, J., Senge, P., Madrazo, C., & Stern, R. (2015). Developing socially, emotionally, and cognitively competent school leaders and learning communities. In J. A. Durlak, C. E. Domitrovich, R. P. Weissberg, & T. P. Gullotta (Eds.), *Handbook of social and emotional learning: Research and practice* (pp. 438–452). The Guilford Press.

Paykamian, B. (2021, March 24). *Virtual Schools to Be Increasingly Common After COVID-19*. GovTech. https://www.govtech.com/education/k-12/virtual-schools-to-be-increasingly-common-after-covid-19.html

Pehrsson, D. E., & McMillen, P. (2007). *Bibliotherapy: Overview and implications for counselors (ACAPCD-02)*. American Counseling Association.

Perfect, M. M., Turley, M. R., Carlson, J. S., Yohanna, J., & Saint Gilles, M. P. (2016). School-related outcomes of traumatic event exposure and traumatic stress symptoms in students: A systematic review of research from 1990 to 2015. *School Mental Health*, *8*(1), 7–43. doi:10.100712310-016-9175-2

Perry, B. D. (2002). Childhood experience and the expression of genetic potential: What childhood neglect tells us about nature and nurture. *Brain and Mind: A Transdisciplinary Journal of Neuroscience and Neurophilosophy*, *3*(2), 79-100.

Perry, B. D. (2000). Traumatized children: How childhood trauma influences brain development. *The Journal of the California Alliance for the Mentally Ill*, *11*(1), 48–51.

Perry, D. L., & Daniels, M. L. (2016). Implementing trauma-informed practices in the school setting: A pilot study. *School Mental Health*, *8*(1), 177–188. doi:10.100712310-016-9182-3

Person, B., Sy, F., Holton, K., Govert, B., Liang, A., Garza, B., Gould, D., Hickson, M., McDonald, M., Meijer, C., Smith, J., Veto, L., Williams, W., & Zauderer, L. (2004). Fear and stigma: The epidemic within the SARS outbreak. *Emerging Infectious Diseases*, *10*(2), 358–363. doi:10.3201/eid1002.030750 PMID:15030713

Pérusse, R., Goodnough, G. E., Donegan, J., & Jones, C. (2004). Perceptions of school counselors and school principals about the National Standards for school counseling programs and the Transforming School Counseling Initiative. *Professional School Counseling*, *7*(3), 152–161.

Petersen, A., Joseph, J., & Feit, M. (Eds.). (2013). *New directions in child abuse and neglect research*. National Academies Press.

Petersilia, J. (2005). From cell to society: Who is returning home? In J. Travis & C. Visher (Eds.), *Prisoner reentry and crime in America* (pp. 15–49). Cambridge University Press. doi:10.1017/CBO9780511813580.002

Peterson, J. S. (2006). Addressing counseling needs of gifted students. *Professional School Counseling, 10*(1), 43–51. doi:10.5330/prsc.10.1.b76h32717q632tqn

Peterson, J. S. (2014). Giftedness, trauma, and development: A qualitative, longitudinal case study. *Journal for the Education of the Gifted, 37*(4), 295–318. doi:10.1177/0162353214552564

Peterson, J. S. (2015). School counselors and gifted kids: Respecting both cognitive and affective. *Journal of Counseling and Development, 93*(2), 153–162. doi:10.1002/j.1556-6676.2015.00191.x

Peterson, J. S., & Morris, C. W. (2010). Preparing school counselors to address concerns related to giftedness: A study of accredited counselor preparation programs. *Journal for the Education of the Gifted, 33*(3), 311–336. doi:10.1177/016235321003300302

Peterson, J. S., & Ray, K. E. (2006). Bullying and the gifted: Victims, perpetrators, prevalence, and effects. *Gifted Child Quarterly, 50*(2), 148–168. doi:10.1177/001698620605000206

Pieterse, A. L., Carter, R. T., Evans, S. A., & Walter, R. A. (2010). An exploratory examination of the associations among racial and ethnic discrimination, racial climate, and trauma-related symptoms in a college student population. *Journal of Counseling Psychology, 57*(3), 255–263. doi:10.1037/a0020040 PMID:21133577

Pincus, R., Hannor-Walker, T., Wright, L., & Justice, J. (2020). COVID-19's Effect on students: How school counselors rise to the rescue. *NASSP Bulletin, 104*(4), 241–256. doi:10.1177/0192636520975866

Platt, M., & Freyd, J. (2012). Trauma and negative underlying assumptions in feelings of shame: An exploratory study. *Psychological Trauma: Theory, Research, Practice, and Policy, 4*(4), 370–378. doi:10.1037/a0024253

Poehlmann, J. (2005). Children of incarcerated mothers: Representations of attachment relationships in children of incarcerated mothers. *Journal of Child Development, 76*(3), 679–696. doi:10.1111/j.1467-8624.2005.00871.x PMID:15892786

Porche, M. V., Costello, D. M., & Rosen-Reynoso, M. (2016). Adverse family experiences, child mental health, and educational outcomes for a national sample of students. *School Mental Health, 8*(1), 44–60. doi:10.100712310-016-9174-3

Porges, S. (2001). The polyvagal theory: Phylogenetic substrates of a social nervous system. *International Journal of Psychophysiology, 42*(2), 123–146. https://doi.org/10.1016/S0167-8760(01)00162-3

Ports, K. A., Ford, D. C., & Merrick, M. T. (2016). Adverse childhood experiences and sexual victimization in adulthood. *Child Abuse & Neglect, 51*, 313–322. doi:10.1016/j.chiabu.2015.08.017 PMID:26386753

Powers-Costello, B., & Swick, K. J. (2011). Transforming teacher constructs of children and families who are homeless. *Early Childhood Education Journal, 39*(3), 207–212. doi:10.100710643-011-0455-z

Preuss, L. J., & Dubrow, E. F. (2004). A comparison between intellectually gifted and typical children in their coping responses to a school and a peer stressor. *Roeper Review, 26*(2), 105–111. doi:10.1080/02783190409554250

Protecting Student Privacy While Using Online Educational Services: Model Terms of Service. Protecting Student Privacy. (2016). https://studentprivacy.ed.gov/resources/protecting-student-privacy-while-using-online-educational-services-model-terms-service

Prout, H. T., & Brown, D. T. (2012). *Counseling and psychotherapy with children and adolescents theory and practice for school and clinical settings*. Wiley.

Rangaswamy, P. (2000). *Namaste America: Indian immigrants in an American metropolis*. Pennsylvania State University Press.

Rawson, S. (2020b). Trauma-Sensitive Schools: Reframing the "Why" Not the "How". In Applying Trauma-Sensitive Practices in School Counseling (pp. 61-76). Routledge.

Rawson, S. (2020a). *Applying Trauma-sensitive Practices in School Counseling: Interventions for Achieving Change*. Routledge.

Razi, A., & Dechillo, N. (2005). High schools respond to crises. *Journal of School Violence, 4*(2), 115–131. doi:10.1300/J202v04n02_07

Read, J., Hammersley, P., & Rudegeair, T. (2007). Why, when and how to ask about childhood abuse. *Advances in Psychiatric Treatment, 13*(2), 101–110. doi:10.1192/apt.bp.106.002840

Redding, S., & Walberg, H. (2015). Indicators of effective SEL practice. In J. A. Durlak, C. E. Domitrovich, R. P. Weissberg, & T. P. Gullotta (Eds.), *Handbook of social and emotional learning: Research and practice* (pp. 37–392). The Guilford Press.

Reed, D., & Reed, E. (1997). Children of incarcerated parents. *Social Justice (San Francisco, Calif.), 24*(3), 152–169. https://www.jstor.org/stable/29767028

Reich, W. (n.d.). *Body Psychotherapy*. Retrieved from Good Therapy. https://www.goodtherapy.org/learn-about-therapy/types/body-psychotherapy

Reinbergs, E. J., & Fefer, S. A. (2018). Addressing trauma in schools: Multitiered service delivery options for practitioners. *Psychology in the Schools, 55*(3), 250–263. doi:10.1002/pits.22105

Reynolds, C. R., & Kamphaus, R. W. (2015). *Behavior Assessment Systems for Children* (3rd ed.). Pearson.

Rhoton, R. (2022, March 28). *Childhood trauma can alter reactivity to real or perceived threat*. Arizona Trauma Institute. Retrieved April 18, 2022, from https://aztrauma.org/childhood-trauma-can-alter-reactivity-real-perceived-threat/

Riddle, T., & Sinclair, S. (2019). Racial disparities in school-based disciplinary actions are associated with county-level rates of racial bias. *Proceedings of the National Academy of Sciences of the United States of America*, *116*(17), 8255–8260. doi:10.1073/pnas.1808307116 PMID:30940747

Rimm-Kaufman, S., & Hulleman, C. (2017). SEL in elementary school settings: identifying mechanisms that matter. In C. E. Domitrovich, R. P. Weissberg, & T. P. Gullotta (Eds.), *Handbook of Social Emotional Learning Research and Practice* (pp. 151–166). The Guilford Press.

Rinn, A. N., Reynolds, M. J., & McQueen, K. S. (2011). Perceived Social Support and the Self-Concepts of Gifted Adolescents. *Journal for the Education of the Gifted*, *34*(3), 367–396. doi:10.1177/016235321103400302

Roberts, J. L. (2004). Leadership is a "Must" for Children Who are Gifted and Talented. *Gifted Child Today*, *27*(1), 5–5. doi:10.1177/107621750402700101

Rogers, C. (1951). *Client-centered therapy: Its current practices, implications, and theory*. Houghton Mifflin.

Rogers, C. R. (1957). The necessary and sufficient conditions of therapeutic personality change. *Journal of Consulting Psychology*, *21*(2), 95–103. doi:10.1037/h0045357 PMID:13416422

Rolon-Arroyo, B., Oosterhoff, B., Layne, C. M., Steinberg, A. M., Pynoos, R. S., & Kaplow, J. B. (2020). The UCLA PTSD Reaction Index for *DSM*-5 Brief Form: A screening tool for trauma-exposed youths. *Journal of the American Academy of Child and Adolescent Psychiatry*, *59*(3), 434–443. doi:10.1016/j.jaac.2019.06.015 PMID:31376502

Rosenblatt, P. C. (2008). Recovery following bereavement: Metaphor, phenomenology, and culture. *Death Studies*, *32*(1), 6–16. doi:10.1080/07481180701741228 PMID:18646394

Rosenbloom, S. R., & Way, N. (2004). Experiences of Discrimination among African American, Asian American, and Latino Adolescents in an Urban High School. *Youth & Society*, *35*(4), 420–451. doi:10.1177/0044118X03261479

Rubenstein, B. Y., Toman, E. L., & Cochran, J. C. (2021). Socioeconomic barriers to child contact with incarcerated parents. *Justice Quarterly*, *38*(4), 725–751. https://doi.org/10.1080/07418825.2019.1606270

Ruiz, E. (2016). Trauma symptoms in a diverse population of sexually abused children. *Psychological Trauma: Theory, Research, Practice, and Policy*, *8*(6), 680–687. doi:10.1037/tra0000160 PMID:27243569

Rumsey, A. D., McCullough, R., & Chang, C. Y. (2020). Understanding the secondary exposure to trauma and professional quality of life of school counselors. *Professional School Counseling*, *24*(1), 1–11. https://doi.org/10.1177/2156759X20973643

Rumsey, A. D., & Milsom, A. (2019). Supporting school engagement and high school completion through trauma-informed school counseling. *Professional School Counseling*, *22*(1), 1–10. doi:10.1177/2156759X19867254

Sable, P. (2013). The pet connection: An attachment perspective. *Clinical Social Work Journal, 41*, 93–99. doi:10.100710615-012-0405-2

Safran, J. D., & Muran, J. C. (2000). *Negotiating the therapeutic alliance: A relational treatment guide*. The Guilford Press.

Sallin, J. H., & Eglinton, K. (2021, November 15). *Conversations on gifted trauma podcast*. InterGifted. Retrieved April 17, 2022, from https://intergifted.com/conversations-gifted-trauma/

Sanchez-Gomez, M., Giorgi, G., Finstad, G. L., Urbini, F., Foti, G., Mucci, N., Zaffina, S., & León-Perez, J. M. (2021). COVID-19 Pandemic as a Traumatic Event and Its Associations with Fear and Mental Health: A Cognitive-Activation Approach. *International Journal of Environmental Research and Public Health, 18*(14), 7422. doi:10.3390/ijerph18147422 PMID:34299873

Santiago, C. D., Raviv, T., & Jaycox, L. (2018). *Creating healing school communities: school-based interventions for students exposed to trauma*. American Psychological Association. doi:10.1037/0000072-000

Satori Learning. (2022). *Satori Alternatives to Managing Aggression (SAMA)*. https://satorilearning.com/courses/

Saunders, B. E., & Adams, Z. W. (2014). Epidemiology of traumatic experiences in childhood. *Child & Adolescent Psychiatric Clinics, 23*(2), 167–184. doi:10.1016/j.chc.2013.12.003 PMID:24656575

Sawyer, C., Peters, M. L., & Willis, J. (2013). Self-Efficacy of Beginning Counselors to Counsel Clients in Crisis. *The Journal of Counselor Preparation and Supervisor, 5*(2), 28–43. doi:10.7729/52.1015

Schaefer, C. E., & Drewes, A. A. (Eds.). (2014). *The therapeutic powers of play: 20 core agents of change* (2nd ed.). Wiley.

Schild, L., Ling, C., Blackburn, J., Stringhini, G., Zhang, Y., & Zannettou, S. (2020). "Go eat a bat, Chang!" An early look on the emergence of sinophobic behavior on web communities in the face of COVID-19. *Computers & Society*, 1–16. https://arxiv.org/pdf/2004.04046.pdf

Schonert-Reichl, K. A., Hanson-Peterson, J., & Hymel, S. (2017). SEL and preservice teachers. In C. E. Domitrovich, R. P. Weissberg, & T. P. Gullotta (Eds.), *Handbook of Social Emotional Learning Research and Practice* (pp. 406–421). The Guilford Press.

Schonfeld, D., & Newgass, S. (2003). *School crisis response initiative*. U.S. Department of Justice, Office of Justice Programs, Office for Victims of Crime. https://ovc.ojp.gov/sites/g/files/xyckuh226/files/publications/bulletins/schoolcrisis/ncj197832.pdf

Schonfeld, D. J., & Quackenbush, M. (2021). *The grieving student: A guide for schools* (2nd ed.). Brookes Publishing.

Schonfeld, D., Lichtenstein, R., Kline Pruett, M., & Speese-Linehan, D. (2002). *How to prepare for and respond to a crisis* (2nd ed.). Association for Supervision and Curriculum Development.

Schore, A. (2001). Effects of a secure attachment relationship on right brain development; Affect regulation and infant mental health. *Infant Mental Health Journal*, *22*(1-2), 7–66. doi:10.1002/1097-0355(200101/04)22:1<7::AID-IMHJ2>3.0.CO;2-N

Schwartz, D., & Gorman, A. (2003). Community violence exposure and children's academic functioning. *Journal of Educational Psychology*, *95*(1), 163–173. doi:10.1037/0022-0663.95.1.163

Scott, E. (2022, January 5). *10 telltale signs you may be a perfectionist*. Verywell Mind. Retrieved April 17, 2022, from https://www.verywellmind.com/signs-you-may-be-a-perfectionist-3145233

Seaton, E. K., Neblett, E. W. Jr, Cole, D. J., & Prinstein, M. J. (2013). Perceived Discrimination and Peer Victimization Among African American and Latino Youth. *Journal of Youth and Adolescence*, *42*(3), 342–350. doi:10.100710964-012-9848-6 PMID:23124713

Segal, J., Smith, M., Robinson, L., & Shubin, J. (2022, February 8). *Improving emotional intelligence (EQ)*. Retrieved November 18, 2021, from https://www.helpguide.org/articles/mental-health/emotional-intelligence-eq.htm

Serpell, J. A., McCune, S., Gee, N., & Griffin, J. A. (2016). Current challenges to research on animal-assisted interventions. *Applied Developmental Science*. Advance online publication. doi:10.1080/10888691.2016.1262775

Shillingford, M., & Edwards, O. (2008). Professional school counselors using choice theory to meet the needs of children of prisoners. *Professional School Counseling*, *12*(1), 62–65. https://www.jstor.org/stable/42732864

Shlafer, R., & Poehlmann, J. (2010). Attachment and caregiving relationships in families affected by parental incarceration. *Attachment & Human Development*, *12*(4), 395–415. doi:10.1080/14616730903417052 PMID:20582847

Shultz, E. (2006) *Furry therapist: The advantages and disadvantages of implementing animal therapy in schools* [Master's Thesis]. University of Wisconsin-Stout.

Sibrava, N. J., Bjornsson, A. S., Pérez Benítez, A. C. I., Moitra, E., Weisberg, R. B., & Keller, M. B. (2019). Posttraumatic stress disorder in African American and Latinx adults: Clinical course and the role of racial and ethnic discrimination. *The American Psychologist*, *74*(1), 101–116. doi:10.1037/amp0000339 PMID:30652903

Silverman, L. K. (2000). *Counseling the gifted and talented*. Love.

Simmen-Janevska, K., Brandstätter, V., & Maercker, A. (2012). The overlooked relationship between motivational abilities and posttraumatic stress: a review. *European Journal of Psychotraumatology*, *3*. doi:10.3402/ejpt.v3i0.18560

Sink, C. (2016). Incorporating a multi-tiered system of support into school counselor preparation. *The Professional Counselor*, *6*(3), 203–219. doi:10.15241/cs.6.3.203

Sisk, D. (2008). Engaging the spiritual intelligence of gifted students to build global awareness in the classroom. *Roeper Review*, *30*(1), 24–30. doi:10.1080/02783190701836296

Skinner-Osei & Levenson. (2018). Trauma-informed services for children with incarcerated parents. *Journal of Family Social Work, 21*(4/5). 421-437. doi:10.1080/10522158.2018.1499064

Skolnick, J. (2019, October 1). *Gifted does not (only) mean smart.* Gifted Does Not (only) Mean Smart | National Association for Gifted Children. Retrieved October 28, 2021, from https://www.nagc.org/blog/gifted-does-not-only-mean-smart

Sorrentino, A. E., Iverson, K. M., Tuepker, A., True, G., Cusack, M., Newell, S., & Dichter, M. E. (2020). Mental health care in the context of intimate partner violence: Survivor perspectives. *Psychological Services.* Advance online publication. doi:10.1037er0000427 PMID:32237873

Spirito, A., & Kazak, A. E. (2006). *Effective and emerging treatments in pediatric psychology.* Oxford Univ. Press.

Stamm, B. H. (2010). The Concise ProQOL Manual (2nd ed.). ProQOL.org.

Starr Commonwealth. (2019). *Children of trauma & resilience guidebook.* Starr Commonwealth.

State of the Profession 2020 ascaresearch report. (n.d.). https://www.schoolcounselor.org/getmedia/bb23299b-678d-4bce-8863-cfcb55f7df87/2020-State-of-the-Profession.pdf

Steele, T. M., Jacokes, D. E., & Stone, C. B. (2014). An Examination Of The Role Of Online Technology In School Counseling. *Professional School Counseling, 18*(1), 125–135. doi:10.1177/2156759X0001800118

Steele, W., Ingle, D., Nelson, M., & Porter, P. (2000). *Trauma response protocol manual for schools* (Rev. ed.). National Institute for Trauma and Loss in Children.

Stein, B. D., Jaycox, L. H., Kataoka, S. H., & Wong, W. T., Elliott, W. M. N., & Fink, A. (2003). A mental health intervention for school-aged children exposed to violence: A randomized controlled trial. *Journal of the American Medical Association, 290*, 603–611. doi:10.1001/jama.290.5.603 PMID:12902363

Stevens, J. E. (2012, May 31). *Massachusetts, Washington State lead U.S. trauma-sensitive school movement* [Blog post]. ACES Too High. https://acestoohigh.com/2012/05/31/massachusetts-washington-state-lead-u-s-trauma-sensitive-school-movement/

Stewart, L.A., Bruneau, L., & Elliott, A. (2016). *The role of animal-assisted interventions in addressing trauma-informed care.* ACA (American Counseling Association) Knowledge Center, VISTA.

Stewart, L. A., Chang, C. Y., Parker, L. K., & Grubbs, N. (2016). *Animal-assisted therapy in counseling competencies.* American Counseling Association, Animal-Assisted Therapy in Mental Health Interest Network.

Stop AAPI Hate Youth Campaign. (2020). *They blamed me because I am Asian: Findings from youth-reported incidents of anti-AAPI hate.* http://www.asianpacificpolicyandplanningcouncil.org/wp-content/uploads/Stop-AAPI-Hate-Youth-Campaign-Report-9.11.20.pdf

Stop AAPI Hate. (2021, February 9). *New data on anti-Asian hate incidents against elderly and total national incidents in 2020.* https://secureservercdn.net/104.238.69.231/a1w.90d.myftpupload.com/wp-content/uploads/2021/02/Press-Statement-re_-Bay-Area-Elderly-Incidents-2.9.2021-1.pdf

Student Discipline in a Virtual Classroom Legal or Board Policy Connection. (n.d.). Retrieved September 26, 2021, from http://thecommons.dpsk12.org/cms/lib/CO01900837/Centricity/Domain/52/SOP%20for%20Student%20Discipline%20in%20a%20Virtual%20Classroom.pdf

Studer, J. R. (2015). The Essential School Counselor in a changing society. *Sage (Atlanta, Ga.).* Advance online publication. doi:10.4135/9781483399881

Stump, K. N., Kupersmidt, J. B., Stelter, R. L., & Rhodes, J. E. (2018). Mentoring program enhancements supporting effective mentoring of children of incarcerated parents. *American Journal of Community Psychology, 62*(1-2), 163–174. https://doi.org/10.1002/ajcp.12250

Substance Abuse and Mental Health Services Administration. (2014). *SAMHSA's concept of trauma and guidance for a trauma informed approach* (HHS Publication No. SMA 14-4884). https://store.samhsa.gov/product/SAMHSA-s-Concept-of-Trauma-and-Guidance-for-a-Trauma-Informed-Approach/SMA14-4884

Substance Abuse and Mental Health Services Administration. (2014). *SAMHSA's concept of trauma and guidance for a trauma-informed approach.* HHS Publication No. (SMA) 14-4884. Substance Abuse and Mental Health Services Administration. https://ncsacw.samhsa.gov/userfiles/files/SAMHSA_Trauma.pdf

Substance Abuse and Mental Health Services Administration. (2014). *SAMHSA's concept of trauma and guidance for a trauma-informed approach.* https://ncsacw.acf.hhs.gov/userfiles/files/SAMHSA_Trauma.pdf

Substance Abuse and Mental Health Services Administration. (2014). *SAMHSA's concept of trauma and guidance for a trauma-informed approach.* Substance Abuse and Mental Health Services Administration. https://ncsacw.samhsa.gov/userfiles/files/SAMHSA_Trauma.pdf

Substance Abuse and Mental Health Services Administration. (2014). *Trauma-informed care in behavioral health services: TIP 57.* Substance Abuse and Mental Health Services Administration. https://store.samhsa.gov/product/TIP-57-Trauma-Informed-Care-in-Behavioral-Health-Services/SMA14-4816

Substance Abuse and Mental Health Services. (2020). *Understanding child trauma.* https://www.samhsa.gov/child-trauma/understanding-child-trauma

Sue, D. W., Sue, D., Neville, H. A., & Smith, L. (2019). *Counseling the culturally diverse: Theory and practice.* John Wiley & Sons.

Sulkowski, M. L., & Michael, K. (2014). Meeting the mental health needs of homeless students in schools: A multi-tiered system of support framework. *Children and Youth Services Review, 44*, 145–151. doi:10.1016/j.childyouth.2014.06.014

Suzuki, B. H. (2002). Revisiting the model minority stereotype: Implications for student affairs practice and higher education. *New Directions for Student Services*, *97*(97), 21–32. doi:10.1002s.36

Sweeney, A., Filson, B., Kennedy, A., Collinson, L., & Gillard, S. (2018). A paradigm shift: Relationships in trauma-informed mental health services. *BJPsych Advances*, *24*(5), 319–333. doi:10.1192/bja.2018.29 PMID:30174829

Sylvester-Nwosu, P. (2020). *Self-care practices, work experience, educational setting, and burnout among school counselors* (Publication No. 28157204) [Doctoral dissertation, Walden University]. ProQuest Dissertations and Theses Global.

Taylor, S. R. (2018). *The body is not an apology: The power of radical self-love*. Berrett-Koehler Publishers.

Taylor, S. S. (2021). Trauma-informed care in schools: A Necessity in the time of COVID-19. *Beyond Behavior*, *30*(3), 124–134. Advance online publication. doi:10.1177/10742956211020841

Teaching Tolerance. (2017). *Responding to hate and bias at school: A guide for administrators, counselors, and teachers*. https://www.learningforjustice.org/sites/default/files/2017-07/Responding%20to%20Hate%20at%20School%202017.pdf

Teaching Tolerance. (2019). *Speak up at school: How to respond to everyday prejudice, biases, and stereotypes*. https://www.learningforjustice.org/magazine/publications/speak-up-at-school

Technology in Schools. (2022). *National Center for Education Statistics*. https://nces.ed.gov/pubs2003/tech_schools/chapter4.asp

Tedeshi, P., & Jenkins, M. (2019). *Transforming Trauma: Resilience and Healing through Our Connection with Animals*. Purdue University Press.

Terry, A. W., Bohnenberger, J. E., Renzulli, J. S., Cramond, B., & Sisk, D. (2008). Vision with action: Developing sensitivity to societal concerns in gifted youth. *Roeper Review*, *30*(1), 61–67. doi:10.1080/02783190701836478

Texas Department of Family and Protective Services. (n.d.). *Family-based support programs*. https://www.dfps.state.tx.us/Child_Protection/Family_Support/default.asp

Texas Education Agency. (2014). *A model comprehensive, developmental guidance and counseling program for Texas public school: A guide for program development pre-K-12th grade*. Author.

Texas Education Agency. (2021). *School mental health practice guide and toolkit*. https://schoolmentalhealthtx.org/

The Case for Michigan's Online Learning Mandate -- THE Journal. (2011). *THE Journal*. https://thejournal.com/articles/2007/01/24/the-case-for-michigans-online-learning-mandate.aspx

The College Board. (2011). *Enhancing the principal-school counselor relationship*. https://secure-media.collegeboard.org/digitalServices/pdf/advocacy/nosca/enhancing-principal-school-counselor-relationship-111018.pdf

The History of Distance Learning: An Online Education Timeline. (2021, June 18). *World Wide Learn*. https://www.worldwidelearn.com/articles/history-of-distance-learning/

The History Of K-12 Online Education??? (2010, February). *Virtual School Meanderings*. https://virtualschooling.wordpress.com/2010/02/01/the-history-of-k-12-online-education/

The NCES Fast Facts Tool provides quick answers to many education questions (National Center for Education Statistics). (2021). *National Center for Education Statistics*. https://nces.ed.gov/fastfacts/display.asp?id=372

The Relationship Between School Attendance and Health. (2016, September). *The Relationship Between School Attendance and Health*. RWJF. https://www.rwjf.org/en/library/research/2016/09/the-relationship-between-school-attendance-and-health.html

The School Counselor and Students with Disabilities - American School Counselor Association (ASCA). (2020). https://schoolcounselor.org/Standards-Positions/Position-Statements/ASCA-Position-Statements/The-School-Counselor-and-Students-with-Disabilities

The School Counselor and Virtual School Counseling - American School Counselor Association (ASCA). (2020). https://www.schoolcounselor.org/Standards-Positions/Position-Statements/ASCA-Position-Statements/The-School-Counselor-and-Virtual-School-Counseling

Thigpen, S., Ellis, S., & Smith, R. (2005). Special education in juvenile residential facilities: Can animals help? *Essays in Education*, *14*(20), 1-16. https://openriver.winona.edu/eie/vol14/iss1/20?utm_source=openriver.winona.edu%2Feie%2Fvol14%2Fiss1%2F20&utm_medium=PDF&utm_campaign=PDFCoverPages

Thomas, A. J., Carey, D., Prewitt, K., Romero, E., Richards, M., & Velsor-Friedrich, B. (2012). African-American youth and exposure to community violence: Supporting Change from the inside. *Journal for Social Action in Counseling and Psychology*, *4*(1), 54–68. doi:10.33043/JSACP.4.1.54-68

Thomas, M. S., Crosby, S., & Vanderhaar, J. (2019). Trauma-informed practices in schools across two decades: An interdisciplinary review of research. *Review of Research in Education*, *43*(1), 422–452. https://doi.org/10.3102/0091732X18821123

Thomas, V., & Ray, K. E. (2006). Counseling exceptional individuals and their families: A systems perspective. *Professional School Counseling*, *10*(1), 58–65. doi:10.5330/prsc.10.1.whr69001g7573m75

Thompson, T. L., & Kiang, L. (2010). The model minority stereotype: Adolescent experiences and links with adjustment. *Asian American Journal of Psychology*, *1*(2), 119–128. https://doi.org/10.1037/a0019966

Thomsen, T., Fritz, V., Mößle, R., & Greve, W. (2015). The impact of accommodative coping on well-being in childhood and adolescence: Longitudinal findings. *International Journal of Behavioral Development*, *39*(5), 467–476. https://doi.org/10.1177/0165025414551762

Tieso, C. L. (2007). Overexcitabilities: A new way to think about talent? *Roeper Review*, *29*(4), 232–239. doi:10.1080/02783190709554417

Toro, P. A., Dworsky, A., & Fowler, P. J. (2007). *Homeless youth in the United States: Recent research findings and intervention approaches.* Paper presented at the National Symposium on Homeless Research, Washington, DC.

Trauma-Informed School Strategies during COVID-19. (n.d.). https://www.nctsn.org/sites/default/files/resources/resource-guide/trauma_informed_school_strategies_during_covid-19.pdf

Trivedi, L., & Peri, J. (1995) Animal facilitated counseling in the elementary school: A literature review and practical considerations. *Elementary School Guidance & Counseling*, *29*, 223-234. http://www.jstor.org/ stable/42871169

Trusty, T., & Brown, D. (2005). Advocacy competencies for professional school counselors. *Professional School Counseling*, *8*(3), 259–265.

Tuma, N. (2018). *The impact of animal-assisted therapy in elementary schools* [Capstone]. Winona State University-Open River. https://openriver.winona.edu/counseloreducationcapstones/74

Turney, K. (2018). Adverse childhood experiences among children of incarcerated parents. *Children and Youth Services Review*, *89*, 218–225. https://doi.org/10.1016/j.childyouth.2018.04.033

Turney, K. (2019). Understanding the needs of children with incarcerated parents: What educators should know. *American Educator*, *43*(2), 22–28. https://www.aft.org/ae/summer2019/turney

Tuttle, M., Ricks, L., & Taylor, M. (2021). *A child abuse reporting framework for early career school counselors.* https://tpcjournal.nbcc.org/a-child-abuse-reporting-framework-for-early-career-school-counselors/

Tuttle, M., Yordy, M., Appling, B., & Hanley, E. (2018). School counselor and school nurse collaboration: Partnering for K-12 student success. *Journal of School Counseling*, *16*(4). http://www.jsc.montana.edu/articles/v16n4.pdf

Tynes, B. M., Rose, C. A., & Williams, D. R. (2010). The development and validation of the online victimization scale for adolescents. *Cyberpsychology (Brno)*, *4*(2). https://cyberpsychology.eu/article/view/4237

U.S. Department of Health and Human Services. (2019). *Child Maltreatment 2019.* https://www.acf.hhs.gov/sites/default/files/documents/cb/cm2019.pdf

U.S. National Institutes of Health. (2021, August 26). *Emotional wellness toolkit.* https://www.nih.gov/health-information/emotional-wellness-toolkit

U.S. News and World Report. (1966). *Success story of one minority group in the U.S.* Author.

United Nations Educational, Scientific, and Cultural Organization. (2021a). *Adverse consequences of school closures.* https://en.unesco.org/covid19/educationresponse/consequences

United Nations Educational, Scientific, and Cultural Organization. (2021b). *Education: From disruption to recovery.* https://en.unesco.org/covid19/educationresponse

United Nations, Human Rights, Office of the High Commissioner. (2020, March 23). *States should take action against COVID-19-related expressions of xenophobia, says UN expert.* https://www.ohchr.org/EN/NewsEvents/Pages/DisplayNews.aspx?NewsID=25739&LangID=

United States Census Bureau. (2021, October 4). *State population by characteristic:2010-2019.* https://www.census.gov/data/tables/time-series/demo/popest/2010s-state-detail.html

United States Department of Homeland Security, Federal Emergency Management Agency. (2006). *Designated counties for Alabama Hurricane Katrina.* Available from: https://www.fema.gov/news/eventcounties.fema?id=4825

van der Kolk, B. (2014). *The body keeps the score: Brain, mind, and body in the healing of trauma.* Viking.

Van der Kolk, B. A. (2015). *The body keeps the score: brain, mind, and body in the healing of trauma.* Penguin Books.

Van Gemert, L. (2017). *Perfectionism: A practical guide to managing "Never good enough".* Gifted Guru Publishing.

Vela-Gude, L., Cavazos, J., Johnson, M., Fielding, C., Cavazos, A., Campos, L., & Rodriguez, I. (2009). "My counselors were never there": Perceptions from Latino college students. *Professional School Counseling, 12*(4), 272–279. doi:10.5330/PSC.n.2010-12.272

Veltman, M. W. M., & Browne, K. D. (2001). Three decades of child maltreatment research: Implications for the school years. *Trauma, Violence & Abuse, 2*(3), 215–239. doi:10.1177/1524838001002003002

Vernon, A. (2009). *Counseling children and adolescents* (4th ed.). Love.

Vernon, A., & Clemente, R. (2005). *Assessment and intervention with children and adolescents: Developmental and cultural approaches.* American Counseling Association.

Virtual Elementary School Counseling - American School Counselor Association (ASCA). (2020). https://www.schoolcounselor.org/Publications-Research/Publications/Free-ASCA-Resources/COVID-19-Resources/Virtual-Elementary-School-Counseling

Virtual High School Counseling - American School Counselor Association (ASCA). (2020). https://www.schoolcounselor.org/Publications-Research/Publications/Free-ASCA-Resources/COVID-19-Resources/Virtual-High-School-Counseling

Vivrett, R., & Bartlett, J. (2020). *Trauma-informed strategies for supporting children and youth in the child welfare system during COVID-19.* ChildTrend.

Von Lintel, J., & Bruneau, L. (2021). Pathways for implementing a school therapy dog program: Steps for success and best practices. *Journal of School Counseling, 19*(14), 2021. www.jsc.montana.edu/articles/v19n14.pdf

Voting with Their Feet: A State-level Analysis of Public Charter School and District Public School Enrollment Trends. (2021, September 22). *National Alliance for Public Charter Schools.* https://www.publiccharters.org/our-work/publications/voting-their-feet-state-level-analysis-public-charter-school-and-district

Wakefield, S., & Wildeman, C. (2013). *Children of the prison boom: Mass incarceration and the future of American inequality.* Oxford University Press. doi:10.1093/acprof:oso/9780199989225.001.0001

Walker, H. M., & Severson, H. H. (1992). *Systematic Screening for Behavior Disorders (SSBD)* (2nd ed.). Sopris West.

Walker, S. L., Connery, C., Blackson, G. N., Divine, T. F., Walker, T. D., Williams, B., Finke, J. A., & Bartel, K. (2020). Developing resilience in youth with incarcerated parents: A bibliotherapeutic blueprint with tween and young adult literature chapter books. *Journal of Correctional Education, 71*(2), 37–56.

Walkley, M., & Cox, T. L. (2013). Building trauma-informed schools and communities. *Children & Schools, 35*(2), 123–126. doi:10.1093/cs/cdt007

Wanless, S., Groark, C., & Hatfield, B. (2015). Assessing organizational readiness. In J. A. Durlak, C. E. Domitrovich, R. P. Weissberg, & T. P. Gullotta (Eds.), *Handbook of social and emotional learning: Research and practice* (pp. 360–376). The Guilford Press.

Wanser, S. H., Vitale, K. R., Thielke, L. E., Brubaker, L., & Udell, M. (2019). Spotlight on the psychological basis of childhood pet attachment and its implications. *Psychology Research and Behavior Management, 2019*(12), 469–479. https://doi.org/10.2147/PRBM.S158998

Warren, J. M., Coker, G. L., & Collins, M. L. (2019). Children of incarcerated parents: Considerations for professional school counselors. *The Professional Counselor, 9*(3), 185–199. https://doi.org/10.15241/jmw.9.3.185

Webb, J. T. (2011, September 14). *Existential depression in gifted individuals.* SENG. Retrieved November 18, 2021, from https://www.sengifted.org/post/existential-depression-in-gifted-individuals

Webb, J. T. (2022, February 25). *Dabrowski's theory and existential depression in gifted children and adults.* Davidson Institute. Retrieved April 18, 2022, from https://www.davidsongifted.org/gifted-blog/dabrowskis-theory-and-existential-depression-in-gifted-children-and-adults/

Wei, M., Wang, K. T., Heppner, P. P., & Du, Y. (2012). Ethnic and mainstream social connectedness, perceived racial discrimination, and posttraumatic stress symptoms. *Journal of Counseling Psychology, 59*, 486–493. https://dx.doi.org/10.1037/a0028000

Weissberg, R. P., Durlak, J., Domitrovich, C. E., & Gullota, T. P. (2017). Social and emotional learning: Past, present, and future. In C. E. Domitrovich, R. P. Weissberg, & T. P. Gullota (Eds.), *Handbook of Social Emotional Learning Research and Practice* (pp. 3–19). The Guilford Press.

Welfare, L. E., Grimes, T. O., Lawson, G., Hori, K., & Asadi, G. (2021). The school to prison pipeline: Quantitative evidence to guide school counselor advocacy. *Journal of Counselor Leadership and Advocacy, 8*(1), 16–29. https://doi.org/10.1080/2326716X.2020.1861490

What is MTSS? (2019, February 27). *PBIS Rewards*. https://www.pbisrewards.com/blog/what-is-mtss/

Wiest-Stevenson, C., & Lee, C. (2016). Trauma-informed schools. *Journal of Evidence-Informed Social Work, 13*(5), 498–503. doi:10.1080/23761407.2016.1166855 PMID:27210273

Wilder, C. (2018). Promoting the role of the school counselor. *Journal of Professional Counseling, Practice, Theory, & Research, 45*(2), 60–68. doi:10.1080/15566382.2019.1646085

Wilkerson, K., & Bellini, J. (2006). Intrapersonal and organizational factors associated with burnout among school counselors. *Journal of Counseling and Development, 84*(4), 440–450. doi:10.1002/j.1556-6678.2006.tb00428.x

Wilkinson, I. G. (2016). Why some children come to school with "baggage": The effects of trauma due to poverty, attachment disruption and disconnection on social skills and relationships. *Canadian Journal of Family and Youth, 8*(1), 173–203. doi:10.29173/cjfy27147

Williams, M. T., Metzger, I. W., Liens, C., & DeLapp, C. (2018). Assessing racial trauma within a DSM-5 framework: The UConn Racial/Ethnic Stress and Trauma Survey. *Practice Innovations (Washington, D.C.), 3*, 242–260. https://dx.doi.org/10.1037/pri0000076

Williamson, A. A., Modecki, K. L., & Guerra, N. G. (2015). SEL programs in high school. In J. A. Durlak, C. E. Domitrovich, R. P. Weissberg, & T. P. Gullotta (Eds.), *Handbook of social and emotional learning: Research and practice* (pp. 181–196). The Guilford Press.

Winfrey, O., & Perry, B. D. (2021). *What happened to you?: Conversations on trauma, resilience, and healing*. Flatiron Books.

Wohlfarth, R., Mutschler, B., Beetz, A., Kreuser, F., & Korsten-Reck, U. (2013). Dogs motivate obese children for physical activity: key elements of a motivational theory of animal-assisted interventions. *Frontiers in Psychology, 4*, 1-7. www.frontiersin.org

Wolpow, R., Johnson, M., Hertel, R., & Kincaid, S. (2016a). *Compassionate Schools – Learning and Teaching Support*. https://www.k12.wa.us/student success/health-safety/mental-social-behavioral-health/compassionate-schools-learning-and-teaching-support

Wolpow, R., Johnson, M., Hertel, R., & Kincaid, S. (2016b). *The heart of learning and teaching: Compassion, resilience, and academic success* (3rd ed.). Office of the Superintendent of Public Instruction. https://www.k12.wa.us/student-success/health-safety/mental-social-behavioral-health/compassionate-schools-learning-and-teaching-support

Wong, M. G., & Hirschman, C. (1983). The new Asian immigrants. In W. C. McCready (Ed.), *Culture, ethnicity, and identity: Current issues in research* (pp. 381–403). Academic Press.

Woo, B., & Jun, J. (2021). COVID-19 racial discrimination and depressive symptoms among Asians Americans: Does communication about the incident matter? *Journal of Immigrant and Minority Health.* doi:10.1007/s10903-021-01167-x

Wu, C., Qian, Y., & Wilkes, R. (2021). Anti-Asian discrimination and the Asian-white mental health gap during COVID-19. *Ethnic and Racial Studies*, *44*(5), 819–835. https://doi.org/10.1080/01419870.2020.1851739

Yalom, I. D. (1995). *Theory and practice of group psychotherapy* (4th ed.). Basic Books.

Yavuz, O., Cayirdag, N., Dahir, C., & Gumuseli, A. I. (2017). Improving student achievement through strengthening principal and school counselor partnership. *International Journal of Educational Reform*, *26*(2), 176–201. doi:10.1177/105678791702600205

Yoo, H. C., Steger, M. F., & Lee, R. M. (2010). Validation of the Subtle and Blatant Racism Scale for Asian American college students (SABRA (2)). *Cultural Diversity & Ethnic Minority Psychology*, *16*, 323–334. https://dx.doi.org/10.1037/a0018674

Young, D., & Smith, C. (2000). When moms are incarcerated: The needs of children, mothers and caregivers. *Families in Society*, *81*(2), 130–141. doi:10.1606/1044-3894.1007

Zalaquett, C., & Chatters, S. (2012). Middle school principals' perceptions of middle school counselors' roles and functions. *American Secondary Education*, *40*(2), 89–103. https://www.jstor.org/stable/43694132

Zeenah, C. H., & Humphreys, K. L. (2019). Child abuse and neglect. *Journal of the American Academy of Child and Adolescent Psychiatry*, *57*, 637–644. https://doi.org/10.1016/j.jaac.2018.06.007

Zents, C. E., Fisk, A. K., & Lauback, C. W. (2017). Paws for intervention: Perceptions about the use of dogs in schools. *Journal of Creativity in Mental Health*, *21*(1), 82–98. http://dx.doi.org.ezp.waldenulibrary.org/10.1080/15401383.2016.1189371

Zolkoski, S. M., Holm, J. M., West, E., Ismail, H., Kennedy, B. R., Votaw, A., Miller, G. J., Stocks, E., & Sass, S. M. (2021). Social-emotional learning in rural schools: Parents' perspectives. *Kappa Delta Pi Record*, *57*(1), 43–46. doi:10.1080/00228958.2021.1851587

Zyromski, B., Hudson, T. D., Baker, E., & Granello, D. H. (2019). Guidance counselors or school counselors: How the name of the profession influences perceptions of competence. *Professional School Counseling*, *22*(1), 1–10. doi:10.1177/2156759X19855654

About the Contributors

Angela M. Powell, Ph.D., is an Associate Professor of Human Services at Lone Star College - Houston North in Houston, Texas. She is a Texas Licensed Professional Counselor-Supervisor and a Texas Certified School Counselor. She has 17 years of counseling experience and has been in the educational field for 20 years. Dr. Powell is an active member of several professional counseling associations. She has been invited to train school counselors in working with students with trauma and has facilitated numerous conference presentations and workshops on the impact of trauma in the African American community. Her research interests include school counseling, youth trauma, anxiety, and depression.

* * *

Kristen Ascencao earned her M.Ed. in School Counseling from Texas Tech University in 1997. She continued her education at Liberty University and graduated in 2009 with her Ed.D. in Educational Leadership. In 2010, she was hired as an Adjunct Professor for Liberty University and currently serves as an Instructional Mentor in the School of Behavioral Sciences. She also has over 25 years of experience in public education in the PK-12 setting and has served as a School Counselor at all three levels. She presents often on topics related to crisis response, foster care, and comprehensive school counseling programs.

Emily C. Brown received her PhD in Counselor Education from the University of Tennessee, Knoxville in 2017. She is a National Certified Counselor, Licensed Professional Counselor, and Registered Play Therapist-Supervisor. She has six years of experience as an urban elementary school counselor. She is currently an Assistant Professor of Counseling and Associate Chair at the University of Missouri - St. Louis. She researches and presents on counseling and advocacy issues for youth experiencing loss, crisis, or trauma, particularly children of incarcerated parents.

Jennifer T. Butcher, Ph.D., is the Director of Diversity, Equity, and Inclusion for Abilene Christian University Dallas. She also serves as Professor in the School of Educational Leadership for ACU Dallas. Dr. Butcher has more than thirty-five years of experience in the educational arena as a public school teacher, school administrator, university professor, and Director of DEI. She has presented at various international, national, regional and state conferences. Dr. Butcher has numerous publications in the area of educational leadership. Her research interests include Social Justice Issues, Special Populations, College Readiness, and Women in Leadership.

Maritza Cha graduated from Garfield High School in East Los Angeles and became the first in her family to attend and graduate from college, the University of California, Los Angeles. She graduated in 2005 with two Bachelor's Degrees in Political Science and History, with a minor in Education. UCLA was so nice she went there twice, earning a Master's Degree in Education, as well as a teaching credential, from UCLA's Teacher Education Program in 2007. She taught social studies at her alma mater, Garfield High School for 4 years. In 2010, Mrs. Cha and several colleagues designed and launched a pilot school within Los Angeles Unified School District – Social Justice Leadership Academy at Esteban Torres High School. Mrs. Cha then decided to work towards her lifelong dream of becoming a college counselor. Mrs. Cha earned her second Master's Degree, a counseling credential and child welfare and attendance credential, from Cal State Dominguez Hills in 2015. Mrs. Cha currently works for Alhambra Unified School District as a school counselor and is a Ph.D. Candidate at Claremont Graduate University in Education/Urban Leadership.

Hulya Ermis-Demirtas, Ph.D., is a licensed school counselor and counselor educator in the Department of Counselor Education at Northeastern Illinois University. Her research interests focus on the path between adverse childhood experiences, sense of emptiness, and suicide risk among adolescents and emerging adults, discrimination and sociocultural trauma among marginalized and/or minoritized youth, creative interventions in school counseling to promote resilience in children, and counseling children and adolescents.

Corey Gurskyj, M.Ed, started her education career in 2007. She taught 1st-4th grades wherein she sought further education as a reading specialist. Mrs. Gurskyj accepted a new role as a Literacy Coach in 2013. She supported many schools in their goal of increasing growth and achievement in Reading/Language Arts/English. In 2015 she was offered a new position as a Literacy Facilitator to support the three elementary and one middle school which were the lowest-performing schools in her district. Mrs. Gurskyj worked tirelessly with administrators, counselors, teachers, students, and other stakeholders for three years. In 2018 Mrs. Gurskyj became a Gifted and Talented Coach where she completed course work and passed the Praxis to earn her Gifted Endorsement. She is currently in this position where she seeks to learn more about gifted students and ways she can support the whole child.

Stacey Guthrie, EdD, LPC/MHSP, NCC, ACS, received her EdD in Counselor, Education, and Supervision from Argosy University in Nashville, TN, in 2014. She is a Licensed Professional School Counselor as well as a Licensed Professional Counselor (LPC) with the Mental Health Service Provider (MHSP) designation for the State of TN. Dr. Guthrie has the National Counselor Credential (NCC) along with being an Approved Clinical Supervisor (ACS). In her practice, she works with children, adolescents, and adults; specializing in addiction, anxiety, and depression. Dr. Guthrie spent 22 years in public education as an elementary teacher and elementary school counselor. She has taught for six years as a Counselor Educator as an Adjunct Professor at Lindsey Wilson College, Carson Newman University, and Capella University now serving in the role as Core Faculty in the School Counseling Department. Dr. Guthrie has eight years of total experience as a LPC/MHSP with five of those years in her private practice. Throughout her career, she has presented numerous times at local, state, and national counseling association conferences. Dr. Guthrie has also been recognized several times with Capella University's Stephen Shank award. At Capella University, she has been a Fieldwork Coordinator, Subject Matter Expert (SME), has designed courses, supervises school counseling interns, and is the School Counseling Program Coordinator. Since the start of her counseling career, she has been a member of SMCA, TCA, ACA, ASCA, ACES, TACES, and NAADAC.

Dylan Hebert is pursuing his Master's degree in School counseling from Auburn University and is anticipating graduating in May 2021. Dylan received his undergraduate degree from the University of Louisiana at Lafayette in Secondary Social Studies Education in May 2020. In his time in graduate school, he has been the Graduate School Council senator for the Department of Special Education, Rehabilitation, and Counseling for two years and is a part of Chi Sigma Iota international honor society.

Donna Hickman is an Assistant Professor and coordinator of the school counseling program at Texas A&M University-Commerce. She is a Licensed Professional Counselor and certified school counselor in the state of Texas. Donna has 22 years of experience in Texas public schools as an elementary school teacher and counselor. She has also worked with children, adolescents, and adults in private practice. She is an active member of several professional counseling associations with presentations on topics such as school counselor supervision, research methods and statistics, sandtray therapy, counselor self-care, and counseling ethics. Her research interest areas include professional school counselor advocacy, graduate student mental health, and counselor self-care and wellness.

Samantha Klassen is an Assistant Professor of Counseling at Texas A&M University-Commerce. She is a Licensed Professional Counselor-Supervisor in the state of Texas. Samantha specializes in crisis work with children, adolescents, and adults. Her clinical expertise and research interests are centered around working with trauma populations; body image and disordered eating; comprehensive behavioral healthcare for children, adolescents, and their families; and infusing mindfulness, meditative practices, and spirituality into counseling and counselor education.

Agnes Luo, Ph.D., is a licensed professional counselor and counselor educator in the Department of Counseling and Higher Education at the University of North Texas. As a bilingual English/Mandarin practitioner, Dr. Luo has worked with children, adolescents, adults, families, and groups in the college campus, community-based agency, and private practice counseling settings. Her research is focused on Asian racial & cultural identities, bilingual and multicultural counseling, and technology use in counseling and counselor education.

Andrea Perez was born and raised in the city of Maywood. Currently, she works as school counselor at Los Angeles Unified School District where she serves 6th-8th grade students. Ms. Perez considers herself to be a transformative school counselor who is committed to support and empower students and families. Before becoming a school counselor, Ms. Perez worked as a college advisor at Educational Talent Search (ETS), a TRIO program, located at California State University in Long Beach. While at ETS, she supported different Los Angeles Unified high school students with college readiness and career exploration. Ms. Perez holds a bachelor's degree in English and Chicana/o Studies from the University of California, Los Angeles; and a master's degree in Counseling and a Pupil Personnel Services Credential from California State University in Long Beach. Currently, Ms. Perez is working on her PhD in Education with a focus on Urban Leadership at Claremont Graduate University. Her research interests include: the school counselor's role in the Multi-tiered system of support; social justice counseling practices in schools; Critical Race Theory and its use in K-12 settings; and students' social and academic development.

Melissa Phelan's areas of interest revolve around Social Justice issues. In particular, Parental Incarceration and those experiencing a family member incarcerated. With over 25 years of experience in the medical field Dr. Phelan is interested in the mental and physical effects incarceration may have on those affected by it. Currently Dr. Phelan is a grant writer working with non-profit organizations in central Texas.

Danielle Render Turmaud, M.S., NCC, PhD in Counseling and Counselor Education, is a Counseling Professional who specializes in working with victims/survivors of trauma. In addition to her work as a counselor, Danielle currently serves as an Assistant Professor of Counseling at Multnomah University. As a Counseling Professional and Counselor Educator, Danielle has a passion for supporting the counseling profession by creating resources and courses, conducting research on, and participating in advocacy efforts that will foster increased competence in the area of trauma-informed counseling. Some of Danielle's advocacy efforts in this area include but are not limited to: serving as an Expert Blog Author on the topic of trauma for Psychology Today, presenting at counseling and counselor education conferences domestically and internationally on trauma, conducting trainings on trauma-informed care, participating as an invited speaker on the topic of trauma on podcasts and other forums, and conducting research related to trauma-informed care counseling and counselor competence on trauma.

Malti Tuttle received her PhD in Counseling and Student Personnel Services, P-16 from the University of Georgia in 2015. She is a National Certified Counselor, National Certified School Counselor, Licensed Professional Counselor, and Certified Professional Counselors Supervisor. She worked as a school counselor for thirteen years in the Metro-Atlanta area. Her research foci include school counselor advocacy, social justice, English Learners, and school counselor collaboration.

Barbara Wilson is a virtual high school counselor with more than 15 years of experience. She is also a licensed therapist in three states and a certified counselor supervisor. Dr. Wilson earned a Ph.D. in Counseling and Student Personnel Services from the University of Georgia. She values opportunities to give back to the fields of counseling and education.

Jia-Rung Wu, Ph.D., is an assistant professor in the Department of Counselor Education at Northeastern Illinois University. She is a certified rehabilitation counselor, a licensed professional counselor, and licensed occupational therapist. Dr. Wu has 11 years of clinical rehabilitation experiences and published 39 refereed journal articles, and five book chapters. Her research interest areas including racial/ethnicity minority student academic and transition success, psychiatric rehabilitation, vocational rehabilitation, health promotion, the International Classification of Functionality, Disability and Health (ICF) model, demand-side employment, evidence-based practice, testing and assessment, and research methodologies.

Index

G

H

I

L

M

N

O

P

R

S

www.ingramcontent.com/pod-product-compliance
Lightning Source LLC
Chambersburg PA
CBHW080501051126
54379CB00005B/136